Download Forms on Nolo.com

You can download the forms in this book at:

 www.nolo.com/back-of-book/EMHA.html

We'll also post updates whenever there's an important change to the law affecting this book—as well as articles and other related materials.

More Resources from Nolo.com

Legal Forms, Books, & Software

Hundreds of do-it-yourself products—all written in plain English, approved, and updated by our in-house legal editors.

Legal Articles

Get informed with thousands of free articles on everyday legal topics. Our articles are accurate, up to date, and reader friendly.

Find a Lawyer

Want to talk to a lawyer? Use Nolo to find a lawyer who can help you with your case.

NOLO The Trusted Name
(but don't take our word for it)

"In Nolo you can trust."

THE NEW YORK TIMES

"Nolo is always there in a jam as the nation's premier publisher of do-it-yourself legal books."

NEWSWEEK

"Nolo publications…guide people simply through the how, when, where and why of the law."

THE WASHINGTON POST

"[Nolo's]…material is developed by experienced attorneys who have a knack for making complicated material accessible."

LIBRARY JOURNAL

"When it comes to self-help legal stuff, nobody does a better job than Nolo…"

USA TODAY

"The most prominent U.S. publisher of self-help legal aids."

TIME MAGAZINE

"Nolo is a pioneer in both consumer and business self-help books and software."

LOS ANGELES TIMES

9th Edition

Create Your Own Employee Handbook

A Legal & Practical Guide for Employers

Lisa Guerin, J.D. & Amy DelPo, J.D.

NINTH EDITION	JUNE 2019
Editor	ELIZABETH GJELTEN
Cover Design	SUSAN PUTNEY
Book Production	SUSAN PUTNEY
Proofreading	IRENE BARNARD
Index	THÉRÈSE SHERE
Printing	BANG PRINTING

Names: Guerin, Lisa, 1964- author. | DelPo, Amy, 1967- author.
Title: Create your own employee handbook : a legal & practical guide for
employers / Lisa Guerin, J.D. & Amy DelPo, J.D.
Description: 9th Edition. | Berkeley, CA : Nolo, [2019] | Revised edition of
the authors' Create your own employee handbook, [2017] | Includes
bibliographical references and index.
Identifiers: LCCN 2018058332 (print) | LCCN 2018060470 (ebook) | ISBN
9781413326321 (ebook) | ISBN 9781413326314 (pbk.)
Subjects: LCSH: Employee orientation. | Employees--Training of. | Employee
rights. | Employee rules.
Classification: LCC HF5549.5.I53 (ebook) | LCC HF5549.5.I53 G84 2019 (print)
| DDC 658.3/01--dc23
LC record available at https://lccn.loc.gov/2018058332

Please note

We believe accurate, plain-English legal information should help you solve many
of your own legal problems. But this text is not a substitute for personalized advice
from a knowledgeable lawyer. If you want the help of a trained professional—and
we'll always point out situations in which we think that's a good idea—consult an
attorney licensed to practice in your state.

Acknowledgments

The authors would like to thank the following people who helped to make this book possible:

- Our editor on the first edition, Ilona Bray, whose good humor and easy nature made the editing process fun—and whose words and insights never failed to improve upon what we gave her
- Our editor on the second edition, Stephanie Bornstein, whose eye for detail and consistency helped us immeasurably
- Editors who have helped on subsequent editions, including Sachi Barreiro, Marcia Stewart, and Elizabeth Gjelten, who have helped us keep the book user-friendly and up to date
- Albin Renauer for his wonderful design ideas—and his ability to think "inside the box"!
- Mary Randolph, for helping us mold and formulate our vision of this book
- Nolo jack-of-all-trades Stan Jacobson, who tirelessly haunted libraries throughout the Bay Area to meet our research needs
- Ella Hirst, for her years of hard work on the 50-state charts that appear in this book; and Alayna Schroeder, Drew Wheaton, Stephen Stine, and the rest of the Nolo legal research team, for graciously picking up where Ella left off
- Andre Zivkovich and Ellen Bitter, who managed to take our printed pages and turn them into forms that people could use on their computers, and
- Terri Hearsh, for working with us on a wonderful book design.

In addition, Amy would like to dedicate her work on this book to her daughter, Sophia, whose early birth delayed the first edition of this book by almost half a year. She is everything and more.

About the Authors

Lisa Guerin is a former Nolo editor specializing in employment and human resources issues. After graduating from the Boalt Hall School of Law at the University of California at Berkeley, Lisa practiced employment law in government, public interest, and private practice. Lisa has represented clients at all levels of federal and state court, in agency hearings, and in mediation and arbitration proceedings. She is the author or coauthor of many Nolo titles, including *The Essential Guide to Workplace Investigations, Smart Policies for Workplace Technologies,* and *The Essential Guide to Family & Medical Leave.*

Amy DelPo brings more than six years of criminal and civil litigation experience to her work at Nolo, having litigated cases at all levels of state and federal courts, including the California Supreme Court and the U.S. Supreme Court. Before joining Nolo's staff in January 2000, Amy specialized in employment law, handling a wide variety of disputes between employers and employees, including sexual harassment, discrimination, and wage-and-hour issues. She has written and edited numerous employment law titles for Nolo, including *Dealing With Problem Employees* (coauthor). Amy received her law degree with honors from the University of North Carolina at Chapel Hill. She lives in Denver, Colorado, with her husband and three children.

Together, the authors have written several books published by Nolo, including *Dealing With Problem Employees* and *The Manager's Legal Handbook.*

our employees, and we consider ourselves to be the premier printing company in the Tri-State Area."

If you do add company-specific information to this welcome statement, keep it brief. Your employees will be getting more detailed information from the policies that follow.

> **CAUTION**
>
> **Don't make big promises in a handbook.** Be careful not to say anything that could create an implied contract with your employees promising to terminate them only for cause. (See Chapter 2 for more about implied contracts and termination for cause.) Avoid statements that promise employees a long future at the company, for example.

1:2 Introduction to the Company

File Name: 01_Introduction.rtf

Include This Policy?

☐ Yes

☐ No

☐ Use our existing policy

☐ Other _____

Alternate Modifications

None

Additional Clauses

None

Related Policies

None

Notes

_____

_____

_____

_____

_____

_____

_____

_____

_____

_____

_____

_____

_____

_____

_____

_____

_____

1:2 Introduction to the Company

The beginning pages of a handbook are a great place to briefly introduce employees to a company's background, history, and culture. (You will delve into your company's history in more detail later. See Policy 1:4, below.) In the Introduction, speak directly to employees and present the company as you want them to see it.

During employees' day-to-day work at your company, information about your company's values and goals will trickle down to them from supervisors, managers, coworkers, and customers. Unfortunately, this means that sometimes employees will hear things about your company that aren't true or that are distorted by the views of the people around them. If these are an employee's first impressions of your company, they will be hard to undo. The Introduction is your opportunity to get in the first word about your company and to make a good first impression.

There is no standard policy language that we can provide to convey your company's unique personality; that's up to you. Here is an example of what an introduction might look like.

> **SAMPLE POLICY LANGUAGE**
>
> Juanita Jones founded this company in 1978 on a very basic principle: Customers will pay for exceptional service and knowledge. Using that principle as her beacon, she took a small independent bookstore and created a chain of 30 stores serving customers throughout the western United States.
>
> Here at J&J Books, we continue to believe that a knowledgeable and courteous staff can sell more books than discount prices can. For this reason, we encourage our employees to read the publishing and literary magazines that you will find in the break room, to use your employee discount to buy and read as many books as possible, and to take advantage of our tuition reimbursement program to take literature and writing classes at local colleges. When our customers come to you with questions, we want you to be able to answer them—with a smile.
>
> We know that only happy and relaxed employees can give the quality and good-natured service that our customers demand. So take all of the breaks you are scheduled for, alert your manager to any problems in your work area, and communicate any ideas you might have for making this a better place to work.
>
> At J&J Books, we want our employees to put the customer first. That's why we, in management, put our employees first. We know that we are only as good as you are.

Drafting Your Own Policy

All sorts of information can go into your Introduction, from a heartfelt description of your company's values to an inventory of the products you create and sell. When you write this policy, imagine sitting across from a single employee. What do you want this person to know about your company? What do you think the essence of your company is? What sort of attitude do you want this employee to have toward customers and clients? What information about your company would be useful to this employee in doing the job?

Consider including the following information in this policy:

- Outline the values that are most important to your company's success, such as customer service, product quality, or high-speed productivity. Be as concrete as possible. Do you always do what the customer wants, no matter how much time and effort it takes? Do you try to fill all orders within one day? Do you always redo orders, no questions asked, if a customer complains?
- Explain why these values are important to your company's success.
- Describe any goals your company has (for example, doubling sales in the next decade or lowering operating costs).
- State the values and goals that each employee should have. For example, it may be more important to your company for employees to develop friendly relationships with customers than to pressure customers into making purchases they don't really need.
- Describe your company culture.
- Give a description of the products your company produces or the services it provides.
- Provide an organizational chart for your company.

1:3 Mission Statement

File Name: 01_Introduction.rtf

Include This Policy?
☐ Yes
☐ No
☐ Use our existing policy
☐ Other _____

Alternate Modifications
None

Additional Clauses
None

Related Policies
None

Notes

_____
_____
_____
_____
_____
_____
_____
_____
_____
_____
_____
_____
_____
_____
_____
_____
_____
_____
_____
_____

1:3   Mission Statement

Most modern businesses and organizations have mission statements as part of their overall business or strategic plan. If you have a mission statement, share it with your employees in your handbook. It is yet another way to educate your employees about your company. It helps them understand why they are there and how they should act. It also helps them see the big picture of what your organization is and what it is trying to accomplish in the world.

If you do not have a mission statement, see the guidelines for drafting one, below.

> **SAMPLE POLICY LANGUAGE**
> The mission of *The Daily News* is to enhance and protect our community through journalism that informs, educates, and inspires.

Drafting Your Own Policy

When writing your mission statement, try to think of the essence of why your organization exists. If you run a business, you certainly want to make money, but there is always more to a business's mission than the mere desire for profit. Ask yourself: Why do I run this business? Why is it in this place? Why is this business important? This should get you in the mindset of articulating your company's mission.

Like the sample above, the mission statement should be short and to the point. Most are no longer than one sentence. Information about your company history and culture can go into other policies. The mission statement should be short enough that employees can memorize it, yet long enough to provide information about:

- what you do
- whom you do it for
- how you do it, and
- why you do it.

1:4   History of the Company

The more pride your employees take in your company as a whole, the more pride they will take in their own performance. Telling the history of your company is one way to instill this pride. It can make employees feel like they are part of something special.

In addition, knowing this history can make employees more effective in their jobs. Anecdotes about your company's noble beginnings can help your employees sell your company to customers and clients. Funny stories from your company's past can make the company seem more human and friendly.

Although you may have previewed this information in the Welcoming Statement and Introduction to the Company (see Policies 1:1 and 1:2, above), now is the time to go into more detail.

Of course, each company has its own history, and you'll have to decide how best to convey those facts. Here is an example of what this kind of policy might look like.

SAMPLE POLICY LANGUAGE

In 1855, Dante DeMarco opened this newspaper's doors at 111 Main Street—right between City Hall and the county courthouse. It was a fitting geographic location for Dante, who always kept both eyes peeled for scandal and corruption among the city's power elite. While he ran this newspaper, he lived and breathed the journalist's creed: "Afflict the comfortable and comfort the afflicted." He often said his proudest moment was the day Mayor Lou Mixon was forced to resign because of the great Black and Tan Scandal of 1925, a scandal uncovered and publicized by "DeMarco's Moles," as the reporters were then called. "I would have gotten away with it if it hadn't been for that meddling paper," Mixon was heard to say on his way up the jailhouse steps.

Here at the *Daily Conscience and News*, we still believe in the ideals that have won this newspaper three Pulitzer Prizes (the first for the Black and Tan Scandal). As Dante said, we must be the conscience of the city. We want reporters with suspicious and inquisitive minds and editors who won't breathe easy until a story is just right. We are committed to hiring the highest-quality staff. We strive to provide the resources our employees need to keep their work at the highest level. We will never bow to pressure from advertisers or civic leaders. In short, we will continue to be the daily conscience of Cedar Falls.

1:4   History of the Company

File Name: 01_Introduction.rtf

Include This Policy?
- ☐ Yes
- ☐ No
- ☐ Use our existing policy
- ☐ Other _____

Alternate Modifications
None

Additional Clauses
None

Related Policies
None

Notes

_____
_____
_____
_____
_____
_____
_____
_____
_____
_____
_____
_____
_____
_____
_____
_____
_____
_____

Drafting Your Own Policy

Try to entertain your employees; tell them a good story. Get them hooked on your company's past and excited to be part of its future. Be as specific as possible. Use concrete details like names, dates, and amounts. If you have pictures from the early days, include them.

In writing your history, don't forget the values and goals that you laid out in the Introduction to the Company section (see Policy 1:2, above). If you can, use the history to illustrate those values and show where they came from.

1:5 Handbook Purpose

Every company should include a purpose statement in its employee handbook. From the beginning, you must make clear to employees that they are expected to read the whole handbook and to incorporate the information they read into their work. After all, what's the use of a handbook if employees don't read it?

There is also a legal reason to include this policy. As we explained in the Introduction to this book, one of the biggest risks of using an employee handbook is that a judge or jury might view it as a contract and hold the company to what it says. One way to minimize this risk is to plainly state that the handbook is not a contract and to emphasize that policies can change at any time, for any reason, and without warning.

The Purpose of This Handbook

We think that employees are happier and more valuable if they know what they can expect from our Company and what our Company expects from them. In the preceding sections, we introduced you to our Company's history, values, culture, and goals. We expect you to incorporate that information into your day-to-day job performance, striving to meet our Company's values in everything you do.

The remainder of this Handbook will familiarize you with the privileges, benefits, and responsibilities of being an employee at our Company. Please understand that this Handbook can only highlight and summarize our Company's policies and practices. For detailed information, you will have to talk to your supervisor or _____ _____ .

In this Company, as in the rest of the world, circumstances are constantly changing. As a result, we may revise, rescind, or supplement these policies from time to time. Nothing in this Handbook is a contract or a promise. The policies can change at any time, for any reason, without warning.

We are always looking for ways to improve communications with our employees. If you have suggestions for ways to improve this Handbook in particular or employee relations in general, please feel free to bring them to _____ _____ .

1:5 The Purpose of This Handbook

File Name: 01_Introduction.rtf

Include This Policy?
- ☐ Yes
- ☐ No
- ☐ Use our existing policy
- ☐ Other _____

Alternate Modifications
None

Additional Clauses
None

Related Policies
None

Notes

_____
_____
_____
_____
_____
_____
_____
_____
_____
_____
_____
_____
_____
_____
_____

How to Complete This Policy

Of course, no handbook can anticipate all of the questions and concerns that your employees might have. For this reason, you must designate people at your company to whom your employees can go for more information. If you have a very small company, there might be only one member of management: you. In larger companies, there might be several levels of management to choose from, or you may want to direct employees to the human resources department, if your company has one. (Policy 1:7 introduces the human resources department.) Adjust this policy to reflect the situation at your company. If possible, name two people (by position, not by name) to whom employees can turn (for example, a supervisor and a human resources director). That way, employees have a choice: If they are uncomfortable with one of their options, they can pick the other. Of course, if you have a small company, there may only be one appropriate person. That's fine, too.

Employee Classifications

In any given workplace, there might be five, ten, 30, or more classifications of employees, including such categories as "regular," "temporary," "on call," "per diem," and so on. The list is as endless as the employer's imagination.

Employers like to group workers into classifications for a wide variety of reasons, most having to do with identifying which employees are entitled to certain wages, benefits, and privileges. For example, an employer who does not want to provide benefits to employees who are scheduled to work fewer than 30 hours per week will likely classify employees as part time or full time and will have a policy that allows only full-time employees to receive benefits.

For the most part, the law does not dictate how you classify employees. For example, you can decide how many hours per week employees have to work to be considered full-time employees. (However, this is not true for health insurance if you are subject to the employer mandate under the Affordable Care Act; see Chapter 8.)

The more complicated your workplace, the more employee classifications you might have. We cannot cover all of the various categories into which different employers group their employees. Instead, we tackle the most common ones. The classifications covered by policies in this chapter will meet the needs of the vast majority of small to midsized businesses.

It is important to understand that these categories are not mutually exclusive. They divide employees up according to different criteria, so you could use all (or none) of these classifications depending on your needs. For example, an employee could be both full time and exempt. This would mean that the employee is scheduled to work at least a minimum number of hours per week (full time) and is not entitled to receive overtime under state or federal law (exempt). We discuss these possibilities further in the descriptions of the various employee classifications throughout this chapter.

5:1 Temporary Employees

File Name: 05_Employee Class.rtf

Include This Policy?
- ☐ Yes
- ☐ No
- ☐ Use our existing policy
- ☐ Other _____

Alternate Modifications
None

Additional Clauses
None

Related Policies
For information and policies about at-will employment, see Chapter 2.

For information and policies on which benefits part-time employees are and are not entitled to, see Chapters 8 and 10.

Notes
_____
_____
_____
_____
_____
_____
_____
_____
_____
_____
_____
_____
_____
_____
_____
_____
_____

5:1   Temporary Employees

Most companies experience times when they need a little extra help. Perhaps you run a retail shop and tend to hire more salespeople during the holidays, or maybe you operate an accounting firm and must hire additional clerical help during tax season.

If you use temporary employees, you must distinguish them from your regular employees. Most companies choose not to extend optional benefits (such as life insurance) or the ability to accrue discretionary leave to temporary employees, and they reserve their right to terminate the employees once the need for their services ends.

Depending on your state law, you may have to extend certain legally mandated benefits to all employees, whether they are hired for a temporary project or for a full-time position. Currently, for example, the District of Columbia and a handful of states (including California and Massachusetts) require employers to provide paid sick leave to their employees. These laws differ in the details, including how long employees must work for their employer before they are entitled to use their accrued paid sick time. Although you may legally preclude temporary employees from your discretionary leave programs (such as vacation time), you may have to include them in your sick leave program if you do business in one of these states.

Similarly, you may have to extend other legally mandated benefits —like workers' compensation and state disability insurance—to temporary employees. Contact your state labor department for details. (See Appendix B for contact information.)

The following policy distinguishes those employees who are working for you on a temporary basis from your regular workforce. It also explains that temporary employees are not entitled to the same benefits and privileges as are regular employees.

How to Complete This Policy

Sometimes, temporary employees will begin to feel that they are regular employees simply by virtue of the length of time that they have spent with a company or because of something a manager has said to them.

It is important that you don't allow the status of temporary employees to change through these informal methods. Otherwise, you may find yourself obligated to provide benefits and discretionary time off to individuals whom you never wanted to hire in the first place.

Of course, you may on occasion find that you do want to hire temporary employees on a more regular basis, so you'll need some method by which you can change the status of temporary employees.

The fourth paragraph of the sample policy, below, warns temporary employees that their status cannot change informally or by implication. It does, however, give you the ability to change their status through a written notification signed by someone within your company. You should designate by position, not by name. Choose a position that handles hiring decisions at your company or oversees employee benefit or leave programs. A human resources manager or an office manager is often a good choice.

Temporary Employees

Periodically, it becomes necessary for us to hire individuals to perform a job or to work on a project that has a limited duration. Typically, this happens in the event of a special project, special time of year, abnormal workload, or emergency.

Individuals whom we hire for such work are temporary employees. They are not eligible to participate in any of our Company benefit programs, nor can they earn or accrue any discretionary time off, such as vacation leave.

Of course, we will provide to temporary employees any and all benefits mandated by law.

Temporary employees cannot change from temporary status to any other employment status by such informal means as remaining in our employ for a long period of time or through oral promises made to them by coworkers, members of management, or supervisors. The only way a temporary employee's status can change is through a written notification signed by _____ .

Like all employees who work for this Company, temporary employees work on an at-will basis. This means that both they and this Company are free to terminate their employment at any time for any reason that is not illegal, even if they have not completed the temporary project for which they have been hired.

Reality Check: Are Those Temporary Employees Really Independent Contractors?

Someone who works for you on a temporary basis may really be an independent contractor, not a temporary employee. If you hire someone for a one-time job that requires special expertise outside your company's purview—like painting the office, redesigning the company's website, or providing an ergonomics audit for employee workspaces—that short-term worker may be an independent contractor. The difference, in a nutshell, is that independent contractors are running their own businesses, typically working for a number of clients, according to their own schedules, with their own work methods, and so on.

Why does it matter whether you classify workers as independent contractors or employees? It's usually in an employer's interest to classify a worker as an independent contractor, if possible, because contractors tend to be less expensive than employees. For example, you don't have to provide benefits for contractors, nor do you have to withhold or pay payroll taxes on their behalf. However, government agencies tend to prefer that employers classify workers as employees, for whom they pay into various insurance programs (like unemployment and workers' compensation) and from whom they withhold taxes up front. If you misclassify an employee as a contractor, you could face lawsuits and fines.

To learn more about employee classification, see *Working with Independent Contractors*, by Stephen Fishman (Nolo).

5:2 Part-Time and Full-Time Employees

If you have some employees who work fewer hours than others, you may want to treat them differently in terms of benefits and other perks. To do this, it's helpful to classify employees as either part time or full time, depending on how many hours they work each week.

Be aware that under some circumstances, state or federal law will govern whether you can deny certain benefits to part-time workers. For example, the Affordable Care Act, or Obamacare (the federal health care reform law), defines full-time employees as those who work at least 30 hours per week. Larger employers must either provide these employees with health insurance meeting a number of requirements or pay a penalty for each employee who isn't adequately covered.

Understanding these benefits laws can be difficult, and determining which workers must be allowed to participate can require complex calculations. Talk to your benefits administrator, accountant, or financial adviser before denying benefits to part-time employees.

Part-Time and Full-Time Employees

Depending on the number of hours per week you are regularly scheduled to work, you are either a part-time or a full-time employee. It is necessary that you understand which of these classifications you fit into, because it will be important in determining whether you are entitled to benefits and leave. (See Section _____ of this Handbook for information about who is entitled to benefits and leave.)

Part-time employees: Employees who are regularly scheduled to work fewer than _____ hours per week are part-time employees.

Full-time employees: Employees who are regularly scheduled to work at least _____ hours per week are full-time employees.

How to Complete This Policy

Your company must decide how many hours per week it requires of employees to entitle them to benefits and leave. Many employers require 40 hours; others require only 32 or 24. You also have the option of prorating benefits and leave. For example, you may call an employee who works 32 hours per week a full-time employee, thereby guaranteeing the employee some benefits and leave, but still prorate the amount of vacation that person is entitled to based on a 40-hour work week. Under such a system, if an employee who works 40 hours per week would earn five vacation days per year, then an employee who works 32 hours per week (four-fifths time) would only earn four (four-fifths of full-time vacation benefits).

5:2 Part-Time and Full-Time Employees

File Name: 05_Employee Class.rtf

Include This Policy?
- ☐ Yes
- ☐ No
- ☐ Use our existing policy
- ☐ Other _____

Alternate Modifications
None

Additional Clauses
None

Related Policies
None

Notes

5:3 Exempt and Nonexempt Employees

Depending on the type of work employees do, they may be entitled to overtime pay for any hours they work in excess of 40 hours in a week (or, in some states, in excess of eight hours in a day). Classifying workers as exempt or nonexempt is not a matter of choice for you; it is a matter of state and federal law. Most likely, you have already determined for payroll purposes which workers fall into which category.

This policy explains to employees that their right to overtime compensation depends on whether they are classified as exempt or nonexempt, and it explains the difference between the two classifications.

Exempt and Nonexempt Employees

Your entitlement to earn overtime pay depends on whether you are classified as an exempt or a nonexempt employee.

Exempt employees are those who do not earn overtime because they are exempt from the overtime provisions of the federal Fair Labor Standards Act and applicable state laws.

Nonexempt employees are those who meet the criteria for coverage by the overtime provisions of the federal Fair Labor Standards Act and applicable state laws.

If you are uncertain about which category you fall into, speak to _____.

Hours

Employers generally want to be able to dictate when their employees will work: what time they will start and finish, when they will take breaks, and how much—if any—overtime they will work. The policies in this chapter will help your company set these standards. Although some state and federal laws impose restrictions on work hours—for example, requiring employers to pay certain employees an overtime premium if they work more than a prescribed number of hours in a day or week, or mandating that employees receive certain breaks during their shifts—employers are generally free to tell their employees when they must work.

6:1 Hours of Work

File Name: 06_Hours.rtf

Include This Policy?
☐ Yes
☐ No
☐ Use our existing policy
☐ Other _____

Alternate Modifications
Include Schedule Information
Choose one: ☐ A ☐ B ☐ C

Additional Clauses
None

Related Policies
None

Notes

_____
_____
_____
_____
_____
_____
_____
_____
_____
_____
_____
_____
_____
_____
_____
_____
_____
_____

6:1 Hours of Work

Your policy on work hours should tell employees when the company is open for business and when they are expected to be at work. This policy will set the stage for company policies on absenteeism and punctuality. (See Chapter 12.) In the blanks, list the start time, end time, and days of operation (for example, "seven days a week").

Hours of Work

Our Company's regular hours of business are from _____

_____ .

Alternate Modifications to Include Schedule Information

To Have Supervisors Provide Schedule

Some employers want company supervisors to set employee work hours, particularly if employees work a variety of schedules or if employee schedules are subject to change. This allows supervisors to make staffing decisions as they see fit. To use this modification, simply add the following language to your policy.

Alternate Modification A

> Your supervisor will let you know your work schedule, including what time you will be expected to start and finish work each day.

To Specify Hours for All Employees

In some companies, all employees work the same hours. For example, if an employer has limited hours (such as a convenience store that caters to office workers or an after-hours nightclub), it may need all employees to start work at the same time and stop work at the same time. You can use this modification to set the schedule for all workers. Simply add the following language to the end of your policy.

Alternate Modification B

> All employees are expected to be here, ready to start work, when we open. Unless you make other arrangements with your supervisor, you are expected to work until closing time.

To Include Shift Schedules

A variety of businesses, from restaurants and stores to manufacturers and hospitals, operate in shifts. If your company assigns workers to shifts with set schedules, you should modify the work hours policy to let employees know when each shift starts and ends. This will not only tell workers when they are expected to work, but will also let them know what other shifts might be available, if they need or want to change their work schedules.

This modification also advises that any shift changes, whether temporary or permanent, must be approved by a supervisor. This will put employees on notice that they may not simply swap shifts with a coworker whenever they wish, which will give the company more control over work schedules.

If you want to include a shift schedule in your policy, add the following modification to the end of your policy. In the blanks, fill in the number of shifts your company uses and the start and end time of each shift. Our modification includes space for three shifts; if your company has more or fewer shifts, you will have to modify this provision accordingly.

Alternate Modification C

Our Company operates in _____ shifts: from _____ to _____ , from _____ to _____ , and from _____ to _____ . Your supervisor will let you know your shift assignment.

If you wish to change shifts permanently, talk to your supervisor. Although the Company will consider all requests to change shifts, we cannot guarantee that any particular request will be granted.

You may exchange shifts with another employee (that is, switch shifts on a one-time basis) only with the prior approval of your supervisor.

6:2 Flexible Scheduling

File Name: 06_Hours.rtf

Include This Policy?

☐ Yes

☐ No

☐ Use our existing policy

☐ Other _____

Alternate Modifications

None

Additional Clauses

None

Related Policies

None

Notes

_____
_____
_____
_____
_____
_____
_____
_____
_____
_____
_____
_____
_____
_____
_____
_____
_____
_____
_____
_____
_____

6:2 Flexible Scheduling ("Flextime")

Many companies offer their employees some form of flexible scheduling, often to accommodate the busy lives of working parents, employees who are attending school, or those who have other pressing needs off the job.

Companies can reap many benefits from allowing their employees to work a flexible schedule. Employees who have sufficient time off work to deal with their outside concerns, be they family commitments, health problems, volunteer work, or school responsibilities, will be better able to concentrate and perform well when they are on the job. Showing concern about employees' lives outside the workplace also goes a long way toward instilling respect and commitment to the company. And some workers simply do a better job—they are more efficient or productive—during certain times of the day. If there are a lot of "morning people" on the payroll, for example, allowing them to start work earlier could boost the bottom line.

If you adopt a flexible scheduling policy, it should tell workers how to request a flexible schedule and what kinds of schedules might be allowed.

Flexible Scheduling

We understand that many employees have to balance the demands of their job with the needs of their families and other outside commitments. Therefore, we offer our employees the opportunity to request a flexible schedule.

If you would like to change your work schedule—for example, to come in and leave a couple of hours earlier or to work more hours on some days and fewer on others—please talk to your supervisor.

The Company will consider flexible scheduling requests on a case-by-case basis. When deciding whether to grant your request, we may consider the nature of your job, your work history, and our staffing needs, among other things.

Reality Check: Deciding Who Gets to Flex

Flexible scheduling can be a tremendous boon to employer and employee alike. However, employers who choose to offer this opportunity must make sure that they dole out the benefits fairly.

An employer that offers a discretionary benefit—that is, a benefit that may be granted for some employees but not for others—must be very careful to have solid business reasons for these decisions. Otherwise, the employer may face legal claims of discrimination. For example, if working mothers are routinely allowed to alter their schedules to meet child care needs but the same benefit isn't always extended to working fathers, an employer could get into trouble. Decision makers must consider each claim for flexible scheduling on its own merits: Can the company accommodate the request without substantial disruption? Does the employee's job lend itself to flexibility? Has the employee demonstrated the responsibility and self-motivation to work outside usual work hours?

CAUTION

Longer days may be costly in some states. A few states have a daily overtime standard. Typically, employers owe overtime to eligible employees who work more than 40 hours in a week. In states with a daily standard, employers owe overtime once an employee works more than eight hours (in California and Alaska) or 12 hours (in Colorado) in a day, even if their weekly hours are less than 40. If you adopt a flexible scheduling policy that allows employees to work more hours on some days and fewer hours on others, you may have to shell out daily overtime pay.

6:3   Meal and Rest Breaks

File Name: 06_Hours.rtf

Include This Policy?
- ☐ Yes
- ☐ No
- ☐ Use our existing policy
- ☐ Other _____

Alternate Modifications
Provide Paid or Unpaid Meal Breaks
Choose one: ☐ A ☐ B

Additional Clauses
None

Related Policies
None

Notes

_____
_____
_____
_____
_____
_____
_____
_____
_____
_____
_____
_____
_____
_____
_____
_____
_____

6:3   Meal and Rest Breaks

Most companies offer their employees some breaks during the day. The laws in some states require employers to provide paid breaks; other states require breaks but don't require employers to pay employees for this time. You can find out what your state requires by consulting "State Meal and Rest Break Laws" at the end of this chapter.

Even if your state doesn't require any breaks, you should adopt a break policy if your company generally allows employees to take breaks. Having a written policy will reduce confusion over how much time can be taken and whether it will be paid or unpaid.

Your policy on meal and rest breaks should let employees know when they get breaks, how long they can take, and whether those breaks are paid. Your policy should also tell employees that they must take their scheduled breaks unless they have made other arrangements with their supervisor. Recently, some employers have faced lawsuits by employees claiming that they were entitled to be paid for breaks they never took (or were never allowed to take). Also, because some state laws require employers to provide breaks at particular intervals, including this language in your policy allows you to make sure your company is complying with applicable law.

Meal and Rest Breaks

Employees are allowed a _____-minute break every _____ hours. These breaks will be _____ .
In addition, all employees who work at least _____ hours in a day are entitled to take a _____-minute meal break. Your supervisor will let you know when you should take your breaks. Breaks are an opportunity to rest and eat during the workday, and they may be required by law. For this reason, employees must take their breaks, as scheduled, unless they make other arrangements with their supervisor. For example, employees may not decide to skip breaks in order to leave early or come in late.

How to Complete This Policy

Federal law doesn't require employers to offer employees breaks of any length during the workday. However, federal law does require employers to pay employees for any breaks of 20 minutes or less that they choose to provide. A handful of states—including California and Washington—currently require employers to provide paid breaks during the workday. State laws are summarized in "State Meal and Rest Break Laws" at the end of this chapter.

To complete this policy, fill in the blanks with the length and frequency of the break your state requires (or the length of the break your company offers, as long as it meets or exceeds your state's legal requirements). Also, indicate whether rest breaks will be paid or unpaid.

Alternate Modifications to Provide for Paid or Unpaid Meal Breaks

To Provide Paid Meal Breaks

Generally, state and federal law do not require paid meal breaks, as long as the employee is entirely relieved of all work during the break; employees who are required to work through a meal period are entitled to be paid for that time. Nonetheless, many employers offer paid meal breaks to employees. If your company chooses to do so, add the language below to the end of the first paragraph of the policy.

Alternate Modification A

Meal breaks will be paid.

To Provide Unpaid Meal Breaks

If your company will not pay employee for their meal breaks, add the language below to the end of the first paragraph of your policy.

Alternate Modification B

Meal breaks are generally unpaid. However, employees who are required to work or remain at their stations during the meal break will be paid for that time.

6:4 Lactation Breaks

File Name: 06_Hours.rtf

Include This Policy?

☐ Yes

☐ No

☐ Use our existing policy

☐ Other _____

Alternate Modifications

Specify Where to Breast-Feed or
Express Breast Milk

Choose one: ☐ A ☐ B

Additional Clauses

None

Related Policies

None

Notes

_____

_____

_____

_____

_____

_____

_____

_____

_____

_____

_____

_____

_____

_____

_____

_____

6:4 Lactation Breaks

The Affordable Care Act of 2010 (Obamacare) includes provisions that promote preventive health care and healthy habits. In keeping with that intent, the law requires employers to allow reasonable break time for nursing mothers to express breast milk at work for up to one year after birth. The employer must also provide private space, other than a bathroom, for this purpose. These requirements apply only to nonexempt employees (see discussion of exempt and nonexempt employees in Chapter 5.

A number of states also require employers to provide lactation breaks. Some require only that employers allow employees to use their regular breaks for this purpose; others go further and require employers to provide additional breaks as needed. Some state laws also require employers to provide an appropriate place for employees to express breast milk. You can find information on your state's requirements in "State Meal and Rest Break Laws," at the end of this chapter.

The federal law applies to all employers, but it includes an exception for employers with fewer than 50 employees, if allowing lactation breaks would impose an "undue hardship," meaning it would entail significant expense or difficulty, considering the employer's size, structure, and resources. Even if you believe your company fits within this exception, however, you still must follow your state's law on lactation breaks, if it has one. Before the health care reform law made lactation breaks mandatory, many employers voluntarily chose to allow them: Allowing nursing mothers to express breast milk at work allows employees to return to work sooner after having a baby, enhances employee loyalty to the company, and provides mothers and babies with the proven health benefits of breast-feeding.

Lactation Breaks

Our Company recognizes the value and importance of breast-feeding, and supports our employees' desire to breast-feed their infants. If you are breast-feeding your child, you may use your meal and rest breaks to express breast milk. If you need more time, please speak to

_____ .

How to Complete This Policy

In the blank, insert the position responsible for reviewing employee requests (for example, "the human resources department" or "your supervisor"). Because the federal health care reform act requires employers to provide reasonable break time for expressing breast milk, your company should grant any employee requests for a longer period.

Tip Credit Notice Form

As a tipped employee, you will be subject to the Company's tip credit. Under the Fair Labor Standards Act, the Company is entitled to pay you a lower hourly wage, crediting a portion of the tips you receive to make up the difference. This form provides information on your wages and the tip credit:

- Your hourly wage (the amount of cash wage the Company will pay you per hour of work) is $_____ .
- The amount of your tips the Company will count as a tip credit per hour is $_____ . We will credit this amount of your tips per hour toward your wages.
- The Company may not claim a tip credit in excess of the tips you actually receive. In other words, if your tips are not sufficient to pay the tip credit amount noted above per hour, the Company must make up the difference.
- All tips you earn belong to you, unless you are required to contribute to a valid tip pool limited only to those employees who customarily and regularly receive their own tips.
- The tip credit will not apply to any employee who has not been notified of these rules.

You are required to contribute to a tip pooling arrangement, limited only to those employees who customarily and regularly receive their own tips. Your required contribution to the tip pool is _____ . Other than this contribution, you have the right to retain all tips you receive. The tip credit will be taken only on the tips you actually receive (in other words, on the amount you receive from the tip pool after you make your contribution and the amount of tips you retain).

Please sign and date this form to acknowledge receipt.

_____   _____
Employee's Signature   Date

_____
Employee's Name (Print)

7:4 Tip Pooling

File Name: 07_Pay Policies.rtf

Include This Policy?
☐ Yes
☐ No
☐ Use our existing policy
☐ Other _____

Alternate Modifications
None

Additional Clauses
None

Related Policies
None

Notes
_____
_____
_____
_____
_____
_____
_____
_____
_____
_____
_____
_____
_____
_____
_____
_____
_____
_____
_____
_____
_____

7:4   Tip Pooling

Tip pooling (also known as "tipping out") is a source of much anxiety and frustration in the tipped workforce. Some employees—particularly those who have to deal most with the customers, such as wait staff or bell persons—deeply resent having to share their tips with employees who have less customer contact. Adopting a policy that explains exactly who is required to share how much of their tips can help ease this problem. If everyone knows ahead of time how the tip pool will work, there is less likelihood of confusion and resentment.

Tip Pooling

Employees in the following positions are required to pool tips:
_____
_____ .

If you hold one of these positions, you must contribute _____% of your tips to the pool at the end of each workday. The pool will be divided among all employees who worked that day and hold one of the positions listed above.

How to Complete This Policy

Which employees can participate in a tip pool? The rules depend on whether your company takes a tip credit. If your company takes a tip credit, only employees who customarily and regularly receive tips, such as wait staff, bussers, bartenders, bellhops, and counter clerks, may take part in the tip pool. Workers who do not receive tips of their own—such as dishwashers, cooks, chefs, and janitors—cannot be included in the pool. In this situation, simply fill in the first blank with the titles of all employees who receive tips and will be required to contribute to the pool.

If your company does not (or cannot, legally) take a tip credit, you may have more leeway to expand the pool. In 2018, Congress amended the FLSA to explicitly allow employers that don't take a tip credit to include non-tipped employees in a tip pool. However, some states have more restrictive rules. In California, for example, only employees that are in the "chain of service" to a particular customer may share that customer's tip.

If your company doesn't take a tip credit, you have a couple of options. First, you may restrict the tip pool to tipped employees. (In other words, even though your company may extend the tip pool to non-tipped employees, it doesn't have to.) If you go this route, complete the first blank by including the titles of all employees who receive tips. Second, you may expand the tip pool to non-tipped employees (whose titles you should also include in the first blank), as long as you comply with your state's law. State laws and court cases may also dictate how the pool must be divided. For instance, although it's legal to allow non-tipped employees to participate in the tip pool, it may not be legal to give them the lion's share of the tips while leaving servers with very little. You can learn more about your state's tip pooling law by contacting your state labor department (see Appendix B for contact information). Because the change to federal law is recent, and the intersection of state and federal law here is not yet clear, this is also an issue you should raise with the attorney who reviews your handbook.

The law also limits how much workers can be required to contribute to a pool. Employees must receive at least the full minimum wage per hour once the pool is shared and divided. To come up with a tip contribution amount, track employee tip amounts for a while to come up with an appropriate percentage. You can also check with a local trade organization to find out what percentage is usual in your industry.

CAUTION

Don't take a dip in the tip pool. All of the money in the tip pool must be shared among the workers who contribute to it, and only those workers. Employers—including managers and supervisors—cannot take any portion of the pooled tips for themselves under any circumstances. Tips belong to employees. If an employer violates this basic rule, the Department of Labor will find its tip pooling arrangement invalid, disallow any tip credit it takes, and require the employer to pay back the money it took from workers, plus interest and penalties.

Who Needs This Policy

Only companies that employ workers who receive tips and require those employees to share their tips with other workers need this policy.

7:5 Shift Premiums

File Name: 07_Pay Policies.rtf

Include This Policy?

☐ Yes

☐ No

☐ Use our existing policy

☐ Other _____

Alternate Modifications

None

Additional Clauses

None

Related Policies

For information and a policy on overtime, see Chapter 6. If employees will be allowed—or required—to put in overtime hours, use this policy to explain the rules.

Notes

_____

_____

_____

_____

_____

_____

_____

_____

_____

_____

_____

_____

_____

_____

_____

_____

7:5 Shift Premiums

A shift premium policy should tell employees whether they'll be paid extra for working certain shifts, if applicable.

Employers in industries that work in shifts often find it difficult to staff shifts that fall outside of the regular 9 a.m. to 5 p.m. workday. Some employers find that offering workers higher pay to work night shifts, swing shifts, or split shifts solves this problem. If your company offers a shift premium, you should adopt a policy explaining the premium in your handbook. After all, the incentive only works if employees know about it.

Shift Premiums

Employees who work the _____ shift will be paid a premium for each shift. This premium will be _____ .

How to Complete This Policy

In the first blank, insert the shifts for which your company pays a premium (for example, night shift, graveyard shift, or 3 p.m. to 11 p.m. shift). In the second blank, insert the premium amount. If all workers make the same wage, you can simply insert the dollar amount these shift workers will receive per hour. If workers earn varying rates, you can insert the dollar amount or percentage by which their pay will be increased for agreeing to work the tough-to-fill shift (for example, two dollars more per hour in addition to their regular hourly pay or an additional 20% of their regular hourly pay).

Some states, including California, require employers to pay their workers a certain premium for working a split shift: working one shift then coming back to work another shift after a relatively short break. Contact your state labor department (you can find contact details in Appendix B) to find out if your state imposes this type of requirement. If so, your company must pay split shift workers this premium, and you should set the premium in your policy to at least meet the minimum amount required by law.

7:6   Pay Docking

Pay docking refers to making deductions from an employee's salary for absences or as a penalty for violating work rules. Generally, employers must pay exempt employees on a salary basis. This means that the employees must receive their full salary for any week in which they perform any work, regardless of how many hours they work or how much work they get done. These rules are a general reflection of the fact that exempt employees are not, by definition, paid by the hour; instead, they must put in as many hours as it takes to get the job done.

There are some exceptions to this general rule, however. The overtime regulations include a longer list of situations when employers can withhold pay from exempt employees. Employers must adhere to this list very carefully: An employer that withholds pay improperly could inadvertently change its exempt employees to nonexempt employees, who are entitled to overtime pay.

The rules also create a "safe harbor" provision for employers who are trying to comply, which is where this policy comes in. Under the safe harbor provision, an employer won't be liable for violating the pay docking rules if it has a written policy prohibiting improper deductions, with a complaint mechanism, and it promptly reimburses any amounts that should not have been withheld.

Your pay docking policy should explain the circumstances under which exempt employees—those who are not entitled to earn overtime—can have their pay docked for missing work. It should also explain what employees can do if they believe their pay has been docked improperly.

7:6   Pay Docking

File Name: 07_Pay Policies.rtf

Include This Policy?
- ☐ Yes
- ☐ No
- ☐ Use our existing policy
- ☐ Other _____

Alternate Modifications
None

Additional Clauses
None

Related Policies
None

Notes

_____
_____
_____
_____
_____
_____
_____
_____
_____
_____
_____
_____
_____
_____
_____
_____
_____

Docking the Pay of Exempt Employees

Our Company is legally required to pay exempt employees—those who are not entitled to earn overtime—on a salary basis. This means, among other things, that exempt employees must receive the same pay for each week in which they perform work, regardless of the quantity or quality of work performed, and regardless of how many hours they actually work, unless an exception applies. (For information on which employees are exempt, see Section _____ of this Handbook.)

Company policy prohibits docking the pay of an exempt employee— that is, paying the employee less than his or her full regular salary— except in the following circumstances:

- The employee takes at least one full day off for sickness or disability, in accordance with _____

  _____ .

- The employee takes at least one full day off for personal reasons other than sickness or disability (for example, for vacation).
- The employee serves an unpaid disciplinary suspension of at least one full day, imposed in good faith for violating a workplace conduct rule.
- The employee takes time off to serve on a jury, as a witness, or in the military; the employee receives money for jury fees, witness fees, or military pay; and the docked pay is an offset of the money received only.
- The employee starts or ends employment with our Company midweek (that is, the employee does not start work first thing Monday morning, or finish employment at the end of the workday on Friday).
- The employee violates a safety rule of major significance, and the amount docked is imposed as a penalty for that violation.
- The employee takes unpaid leave pursuant to the Family and Medical Leave Act.

If you are an exempt employee and you believe that pay has been improperly deducted from your salary in violation of these rules, please report it immediately using the Company's complaint policy. (See Section _____ of this Handbook.) Your complaint will be investigated and, if we find that your pay was improperly docked, you will be reimbursed for any amounts that should not have been withheld.

Who Needs This Policy

All companies that employ exempt employees *must* use this policy if they want the benefit of the safe harbor provision in the overtime rules.

How to Complete This Policy

In the first and third blanks, insert the appropriate section numbers for your Handbook's Employee Classification (see Chapter 5) and Complaint policies (see Chapter 20). In the second blank, insert the name of your company's plan or policy that provides paid time off for sickness or disability. For example, if your company offers paid sick leave, you should insert, "our sick leave policy." You may dock the employee's pay for this time only if you have a plan or policy that provides compensation for this time off.

RESOURCE

For more information on these rules. The Department of Labor has posted lots of resources on the overtime rules at its "Overtime Pay" page, www.dol.gov/whd/overtime_pay.htm.

7:7 Payroll Deductions

File Name: 07_Pay Policies.rtf

Include This Policy?
- ☐ Yes
- ☐ No
- ☐ Use our existing policy
- ☐ Other _____

Alternate Modifications
None

Additional Clauses
None

Related Policies
None

Notes
_____
_____
_____
_____
_____
_____
_____
_____
_____
_____
_____
_____
_____
_____
_____
_____
_____
_____
_____
_____
_____

7:7   Payroll Deductions

Your payroll deduction policy should explain the mandatory deductions that will be taken from employees' paychecks, as well as the deductions an employee can request. Although all the information is usually right there on the pay stub, a policy can help clarify the reasons why deductions are taken (and why that paycheck is always so much smaller than the worker thinks it will be).

Payroll Deductions

Your paycheck reflects your total earnings for the pay period, as well as any mandatory or voluntary deductions from your paycheck. Mandatory deductions are deductions that we are legally required to take. Such deductions include federal income tax, Social Security tax (FICA), and any applicable state taxes. Voluntary deductions are deductions that you have authorized. Such deductions might include

_____
_____ .

   If you have any questions about your deductions, or wish to change your federal withholding form (Form W-4), contact _____
_____ .

How to Complete This Policy

In the space for voluntary deductions, list any contributions employees are allowed to make through payroll withholding, such as:
- insurance premiums
- flexible spending accounts
- contributions to pensions, 401(k)s, or other retirement accounts
- union dues
- charitable contributions, or
- contributions to credit unions or savings accounts.

   In the second blank, insert the name of the person or position that handles payroll matters. This might be the payroll administrator, human resources department, benefits coordinator, or whoever makes sure that paychecks go out on time or reports employee compensation to the IRS.

7:8   Wage Garnishments

Any employer can be required—by a court order, the IRS, or another government agency—to garnish an employee's wages. Most employers dislike these orders because wage garnishments are a payroll hassle. An employer who receives one will have to deduct the prescribed amount from the employee's wages, either for a limited amount of time (for example, when the employee owes a specified amount of money in unpaid taxes or student loans) or indefinitely (for example, for garnishments relating to child or spousal support), depending on the order.

No matter how much an employer dislikes having to deal with a wage garnishment order, the employee whose wages will be garnished likes it even less. Adopting a policy lets employees know that the company has no choice but to comply with these orders. Employees will know that there's not much point asking the employer to reduce, forgive, or postpone the garnishment; it's out of the company's hands. And hopefully, employees who are upset about a garnishment will take their complaints to the responsible person or agency, rather than to someone who can't change the situation (you).

Your wage garnishment policy should explain what a wage garnishment is and why an employee's wages might be garnished. It should also inform employees that the company must comply with orders to garnish wages.

Wage Garnishments

A wage garnishment is an order from a court or a government agency directing us to withhold a certain amount of money from an employee's paycheck and send it to a person or agency. Wages can be garnished to pay child support, spousal support or alimony, tax debts, outstanding student loans, or money owed as a result of a judgment in a civil lawsuit.

If we are instructed by a court or agency to garnish an employee's wages, the employee will be notified of the garnishment at once. Please note that we are legally required to comply with these orders. If you dispute or have concerns about the amount of a garnishment, you must contact the court or agency that issued the order.

7:8   Wage Garnishments

File Name: 07_Pay Policies.rtf

Include This Policy?

☐ Yes

☐ No

☐ Use our existing policy

☐ Other _____

Alternate Modifications

None

Additional Clauses

None

Related Policies

None

Notes

_____

_____

_____

_____

_____

_____

_____

_____

_____

_____

_____

_____

_____

_____

_____

_____

_____

_____

_____

_____

RESOURCE

Want more information on wage garnishments? The Department of Labor's website offers a helpful fact sheet on related federal law, including how much of an employee's wages can be garnished. You can download it at www.dol.gov/compliance/guide/garnish.htm.

7:9   Expense Reimbursement

Expenses often become a source of conflict between workers and management. Workers don't want to incur work-related expenses that the company refuses to pay. They want to know ahead of time what they will be reimbursed for, what they need to do to get reimbursed, and when they can expect repayment. Just as understandably, employers don't want to get hit with requests for reimbursement for extravagant, fraudulent, or unnecessary expenses. Employers also want some proof that the worker actually incurred the expenses claimed. An expense reimbursement policy can help you set things straight before your employees incur any expenses on behalf of the company.

Your expense reimbursement policy should tell employees which expenses will be reimbursed, how to get authorization to incur expenses, and the procedures for requesting reimbursement.

Expense Reimbursement

From time to time, employees may incur expenses on behalf of our Company. We will reimburse you for the actual work-related expenses you incur, as long as those expenses are reasonable. You must follow these procedures to get reimbursed:

- Get permission from your supervisor before incurring an expense.
- Spend the Company's money wisely. Make an effort to save money and use approved vendors if possible.
- Keep a receipt or some other proof of payment for every expense.
- Submit your receipts, along with an expense report, to your supervisor for approval within 30 days of incurring an expense.
- Your supervisor is responsible for submitting your expense report to _____ _____ .

If your report is approved, you will receive your reimbursement

_____ .

Remember that you are spending the Company's money when you pay for business-related expenses. We expect you to save money wherever possible. Your supervisor can assist you in deciding whether an expense is appropriate.

7:9   Expense Reimbursement
File Name: 07_Pay Policies.rtf

Include This Policy?
- ☐ Yes
- ☐ No
- ☐ Use our existing policy
- ☐ Other _____

Alternate Modifications
None

Additional Clauses
Require Employees to Use Particular Vendors
  Insert?:   ☐ Yes   ☐ No
Include More Detail on Travel Expenses
  Insert?:   ☐ Yes   ☐ No
Allow Mileage Reimbursement
  Insert?:   ☐ Yes   ☐ No

Related Policies
None

Notes

_____
_____
_____
_____
_____
_____
_____
_____
_____
_____
_____
_____

Reality Check: An Expense by Any Other Name

Sometimes, state law dictates whether the employer or employee has to pay for a particular expense. For example, some states require employers to pay the cost of everything an employee needs in order to do the job, including uniforms and tools. Other states don't have such strict requirements; they allow employers to pass these costs on to their employees (or to refuse to reimburse these expenses, as the case may be). Contact your state labor department (you can find contact information in Appendix B) to find out what your state requires.

How to Complete This Policy

In the first blank, insert the position or department responsible for payroll matters (for example, the payroll department, the accounting department, or human resources). In the second blank, indicate when and how employees will receive their reimbursements (for example, "with your next paycheck" or "within 14 days").

Additional Clause to Require Employees to Use Particular Vendors

If your company has business accounts with particular vendors, such as messengers, caterers, or suppliers, you may want to modify our standard policy to require employees to do business with those vendors, if possible. This will save time and money: The company will know it's getting a good deal, and workers won't have to shop around. If you want to make this addition, insert the additional clause at the end of the list in our sample policy. Fill in the blank with the name of the position or department that handles payroll.

Additional Clause

- The Company maintains a list of preferred vendors for various work-related items and services. You must use these vendors, if possible. You can get a current copy of the list from _____
_____ .

Leave and Time Off

A little time off is a good thing, for employer and employee alike. Workers get a chance to have fun; deal with personal, civic, and family obligations; and recharge their batteries. Your company benefits, too: The business will be more productive if employees are healthy, rested, and focused on their jobs.

By now, offering at least some paid time off—for sickness and vacation—has become the nationwide standard. In fact, a growing number of states require employers to provide paid sick leave. Also, an employer may be legally required to let employees take unpaid leave in certain circumstances. No matter what type of leave program your company decides to adopt, the policies in this chapter will help you set rules that are consistent, sensible, and easy to follow.

CONTENTS

10:1 Vacation

File Name: 10_Time Off.rtf

Include This Policy?
☐ Yes
☐ No
☐ Use our existing policy
☐ Other _____

Alternate Modifications
None

Additional Clauses
Cap Accrual of Vacation Time
Insert?:   ☐ Yes ☐ No
Pay Unused Vacation at Termination
Insert?:   ☐ Yes ☐ No

Related Policies
None

Notes
_____
_____
_____
_____
_____
_____
_____
_____
_____
_____
_____
_____
_____
_____
_____
_____
_____
_____
_____

10:1 Vacation

Most employers offer paid vacation benefits to at least some of their employees, even though they aren't legally required to do so. Paid vacation has become standard business practice in this country. Employers who don't offer some paid days off for rest and relaxation will almost certainly have trouble attracting and retaining good employees.

Your vacation policy should explain who is eligible for vacation, how vacation time accrues, and how the employee can schedule time off.

Vacation

Our Company recognizes that our employees need to take time off occasionally to rest and relax, enjoy a vacation, or attend to personal matters. That's why we offer a paid vacation program.

_____

are eligible to participate in the paid vacation program.

Eligible employees accrue vacation time according to the following schedule:

Years of Employment	Vacation Accrual
_____	_____
_____	_____
_____	_____
_____	_____
_____	_____
_____	_____
_____	_____
_____	_____
_____	_____
_____	_____
_____	_____

Employees must schedule their vacations _____ in advance, with their supervisor. We will try to grant every employee's vacation request for the days off of their choice. Because we must have enough workers to meet our day-to-day needs, however, we might not be able to grant every vacation request, especially during holiday periods.

How to Complete This Policy

In the first blank space, indicate which employees will be eligible to participate in the vacation program (for example, "Full-time employees," "Employees who work at least 32 hours per week," or "Employees who have been with the company for at least three months"). Some employers limit these benefits to full-time employees or require employees to complete a waiting period before they can accrue or use vacation benefits. (For information and policies on these employee classifications, see Chapter 5.)

In the second blank, write in the schedule by which employees will accrue benefits. Many employers provide increases in benefits to employees who stay with the company over time. For example, a worker might accrue ten days of vacation during the first year or two of employment, then move up to 15 the next year, then 20. Once you figure out how many days of vacation employees will accrue, divide that number by 12 to figure out how many days of vacation they accrue each month. The sample accrual schedule below allows employees to accrue ten days of vacation during their first and second years of employment, 15 during their third and fourth years, and 20 during each year thereafter.

SAMPLE POLICY LANGUAGE

Years of Employment	Vacation Accrual
0–2	10 days per year, at the rate of $5/6$ of a day per month
2–4	15 days per year, at the rate of 1¼ days per month
4 or more	20 days per year, at the rate of $1^2/_3$ days per month

Of course, if your company provides the same number of vacation days to all employees, you can delete this schedule and replace it with your company's rule, such as "Eligible employees accrue 1 day of vacation per month."

In the third blank, insert how many days of notice your company requires employees to give (for example, "30 days").

Additional Clause to Cap Accrual of Vacation Time

Your company can encourage employees to use their vacation regularly—and avoid having employees out for weeks of collected vacation at a time—by capping how much vacation time employees can accrue. Employees who reach this limit won't earn any more vacation time until they take some vacation and bring themselves back down below the cap. To cap how much vacation time an employee can accrue, add this clause to your policy immediately after the accrual schedule. In the blank space, insert the cap: how many hours or days of vacation time an employee will be allowed to accrue.

Additional Clause

> Employees may not accrue more than _____ of vacation time. Once an employee's vacation balance reaches this limit, an employee may accrue more vacation only by taking some vacation time to bring the employee's balance back below the limit.

CAUTION

"Use it or lose it" policies are illegal in some states. An employer is legally entitled to cap how much vacation time an employee can accrue. However, some states forbid "use it or lose it" policies, by which an employee must forfeit accrued but unused vacation time over a certain limit or past a certain date. Because these states view earned vacation time as a form of compensation, which must be cashed out when the employee quits or is fired, a policy that takes vacation time away is seen as illegally failing to pay employees money that they have already earned. Although the difference may seem merely technical, an accrual cap is legal in these states, because it prohibits the employee from earning vacation time in the first place, rather than taking away vacation time after the employee has earned it. Contact your state labor department to find out about your state's rules. (See Appendix B for contact information.)

Additional Clause to Pay Unused Vacation at Termination

Some states have passed laws addressing an employer's obligation to cash out unused, accrued vacation time when an employee quits or is fired. These laws take a few forms. State law might simply require employers to pay out unused vacation. A few states explicitly do not require employers to pay out unused vacation. In a number of states, however, your policy determines whether you are obliged to pay out unused vacation. For instance, Kansas employers must pay out unused vacation time if required by their policies or practices. In contrast, New York requires employers to pay out unused vacation time unless they have adopted a contrary policy. You can find out your state's rule by checking "State Laws That Control Final Paychecks" at the end of Chapter 21.

Depending on your state's rules, you may want to modify the policy to inform employees that they will or will not receive payment for unused vacation. To do so, simply select the appropriate language and add the clause below as the final paragraph of the policy.

Additional Clause

Employees *[will/will not]* be paid for any accrued and unused vacation when their employment terminates.

10:2 Holidays

File Name: 10_Time Off.rtf

Include This Policy?

☐ Yes

☐ No

☐ Use our existing policy

☐ Other _____

Alternate Modifications

None

Additional Clauses

Allow Floating Holidays

Insert?:　☐ Yes　☐ No

Related Policies

None

Notes

_____
_____
_____
_____
_____
_____
_____
_____
_____
_____
_____
_____
_____
_____
_____
_____
_____
_____

10:2 Holidays

Most companies offer their employees paid time off on certain holidays, such as New Year's Day, Independence Day, and Thanksgiving. Your holiday policy should tell employees which holidays the company observes and what happens when a holiday falls on a weekend.

Holidays

Our Company observes the following holidays each year:

_____
_____
_____
_____
_____
_____
_____
_____
_____

　If a holiday falls on a weekend, the Company will inform you when the holiday will be observed. Ordinarily, holidays falling on a Saturday will be observed the preceding Friday; holidays falling on a Sunday will be observed the following Monday.

How to Complete This Policy

In the blank space, list the holidays that your company observes. The days you choose will, of course, depend on when your company is open. Most employers offer some combination of the following paid holidays: New Year's Day, Martin Luther King Jr. Day, President's Day, Good Friday, Memorial Day, Independence Day, Labor Day, Columbus Day, Veterans' Day, Thanksgiving, the Friday following Thanksgiving, Christmas Eve, Christmas Day, and New Year's Eve.

Additional Clause to Allow Floating Holidays

Some employees may not observe the religious holidays your company chooses to offer—for example, Christmas or Good Friday—and may wish to take a holiday on a day of significance to their own religion. Employers are legally obligated to accommodate their workers' religious practices, which in some cases may require an employer to give these workers time off for important religious holidays. Rather than requiring workers to come to management with these requests, your company can make floating holidays available to all workers, to allow them to participate in religious activities or attend to other personal matters.

Some employers offer only one or two floating holidays per year; others offer more floating holidays but trim the list of company-recognized holidays accordingly. If your company will offer floating holidays, add the clause below as the second paragraph of the policy, immediately after the list of holidays your company observes. In the blank, insert the number of floating holidays employees will be allowed to take each year.

Additional Clause

Eligible employees are also entitled to take _____ floating holidays each year. These holidays may be used to observe a religious holiday, to celebrate your birthday, or simply to take a day off for personal reasons. You must schedule your floating holidays with your supervisor in advance. If you do not use your floating holidays during the year, you may not carry them over to the next year.

10:3 Sick Leave

File Name: 10_Time Off.rtf

Include This Policy?

☐ Yes

☐ No

☐ Use our existing policy

☐ Other _____

Alternate Modifications

None

Additional Clauses

Limit Carryover or Cap Accrual of Sick Leave

Insert?: ☐ Yes ☐ No

If yes, choose one: ☐ A ☐ B

Cap Use of Sick Leave in One Year

Insert?: ☐ Yes ☐ No

Allow Other Uses for Sick Leave

Insert?: ☐ Yes ☐ No

Related Policies

None

Notes

_____

_____

_____

_____

_____

_____

_____

_____

_____

_____

_____

_____

10:3 Sick Leave

It's common practice for employers to provide paid sick days. In an increasing number of states and localities, it may also be the law. A number of cities require employers that do business within the city limits to provide some paid sick time to their employees. And several states have passed laws requiring employers to provide some paid sick leave: Arizona, Calfornia, Connecticut, Maryland, Massachusetts, Michigan, New Jersey, Oregon, Rhode Island, Vermont, and Washington, plus the District of Columbia.

Even if your state or local government does not require you to offer paid sick time, it's a good idea. Paid sick days help workers who live paycheck to paycheck make ends meet, create fewer payroll hassles, and, perhaps most important, encourage sick workers to stay home rather than coming to work to infect the rest of the workforce or perform at a substandard level.

Your sick leave policy should explain who is eligible for leave, how much leave employees can take, and any notice requirements the company will impose.

Sick Leave

Our Company provides paid sick leave to _____.
Eligible employees accrue sick leave according to the following schedule: _____.
You may use your sick leave _____.

Employees should use sick leave when they are unable to work due to illness or injury. Please do not report to work if you are feeling too ill to do your job, you have a fever, or you have a contagious illness, such as influenza. By staying home and using paid sick leave, you are supporting your own health and preventing transmission of communicable illness to coworkers and customers. If your supervisor determines that you are not feeling well enough to work, you will be sent home.

You must report to your supervisor if you will need to take sick leave. We ask that employees call in as soon as they realize that they will be unable to work, before the regular start of their workday. You must report to your supervisor by phone each day you are out on leave.

Sick leave is not to be used as extra vacation time, personal days, or "mental health" days. Any employee who abuses sick leave may be subject to discipline.

The Company will not pay employees for sick leave that has accrued but has not been used when employment ends.

State Family and Medical Leave Laws (continued)

Connecticut

Conn. Gen. Stat. §§ 31-51kk–31-51qq, 31-57r–31-57t, 46a-60

Family and Medical Leave: Employers with 75 or more employees must provide up to 16 weeks during any 24-month period for childbirth, adoption, the employee's serious health condition, a family member's serious health condition, bone marrow or organ donation, or a qualifying exigency arising out of a family member's active duty in the military.

Employee may take up to 26 weeks in a 12-month period for a family member who is a current member of the armed forces and is undergoing medical treatment for a serious illness or injury. Employees are eligible if they have worked for the employer for one year and have worked 1,000 hours in the last year.

Pregnancy Disability Leave: Employers with three or more employees must provide a reasonable amount of leave to employees who are unable to work due to pregnancy.

Paid Sick Leave: Employers in the service industry with 50 or more employees must provide employees with one hour of paid sick leave for every 40 hours worked, but may cap accrual at 40 hours per year. Employees may use leave for their own illness or to care for an ill family member.

District of Columbia

D.C. Code §§ 32-501 and following, 32-1202, 32-131.01 and following

Family and Medical Leave: Employers with 20 or more employees must provide up to 16 weeks in a 24-month period for the birth of a child, adoption, foster care, placement of a child with the employee for whom the employee permanently assumes and discharges parental responsibility, or to care for family member with a serious health condition. Employees may take an additional 16 weeks in a 24-month period for their own serious health conditions. Employees must have worked for the employer for at least one year and worked at least 1,000 hours in the year before the start of leave.

School Activities: All employers must provide up to 24 hours of unpaid leave per year for an employee to attend a child's school activities.

Domestic Violence: Paid sick leave may also be used for employee or family member who is a victim of stalking, domestic violence, or abuse to get medical attention, get services, seek counseling, relocate, take legal action, or take steps to enhance health and safety.

Paid Sick Leave: All employers must provide paid sick leave for employees to use for their own illness or to care for a family member. Amount of paid leave ranges from three days to seven days per year, depending on size of the employer. Sick leave may be used for the employee's illness, to care for an ill family member, or to deal with the effects of stalking, domestic violence, or abuse against the employee or a family member.

Paid Family Leave: Beginning on July 1, 2020, employees will be eligible to receive paid family leave benefits from the district when taking leave for their own serious health conditions (two weeks), to care for a family member with a serious health condition (six weeks), or to bond with a new child (eight weeks).

Florida

Fla. Stat. Ann. § 741.313

Domestic Violence: Employers with at least 50 employees must provide up to three days of unpaid leave each year to employees who are the victims of domestic violence or sexual abuse or whose family members are victims. Employees are eligible if they have worked for the employer for at least three months.

Georgia

Ga. Code Ann. § 34-1-10

Family and Medical Leave: No requirement to provide sick leave, but employers with 25 or more employees that choose to do so must allow up to five days each year to be used to care for a sick immediate family member.

Hawaii

Haw. Rev. Stat. §§ 378-1, 378-71–378-74, 392-23, 398-1–398-11

Family and Medical Leave: Employers with 100 or more employees must provide up to four weeks of unpaid leave each year for the birth of a child or adoption, or to care for family member with a serious health condition. (If employer provides paid sick leave, up to ten days may be used for these purposes.) Employees are eligible if they have worked for the employer for six months.

Pregnancy Disability Leave: All employers must provide a reasonable period of time off for disability resulting from pregnancy, childbirth, or a related condition.

Domestic Violence: All employers must provide domestic violence leave. Employers with 50 or more employees must allow up to 30 days' unpaid leave per year for employee who is a victim of domestic or sexual violence or if employee's minor child is a victim. Employer with 49 or fewer employees must allow up to five days' leave.

Organ and Bone Marrow Donation: Employers with 50 or more employees must provide up to seven days of unpaid leave for bone marrow donation and 30 days' unpaid leave for organ donation.

Temporary Disability Insurance: Eligible employees who are temporarily unable to work because of illness or injury (including pregnancy) may collect up to 26 weeks of benefits through the state disability insurance program.

Illinois

820 Ill. Comp. Stat. §§ 147/1 and following, 180/1 and following

School Activities: Employers with 50 or more employees must provide eight hours per year, but not more than four hours in a day, for employees to participate in a child's school activities. Employees are eligible if they have worked for the employer at least half time for six months and have no paid leave available.

Domestic Violence: All employers must provide unpaid leave each year to an employee who is a victim of domestic violence or sexual assault or whose family or household member is a victim. Employers with 50 or more employees must provide 12 weeks of leave; employers with 15 to 49 employees must provide eight weeks of leave; and employers with 14 or fewer employees must provide four weeks of leave.

Iowa

Iowa Code § 216.6

Pregnancy Disability Leave: Employers with four or more employees must provide eight weeks of leave for disability due to pregnancy, childbirth, or related conditions.

Kentucky

Ky. Rev. Stat. § 337.015

Family and Medical Leave: All employers must provide six weeks of leave to employees adopting a child under seven years old.

Louisiana

La. Rev. Stat. §§ 23:341–23:342, 23:1015 and following, 40:1263.4

Pregnancy Disability Leave: Employers with 25 or more employees must provide a reasonable period of time off for disability due to pregnancy and childbirth, not to exceed six weeks for normal pregnancy or eight weeks for complicated pregnancy.

School Activities: All employers must provide 16 hours of leave each year to attend a child's school or daycare activities.

Paid Sick Leave: Employers with 20 or more employees must provide 40 hours of paid leave each year for employees to donate bone marrow. Employees are eligible if they work at least 20 hours per week.

Maine

Me. Rev. Stat. tit. 26, §§ 843 and following, 850

Family and Medical Leave: Employers with 15 or more employees at one location must provide ten weeks of leave in a two-year period for the birth of a child, adoption (for child 16 or younger), the employee's serious health condition, a family member's serious health condition, organ donation, or the death or serious health condition of a family member incurred while on active military duty. Employees are eligible if they have worked for the employer for at least one year.

Domestic Violence: All employers must provide reasonable and necessary leave to an employee who is the victim of domestic violence, sexual assault, or stalking, or whose parent, spouse, or child is a victim. Leave may be used to prepare for and attend court, for medical treatment, and for other necessary services.

Maryland

Md. Code, Lab. & Empl. §§ 3-1301–3-1311, 3-801–3-803

Family and Medical Leave: Employers with 15 or more employees must provide the same leave for adoption as allowed for the birth of a child. Employers with 50 or more employees must give employees a day off when an immediate family member leaves for or returns from active military duty outside the United States. Employees are eligible if they have worked for the employer for at least 12 months and worked at least 1,250 hours in the last year.

Paid Sick Leave: Employers with 15 or more employees must provide sick leave; smaller employers must provide unpaid sick leave. Employees accrue one hour of sick leave for every 30 hours worked. However, employers may cap accrual at 40 hours per year and use at 64 hours per year. Employees may use sick leave for their own illnesses, to care for an ill family member, for preventative medical care for the employee or a family member, for maternity or paternity leave, or to deal with the effects of domestic violence.

State Family and Medical Leave Laws (continued)

Massachusetts

Mass. Gen. Laws ch. 149, §§ 52D, 105D, 148C; ch. 151B, § 1(5)

Family and Medical Leave: Employers with six or more employees must provide eight weeks of unpaid leave to employees for the birth of a child or the adoption of a minor. Employees are eligible once they have completed their initial probationary period of employment, as long as it doesn't exceed three months.

Employers with 50 or more employees must provide 24 hours of leave each year to take a minor child or relative who is 60 or older to medical or dental appointment (combined with school activities leave). Employees must meet the same eligibility requirements of the FMLA.

School Activities: Employers with 50 or more employees must provide 24 hours of leave each year for an employee to attend a child's school activities (combined with family and medical leave for medical appointments). Employees must meet the same eligibility requirements of the FMLA.

Domestic Violence: Employers with 50 or more employees must provide 15 days of unpaid leave in a 12-month period if the employee, or the employee's family member, is a victim of abusive behavior. Leave may be used to seek medical attention or counseling, obtain a protective order from a court, attend child custody proceedings, and other related purposes. Employees must meet the same eligibility requirements of the FMLA.

Paid Sick Leave: All employers must provide one hour of sick leave for every 30 hours worked, although employers may cap annual accrual at 40 hours. Employers with 11 or more employees must provide paid time off; employers with ten or fewer employees may provide unpaid time off. Employees may use leave for their own illnesses, to care for an ill family member, or domestic violence reasons.

Michigan

Mich. Comp. Laws §§ 408.961 and following

Paid Sick Leave: Beginning in late March 2019, employers with 50 or more employees must provide paid medical leave. Employees accrue one hour of paid leave for every 35 hours worked, but not more than one hour of paid leave per workweek. Employers may cap accrual and use at 40 hours per year. Employees may use sick leave for their own illnesses or preventative care; a family member's illness or preventative care; to deal with the effects of domestic violence or sexual assault; or due to the closure of the employee's workplace or a child's school due to a public health emergency.

Minnesota

Minn. Stat. §§ 181.940 and following

Family and Medical Leave: Employers with 21 or more employees at one site must provide 12 weeks of leave for the birth of a child or adoption. Employees may also use accrued sick leave to care for an ill family member. Employees are eligible if they have worked at least half time for one year.

School Activities: All employers must provide 16 hours in a 12-month period to attend a child's activities related to child care, preschool, or special education. Employees are eligible if they have worked half time for at least one year.

Domestic Violence: Employers with 21 or more employees must allow accrued sick leave to be used to seek assistance due to sexual assault, domestic violence, or stalking.

Organ and Bone Marrow Donation: Employers with 20 or more employees must provide 40 hours of paid leave each year to donate bone marrow. Employees are eligible if they work at least 20 hours per week.

Montana

Mont. Code §§ 49-2-310, 49-2-311

Pregnancy Disability Leave: All employers must provide a reasonable leave of absence for pregnancy disability and childbirth.

Nebraska

Neb. Rev. Stat. § 48-234

Family and Medical Leave: Employers that allow employees to take leave for the birth of a child must give the same leave for adoption of a child no older than eight, or a child no older than 18 if the child has special needs (does not apply to stepparent or foster parent adoptions).

Nevada

Nev. Rev. Stat. §§ 392.920, 392.4577, 608.0198, 613.4383

Pregnancy Disability Leave: Employers that provide sick or disability leave to employees with other medical conditions must provide the same leave for pregnancy, miscarriage, childbirth and related medical conditions.

School Activities: Employers with 50 or more employees must provide employees with a child in public school four hours of leave per school year to attend parent-teacher conferences, school-related activities during regular school hours, school-sponsored events, or to volunteer or be involved at the school. All employers may not fire or threaten to fire a parent, guardian, or custodian for attending a school conference or responding to a child's emergency.

Domestic Violence: All employers must provide 160 hours of unpaid leave within one year of an incident of domestic violence for the following purposes: to seek medical treatment, to obtain counseling, to participate in court proceedings, or to create a safety plan. Employees are eligible if they have worked for at least 90 days and if they are victims of domestic violence or have a family member who is a victim.

New Hampshire

N.H. Rev. Stat. § 354-A:7(VI)

Pregnancy Disability Leave: Employers with six or more employees must provide temporary disability leave for pregnancy, childbirth, or a related medical condition.

New Jersey

N.J. Stat. §§ 34:11B-1 and following, 34-11C1 and following, 34:11D-1 and following, 43:21-1 and following

Family and Medical Leave: Employers with 50 or more employees must provide 12 weeks of leave (or 24 weeks reduced leave schedule) in any 24-month period for the birth or adoption of a child or to care for a family member with a serious health condition. Employees are eligible if they have worked for at least one year and at least 1,000 hours in the previous 12 months.

Domestic Violence: Employers with 25 or more employees must provide 20 unpaid days in one 12-month period for employee who is (or whose family member is) a victim of domestic violence or a sexually violent offense. Employees are eligible if they have worked for at least one year and worked at least 1,000 hours in the last 12 months.

Paid Sick Leave: All employers must provide paid sick leave to their employees. Employees accrue one hour of paid sick leave for every 30 hours worked. However, employers may cap accrual and use at 40 hours per year. Employees may use sick leave for their own illnesses, to care for an ill family member, for preventative medical care for themselves or a family member, to attend a child's school events, to deal with the effects of domestic violence, or due to the closure of the employee's workplace or child's school due to a public health emergency.

Paid Family Leave: Employees may receive paid family leave benefits from the state for six weeks of leave per year to care for a seriously ill family member (including a registered domestic partner) or to bond with a new child.

Temporary Disability Insurance: Employees may receive temporary disability benefits from the state for up to 26 weeks when they are unable to work due to disability.

New Mexico

N.M. Stat. §§ 50-4A-1 and following.

Domestic Violence: All employers must provide intermittent leave for up to 14 days each calendar year, but no more than eight hours in one day, to obtain an order of protection or other judicial relief from domestic abuse, to meet with law enforcement officials, to consult with attorneys or district attorneys' victim advocates, or to attend court proceedings related to the domestic abuse of an employee or an employee's family member.

New York

N.Y. Lab. Law §§ 201-c, 202-a; N.Y. Workers' Comp. Law §§ 200 and following

Family and Medical Leave: Employers that allow employees to take leave for the birth of a child must provide the same leave to employees adopting a child of preschool age or younger (or no older than 18 if disabled).

All employers must provide time off to employees to bond with a new child, take care of a family member with a serious health condition, or for qualifying exigencies arising out of a family member's call to active military duty. The maximum amount of leave in a 52-week period: eight weeks in 2018, ten weeks in 2019 and 2020, and 12 weeks in 2021 and beyond. Full-time employees are eligible once they have been employed for 26 weeks; part-time employees are eligible once they have worked 175 days.

Organ and Bone Marrow Donation: Employers with 20 or more employees at one site must provide 24 hours' leave to donate bone marrow. Employees are eligible if they work at least 20 hours per week.

Paid Family Leave: Employees may also receive paid family leave benefits from the state when taking leave to care for a family member with a serious health condition, to bond with a new child, or for qualifying exigency arising out of a family member's call to active duty in the military. The maximum benefit in 2018 is 50% of employee's average weekly wage or state average weekly wage. This increases to 55% in 2019, 60% in 2020, and 67% in 2021.

State Family and Medical Leave Laws (continued)

Temporary Disability Insurance: Employees who have worked for a covered employer for at least four consecutive weeks may receive temporary disability insurance benefits from the state for up to 26 weeks while unable to work due to disability (including pregnancy).

North Carolina

N.C. Gen. Stat. §§ 50B-5.5, 95-28.3

School Activities: All employers must give employees four hours of leave per year to parents or guardians of school-aged children to participate in school activities.

Domestic Violence: All employers must provide reasonable time off to obtain or attempt to obtain relief from domestic violence and sexual assault.

Oregon

Or. Rev. Stat. §§ 659A.029, 659A.150 and following, 659A.270 and following, 659A.312, 653.601 and following

Family and Medical Leave: Employers with 25 or more employees must provide 12 weeks off per year for the birth or adoption of a child (parental leave), the employee's serious health condition, to care for a family member with a serious health condition, to care for a child with an illness or injury that requires home care (sick child leave), or to deal with the death of a family member (bereavement leave). Bereavement leave is capped at two weeks. Employees can take 12 weeks of parental leave and an additional 12 weeks for sick child leave. Employees are eligible if they have worked 25 or more hours per week for at least 180 days (except parental leave, which only requires that the employee has worked 180 days).

Pregnancy Disability Leave: Employers with 25 or more employees must provide 12 weeks off per year for pregnancy disability. This is in addition to 12 weeks for parental leave and 12 weeks for sick child leave. Employees are eligible if they have worked 25 or more hours per week for at least 180 days.

Domestic Violence: Employers with six or more employees must provide reasonable leave to employee who is victim of, or whose minor child is a victim of, domestic violence, harassment, sexual assault, or stalking. Leave may be used to seek legal treatment, medical services, counseling, or to relocate or secure existing home.

Organ and Bone Marrow Donation: All employers must allow the employee to use accrued leave or must provide the employee with 40 hours of unpaid leave, whichever is less, to donate bone marrow. Employees are eligible if they work at least 20 hours per week.

Paid Sick Leave: All employers must provide one hour of sick leave for every 30 hours worked, although employers may cap accrual and use at 40 hours per year. Up to 40 hours of accrued leave must carry over to the next year. Employers with ten or more employees must provide paid time off; employers with nine or fewer employees may provide unpaid time off. Employees may use leave for their own illnesses, to care for an ill family member, to deal with domestic violence issues, or for any purpose described under the "Family Medical Leave" section.

Rhode Island

R.I. Gen. Laws §§ 28-48-1 and following, 28-41-34–28-41-42, 28-57-1 and following

Family and Medical Leave: Employers with 50 or more employees must provide 13 weeks of leave in a two-year period for the birth of a child, adoption of child up to 16 years old, the employee's serious health condition, or to care for family member with serious health condition. Employees must have worked an average of 30 or more hours a week for at least 12 consecutive months.

School Activities: Employers with 50 or more employees must provide up to ten hours a year to attend a child's school conferences or other activities.

Paid Sick Leave: Employers with 18 or more employees must provide one hour of paid sick leave for every 35 hours worked, up to a maximum of 24 hours in 2018, 32 hours in 2019, and 40 hours in 2020 and beyond. Employers with fewer than 18 employees must provide the same amount of unpaid sick leave. Sick leave may be used for the employee's own illness, to care for an ill family member, for reasons relating to domestic violence, or due to the closure of the employee's work or a child's school due to a public health emergency.

Paid Family Leave: Employees who take time off to bond with a new child or care for a family member with a serious health condition may receive four weeks of temporary caregiver benefits from the state.

Temporary Disability Insurance: Employees who are unable to work due to illness, injury, or pregnancy may collect up to 30 weeks of benefits from the state through its short-term disability insurance program (temporary caregiver benefits are counted against the 30 weeks).

State Family and Medical Leave Laws (continued)

South Carolina

S.C. Code § 44-43-80

Organ and Bone Marrow Donation: Employers with 20 or more employees in the state at one site may—but are not required to—allow employees to take up to 40 hours' paid leave per year to donate bone marrow. Employees are eligible if they work at least 20 hours per week.

Tennessee

Tenn. Code § 4-21-408

Family and Medical Leave: Employers with 100 or more employees must provide up to four months of unpaid leave for pregnancy, childbirth, nursing, and adoption. Employees must give three months' notice unless a medical emergency requires the leave to begin sooner. Employees are eligible if they have worked full-time for the employer for 12 consecutive months.

Texas

Tex. Lab. Code § 21.0595

Family and Medical Leave: Employers with 15 or more employees that provide leave to care for a sick child must also allow leave to care for a sick foster child.

Vermont

Vt. Stat. tit. 21, §§ 471 and following, 481 and following

Family and Medical Leave: Employers with ten or more employees must provide unpaid leave for pregnancy, childbirth, or parental leave for the birth of a child or adoption of a child 16 or younger. Employers with 15 or more employees must also provide unpaid leave for the employee's serious health conditions or to care for family member with a serious health condition. Employees may take up to 12 weeks each year for any of these purposes. Employers with 15 employees must provide an additional four hours of leave in a 30-day period, but not more than 24 hours per year, to take a family member to a medical, dental, or professional well-care appointment or respond to a family member's medical emergency (combined with school activities leave). Employees are eligible if they have worked an average of 30 hours per week for one year.

School Activities: Employers with 15 or more employees must provide employees with four hours of leave in a 30-day period, but not more than 24 hours per year, to participate in a child's school activities (combined with leave to take a family member to medical appointments). Employees are eligible if they have worked an average of 30 hours per week for one year.

Domestic Violence: Unpaid leave for victims of crime, including domestic violence and sexual assault, to attend certain legal proceedings.

Paid Sick Leave: All employers must provide one hour of paid sick leave for every 52 hours worked. Employers may cap accrual at 24 hours per year in 2018 and 40 hours per year in 2019. Employees are eligible if they have worked for a covered employer for an average of 18 hours per week for at least 20 weeks. Employees may use sick leave for their own illnesses, to care for an ill family member, for preventative medical care for themselves or a family member, to arrange long-term care for a family member, to deal with the effects of domestic violence on themselves or a family member, or to care for a family member when a school or business is closed due to a public health emergency.

Washington

Wash. Rev. Code §§ 49.12.265 and following, 49.12.350 and following, 49.46.200 and following, 49.76.010 and following, 49.78.010 and following

Family and Medical Leave: Employers with 50 or more employees must provide 12 weeks of leave during any 12-month period for the birth or placement of a child (through adoption or foster placement), the employee's serious health condition, or to care for a family member with a serious health condition. Employees are eligible if they have worked for the employer for at least 12 months and have worked at least 1,250 hours in the previous year. Employers must offer the same parental leave to adoptive parents and stepparents as biological parents.

Pregnancy Disability Leave: Employers with eight or more employees must provide leave for the period of time when an employee is temporarily disabled due to pregnancy or childbirth. This is in addition to any leave available under federal FMLA and state family and medical leave laws.

Domestic Violence: All employers must provide reasonable leave from work to employees who are victims of domestic violence, sexual assault, or stalking—or whose family member is a victim—to prepare for and attend court, for medical treatment, and for other necessary services.

State Family and Medical Leave Laws (continued)

Paid Sick Leave: All employers must provide one hour of paid sick leave for every 40 hours worked. No annual cap on accrual, but employees may only carry over 40 hours of accrued leave from year to year. Employees may use sick leave for their own illness, the illness of a family member, the closure of a child's school or day care due to a public health emergency, and to seek services relating to domestic violence. Washington has a state-run paid family leave program, but benefits won't be available until January 2020.

Paid Family Leave: Beginning in January 2020, employees may receive 12 weeks of paid family leave benefits while taking time off to bond with a new child, recover from an illness, care for an ill family member, or attend to certain military-related events.

Wisconsin

Wis. Stat. § 103.10

Family and Medical Leave: Employers with 50 or more employees must provide six weeks of leave per 12-month period for pregnancy, childbirth, and to bond with a baby arriving by birth or adoption. These employers must provide an additional two weeks off each year for the employee's own serious health condition and an additional two weeks each year to care for a family member with a serious health condition. Employees are eligible if they have worked for at least one year and have worked 1,000 hours in the preceding 12 months.

State Laws on Military Leave

Alabama

Ala. Code §§ 31-12-1–31-12-4

Members of the Alabama National Guard, or the national guard of another state, called to active duty or for federally funded duty for service other than training have the same leave and reinstatement rights and benefits guaranteed under USERRA (doesn't apply to normal annual training, weekend drills, and required schools).

Alaska

Alaska Stat. § 26.05.075

Employees called to active service in the state militia or the National Guard of another state are entitled to unlimited unpaid leave and reinstatement to their former or a comparable position, with the pay, seniority, and benefits the employee would have had if not absent for service. Reinstatement is not required if it would pose an undue hardship on the employer or would be impossible or unreasonable due to the employer's changed circumstances. Employee must return to work on next workday, after time required for travel. Disabled employee must request reemployment within 30 days of release; if disability leaves the employee unable to do the job, employee must be offered a position with similar pay and benefits.

Arizona

Ariz. Rev. Stat. §§ 26-167, 26-168

Members of the National Guard of Arizona or any other state, or the U.S. National Guard and Reserve, called to training or active duty have the same leave and reinstatement rights and benefits guaranteed under USERRA. When called to active duty or to attend camps, formations, maneuvers, or drills, military members are entitled to unlimited unpaid leave and reinstatement to their former or a higher position with the same seniority and vacation benefits. Employers may not dissuade employees from enlisting in state or national military forces by threatening economic reprisal.

Arkansas

Ark. Code § 12-62-413

Employees called to active state duty as a member of the armed forces (which includes the national guard, militia, and reserves) of Arkansas or any other state have the same leave and reinstatement rights and benefits guaranteed under USERRA.

California

Cal. Mil. & Vet. Code §§ 394, 394.5, 395.06

Members of the California National Guard, or the national guard of any state, called to active duty are entitled to unlimited unpaid leave and reinstatement to their former position or to a position of similar seniority, status, and pay. Full-time employees must be reinstated (without loss of retirement or other benefits), unless the employer's circumstances have so changed as to make reinstatement impossible or unreasonable. Part-time employees must be reinstated if an open position exists. Reinstated employees cannot be terminated without cause for one year. Full-time employees must apply for reinstatement within 40 days of discharge, while part-time employees must apply for reinstatement within five days of discharge.

Employees in the U.S. National Guard and Reserve or Naval Militia are entitled to 17 days' unpaid leave per year for military training, drills, encampment, naval cruises, special exercises, or similar activities. Employer may not terminate employee or limit any benefits or seniority because of a temporary disability resulting from duty in the National Guard, Naval Militia, State Military Reserve, or the federal reserve components of the U.S. Armed Forces (up to 52 weeks).

Employers may not fire or otherwise discriminate against employees because of their performance of any ordered military duty or training or due to their membership in the state military, state naval forces, or the federal reserve components of the U.S. Armed Forces.

Colorado

Colo. Rev. Stat. §§ 28-3-609, 28-3-610, 28-3-610.5

Members of the Colorado National Guard or the U.S. National Guard and Reserve are entitled to 15 days' unpaid leave per year for training. Employees called to active state duty in the Colorado National Guard are entitled to unlimited unpaid leave. Employees on leave for training and active duty must be reinstated to their former positions or a similar position with the same status, pay, and seniority, and they must receive the same vacation, sick leave, bonuses, benefits, and other advantages they would have had if not absent for service.

State Laws on Military Leave (continued)

Connecticut

Conn. Gen. Stat. §§ 27-33a, 27-34a

Members of the Connecticut National Guard, or the national guard of any state, ordered into active state service by the governor are entitled to the same rights and benefits guaranteed under USERRA, except those pertaining to life insurance. Employees who are members of the state armed forces, any reserve component of the U.S. Armed Forces, or the national guard of any states, are entitled to take leave to perform ordered military duty, including meetings or drills, that take place during regular work hours, without loss or reduction of vacation or holiday benefits. Employer may not discriminate in terms of promotion or continued employment.

Delaware

Del. Code tit. 20, § 905

National guard members who are called to state active duty shall be entitled to the same rights, privileges, and protections as they would have had if called for military training under federal law protecting reservists and National Guard members.

Florida

Fla. Stat. §§ 250.481, 250.482, 252.55, 627.6692(5)

Employees who are called to active duty in the national guard, or into active duty by the laws of any other state, may not be penalized for absence from work. Upon return from service, employees are entitled to reinstatement with full benefits unless employer's circumstances have changed to make reinstatement impossible or unreasonable or it would impose an undue hardship. Reinstated employees may not be terminated without cause for one year.

If a member of the national guard or reserves is receiving COBRA benefits when called to active duty, the period of time when that service member is covered by TRICARE (military health benefits) won't count against his or her COBRA entitlement. Discrimination against members of the national guard or reserves is prohibited.

Employers with 15 or more employees must provide up to 15 days of unpaid leave to members of the Civil Air Patrol. Employers must reinstate an employee after the leave, unless the employer's circumstances have changed such that it would be unreasonable or impossible or it would cause an undue hardship. Returning employees may not be fired without cause for one year.

Georgia

Ga. Code § 38-2-280

Discrimination against members of the U.S. military reserves or state militia is prohibited. Employees called to active duty in the U.S. uniformed services, the Georgia National Guard, or the national guard of any other state, are entitled to unlimited unpaid leave for active service and up to six months' leave in any four-year period for service school or annual training. Employee is entitled to reinstatement with full benefits unless employer's circumstances have changed to make reinstatement impossible or unreasonable. Employee must apply for reinstatement within 90 days of discharge or within ten days of completing school or training.

Hawaii

Haw. Rev. Stat. § 121-43

Members of the national guard are entitled to unlimited unpaid leave while performing ordered national guard service and while going to and returning from service, and reinstatement to the same or a position comparable in seniority, status, and pay. If an employee is not qualified for his or her former position because of a disability sustained during service but is qualified for another position, the employee is entitled to the position that is most similar to his or her former position, unless employer's circumstances have changed to make reinstatement impossible or unreasonable. Employee cannot be terminated without cause for one year after reinstatement. Employer cannot discriminate against employee because of any obligation as a member of the national guard.

Idaho

Idaho Code §§ 46-224, 46-225, 46-407, 46-409

Members of the Idaho National Guard, or the national guard of another state, who are called to active duty by the governor or president in time of war, armed conflict, or emergency, are entitled to the same protections as USERRA. Once their leave is over, employees are entitled to reinstatement to their former position or a comparable position with like seniority, status, and pay. If an employee is not qualified for his or her former position because of a disability sustained during service, the employee is entitled to the position that is most similar to his or her former position in terms of seniority, status, and pay (provided that the employee is qualified). Reinstated employees may not be fired without cause for one year.

State Laws on Military Leave (continued)

Members of the U.S. National Guard Reserve may take up to 15 days' unpaid leave per year for training without affecting the employee's rights to vacation, sick leave, bonus, advancement, and other advantages of employment. Employees must give 90 days' notice of training dates.

Illinois

330 Ill. Comp. Stat. § 61/1-1 and following; 820 Ill. Comp. Stat. §§ 148/10, 148/15, 148/20

Members of the U.S. Armed Forces, Illinois State Guard, and national guard of any state are entitled to the same leave and reinstatement rights and benefits guaranteed under USERRA for military service. This includes service in a federally recognized auxiliary of the U.S. Armed Forces when performing official duties in support of military or civilian authorities in an emergency. Service members are also protected while absent from work and receiving medical or dental treatment related to a condition incurred or aggravated during active service.

Employers with at least 15 employees must provide up to 15 days of unpaid Civil Air Patrol leave to employees performing a Civil Air Patrol mission. Employers with at least 50 employees must provide up to 30 days of unpaid leave for the same purposes. Employees must be reinstated to the same position with the same pay, benefits, and seniority.

Indiana

Ind. Code §§ 10-16-7-4 , 10-16-7-6, 10-16-7-23; 10-17-4-1 to 10-17-4-5

Members of the Indiana National Guard, or the national guard of any other state, who are called to state active duty have the same leave and reinstatement rights and benefits guaranteed under USERRA. Employers may not refuse to allow members of the Indiana National Guard to attend assembly for drills, training, or other duties.

Members of the U.S. armed force reserves may take up to 15 days' unpaid leave per year for training. Employees must provide evidence of dates of departure and return 90 days in advance, and proof of completion of the training upon return. Leave does not affect vacation, sick leave, bonus, or promotion rights. At the end of training, employee must be reinstated to former or a similar position with no loss of seniority or benefits.

Iowa

Iowa Code § 29A.43

Members of the Iowa National Guard, the national guard of any other state, the organized reserves of the U.S. Armed Forces, or the Civil Air Patrol who are called into temporary duty are entitled to reinstatement to former or a similar position. Leave does not affect vacation, sick leave, bonuses, or other benefits. Employee must provide evidence of satisfactory completion of duty and of qualifications to perform the job's duties. Employers may not discriminate against these employees or discharge them due to their military affiliations.

Kansas

Kan. Stat. §§ 48-222, 48-517

Employees called into active duty by the state of Kansas, or any other state, are entitled to unlimited leave and reinstatement to the same position or a comparable position with like seniority, status, and pay. Reemployment not required if employer's circumstances have changed so as to make reemployment impossible/unreasonable or if reemployment would impose undue hardship on employer. Reinstated employees may not be discharged without cause for one year. Members of the Kansas National Guard are entitled to five to ten days' leave each year to attend annual muster and camp of instruction. Employer's failure to allow employee to attend or punishing employee who attends is a misdemeanor.

Kentucky

Ky. Rev. Stat. §§ 38.238, 38.460

Members of national guard are entitled to unlimited unpaid leave for active duty or training and reinstatement to former position with no loss of seniority or benefits. Employer may not in any way discriminate against employee or use threats to prevent employee from enlisting in the Kentucky National Guard, the national guard of any other state, or active militia.

Louisiana

La. Rev. Stat. §§ 29:38, 29:38.1

Employees called into active duty in national guard, state militia, or any branch of the state military forces of Louisiana or any other state are entitled to reinstatement to same or comparable position with same seniority, status, benefits, and pay. If employee is not qualified for former position because of disability sustained during active duty, but is otherwise qualified to perform another position, employer or successor shall employ person in other or comparable position with like seniority, status, benefits, and pay provided the employment does not pose a direct threat or significant risk to the health and safety of the individual or others that cannot be eliminated by reasonable accommodation. Employees on leave are entitled to the benefits offered to employees who take leave for other reasons. Employee must report to work within 72 hours of release or recovery from service-related injury or illness and cannot be fired, except for cause, for one year after reinstatement. Employer cannot discriminate against employee because of any obligation as a member of the Louisiana National Guard or the U.S. National Guard and Reserve.

Maine

Me. Rev. Stat. tit. 26, §§ 811 to 813, tit. 37-B, § 342;

Employer may not discriminate against employee for membership or service in the U.S. National Guard and Reserve. Employees in the national guard or reserves are entitled to military leave in response to state or federal military orders. Upon completion of service, employees must be reinstated, at the same pay, seniority, benefits, and status, and must receive all other employment advantages as if they had been continuously employed.

For the first 30 days of an employee's military leave, the employer must continue the employee's health, dental, and life insurance at no additional cost to the employee. After 30 days, the employee may continue these benefits at his or her own expense (paying the employer's group rates).

Maryland

Md. Code, Public Safety, § 13-704; Lab. & Empl., § 3-1001–3-1007

Members of the Maryland National Guard and Maryland Defense Force ordered to military duty have the same leave and reinstatement rights and benefits guaranteed under USERRA. Maryland employers with 15 or more employees must allow employees who have been employed for at least 90 days to take at least 15 days off each year to respond to an emergency mission of the Maryland Wing of the Civil Air Patrol.

Employees must give as much notice as possible of their need for this leave. After arriving at the emergency location, employees must notify their employer and estimate how long the mission will take. Employees are entitled to reinstatement upon their return from this type of leave. Employers may not penalize employees for exercising their rights under this law, nor may they retaliate against employees who complain that an employer has violated the law.

Massachusetts

Mass. Gen. Laws ch. 151B, § 4; ch. 33, § 13

Employers may not discriminate against employees and applicants based on their membership in, application to perform, or obligation to perform military service, including service in the national guard. Employees who are members of the armed forces are entitled to the same rights and protections granted under USERRA.

Michigan

Mich. Comp. Laws §§ 32.271–32.274

Employees who are called to active duty in the U.S. Armed Forces, National Guard, or Reserve, or the military forces of any state, are entitled to take unpaid leave, and to be reinstated when their service has ended. Reinstatement is not required for military service that exceeds five years, except in certain cases. Employers may not discriminate against employees based on their military service, use threats to prevent employees from enlisting, or prevent employees from attending military encampments or other places of drills or instruction.

Minnesota

Minn. Stat. § 192.34

Employer may not discharge employee, interfere with military service, or dissuade employee from enlisting by threatening employee's job. Applies to employees who are members of the U.S., Minnesota, or any other state military or naval forces.

Mississippi

Miss. Code §§ 33-1-15, 33-1-19

Employers may not discriminate against employees or applicants based on their current membership in the reserves of the U.S. Armed Forces or their former membership in the U.S. Armed Forces. Employers may not threaten employees to dissuade them from enlisting.

Members of the U.S. National Guard and Reserve or U.S. military veterans may take time off for military training or duty with the armed forces of the U.S., Mississippi, or any other state. Once their leave is over, these employees are entitled to be reinstated to their former position or a similar position. Employees must provide evidence that they have completed their training.

Missouri

Mo. Rev. Stat. §§ 40.490, 41.730

State Laws on Military Leave (continued)

Members of the Missouri military forces, the national guard of any other state, or a reserve component of the U.S. Armed Forces who are called to active duty are entitled to the same leave and reinstatement rights provided under USERRA. Employer may not discharge employee, interfere with employee's military service, or use threats to dissuade employee from enlisting in the state organized militia.

Montana
Mont. Code §§ 10-1-1005, 10-1-1006, 10-1-1007

Employees who are ordered to federally funded military service are entitled to all rights available under USERRA. Members of the Montana National Guard, or the national guard of any other state, who are called to state military duty are entitled to leave for duration of service. Leave may not be deducted from sick leave, vacation, or other leave, although employee may voluntarily use that leave. Returning employee is entitled to reinstatement to same or similar position with the same seniority, status, pay, health insurance, pension, and other benefits, provided that the employee told the employer of membership in the military at the time of hire, or if the employee enlisted during employment, at the time of enlistment. Employer may not in any way discriminate against employee or dissuade employee from enlisting in the state organized militia.

Nebraska
Nev. Rev. Stat. §§ 55-161

Employees who are called into active duty in the Nevada National Guard, or the national guard of another state, have the same leave and reinstatement rights and benefits guaranteed under USERRA.

Nevada
Nev. Rev. Stat. §§ 412.139, 412.606

Employers may not discriminate against members of the Nevada National Guard, or the national guard of another state, and may not discharge any employee because he or she assembles for training, participates in field training, is called to active duty, or otherwise meets as required for ceremonies, maneuvers, and other military duties.

New Hampshire
N.H. Rev. Stat. §§ 110-B:65, 110-C:1

Members of the state national guard or militia called to active duty by the governor have the same leave and reinstatement rights and benefits guaranteed under USERRA.

Employer may not discriminate against employee because of connection or service with state national guard or militia; may not dissuade employee from enlisting by threatening job.

New Jersey
N.J. Stat. § 38:23C-20

An employee is entitled to take unpaid leave for active service in the U.S. or state military services. Upon return, employee must be reinstated to the same or a similar position, unless employer's circumstances have changed to make reinstatement impossible or unreasonable. If same or similar position is not possible, employer shall restore such person to any available position, if requested by such person, for which the person is capable and qualified to perform the duties. Employee must apply for reinstatement within 90 days of release from service. Employee may not be fired without cause for one year after returning from service. Employee is also entitled to take up to three months' leave in four-year period for annual training or assemblies relating to military service, or to attend service schools conducted by the U.S. Armed Forces. Employee must apply for reinstatement within ten days.

New Mexico
N.M. Stat. §§ 20-4-6, 28-15-1, 28-15-2,

Members of the U.S. Armed Forces, organized reserves, or national guard of any state may take up to five years of unpaid leave for service, as long as they've given advance notice (unless that notice is impossible or unreasonable). Employees must request reinstatement within 90 days after being released from duty or discharged from up to two years of hospitalization and convalescence following duty. Employees who are still qualified must be reinstated in former or similar position with same status, seniority, and pay unless employers' circumstances have changed to make reinstatement impossible or unreasonable. Employees may not be fired without cause for one year after returning from service. Employers may not prevent employees from performing military service or discriminate against or discharge employees because of membership in national guard.

New York
N.Y. Mil. Law §§ 251, 252, 317, 318

Members of the U.S. Armed Forces or organized militia are entitled to unpaid leave for active service; reserve drills or annual training; service school; or initial full-time or active duty training. Returning employee is entitled

State Laws on Military Leave (continued)

to reinstatement to previous position, or to one with the same seniority, status, and pay, unless the employer's circumstances have changed and reemployment is impossible or unreasonable. Employee must apply for reinstatement within 90 days of discharge from active service, ten days of completing school, reserve drills, or annual training, or 60 days of completing initial full-time or active duty training. Employee may not be discharged without cause for one year after reinstatement. Employers may not discriminate against persons subject to state or federal military duty.

North Carolina

N.C. Gen. Stat. §§ 127A-201, 127A-202, 127A-202.1, 127B-14

Members of the North Carolina National Guard, or the national guard of any other state, who are called to active state duty by a state governor are entitled to take unpaid leave. Within five days of release from state duty, employee must be restored to previous position or one of comparable seniority, status, and salary, unless the employer's circumstances now make it unreasonable. Employees who are no longer qualified for their jobs must be placed in another position with appropriate seniority, status, and salary. For service of 30 days or less, the employee must apply for reinstatement in writing on the next regularly scheduled workday at least 24 hours after traveling home. For service of more than 30 days, the employee must apply in writing within 14 days of release from duty. (If the employee is hospitalized due to an injury or illness sustained in active duty, different rules apply.)

Employers may not discriminate against or fire an employee because of membership in the national guard of any state or fire an employee called up for emergency military service.

North Dakota

N.D. Cent. Code. §§ 37-29-01, 37-29-03

Employers may not terminate, demote, or otherwise discriminate against volunteer members of the North Dakota National Guard or North Dakota Air National Guard, or volunteer civilian members of the Civil Air Patrol. The employer must allow such employees to be absent or tardy from work for up to 20 days in a calendar year because they are responding to a disaster or national emergency (20-day limit does not apply to involuntarily activated members of the North Dakota National Guard). An employee who needs this leave must make a reasonable effort to notify the employer. Upon request, the employee must also provide written verification of the dates and times of service.

Ohio

Ohio Rev. Code §§ 5903.01, 5903.02

Employees who are members of the Ohio organized militia or national guard or in the organized militia of another state called for active duty or training; members of the commissioned public health service corps; or any other uniformed service called up in time of war or emergency; have the same leave and reinstatement rights and benefits guaranteed under USERRA.

Oklahoma

Okla. Stat. tit. 44, §§ 71, 208.1

Employees in the Oklahoma National Guard who are ordered to state active duty or full-time guard duty have the same reinstatement rights and other benefits guaranteed by USERRA. Members of the Oklahoma National Guard must be allowed to take time off to attend guard drills, instruction, encampment, maneuvers, ceremonies, exercises, or other duties.

Oregon

Or. Rev. Stat. §§ 659A.082, 659A.086

Members of Oregon or other states' organized militias called into active state service or state active duty may take unpaid leave for term of service. Returning employee is entitled to reinstatement with no loss of seniority or benefits including sick leave, vacation, or service credits under a pension plan. Employee must return to work within seven calendar days of release from service.

Pennsylvania

51 Pa. Cons. Stat. §§ 7301–7309

Employees who enlist or are drafted during a time of war or emergency called by the president or governor, along with reservists or members of Pennsylvania National Guard called into active duty, are entitled to unpaid military leave. Leave expires 90 days after enlistment/draft period, 90 days after military duty for reservists, 30 days after state duty for Pennsylvania National Guard members. Returning employee must be reinstated to same or similar position with same status, seniority, and pay. If no longer qualified due to disability sustained during military duty, employer must restore to position with like seniority, status, and pay unless employer or successor's circumstances have changed so as to make it impossible or unreasonable to do so. Employers may not discharge or discriminate against any employee because of membership or service in the military.

State Laws on Military Leave (continued)

Employees called to active duty are entitled to 30 days' health insurance continuation benefits at no cost.

Rhode Island

R.I. Gen. Laws §§ 30-11-2–30-11-9; 30-21-1

Members of state military forces and national guard of any state who are called to active duty have the same leave and reinstatement rights and benefits guaranteed under USERRA. Members of the national guard or reserve units of U.S. Armed Forces are entitled to unpaid leave for training and are entitled to reinstatement with the same status, pay, and seniority. Employees in the U.S. Armed Forces are entitled to reinstatement to the same position or a position with similar seniority, status, and pay unless the employer's circumstances make reinstatement impossible or unreasonable. Employee must request reinstatement within 40 days. Employer may not discriminate against or discharge employee because of membership in the state military forces or U.S. reserves, interfere with employee's military service, or dissuade employee from enlisting by threatening employee's job.

South Carolina

S.C. Code §§ 25-1-2310–25-1-2340, 25-1-2350

Members of the South Carolina National Guard or State Guard, or the national or state guard of any state, who are called to active duty by a state governor are entitled to unpaid leave for service. Upon honorable discharge from service, the employee must be reinstated to the same position or a position with similar seniority, status, and pay. Employee must apply for reinstatement in writing, within five days of release from service or related hospitalization. Employer has no duty to reinstate if the employer's circumstances make reinstatement unreasonable.

South Dakota

S.D. Codified Laws § 33A-2-9

Members of the South Dakota National Guard, or the national guard of any state, ordered to active duty by the governor or president have the same leave and reinstatement rights and benefits guaranteed under USERRA.

Tennessee

Tenn. Code § 58-1-604

Employer may not terminate or refuse to hire an employee because of Tennessee National Guard membership or because employee is absent for a required drill, including annual field training.

Texas

Tex. Gov't Code §§ 437.204, 437.213

Members of the state military forces are entitled to the same leave and reinstatement protections granted under USERRA. Employers may not discriminate against members of the Texas military forces, or the military forces of any other state, and have the right to be reinstated following a call to active duty or training. Employees are entitled to be reinstated to the same position they held before leaving, with no loss of time, efficiency rating, vacation time, or other benefits. An employee must give notice of his or her intent to return to work as soon as practicable after release from duty.

Utah

Utah Code § 39-1-36

Members of U.S. National Guard and Reserve who are called to active duty, active duty for training, inactive duty training, or state active duty may take up to five years of unpaid leave. Upon return, employee is entitled to reinstatement to previous employment with same seniority, status, pay, and vacation rights. Employer may not discriminate against an employee based on membership in armed forces reserves.

Vermont

Vt. Stat. tit. 20, § 608; tit. 21, § 491, Vt. Stat. Ann.

Employees who are members of U.S. National Guard and Reserve, an organized unit of the National Guard of Vermont or any other state, or the ready reserves are entitled to 15 days per year of unpaid leave for military drills, training, or other temporary duty under military authority. Returning employee must be reinstated to former position with the same status, pay, and seniority, including any seniority that accrued during the leave of absence. Employer may not discriminate against an employee who is a member or an applicant for membership in the National Guard of Vermont or any other state. Members of the National Guard of Vermont or any other state ordered to state active duty by the governor have the right to take unpaid leave from civilian employment, and cannot be required to exhaust their vacation or other accrued leave.

Virginia

Va. Code §§ 40.1-28.7:6, 44-93.2–44-93.4

Members of the Virginia National Guard, Virginia Defense Force, or the national guard of another state, called to

State Laws on Military Leave (continued)

active duty by the governor are entitled to take unpaid leave and may not be required to use vacation or any other accrued leave (unless employee wishes). Returning employee whose absence does not exceed five years must be reinstated to previous position or one with same seniority, status, and pay; if position no longer exists, then to a comparable position unless employer's circumstances would make reemployment unreasonable. Employee must apply for reinstatement, in writing, within (a) 14 days of release from service or related hospitalization if service length did not exceed 180 days, or (b) 90 days of release from service or related hospitalization if service length exceeded 180 days. Employer cannot discriminate against employees because of membership in state military service.

Members of the Virginia Civil Air Patrol are entitled to up to 30 workdays of leave while responding to an emergency mission and up to ten workdays of leave for training for emergency missions, without loss of seniority or other benefits.

Washington
Wash. Rev. Code §§ 73.16.032–73.16.035

Employees in Washington who are members of the armed forces or the national guard of any state are entitled to take leave when called to active duty for training, inactive duty training, full-time national guard duty, or state active duty. Employees are entitled to be reinstated, following their military duty, to the position they previously held or one with like seniority, status, and pay. The time limit for requesting reinstatement depends on the length of the employee's military leave.

Employers may not discriminate against employees based on their membership in any branch of the uniformed services.

West Virginia
W. Va. Code §§ 15-1F-8, 15-1K-1–15-1K-9

Employees who are members of the organized militia in active service of the state of West Virginia or any other state have the same leave and reinstatement rights and benefits guaranteed under USERRA.

Employers with 15 or more employees must provide up to ten days of leave to members of the Civil Air Patrol for training for emergency missions and up to 30 days for responding to an emergency mission. Employers may not discriminate against employees who have been employed for at least 90 days due to their membership in the Civil Air Patrol.

Wisconsin
Wis. Stat. §§ 111.321, 321.64, 321.65, 321.66

Employees who enlist, are inducted, or are ordered to serve in the U.S. Armed Forces for 90 days or more, or civilian employees who are asked to perform national defense work during an officially proclaimed emergency, may take leave for military service and/or training. Employees who are called to state active duty in the Wisconsin National Guard or the national guard of any state or U.S. territory, or called to active service with the state laboratory of hygiene during a public health emergency, are also entitled to take military leave. Upon completion of military leave, employees are entitled to reinstatement to their prior position or to one with equivalent seniority, status, and pay. A reinstated employee may not be discharged without cause for up to one year. Employers may not discriminate against employees based on their military service.

Employers with 11 or more employees must provide up to 15 days of unpaid leave (but not more than five consecutive days at a time) to members of the Civil Air Patrol for an emergency service operation, if it wouldn't unduly disrupt the employer's operations.

Wyoming
Wyo. Stat. §§ 19-11-103, 19-11-104, 19-11-107, 19-11-111

Employees of the armed forces or national guard of any state who report for active duty, training, or a qualifying physical exam may take up to five years' leave of absence. Employee must give advance notice of service. Employee may use vacation or any other accrued leave but is not required to do so. Returning employee is entitled to reemployment with the same seniority, rights, and benefits, plus any additional seniority and benefits that employee would have earned if there had been no absence, unless employer's circumstances have changed so that reemployment is impossible or unreasonable or would impose an undue hardship. Time limits set forth governing written application for reinstatement based on length of uniformed service. Employee is entitled to complete any training program that would have been available to employee's former position during period of absence. Employee may not be terminated without cause for one year after returning to work. Employer cannot discriminate against applicant or member of the uniformed services.

State Laws on Taking Time Off to Vote

Note: The states of Connecticut, Delaware, Florida, Idaho, Indiana, Louisiana, Maine, Michigan, Mississippi, Montana, New Hampshire, New Jersey, North Carolina, Oregon, Pennsylvania, Rhode Island, South Carolina, Vermont, Virginia, Washington, and the District of Columbia are not listed in this chart because they do not have laws or regulations on time off to vote that govern private employers. Check with your state department of labor if you need more information. (See Appendix B for contact list.)

Alabama
Ala. Code § 17-1-5

Time off work for voting: Necessary time up to one hour. The employer may decide when hours may be taken.

Time off not required if: Employee has two nonwork hours before polls open or one nonwork hour after polls are open.

Time off is paid: No.

Employee must request leave in advance: "Reasonable notice."

Alaska
Alaska Stat. § 15.56.100

Time off work for voting: Not specified.

Time off not required if: Employee has two consecutive nonwork hours at beginning or end of shift when polls are open.

Time off is paid: Yes.

Arizona
Ariz. Rev. Stat. § 16-402

Time off work for voting: As much time as will add up to three hours when combined with nonwork time. Employer may decide when hours are taken.

Time off not required if: Employee has three consecutive nonwork hours at beginning or end of shift when polls are open.

Time off is paid: Yes.

Employee must request leave in advance: Prior to the day of the election.

Arkansas
Ark. Code § 7-1-102

Time off work for voting: Employer must schedule employees' work schedules on election days to enable employees to vote.

Time off is paid: No.

California
Cal. Elec. Code § 14000

Time off work for voting: Up to two hours at beginning or end of shift, whichever gives employee most time to vote and takes least time off work.

Time off not required if: Employee has sufficient time to vote during nonwork time.

Time off is paid: Yes (up to two hours).

Employee must request leave in advance: two working days before election.

Colorado
Colo. Rev. Stat. § 1-7-102

Time off work for voting: Up to two hours. Employer may decide when hours are taken, but employer must permit employee to take time at beginning or end of shift, if employee requests it.

Time off not required if: Employee has three nonwork hours when polls are open.

Time off is paid: Yes (up to two hours).

Employee must request leave in advance: Prior to election day.

Georgia
Ga. Code § 21-2-404

Time off work for voting: Up to two hours. Employer may decide when hours are taken.

Time off not required if: Employee has two nonwork hours at beginning or end of shift when polls are open.

Time off is paid: No.

Employee must request leave in advance: "Reasonable notice."

Hawaii
Haw. Rev. Stat. § 11-95

Time off work for voting: two consecutive hours excluding meal or rest breaks. Employer may not change employee's regular work schedule.

Time off not required if: Employee has two consecutive nonwork hours when polls are open.

Time off is paid: Yes.

Employee required to show proof of voting: Only if employer is verifying whether employee voted when they

State Laws on Taking Time Off to Vote (continued)

took time off to vote. A voter's receipt is proof of voting by the employee. If employer verifies that employee did not vote, hours off may be deducted from pay.

Illinois

10 Ill. Comp. Stat. §§ 5/7-42, 5/17-15

Time off work for voting: two hours. Employer may decide when hours are taken except that employer must permit a two-hour absence during working hours if employee's working hours begin less than two hours after opening of polls and end less than two hours before closing of polls.

Time off is paid: Yes.

Employee must request leave in advance: Prior to the day of election. One day in advance (for general or state election). Employer must give consent (for primary).

Iowa

Iowa Code § 49.109

Time off work for voting: As much time as will add up to three hours when combined with nonwork time. Employer may decide when hours are taken.

Time off not required if: Employee has three consecutive nonwork hours when polls are open.

Time off is paid: Yes.

Employee must request leave in advance: In writing "prior to the date of the election."

Kansas

Kan. Stat. § 25-418

Time off work for voting: Up to two hours or as much time as will add up to two hours when combined with nonwork time. Employer may decide when hours are taken, but it may not be during a regular meal break.

Time off not required if: Employee has two consecutive nonwork hours when polls are open.

Time off is paid: Yes.

Kentucky

Ky. Const. § 148; Ky. Rev. Stat. § 118.035

Time off work for voting: "Reasonable time," but not less than four hours. Employer may decide when hours are taken.

Time off is paid: No.

Employee must request leave in advance: One day before election.

Employee required to show proof of voting: No proof specified, but employee who takes time off and does not vote may be subject to disciplinary action.

Maryland

Md. Code, Elec. Law § 10-315

Time off work for voting: two hours.

Time off not required if: Employee has two consecutive nonwork hours when polls are open.

Time off is paid: Yes.

Employee required to show proof of voting: Yes; also includes attempting to vote. Must use state board of elections form.

Massachusetts

Mass. Gen. Laws ch. 149, § 178

Time off work for voting: First two hours that polls are open. (Applies to workers in manufacturing, mechanical, or retail industries.)

Time off is paid: No.

Employee must request leave in advance: Must apply for leave of absence (no time specified).

Minnesota

Minn. Stat. § 204C.04

Time off work for voting: May be absent for the time necessary to appear at the employee's polling place, cast a ballot, and return to work.

Time off is paid: Yes.

Missouri

Mo. Rev. Stat. § 115.639

Time off work for voting: three hours. Employer may decide when hours are taken.

Time off not required if: Employee has three consecutive nonwork hours when polls are open.

Time off is paid: Yes (if employee votes).

Employee must request leave in advance: "Prior to the day of election."

Employee required to show proof of voting: None specified, but pay contingent on employee actually voting.

State Laws on Taking Time Off to Vote (continued)

Nebraska

Neb. Rev. Stat. § 32-922

Time off work for voting: As much time as will add up to two consecutive hours when combined with nonwork time. Employer may decide when hours are taken.

Time off not required if: Employee has two consecutive nonwork hours when polls are open.

Time off is paid: Yes.

Employee must request leave in advance: Prior to or on election day.

Nevada

Nev. Rev. Stat. § 293.463

Time off work for voting: If it is impracticable to vote before or after work: Employee who works two miles or less from polling place may take one hour; two to ten miles, two hours; more than ten miles, three hours. Employer will decide when hours are taken.

Time off not required if: Employee has sufficient nonwork time when polls are open.

Time off is paid: Yes.

Employee must request leave in advance: Prior to election day.

New Mexico

N.M. Stat. § 1-12-42

Time off work for voting: two hours. (Includes Indian nation, tribal, and pueblo elections.) Employer may decide when hours are taken.

Time off not required if: Employee's workday begins more than two hours after polls open or ends more than three hours before polls close.

Time off is paid: Yes.

New York

N.Y. Elec. Law § 3-110

Time off work for voting: As many hours at beginning or end of shift as will give employee enough time to vote when combined with nonwork time. Employer may decide when hours are taken.

Time off not required if: Employee has four consecutive nonwork hours at beginning or end of shift when polls are open.

Time off is paid: Yes (up to two hours).

Employee must request leave in advance: Not more than ten or less than two working days before election.

North Dakota

N.D. Cent. Code § 16.1-01-02.1

Time off work for voting: Employers are encouraged to give employees time off to vote when regular work schedule conflicts with times polls are open.

Time off is paid: No.

Ohio

Ohio Rev. Code § 3599.06

Time off work for voting: "Reasonable time."

Time off is paid: Yes.

Oklahoma

Okla. Stat. tit. 26, § 7-101

Time off work for voting: two hours, unless employee lives so far from polling place that more time is needed. Employer may decide when hours are taken or may change employee's schedule to give employee nonwork time to vote.

Time off not required if: Employee's workday begins at least three hours after polls open or ends at least three hours before polls close.

Time off is paid: Yes.

Employee must request leave in advance: One day before election, either orally or in writing.

Employee required to show proof of voting: Yes.

South Dakota

S.D. Codified Laws § 12-3-5

Time off work for voting: two consecutive hours. Employer may decide when hours are taken.

Time off not required if: Employee has two consecutive nonwork hours when polls are open.

Time off is paid: Yes.

Tennessee

Tenn. Code § 2-1-106

Time off work for voting: "Reasonable time" up to three hours during the time polls are open. Employer may decide when hours are taken.

Time off not required if: Employee's workday begins at least three hours after polls open or ends at least three hours before polls close.

State Laws on Taking Time Off to Vote (continued)

Time off is paid: Yes.

Employee must request leave in advance: Before noon on the day before the election.

Texas

Tex. Elec. Code § 276.004

Time off work for voting: Employer may not refuse to allow employee to take time off to vote, but no time limit specified.

Time off not required if: Employee has two consecutive nonwork hours when polls are open.

Time off is paid: Yes.

Utah

Utah Code § 20A-3-103

Time off work for voting: two hours at beginning or end of shift. Employer may decide when hours are taken.

Time off not required if: Employee has at least three nonwork hours when polls are open.

Time off is paid: Yes.

Employee must request leave in advance: "Before election day."

West Virginia

W. Va. Code § 3-1-42

Time off work for voting: Up to three hours. (Employers in health, transportation, communication, production, and processing facilities may change employee's schedule so that time off doesn't impair essential operations but must allow employee sufficient and convenient time to vote.)

Time off not required if: Employee has at least three nonwork hours when polls are open.

Time off is paid: Yes (if employee votes).

Employee must request leave in advance: Written request at least three days before election.

Employee required to show proof of voting: None specified, but time off will be deducted from pay if employee does not vote.

Wisconsin

Wis. Stat. § 6.76

Time off work for voting: Up to three consecutive hours. Employer may decide when hours are taken.

Time off is paid: No.

Employee must request leave in advance: "Before election day."

Wyoming

Wyo. Stat. § 22-2-111

Time off work for voting: One hour, other than a meal break. Employer may decide when the hour is taken.

Time off not required if: Employee has at least three consecutive nonwork hours when polls are open.

Time off is paid: Yes (if employee votes).

Employee required to show proof of voting: None specified, but pay contingent on employee voting.

State Laws on Jury Duty

Alabama

Ala. Code §§ 12-16-8–12-16-8.1

Paid leave: Full-time employees are entitled to usual pay.

Notice employee must give: Must show supervisor jury summons the next working day; must return to work the next scheduled hour after discharge from jury duty.

Employer penalty for firing or penalizing employee: Liable for actual and punitive damages.

Note: Employers with five or fewer full-time employees: Court must postpone an employee's jury service if another employee is already serving as a juror.

Alaska

Alaska Stat. § 09.20.037

Unpaid leave: Yes.

Additional employee protections: Employee may not be threatened, coerced, or penalized.

Employer penalty for firing or penalizing employee: Liable for lost wages and damages; may be required to reinstate the fired employee.

Arizona

Ariz. Rev. Stat. § 21-236

Unpaid leave: Yes.

Additional employee protections: Employee may not lose vacation rights, seniority, or precedence. Employer may not require employee to use annual, sick, or vacation hours.

Employer penalty for firing or penalizing employee: Class 3 misdemeanor, punishable by a fine of up to $500 or up to 30 days' imprisonment.

Note: Employers with five or fewer full-time employees: Court must postpone an employee's jury service if another employee is already serving as a juror.

Arkansas

Ark. Code § 16-31-106

Unpaid leave: Yes.

Additional employee protections: Absence may not affect sick leave and vacation rights.

Notice employee must give: Reasonable notice.

Employer penalty for firing or penalizing employee: Class A misdemeanor, punishable by a fine of up to $2,500.

California

Cal. Lab. Code §§ 230, 230.1

Unpaid leave: Employee may use vacation, personal leave, or comp time.

Notice employee must give: Reasonable notice.

Employer penalty for firing or penalizing employee: Employer must reinstate employee with back pay and lost wages and benefits. Willful violation is a misdemeanor.

Colorado

Colo. Rev. Stat. §§ 13-71-126, 13-71-133–13-71-134, 18-1.3-501

Paid leave: All employees (including part-time and temporary who were scheduled to work for the three months preceding jury service): regular wages up to $50 per day for first three days of jury duty. Must pay within 30 days of jury service.

Additional employee protections: Employer may not make any demands on employee that will interfere with effective performance of jury duty.

Employer penalty for firing or penalizing employee: Class two misdemeanor, punishable by a fine of $250 to $1,000 or three to 12 months' imprisonment, or both. May be liable to employee for triple damages and attorneys' fees.

Connecticut

Conn. Gen. Stat. §§ 51-247, 51-247a

Paid leave: Full-time employees: regular wages for the first five days of jury duty; after five days, state pays up to $50 per day.

Additional employee protections: Once employee serves eight hours of jury duty, employer may not require employee to work more hours on the same day.

Employer penalty for firing or penalizing employee: Criminal contempt: punishable by a fine of up to $500 or up to 30 days' imprisonment, or both. Liable for up to ten weeks' lost wages for discharging employee. If employer fails to pay the employee as required, may be liable for treble damages and attorneys' fees.

Delaware

Del. Code tit. 10, §§ 4514, 4515

Unpaid leave: State pays $20 per diem for travel, parking, other out-of-pocket expenses. State pays certain other expenses if jury is sequestered.

State Laws on Jury Duty (continued)

Employer penalty for firing or penalizing employee:
Criminal contempt: punishable by a fine of up to $500 or up
to six months' imprisonment, or both. Liable to discharged
employee for lost wages and attorneys' fees and may be
required to reinstate the fired employee.

District of Columbia

D.C. Code §§ 11-1913, 15-718

Paid leave: Full-time employees: regular wages for the
first five days of jury duty, less jury fee from state. State
attendance fee: $30, if not paid full regular wages by
employer. State travel allowance: $2 per day.

Employer penalty for firing or penalizing employee:
Criminal contempt: punishable by a fine of up to $300 or
up to 30 days' imprisonment, or both, for a first offense; up
to $5,000 or up to 180 days' imprisonment, or both, for any
subsequent offense. Liable to discharged employee for lost
wages and attorneys' fees and may be required to reinstate
the fired employee.

Florida

Fla. Stat. §§ 40.24, 40.271

Unpaid leave: Yes. State pays $15 per day for first three days
of service if juror does not receive regular wages those days.
State pays $30 per day for the fourth and subsequent days.

Additional employee protections: Employee may not be
threatened with dismissal.

Employer penalty for firing or penalizing employee:
Threatening employee is contempt of court. May be liable
to discharged employee for compensatory and punitive
damages and attorneys' fees.

Georgia

Ga. Code § 34-1-3

Paid leave: According to Opinion of the Attorney General
Number 89-55, issued in 1989, employers must pay an
employee's wages while on jury duty, minus any funds the
employee receives for jury service.

Additional employee protections: Employee may not
be discharged, penalized, or threatened with discharge or
penalty for responding to a subpoena or making a required
court appearance.

Notice employee must give: Reasonable notice.

Employer penalty for firing or penalizing employee: Liable
for actual damages and reasonable attorneys' fees.

Hawaii

Haw. Rev. Stat. § 612-25

Unpaid leave: Yes.

Employer penalty for firing or penalizing employee: Petty
misdemeanor: punishable by a fine of up to $1,000 or up to
30 days' imprisonment. May be liable to discharged employee
for up to six weeks' lost wages, reasonable attorneys' fees, and
may be required to reinstate the fired employee.

Idaho

Idaho Code § 2-218

Unpaid leave: Yes.

Employer penalty for firing or penalizing employee:
Criminal contempt: punishable by a fine of up to $300.
Liable to discharged employee for triple lost wages and
reasonable attorneys' fees. May be ordered to reinstate the
fired employee.

Illinois

705 Ill. Comp. Stat. § 310/10.1

Unpaid leave: Yes.

Additional employee protections: A regular night shift
employee may not be required to work if serving on a jury
during the day. May not lose any seniority or benefits.

Notice employee must give: Must give employer a copy of
the summons within ten days of issuance.

Employer penalty for firing or penalizing employee:
Employer will be charged with civil or criminal contempt, or
both; liable to employee for lost wages and benefits; may be
ordered to reinstate employee.

Indiana

Ind. Code §§ 34-28-4-1, 35-44.1-2-11

Unpaid leave: Yes.

Additional employee protections: Employee may not be
deprived of benefits or threatened with the loss of them.

Employer penalty for firing or penalizing employee:
Class B misdemeanor: punishable by up to 180 days'
imprisonment; may also be fined up to $1,000. Liable to
discharged employee for lost wages and attorneys' fees and
may be required to reinstate the fired employee.

State Laws on Jury Duty (continued)

Iowa

Iowa Code § 607A.45

Unpaid leave: Yes.

Additional employee protections: Employer may not threaten or coerce employee based on jury notice or jury duty.

Employer penalty for firing or penalizing employee: Contempt of court. Liable to discharged employee for up to six weeks' lost wages and attorneys' fees and may be required to reinstate the fired employee.

Kansas

Kan. Stat. § 43-173

Unpaid leave: Yes.

Additional employee protections: Employee may not lose seniority or benefits. (Basic and additional protections apply to permanent employees only.)

Employer penalty for firing or penalizing employee: Liable for lost wages and benefits, damages, and attorneys' fees and may be required to reinstate the fired employee.

Kentucky

Ky. Rev. Stat. §§ 29A.160, 29A.990

Unpaid leave: Yes.

Additional employee protections: Employer may not threaten or coerce employee based on jury notice or jury duty.

Employer penalty for firing or penalizing employee: Class B misdemeanor: punishable by up to 89 days' imprisonment or fine of up to $250, or both. Liable to discharged employee for lost wages and attorneys' fees. Must reinstate employee with full seniority and benefits.

Louisiana

La. Rev. Stat. § 23:965

Paid leave: Regular employee entitled to one day full compensation for jury service. May not lose any sick, vacation, or personal leave or other benefit.

Additional employee protections: Employer may not create any policy or rule that would discharge employee for jury service.

Notice employee must give: Reasonable notice.

Employer penalty for firing or penalizing employee: For each discharged employee: fine of $100 to $1,000; must reinstate employee with full benefits. For not granting paid leave: fine of $100 to $500; must pay full day's lost wages.

Maine

Me. Rev. Stat. tit. 14, § 1218

Unpaid leave: Yes.

Additional employee protections: Employee may not lose or be threatened with loss of employment or health insurance coverage.

Employer penalty for firing or penalizing employee: Class E crime: punishable by up to six months in the county jail or a fine of up to $1,000. Liable for up to six weeks' lost wages, benefits, and attorneys' fees. Employer may be ordered to reinstate the employee.

Maryland

Md. Code., Cts. & Jud. Proc. §§ 8-501, 8-502

Unpaid leave: Yes.

Additional employee protections: Employer cannot threaten or coerce an employee. An employee may not be required to use annual, sick, or vacation leave. An employee who spends at least four hours on jury service (including travel time) may not be required to work a shift that begins on or after 5 p.m. that day or before 3 a.m. the following day.

Employer penalty for firing or penalizing employee: Employer penalty for violating these provisions is a fine up to $1,000.

Massachusetts

Mass. Gen. Laws ch. 234A, §§ 48 and following

Paid leave: All employees (including part-time and temporary who were scheduled to work for the three months preceding jury service): regular wages for first three days of jury duty. If paid leave is an "extreme financial hardship" for employer, state will pay. After first three days, state will pay $50 per day.

Michigan

Mich. Comp. Laws § 600.1348

Unpaid leave: Yes.

Additional employee protections: Employee may not be threatened or disciplined; may not be required to work in addition to jury service, if extra hours would mean working overtime or beyond normal quitting time.

Employer penalty for firing or penalizing employee: Misdemeanor, punishable by a fine of up to $500 or up to 90 days' imprisonment, or both. Employer may also be punished for contempt of court, with a fine of up to $7,500 or up to 93 days' imprisonment, or both.

State Laws on Jury Duty (continued)

Minnesota

Minn. Stat. § 593.50

Unpaid leave: Yes.

Additional employee protections: Employer may not threaten or coerce employee.

Employer penalty for firing or penalizing employee: Criminal contempt: punishable by a fine of up to $700 or up to six months' imprisonment, or both. Also liable to employee for up to six weeks' lost wages and attorneys' fees and may be required to reinstate the fired employee.

Mississippi

Miss. Code §§ 13-5-23, 13-5-35

Unpaid leave: Yes.

Additional employee protections: Employee may not be intimidated or threatened. Employee may not be required to use annual, sick, or vacation leave for jury service.

Notice employee must give: Reasonable notice is required.

Employer penalty for firing or penalizing employee: If found guilty of interference with the administration of justice: at least one month in the county jail or up to two years in the state penitentiary, or a fine of up to $500, or both. May also be found guilty of contempt of court, punishable by a fine of up to $1,000 or up to six months' imprisonment, or both.

Note: Employers with five or fewer full-time employees: Court must postpone an employee's jury service if another employee is already serving as a juror.

Missouri

Mo. Rev. Stat. § 494.460

Unpaid leave: Yes.

Additional employee protections: Employer may not take or threaten to take any adverse action. Employee may not be required to use annual, sick, vacation, or personal leave.

Employer penalty for firing or penalizing employee: Employer may be liable for lost wages, damages, and attorneys' fees and may be required to reinstate the fired employee.

Montana

Mont. Admin. R. 24.16.2520

Paid leave: No paid leave laws regarding private employers.

Nebraska

Neb. Rev. Stat. § 25-1640

Paid leave: Normal wages minus any compensation (other than expenses) from the court.

Additional employee protections: Employee may not lose pay, sick leave, or vacation or be penalized in any way; may not be required to work evening or night shift.

Notice employee must give: Reasonable notice.

Employer penalty for firing or penalizing employee: Class IV misdemeanor, punishable by a fine of up to $500.

Nevada

Nev. Rev. Stat. §§ 6.190, 193.140

Unpaid leave: Yes.

Additional employee protections: Employer may not recommend or threaten termination; may not dissuade or attempt to dissuade employee from serving as a juror, and cannot require the employee to work within eight hours before jury duty or if employee's duty lasts four hours or more (including travel time to and from the court), between 5 p.m. that day and 3 a.m. the next day. Cannot be required to take paid leave.

Notice employee must give: At least three days' notice.

Employer penalty for firing or penalizing employee: Terminating or threatening to terminate is a gross misdemeanor, punishable by a fine of up to $2,000 or up to 364 days' imprisonment, or both; in addition, employer may be liable for lost wages, damages equal to lost wages, and punitive damages to $50,000 and must reinstate employee. Dissuading or attempting to dissuade is a misdemeanor, punishable by a fine of up to $1,000 or up to six months in the county jail, or both.

New Hampshire

N.H. Rev. Stat. § 500-A:14

Unpaid leave: Yes.

Additional employee protections: Employer cannot threaten or coerce employee.

Employer penalty for firing or penalizing employee: Employer may be found guilty of contempt of court; also liable to employee for lost wages and attorneys' fees and may be required to reinstate the fired employee.

New Jersey

N.J. Stat. § 2B:20-17

Unpaid leave: Yes.

Additional employee protections: Employer cannot threaten or coerce employee.

State Laws on Jury Duty (continued)

Employer penalty for firing or penalizing employee: Employer may be found guilty of a disorderly persons offense, punishable by a fine of up to $1,000 or up to six months' imprisonment, or both. May also be liable to employee for economic damages and attorneys' fees and may be ordered to reinstate the fired employee.

New Mexico
N.M. Stat. §§ 38-5-10.1, 38-5-18–38-5-19

Unpaid leave: Yes.

Additional employee protections: Employer cannot threaten or coerce employee. An employee may not be required to use annual, sick, or vacation leave.

Employer penalty for firing or penalizing employee: Petty misdemeanor, punishable by a fine of up to $500 or up to six months in the county jail, or both.

Note: Court must postpone an employee's jury service if the employer has five or fewer full-time employees and another employee has already been summoned to appear during the same period, or if the employee is the only person performing essential services that the employer cannot function without.

New York
N.Y. Jud. Ct. Acts Law § 519

Unpaid leave: Yes.

Paid leave: Employers with more than ten employees must pay first $40 of wages for the first three days of jury duty.

Notice employee must give: Must notify employer prior to beginning jury duty.

Employer penalty for firing or penalizing employee: May be found guilty of criminal contempt of court, punishable by a fine of up to $1,000 or up to 30 days in the county jail, or both.

North Carolina
N.C. Gen. Stat. § 9-32

Unpaid leave: Yes.

Additional employee protections: Employee may not be demoted.

Employer penalty for firing or penalizing employee: Liable to discharged employee for reasonable damages; must reinstate employee to former position.

North Dakota
N.D. Cent. Code § 27-09.1-17

Unpaid leave: Yes.

Additional employee protections: Employee may not be laid off, penalized, or coerced because of jury duty, responding to a summons or subpoena, serving as a witness, or testifying in court.

Employer penalty for firing or penalizing employee: Class B misdemeanor, punishable by a fine of up to $1,500 or up to 30 days' imprisonment, or both. Liable to employee for up to six weeks' lost wages and attorneys' fees, and may be required to reinstate the fired employee.

Ohio
Ohio Rev. Code §§ 2313.15, 2313.19, 2313.99

Unpaid leave: Yes.

Additional employee protections: An employee may not be required to use annual, sick, or vacation leave.

Notice employee must give: Reasonable notice. Absence must be for actual jury service.

Employer penalty for firing or penalizing employee: May be found guilty of contempt of court, punishable by a fine of up to $250 or 30 days' imprisonment, or both, for first offense.

Note: Employers with 25 or fewer full-time employees: Court must postpone an employee's jury service if another employee served within thirty days prior.

Oklahoma
Okla. Stat. tit. 38, §§ 34, 35

Unpaid leave: Yes.

Additional employee protections: Employee can't be subject to any adverse employment action, and can't be required to use annual, sick, or vacation leave.

Notice employee must give: Reasonable notice.

Employer penalty for firing or penalizing employee: Misdemeanor, punishable by a fine of up to $5,000. Liable to discharged employee for actual and exemplary damages; actual damages include past and future lost wages, mental anguish, and costs of finding suitable employment.

State Laws on Jury Duty (continued)

Oregon

Or. Rev. Stat. §§ 10.090, 10.092

Unpaid leave: Yes (or according to employer's policy).

Additional employee protections: Employee may not be threatened, intimidated, or coerced, and can't be required to use annual, sick, or vacation leave. Employers with ten or more employees that provide health, disability, life, or other insurance benefits must continue coverage during jury service at the election of the employee.

Employer penalty for firing or penalizing employee: Court may order reinstatement with or without back pay, and a $720 civil penalty.

Pennsylvania

42 Pa. Cons. Stat. § 4563; 18 Pa. Cons. Stat. § 4957

Unpaid leave: Yes (applies to retail or service industry employers with 15 or more employees and to manufacturers with 40 or more employees).

Additional employee protections: Employee may not be threatened or coerced, or lose seniority or benefits. (Any employee who would not be eligible for unpaid leave will be automatically excused from jury duty.)

Employer penalty for firing or penalizing employee: Liable to employee for lost benefits, wages, and attorneys' fees; may be required to reinstate the fired employee.

Rhode Island

R.I. Gen. Laws § 9-9-28

Unpaid leave: Yes.

Additional employee protections: Employee may not lose wage increases, promotions, length of service, or other benefit.

Employer penalty for firing or penalizing employee: Misdemeanor punishable by a fine of up to $1,000 or up to one year's imprisonment, or both.

South Carolina

S.C. Code § 41-1-70

Unpaid leave: Yes.

Employer penalty for firing or penalizing employee: For discharging employee, liable for one year's salary; for demoting employee, liable for one year's difference between former and lower salary.

South Dakota

S.D. Codified Laws §§ 16-13-41.1, 16-13-41.2

Unpaid leave: Yes.

Additional employee protections: Employee may not lose job status, pay, or seniority.

Employer penalty for firing or penalizing employee: Class 2 misdemeanor, punishable by a fine of up to $500 or up to 30 days in the county jail, or both.

Tennessee

Tenn. Code § 22-4-106

Paid leave: Regular wages minus jury fees, as long as the employer has at least five employees, and the employee is not a temporary worker who has been employed for less than six months.

Additional employee protections: Employer may not demote, suspend, or discriminate against employee. Night shift employees are excused from shift work during and for the night before the first day of jury service.

Notice employee must give: Employee must show summons to supervisor the next work day after receiving it.

Employer penalty for firing or penalizing employee: Employees are entitled to reinstatement and reimbursement for lost wages and work benefits. Violating employee rights or any provisions of this law is a Class A misdemeanor, punishable by up to 11 months, 29 days' imprisonment or a fine up to $2,500, or both. Liable to employee for lost wages and benefits and must reinstate employee.

Texas

Tex. Civ. Prac. & Rem. Code §§ 122.001, 122.002

Unpaid leave: Yes.

Notice employee must give: Employee must notify employer of intent to return after completion of jury service.

Employer penalty for firing or penalizing employee: Liable to employee for not less than one year's nor more than five years' compensation and attorneys' fees. Must reinstate employee.

Note: Only applies to permanent employees.

State Laws on Jury Duty (continued)

Utah

Utah Code § 78B-1-116

Unpaid leave: Yes.

Additional employee protections: Employer may not threaten or coerce employee or take any adverse employment action against employee. Employee may not be requested or required to use annual or sick leave or vacation.

Employer penalty for firing or penalizing employee: May be found guilty of criminal contempt, punishable by a fine of up to $500 or up to six months' imprisonment, or both. Liable to employee for up to six weeks' lost wages and attorneys' fees and may be required to reinstate the fired employee.

Vermont

Vt. Stat. tit. 21, § 499

Unpaid leave: Yes.

Additional employee protections: Employee may not be penalized or lose any benefit available to other employees; may not lose seniority, vacation credit, or any fringe benefits.

Employer penalty for firing or penalizing employee: Fine of up to $200.

Virginia

Va. Code § 18.2-465.1

Unpaid leave: Yes.

Additional employee protections: Employee may not be subject to any adverse personnel action and may not be forced to use sick leave or vacation. Employee who has appeared for four or more hours cannot be required to start a shift after 5 p.m. that day or before 3 a.m. the next morning.

Notice employee must give: Reasonable notice.

Employer penalty for firing or penalizing employee: Class 3 misdemeanor, punishable by a fine of up to $500.

Washington

Wash. Rev. Code § 2.36.165

Unpaid leave: Yes.

Additional employee protections: Employee may not be threatened, coerced, harassed, or denied promotion.

Employer penalty for firing or penalizing employee: Intentional violation is a misdemeanor, punishable by a fine of up to $1,000 or up to 90 days' imprisonment, or both; also liable to employee for damages and attorneys' fees and may be required to reinstate the fired employee.

West Virginia

W. Va. Code § 52-3-1

Unpaid leave: Yes.

Additional employee protections: Employee may not be threatened or discriminated against; regular pay cannot be cut.

Employer penalty for firing or penalizing employee: May be found guilty of civil contempt, punishable by a fine of $100 to $500. May be required to reinstate the fired employee. May be liable for back pay and for attorneys' fees.

Wisconsin

Wis. Stat. § 756.255

Unpaid leave: Yes.

Additional employee protections: Employee may not lose seniority or pay raises; may not be disciplined.

Employer penalty for firing or penalizing employee: Fine of up to $200. May be required to reinstate the fired employee with back pay.

Wyoming

Wyo. Stat. § 1-11-401

Unpaid leave: Yes.

Additional employee protections: Employee may not be threatened, intimidated, or coerced.

Employer penalty for firing or penalizing employee: Liable to employee for up to $1,000 damages for each violation, costs, and attorneys' fees. May be required to reinstate the fired employee with no loss of seniority.

Health and Safety

Workplace safety is of paramount concern to savvy employers. And for good reason: Dangerous situations, accidents, violence, or breaches of security can have disastrous workplace consequences, including lost productivity, raised insurance premiums, stolen or damaged equipment, employee injuries, or even deaths.

What's more, the government regulates workplace safety issues very heavily. Both federal and state laws require employers to provide a workplace free of hazards that could cause serious harm to their employees. These laws also require employers to investigate and report workplace accidents, provide employees with safety training for their jobs, and keep records on workplace safety. Depending on the type of business an employer runs, virtually every aspect of its operations may be subject to detailed safety rules.

Although no employer can guarantee an accident-free workplace, policies that promote workplace safety are a good start.

13:1 Safety Policy

File Name: 13_Health Safety.rtf

Include This Policy?

☐ Yes

☐ No

☐ Use our existing policy

☐ Other _____

Alternate Modifications

None

Additional Clauses

Give Specific Safety Instructions

Insert?:   ☐ Yes   ☐ No

Related Policies

Chapter 12 provides policies on workplace behavior—including horseplay, fighting, and professional conduct.

Notes

_____
_____
_____
_____
_____
_____
_____
_____
_____
_____
_____
_____
_____
_____
_____
_____
_____
_____

13:1 Workplace Safety

A basic safety policy is a must for every employer, in every type of business. Federal and state laws require employers to keep their workplace free of hazards, investigate accidents quickly, and keep proper safety records. An employer cannot meet these legal requirements unless its employees follow safe work habits and report workplace accidents and injuries.

Your workplace safety policy should tell employees that safety is a top concern for your company, let employees know about safety rules, and explain how to report accidents or injuries.

CAUTION

Some states require particular policy language. The federal law that regulates health and safety on the job is called the Occupational Safety and Health Act, or OSHA (29 U.S.C. §§ 651 and following). In addition, almost half of the states have adopted their own workplace safety laws that are at least as strict as OSHA. Although OSHA doesn't require employers to adopt a written workplace safety policy, some of these state laws do. For example, California employers must adopt a written "injury and illness prevention program." To find out what your state requires, contact your state labor department (see Appendix B for contact information) or consult with an experienced employment attorney.

Safety Policy

Our Company takes employee safety very seriously. In order to provide a safe workplace for everyone, every employee must follow our safety rules:

- Horseplay, roughhousing, and other physical acts that may endanger employees or cause accidents are prohibited.
- Employees must follow their supervisors' safety instructions.
- Employees in certain positions may be required to wear protective equipment, such as hair nets, hard hats, safety glasses, work boots, ear plugs, or masks. Your supervisor will let you know if your position requires protective gear.
- Employees in certain positions may be prohibited from wearing dangling jewelry or apparel, or may be required to pull back or cover their hair, for safety purposes. Your supervisor will tell you if you fall into one of these categories.
- All equipment and machinery must be used properly. This means all guards, restraints, and other safety devices must be used at all times. Do not use equipment for other than its intended purpose.
- All employees must immediately report any workplace condition that they believe to be unsafe to their supervisor. The Company will look into the matter promptly.
- All employees must immediately report any workplace accident or injury to _____

_____ .

Additional Clause to Give Specific Safety Instructions

Every type of industry has its own unique safety hazards. Our basic standard policy can be modified to include safety rules particular to your company. For example, you might want to include rules on the proper use of certain types of equipment and machinery; proper techniques for physical labor, such as lifting and carrying heavy objects; or ergonomic rules for those who operate computers or cash registers or perform other types of repetitive motions. If so, simply add these rules to the end of the policy.

Of course, the specific rules you adopt will depend on what your company's employees do and the resources you have available to assist them; we can't provide standard policy language that will work for everyone. Here is an example of policy language that provides ergonomics information for employees who use computers.

SAMPLE POLICY LANGUAGE

Most of our Company's employees work at computers, some for nearly the full workday. We recognize that proper equipment, furnishings, and body positioning can help employees avoid discomfort or injury while working at computers. To help employees work comfortably and efficiently, without putting unnecessary stress and strain on their bodies, our Company has an ergonomics program.

When you begin working at our Company, a trained member of the ergonomics team will assess your workstation. You will be provided the equipment necessary to work comfortably. Your equipment and furnishings (for example, chair height, position of keyboard and mouse, monitor height and tilt, and so on) will be adjusted to fit your physical requirements. You will also receive training and handouts on avoiding computer-related injuries. If you have any special ergonomics needs, please raise them at this time.

If at any time you have ergonomics questions or concerns, you would like to request special equipment, or you would like a reassessment of your workspace, feel free to contact a member of the ergonomics team.

13:2 Workplace Security

A workplace security policy explains what measures the company expects employees to take to keep its premises and property safe from intruders. Clearly, what you include in the policy will depend on the nature of your workplace: An office building in a bustling metropolis will have different security concerns from a farming operation. However, any security policy should include rules on securing the premises (locking up, closing gates, shutting off machinery, or securing tools, for example), rules on after-hours access to the workplace, and rules on workplace visitors.

Workplace Security

It is every employee's responsibility to help keep our workplace secure from unauthorized intruders. Every employee must comply with these security precautions.

When you leave work for the day, please do all of the following:

_____

_____

_____ .

After-hours access to the workplace is limited to those employees who need to work late. If you are going to be working past our usual closing time, please let your supervisor know.

Employees are allowed to have an occasional visitor in the workplace, but workplace visits should be the exception rather than the rule. If you are anticipating a visitor, please let _____

_____

know. When your visitor arrives, you will be notified.

How to Complete This Policy

In the first blank space, list all of the things employees are expected to do before they leave for the day. For example, the policy might tell employees to shut off their computers, turn off equipment, turn off lights, close and lock office windows, store and secure tools, lock and garage company vehicles, or lock any area that won't be used any more that day.

In the second blank space, list the position of the person who will greet visitors to your company. This might be a receptionist, security guard, or front desk attendant.

If you have additional security rules, you can add them at the end of the policy.

13:2 Workplace Security

File Name: 13_Health Safety.rtf

Include This Policy?

☐ Yes

☐ No

☐ Use our existing policy

☐ Other _____

Alternate Modifications

None

Additional Clauses

Require Escorts for Visitors

Insert?:   ☐ Yes   ☐ No

Require Badges for Visitors

Insert?:   ☐ Yes   ☐ No

Instructions for Employees Who Are the Last to Leave the Workplace

Insert?:   ☐ Yes   ☐ No

Related Policies

None

Notes

_____

_____

_____

_____

_____

_____

_____

_____

_____

_____

_____

_____

_____

_____

_____

_____

Additional Clause to Require Escorts or Badges for Visitors

Our sample policy allows employees to have visitors but asks them to keep visitors to a minimum. Some businesses, particularly large companies and companies that have industrial operations, put more restrictions on visitors in the workplace. Visitors might be required to wear a badge or other identification, or the employee who invited the visitor might be required to accompany the visitor at all times on company premises and escort the visitor to and from the entrance. If you wish to adopt either of these policies, simply add one or both of the modifications below at the end of the policy, after the paragraph on visitors.

Additional Clause

Visitors must wear an identification badge at all times when they are in our workplace. Visitors can get a badge at _____

_____ .

They must return the badge when they leave Company premises.

Additional Clause

Do not leave your visitor unattended in the workplace. If you have a visitor, you must accompany your visitor at all times. This includes escorting your visitor to and from the entrance to our Company.

Additional Clause to Give Instructions to Employees Who Are the Last to Leave the Workplace

In many companies, supervisors, managers, or the owner are always the last to leave the workplace. And some workplaces (such as 24-hour convenience stores or factories that operate round the clock) never close. However, if employees at your company are sometimes the last ones at work, you should modify this policy to let them know how to secure the premises. Insert the sample modification, below, filling in the blanks to tell employees what is expected of them. For example, the policy might direct employees to lock the building or security gates, set an alarm, make sure all windows are closed and locked, or turn off all equipment and lights.

Additional Clause

If you are the last to leave the workplace for the evening, you are responsible for doing all of the following: _____

_____

_____

_____ .

If you have questions about any of these responsibilities, please talk to your supervisor.

13:3 What to Do in an Emergency

File Name: 13_Health Safety.rtf

Include This Policy?

☐ Yes

☐ No

☐ Use our existing policy

☐ Other _____

Alternate Modifications

None

Alternate Modifications

None

Additional Clauses

Location of Emergency Supplies

Insert?: ☐ Yes ☐ No

Related Policies

None

Notes

_____
_____
_____
_____
_____
_____
_____
_____
_____
_____
_____
_____
_____
_____

13:3 What to Do in an Emergency

Every business should have a written policy letting employees know what to do in case of emergency. Employees should be familiar with evacuation routes and procedures to ensure their safety should disaster strike. Employees should also be told where to congregate once they have left the workplace. This will help management—and rescue workers—figure out whether anyone is missing and may need assistance getting out of the workplace.

In this policy, you can describe evacuation plans, the location of emergency equipment (such as first aid supplies or fire extinguishers) kept on site, and where employees should go if they are forced to leave the workplace. In the policy, you should also let employees know whom they can call to find out what to do if disaster or emergency strikes when they are not at work.

What to Do in an Emergency

In case of an emergency at work, such as a fire, earthquake, or accident, your first priority should be your own safety. In the event of an emergency causing serious injuries, IMMEDIATELY DIAL 9-1-1 to alert police and rescue workers of the situation.

If you hear a fire alarm or in case of an emergency that requires evacuation, please proceed quickly and calmly to the emergency exits. The Company will hold periodic drills to familiarize everyone with the routes they should take. Remember that every second may count. Don't return to the workplace to retrieve personal belongings or work-related items. Once you have exited the building, head toward the _____

_____.

(For our Company's policy on workplace violence, see Section _____ of this Handbook.)

If you are not at work when a disaster or an emergency strikes, please call _____ before returning to the workplace.

How to Complete This Policy

In the first blank, let employees know what to do once they leave the workplace. What you say here will depend on your local geography. For example, you might tell employees to congregate in the parking lot or on the corner outside. In the second blank, you'll need to name someone (by position) for the employee to call in case of an emergency that strikes outside of work hours. You might ask employees to call their manager, the HR department, or the Chief Operating Officer, for example. Some companies have a phone tree system for notifying employees of the company's status and the employee's work schedule following a disaster. If yours is one of them, you'll need to modify the language of the policy slightly to let employees know they can expect a phone call rather than having to make one.

Reality Check: Fire Drills Are Not Just for Kids

All of us probably remember the fire drills of grade school, but when was the last time your company held a fire drill? Emergency drills are vitally important for every business. They help workers learn emergency evacuation procedures, so they'll know what to do if a real disaster strikes. Of course, these drills disrupt business and may take 15 or 20 minutes to conduct. But if that advance planning later saves lives or prevents serious injuries, the inconvenience will seem a very small price to pay.

Additional Clause to Include Location of Emergency Supplies

Many businesses keep a store of emergency supplies in the workplace. If your company takes this very sensible precaution, modify the policy to let employees know where the supplies are kept. You can add the modification below, filling in the blanks to indicate the location of the supplies. If your company keeps additional types of supplies that are not listed below, add them on at the end.

Additional Clause

Our Company keeps emergency supplies on hand. First aid kits are located _____

_____ .

Fire extinguishers can be found _____

_____ .

Earthquake preparedness kits are kept _____

_____ .

We also keep a supply of flashlights in _____

_____ .

13:4 Smoking

File Name: 13_Health Safety.rtf

Include This Policy?
- ☐ Yes
  - *Choose one:* ☐ A ☐ B
- ☐ No
- ☐ Use our existing policy
- ☐ Other _____

Alternate Modifications

None

Additional Clauses

Regulate E-Cigarettes (Vaping)
- *Insert?:* ☐ Yes ☐ No

Regulate When Employees May Smoke
- *Insert?:* ☐ Yes ☐ No

Help Employees Quit Smoking
- *Insert?:* ☐ Yes ☐ No
- *If yes, choose one:* ☐ A ☐ B

Prohibit Discrimination Against Smokers
- *Insert?:* ☐ Yes ☐ No

Related Policies

None

Notes

_____
_____
_____
_____
_____
_____
_____
_____
_____

13:4 Smoking

Smoking can be a divisive workplace issue. Smokers want the freedom to enjoy a cigarette without having to stand outside in the cold; nonsmokers want to work comfortably, without smoke irritating their eyes and throats, and without the increased health risks attributable to secondhand smoke. It is the employer's unfortunate job to balance these interests.

There are a few legal guidelines that can help. In all states, employers may ban smoking in the workplace. If your company wants to prohibit employees from lighting up, it can do so. However, if your company wants to allow smoking or allow it in certain areas, you will have to check your state and local laws to find out exactly what is allowed. These laws are summarized in "State Laws on Smoking in the Workplace" at the end of this chapter. Some states require employers to ban smoking, at least in certain kinds of businesses. For example, California bans smoking in the workplace, public or private. And other states prohibit smoking in certain kinds of business establishments, such as hospitals or restaurants. You will also need to check local laws.

Because of these variations, we offer you two sample policies to choose from. Policy A bans smoking altogether; Policy B allows smoking in designated areas.

Policy A

Smoking Is Prohibited

For the health, comfort, and safety of our employees, smoking is not allowed on Company property.

Policy B

Smoking Policy

To accommodate employees who smoke as well as those who do not, the Company has created smoking and nonsmoking areas. Smoking is allowed only in _____

_____ .

The Company has posted signs designating smoking and nonsmoking areas. Employees who smoke are required to observe these signs and to smoke in designated areas only.

Reality Check: Special Rules for Smoking Areas

States that allow smoking on the job often impose strict rules to prevent smoke from spreading to the rest of the workplace. Some require that any workplace smoking area have a separate ventilation system, so the smoky air does not recirculate to the rest of the office. Others require physical barriers—such as walls or partitions—to separate smoking and nonsmoking areas.

Even if your state does not impose these requirements, however, it's a good idea to keep smoking areas separate from the rest of the workplace. Nonsmokers who are physically troubled by smoke can complain to the Occupational Safety and Health Administration (OSHA) and may even have a legal claim under the Americans with Disabilities Act (ADA). There's no need to invite this kind of problem: If your company allows smoking, keep the air clean for nonsmokers by designating a smoking area that won't allow smoke to enter the rest of the workplace.

Who Needs This Policy

This is one of the few policies that is mandatory, at least in some states. If your company plans to allow smoking anywhere in the workplace, certain states require employers to adopt a written smoking policy. In states that require a smoking policy, the rules vary as to what the policy must include. Check "State Laws on Smoking in the Workplace" at the end of this chapter to see what your state requires.

Additional Clause to Include E-Cigarettes ("Vaping")

Electronic cigarettes (e-cigarettes) are small, battery-operated devices that allow users to inhale a vapor containing nicotine. Referred to as "vaping" rather than "smoking," use of these devices in the workplace can be controversial. On the one hand, some experts claim that use of e-cigarettes can help smokers quit or cut way back, which has a number of health benefits. On the other hand, e-cigarettes contain nicotine and other potentially harmful chemicals, and the vapor they release can be bothersome to other employees.

Every year, more states and local governments regulate e-cigarettes. Some simply include them in workplace smoking bans. In California, for example, employees may not smoke or vape in the workplace, period. Some states and local governments don't regulate use of e-cigarettes. And some are in between, perhaps limiting their

14:2 Telephone Monitoring

If your company will monitor employees' telephone calls, you must adopt a policy to let employees know about it. Federal law allows employers to monitor employee phone calls "in the ordinary course of business" (for example, to keep tabs on customer service). However, some states require the consent of one or both parties to the conversation for monitoring to be legal. By adopting a policy and requiring employees to consent, in writing, to monitoring, your company will be protected from lawsuits claiming invasion of privacy.

Your telephone policy should let employees know whether the company plans to monitor calls on work telephones and under what circumstances.

Telephone Monitoring

The Company reserves the right to monitor calls made from or received on Company telephones. Therefore, no employee should expect that conversations made on Company telephones will be private.

Additional Clause to Designate Nonmonitored Phones

If your company chooses to monitor employee phone calls, it may want to designate specified phones that are not monitored for employees to use for personal calls. By doing this, an employer can avoid employee claims of invasion of privacy by giving them an opportunity to make personal calls that won't be overheard. Employees who fail to use the designated phones have no cause for complaint if their personal calls from nondesignated work phones are monitored.

To insert this additional clause, simply add this language to the end of your telephone policy.

Additional Clause

The Company has designated telephones that employees may use for personal calls. Calls made from these phones will not be monitored. Employees may make personal calls during their breaks; if you must make a personal call during your work hours, you are expected to keep the conversation brief.

Telephones for personal calls are located _____

_____ .

14:2 Telephone Monitoring

File Name: 14_Privacy.rtf

Include This Policy?
- ☐ Yes
- ☐ No
- ☐ Use our existing policy
- ☐ Other _____

Alternate Modifications
None

Additional Clauses
Designate Nonmonitored Phones
Insert?:   ☐ Yes   ☐ No

Related Policies
Policy 9:3 covers employee use of company phones.

Notes

_____

_____

_____

_____

_____ _____

_____

_____

_____

_____

_____

_____

_____

_____

_____

_____

Reality Check: How to Monitor Telephone Calls

If your company plans to monitor employee phone calls, it must make sure not to violate the privacy of the employee or the person on the other end of the line. Although the law of telephonic monitoring is still in flux, a few clear guidelines have emerged:

- **Make a monitoring announcement.** We've all called a bank, utility company, or other institution and heard that "calls may be monitored for quality assurance." The purpose of this message is simple: to tell the person outside the company that their call may be recorded or overheard. Your company policy will let employees know what to expect, but the company must also tell the other party to the phone call that the conversation may be monitored. In fact, some states allow eavesdropping only if all parties to the call consent. A monitoring announcement lets everyone on the line know that they may have a silent partner.

- **If the call is personal, get off the line.** Federal law allows monitoring for clear business purposes. However, courts have held that employers no longer have a business purpose to monitor once they realize that they are listening in on a private conversation. Whoever is listening in should stop monitoring as soon as he or she finds out that a call is personal.

- **Choose monitors carefully.** The people who actually listen to employee phone calls must be discreet and professional. Even if an employer has a solid business reason for monitoring calls, it will be on shaky legal ground if its monitors blab what they overhear to all who care to listen. Choose monitors who can keep their mouths shut, and use as few monitors as possible.

Form E: Telephone Monitoring Policy Acknowledgment

If your company decides to adopt a policy allowing it to monitor employee telephone calls, you should ask employees to sign a form acknowledging that they have read the policy and understand that their calls can be monitored.

Using an acknowledgment form helps ensure that employees actually read the policy and take steps to keep their personal calls private (for example, by making them on designated phones, on personal cellphones, or outside of work altogether). Employees who sign the form will have a very tough time arguing that their privacy was violated because they didn't know that their telephone calls could be monitored.

How to Complete This Form

Our form assumes that you have designated phones that will not be monitored for employees to use for personal calls. If you do not have such phones and you have not adopted the additional clause on designated phones in your policy, you should delete the last paragraph of the form, immediately before the signature and date lines.

If you have designated phones that will not be monitored, complete the policy by inserting the location of these phones; use the same language you used in the policy.

You can find this and all other forms (and policies) at this book's online companion page (see Appendix A for information on accessing these materials).

Telephone Monitoring Policy Acknowledgment

My signature on this form indicates that I have read the Company's telephone monitoring policy and I agree to abide by its terms. I understand that telephone calls I make or receive on Company phones are not private, and that the Company may monitor these calls at any time.

   I also understand that I may make or receive personal calls on the telephones located

_____

_____,

and that these calls will not be monitored. I agree to abide by the Company's policy regarding personal calls.

_____   _____
Signature   Date

_____
Print Name

14:3 Cameras and Camera Phones

Today, even the most basic cellphones come with recording devices, such as cameras or video capability. While these can be great features outside of the workplace, they pose considerable challenges on the job. Employers have become increasingly concerned about employees violating their coworkers' privacy by photographing them surreptitiously at work. And employers who have visible trade secrets to protect—whether in the form of documents, devices, processes, or personnel—are understandably worried that employees might use these small recording devices to steal or transmit confidential information.

We have provided two sample policies below. Policy A allows employees to have recording devices, including cellphones with recording capabilities, in the workplace, but prohibits employees from bringing them into certain areas of the workplace. If you adopt this policy, you must complete it by listing the areas where employees may not bring their camera phones and other recording devices (for example, company restrooms, changing areas, research facilities, and so on).

Policy A also includes some commonsense rules for employees who take photographs or make recordings at work. For example, the policy clarifies that employees may not photograph or record confidential information, may not violate the privacy of others, and so on.

Policy B prohibits cameras and cellphones with recording capabilities outright. This policy might make more sense for a company that has valuable trade secrets to protect, such as a high-tech engineering company, research and development company, or manufacturing company that closely guards its production process. As you can see, this policy allows employees to ask their supervisors for permission to bring a cellphone with recording capabilities to work if their personal situation requires it. If you adopt this policy, you will have to insert the place where employees can leave their recording devices while at work (for example, with the receptionist or office manager).

14:3 Cameras and Camera Phones

File Name: 14_Privacy.rtf

Include This Policy?
- ☐ Yes
    - *Choose one:* ☐ A   ☐ B
- ☐ No
- ☐ Use our existing policy
- ☐ Other _____

Alternate Modifications
None

Alternate Modifications
None

Additional Clauses
None

Related Policies
None

Notes

_____
_____
_____
_____
_____
_____
_____
_____
_____
_____
_____
_____
_____
_____
_____
_____
_____

Alternate Policy A

Camera Phones and Other Recording Devices

Employees may not bring cameras, video and audio recording devices, or digital devices (such as cellphones) that have recording capability, to any of the following areas:_____

_____ .

Guidelines for Camera and Recording Device Use

Employees who use cameras, camera phones, or other digital devices to capture photos, audio, or video on Company property or at Company events must follow these rules:

1. Employees may record or take pictures of other employees, customers, clients, or visitors only with their permission. If you intend to publicize the pictures or other recordings—for example, by posting them on the Internet, using them in a Company newsletter, or submitting them to a photography contest—you must disclose this to the subjects.

2. Employees may not record or take pictures of Company trade secrets or other confidential information. This includes, but is not limited to, [*list the most common types of trade secrets your company has, such as "customer lists," "pricing information," "recipes," "design plans," "software code," and so on*].

3. Employees may not take or use pictures or recordings to harass others. All Company policies—including the Company's policies on harassment, discrimination, and threats—apply to workplace photographs and recordings.

4. If you have any questions about whether it's appropriate to record or take a photograph at work or use a workplace photograph or recording in a particular way, please ask your supervisor.

Alternate Policy B

Camera Phones and Other Recording Devices

The use of cameras, video and audio recording devices, or digital devices (such as cellphones) that have recording capability can cause violations of privacy and breaches of confidentiality.

For that reason, we do not allow cameras, video or audio recording equipment, or cellphones or other digital devices that have these capabilities, on Company property. If you have such a device with you, you may either leave it in your car or _____

_____ .

If you believe that your personal circumstances require you to have your cell phone at work, and your cellphone has a camera or other recording capability, please talk to your supervisor.

Computers, Email, and the Internet

Computers can be an employer's best friend or worst nightmare. On the one hand, computers are essential in many workplaces. On the other hand, computers give employees the opportunity to spend their days sending harassing or threatening email, downloading pornographic images or pirated software, and shopping online.

So how does a savvy employer get the benefits without the downside? By adopting comprehensive policies that govern how employees may use computer equipment, including email, Internet access, and software. In this chapter, we show you how to create policies that tell employees how the company expects them to use its computer equipment and that will allow management to read email and monitor Internet traffic, to make sure that employees follow the rules. We also provide policy language dealing with something employees might do on their own computers that could have a significant impact on the company: blogging, social networking, and other online posts.

15:1 Email

File Name: 15_Computers.rtf

Include This Policy?
- ☐ Yes
- ☐ No
- ☐ Use our existing policy
- ☐ Other _____

Additional Clauses

Monitoring
  Insert?:   ☐ Yes   ☐ No
Email Rules and Style
  Insert?:   ☐ Yes   ☐ No

Related Policies

Chapter 14 explains privacy issues in detail.

Notes

_____
_____
_____
_____
_____
_____
_____
_____
_____
_____
_____
_____
_____
_____
_____
_____
_____
_____

15:1 Email

Any company that makes electronic communications equipment available to employees is asking for trouble if it doesn't have a policy explaining the company's rules for email use and allowing the company to monitor messages sent on that equipment. Even an employer that has never read employee email and doesn't plan to set up a regular system of monitoring should protect its right to do so. If your company is ever faced with a problem involving employee email—an employee who sends sexually explicit images, proselytizes other employees to join a religious group, transmits trade secrets to a competitor, or gets involved in a "flame war" with a client, for example—a company official will have to read the messages involved to figure out what to do. If your company doesn't have a policy warning employees that the company can read their messages at any time, an employee might sue for violation of privacy.

Your email policy should tell employees what the company considers proper use of its email system, reserve the company's right to read employee email at any time, and establish a schedule for purging the email system.

CAUTION

Make sure employees know that their computer use is not private. Perhaps the most important goal of computer policies is to reserve the company's right to monitor employee communications when necessary. The policies must tell employees that they should not expect their email or Internet use to be private.

Email

Use of the Email System

The email system is intended for official Company business. Although you may use the email system occasionally for personal messages, you may do so during nonwork hours only.

Email Is Not Private

Email messages, including attachments, sent and received on Company equipment are the property of the Company. We reserve the right to access, monitor, read, and/or copy email messages at any time, for any reason. You should not expect privacy for any email you send using Company equipment, including messages that you consider to be personal or label with a designation such as "Personal" or "Private."

All Conduct Rules Apply to Email

All of our policies and rules of conduct apply to employee use of the email system. This means, for example, that you may not use the email system to send harassing or discriminatory messages, including messages with explicit sexual content or pornographic images; to send threatening messages; or to reveal company trade secrets.

Email Security

To avoid email viruses and other threats, employees should not open email attachments or click on links in email from people and businesses they don't recognize, particularly if the email appears to have been forwarded multiple times or has a nonexistent or peculiar subject heading. Even if you know the sender, do not open an email attachment or click a link that has a strange name or is not referenced in the body of the email. It may have been transmitted automatically, without the sender's knowledge.

If you believe your computer has been infected by a virus, worm, or other security threat to the Company's system, you must inform the IT department immediately.

Employees may not share their email passwords with anyone, including coworkers or family members. Revealing passwords to the Company's email system could allow an outsider to access the Company's network.

Retaining and Deleting Email Messages

Because email messages are electronic records, certain messages must be retained for compliance purposes. Please refer to our record-keeping policy for guidance on which records must be kept, and for how long. If you have any questions about whether and how to retain a particular email message, please ask your manager.

Because of the large volume of emails our Company sends and receives each day, we discourage employees from storing large numbers of email messages that are not subject to the retention rules explained above. Please make a regular practice of deleting email messages once you have read and/or responded to them. If you need to save a particular message, you may print out a paper copy, archive the email, or save it on your hard drive or disk. The Company will purge email messages that have not been archived after _____ days.

The Company may have occasion to suspend our usual rules about deleting email messages (for example, if the company is involved in a lawsuit requiring it to preserve evidence). If this happens, employees will be notified of the procedures to follow to save email messages. Failing to comply with such a notice could subject the company to serious legal consequences, and will result in discipline, up to and including termination.

Violations

Any employee who violates this policy can be subject to discipline, up to and including termination.

How to Complete This Policy

Many email policies provide that messages will be purged every 60 to 90 days. (For more on the importance of purging email, see "Reality Check: Don't Fight the Urge to Purge Email," below.) Select a time period that makes sense for your company, given its rate of email traffic, the capacities of the system, and how quickly employees read (and respond to) their email.

Reality Check: Don't Fight the Urge to Purge Email

There are two very good reasons to purge your company's email system by deleting older messages regularly. First, if employees don't delete messages, the company will eventually have a storage problem on its hands. Many employees simply don't get around to deleting old messages, no matter what the company's policy asks them to do. If your company has a lot of email traffic, the system's capacity to store information will be overwhelmed unless it is cleaned out periodically.

Second, purging emails can reduce your company's legal liability and its legal obligations if it faces a lawsuit. In many kinds of business lawsuits, including lawsuits brought by employees, customers, or other businesses, email becomes evidence. Realizing this, lawyers who sue businesses routinely ask for months, or even years, of the company's email messages in "discovery," the legal process by which parties to a lawsuit gather documents and information from each other and from third parties. Although courts often put limits on what companies have to hand over (for example, they may require a company to disclose only emails on a certain subject matter or emails for a limited time period), businesses that don't purge regularly can spend a lot of time trying to pull together the requested documents.

Once the company learns that it is (or might soon be) facing a lawsuit, however, the rules change. The company has a legal duty to preserve all evidence that might be relevant to the case. If this happens at your company, you'll have to override your usual purge rules and make sure you hang on to every relevant document.

 CAUTION

Banning personal use of email is legally risky. Some employers don't want employees using the company email system for personal messages under any circumstances. Although such a policy might seem reasonable, it's fraught with legal risk. Because these bans are often violated, they are seldom enforced. Inconsistent enforcement can lead to legal claims (for retaliation or discrimination, for example) by employees who believe they were unfairly singled out for discipline. Also, the NLRB has held that employers may not prohibit employees from using the company email system, during nonwork hours, to discuss the terms and conditions of their employment, unless such a ban is necessary to maintain productivity or discipline. For these reasons, you should talk to an attorney if you are considering banning personal use of the company's email system.

Additional Clause on Monitoring

Your email policy absolutely must inform employees that their messages are not private and must reserve the company's right to monitor and read messages at any time, as our policy does.

If the company has monitoring software it plans to use, or if someone will be assigned to read employee email on a regular basis, you should add language to the policy to let employees know. After all, the purpose of an email policy is not only to allow the company to read those problematic messages after they've been sent, but also to deter employees from sending them in the first place. Telling employees that their messages will be monitored and/or read will almost certainly help accomplish this second goal.

Whether your company should regularly monitor employee email is a tough issue to sort through. Doing so will force employees to take the email policy seriously and thereby make them less likely to send messages that are harassing, threatening, or otherwise in violation of your policy. It's just human nature: We aren't as quick to break the rules if we think we will get caught.

But there are some serious downsides as well, with employee dissatisfaction topping the list. Employees don't want to feel like the company doesn't trust them or plans to check up on their every keystroke. Monitoring also costs time and money: The company will have to invest in monitoring software and assign someone the task of actually reviewing or reading messages. And some employers just find monitoring distasteful. They don't want to be cast in the role of Big Brother.

Ultimately, the company's philosophy, workforce, and needs will determine whether the benefits of monitoring outweigh the disadvantages. If your company has no immediate plans to monitor or read employee email, you need not add monitoring language. The provision on privacy that's already in the policy is sufficient.

However, if your company plans to regularly monitor messages, you should add that information to your policy at the end of the "Email Is Not Private" provision. The exact language of your policy will depend on how you will monitor. Here are some sample policy provisions to consider:

16:4 Inspection of Personnel Records

Although many employers would rather not have employees inspecting their own personnel records, state laws may require that employees be granted access. These laws vary greatly in the details. In some states, employees may review their files only at specified hours. In other states, only past employees, not current employees, have the right to inspect their files.

Typically, these laws state who can inspect, when they can inspect, whether they have to give notice, whether they can photocopy their file, and whether they have to pay for the copies. To find out about your state's law, refer to "State Laws on Access to Personnel Records" at the end of this chapter. You can also check with your state labor department. (See Appendix B for contact information.)

Because the laws vary so much, we cannot provide a standard policy for you to use. The following is an example of what your policy might look like.

SAMPLE POLICY LANGUAGE

Current employees who want to inspect their personnel files must make an appointment with the Human Resources Department. Appointments will typically take place Monday through Friday between 1 p.m. and 5 p.m. Although we will make every effort to give employees an appointment quickly, it may take up to 48 hours. If an employee would like a representative to view his or her file, the employee must make the request in writing.

Former employees who would like to inspect their files must make a written request to do so. Upon receiving the written request, the Human Resources Department will call the former employee to schedule an appointment.

We do not allow current or former employees to photocopy their file. If you would like a copy of a document in the file, the Human Resources Department will copy it for you at a price of 10¢ per page.

If you have any questions about this policy, please contact the Human Resources Manager.

16:4 Inspecting Your Records

File Name: 16_Records.rtf

Include This Policy?
- [ ] Yes
- [ ] No
- [ ] Use our existing policy
- [ ] Other _____

Alternate Modifications

None

Additional Clauses

None

Related Policies

None

Notes

_____
_____
_____
_____
_____
_____
_____
_____
_____
_____
_____
_____
_____
_____
_____
_____
_____
_____

Drafting Your Own Policy

When drafting your own policy on employee access to personnel records, be sure to check your state's law so that you don't create a policy that is contrary to legal requirements. A typical inspection policy will state:

- who can inspect the file (current employees, former employees, designated representatives, and so on)
- when they can inspect the file
- where they can inspect the file
- whether they need to make a request
- whether their request must be in writing
- whether they can photocopy the file, and
- how much you will charge for photocopying.

16:5 Work Eligibility Records

Federal law requires employers to make sure their employees are legally authorized to work in the United States. As part of this process, the employer has to complete a form issued by a federal agency, the United States Citizenship and Immigration Services ("USCIS"), called Form I-9. Employers should not keep Form I-9 or other work eligibility forms in employee personnel files. The USCIS is entitled to inspect these forms. If the forms are kept in a worker's personnel file, the USCIS will be able to see all the other documents in the file as well. Not only does this compromise a worker's privacy, but it could also open the company up to additional questions and investigation.

The following policy reassures employees that their work status records will not be kept in their personnel files.

Work Eligibility Records

In compliance with federal law, all newly hired employees must present proof that they are legally eligible to work in the United States. We must keep records related to that proof, including a copy of the USCIS Form I-9 that each employee completes for us.

Those forms are kept as confidential as possible. We do not keep them in your personnel file.

If you would like more information about your I-9 Form, see Section _____ of this Handbook or contact _____ _____ .

16:5 Work Eligibility Records
File Name: 16_Records.rtf

Include This Policy?
☐ Yes
☐ No
☐ Use our existing policy
☐ Other _____

Alternate Modifications
None

Additional Clauses
None

Related Policies
4:3 Proof of Work Eligibility

Notes
_____
_____
_____
_____
_____
_____
_____
_____
_____
_____
_____
_____
_____
_____
_____
_____
_____
_____
_____
_____

16:6 Medical Records

File Name: 16_Records.rtf

Include This Policy?
- ☐ Yes
- ☐ No
- ☐ Use our existing policy
- ☐ Other _____

Alternate Modifications

None

Additional Clauses

None

Related Policies

None

Notes

_____
_____
_____
_____
_____
_____
_____
_____
_____
_____
_____
_____
_____
_____
_____
_____
_____
_____
_____
_____

16:6 Medical Records

Employers come into possession of worker medical records for a variety of reasons. Perhaps an employee has requested an accommodation for a disability and has presented your company with a medical evaluation verifying the disability. Or maybe an employee has requested medical leave and has given your company documentation to show the seriousness of the medical condition.

Medical records should not go into a worker's personnel file. The federal Americans with Disabilities Act includes strict rules on how to handle records relating to an employee's disability: Medical information must be kept separate from nonmedical records, and medical files must be stored in a locked cabinet. Your state might have a similar, or perhaps even stricter, law requiring confidential handling of employee medical records. Whether your state's law goes beyond the federal requirements or not, it's a good practice to keep all medical records confidential and in a separate, locked file cabinet.

The following standard policy informs employees that their medical records will be kept separate from their personnel files.

Medical Records

Employee medical records, including but not limited to workers' compensation information, medical certifications and authorizations, and information pertaining to disabilities and accommodations, are not kept in an employee's regular personnel file. Instead, we keep each employee's medical records in a separate, confidential file. We make these records available only as required or allowed by law.

If you have any questions about the storage of your medical records or about inspecting your medical records, contact

_____ .

State Laws on Access to Personnel Records

This chart deals with only those states that authorize access to personnel files. Generally, an employee is allowed to see evaluations, performance reviews, and other documents that determine a promotion, bonus, or raise; access usually does not include letters of reference, test results, or records of a criminal or workplace violation investigation. Under other state laws, employees may have access to their medical records and records of exposure to hazardous substances; these laws are not included in this chart.

Alaska

Alaska Stat. § 23.10.430

Employers affected: All.

Employee access to records: Employee or former employee may view and copy personnel files.

Conditions for viewing records: Employee may view records during regular business hours under reasonable rules.

Copying records: Employee pays (if employer requests).

California

Cal. Lab. Code §§ 432; 1198.5

Employers affected: All employers subject to wage and hour laws.

Employee access to records: Employee or former employee has right to inspect personnel records relating to performance or to a grievance proceeding, within 30 days of making a written request for records. Employer may redact the names of any nonmanagerial employees. Employer need not comply with more than one request per year from a former employee. If employee files a lawsuit against employer that relates to a personnel matter, the right to review personnel records ceases while the suit is pending.

Written request required: Yes. If employee makes an oral request, the employer must supply a form to make a written request.

Conditions for viewing records: Employee may view personnel file at reasonable times, during break or nonwork hours. If records are kept offsite or employer does not make them available at the workplace, then employee must be allowed to view them at the storage location without loss of pay. If former employee was terminated for reasons relating to harassment or workplace violence, employer may provide copy of records or make them available offsite.

Copying records: Employee or former employee also has a right to a copy of personnel records, at the employee's cost, within 30 days of making a written request.

Colorado

Colo. Rev. Stat. § 8-2-129

Employers affected: All.

Employee access to records: Upon request, current employee may inspect personnel file at least once per year. Former employee may inspect personnel file once after termination of employment.

Conditions for viewing records: Employer must make personnel file available at its place of business at a time convenient to employee and employer. Employer may have a designated representative present at the time of inspection.

Copying records: Employee or former employee may request a copy of the personnel file. Employer can require the employee to pay reasonable copying costs.

Connecticut

Conn. Gen. Stat. §§ 31-128a–31-128h

Employers affected: All.

Employee access to records: Employee has right to inspect personnel files within seven business days after making a request, but not more than twice a year. Former employee has right to inspect personnel files within ten business days after making a request.

Written request required: Yes.

Conditions for viewing records: Employee may view records during regular business hours in a location at or near worksite. Employer may require that files be viewed in the presence of designated official.

Copying records: Employer must provide copies within seven days (current employee) or ten days (former employee) after receiving employee's written request; request must identify the materials employee wants copied. Employer may charge a fee that is based on the cost of supplying documents. Employee is entitled to a copy of any disciplinary action against the employee within one business day after it is imposed; employer must immediately provide terminated employee with a copy of the termination notice.

Employee's right to insert rebuttal: If employee disagrees with information in personnel file and cannot reach an agreement with employer to remove or correct it, employee may submit an explanatory written statement (a "rebuttal"). Rebuttal must be maintained as part of the file. Employer must inform employee of the right to submit a rebuttal in evaluation, discipline, or termination paperwork.

State Laws on Access to Personnel Records (continued)

Delaware

Del. Code tit. 19, §§ 730–735

Employers affected: All.

Employee access to records: Current employee, employee who is laid off with reemployment rights, or employee on leave of absence may inspect personnel record; employee's agent is not entitled to have access to records. Unless there is reasonable cause, employer may limit access to once a year.

Written request required: At employer's discretion. Employer may require employee to file a form and indicate either the purpose of the review or what parts of the record employee wants to inspect.

Conditions for viewing records: Records may be viewed during employer's regular business hours. Employer may require that employees view files on their own time and may also require that files be viewed on the premises and in the presence of a designated official.

Copying records: Employer is not required to permit employee to copy records. Employee may take notes.

Employee's right to insert rebuttal: If employee disagrees with information in personnel file and cannot reach an agreement with employer to remove or correct it, employee may submit an explanatory written statement (a "rebuttal"). Rebuttal must be maintained as part of the personnel file.

Illinois

820 Ill. Comp. Stat. §§ 40/1–40/12

Employers affected: Employers with five or more employees.

Employee access to records: Current employee, or former employee terminated within the past year, is permitted to inspect records twice a year at reasonable intervals, unless a collective bargaining agreement provides otherwise. An employee involved in a current grievance may designate a representative of the union or collective bargaining unit, or other agent, to inspect personnel records that may be relevant to resolving the grievance. Employer must make records available within seven working days after employee makes request (if employer cannot meet deadline, may be allowed an additional seven days).

Written request required: At employer's discretion. Employer may require use of a form.

Conditions for viewing records: Records may be viewed during normal business hours at or near worksite or, at employer's discretion, during nonworking hours at a different location if more convenient for employee.

Copying records: After reviewing records, employee may get a copy. Employer may charge only actual cost of duplication. If employee is unable to view files at worksite, employer, upon receipt of a written request, must mail employee a copy.

Employee's right to insert rebuttal: If employee disagrees with any information in the personnel file and cannot reach an agreement with employer to remove or correct it, employee may submit an explanatory written statement (a "rebuttal"). Rebuttal must remain in file with no additional comment by employer.

Iowa

Iowa Code §§ 91A.2, 91B.1

Employers affected: All employers with salaried employees or commissioned salespeople.

Employee access to records: Employee may have access to personnel file at time agreed upon by employer and employee.

Conditions for viewing records: Employer's representative may be present.

Copying records: Employer may charge copying fee for each page that is equivalent to a commercial copying service fee.

Maine

Me. Rev. Stat. tit. 26, § 631

Employers affected: All.

Employee access to records: Within ten days of submitting request, employee, former employee, or authorized representative may view and copy personnel files.

Written request required: Yes.

Conditions for viewing records: Employee may view records during normal business hours at the location where the files are kept, unless employer, at own discretion, arranges a time and place more convenient for employee. If files are in electronic or any other nonprint format, employer must provide equipment for viewing and copying.

Copying records: Employee entitled to one free copy of personnel file during each calendar year, including any material added to file during that year. Employee must pay for any additional copies.

State Laws on Access to Personnel Records (continued)

Massachusetts

Mass. Gen. Laws ch. 149, § 52C

Employers affected: All.

Employee access to records: Employee or former employee must have opportunity to review personnel files within five business days of submitting request, but not more than twice a calendar year. (Law does not apply to tenured or tenure-track employees in private colleges and universities.) Employer must notify an employee within ten days of placing in the employee's personnel record any information to the extent that the information is, has been, or may be used, to negatively affect the employee's qualification for employment, promotion, transfer, additional compensation, or the possibility that the employee will be subject to disciplinary action. (This notification does not count toward employee's two allotted opportunities to view personnel file.)

Written request required: Yes.

Conditions for viewing records: Employee may view records at workplace during normal business hours.

Copying records: Employee must be given a copy of record within 5 business days of submitting a written request.

Employee's right to insert rebuttal: If employee disagrees with any information in personnel record and cannot reach an agreement with employer to remove or correct it, employee may submit an explanatory written statement (a "rebuttal"). Rebuttal becomes a part of the personnel file.

Michigan

Mich. Comp. Laws §§ 423.501–423.505

Employers affected: Employers with four or more employees.

Employee access to records: Current or former employee is entitled to review personnel records at reasonable intervals, generally not more than twice a year, unless a collective bargaining agreement provides otherwise.

Written request required: Yes. Request must describe the record employee wants to review.

Conditions for viewing records: Employee may view records during normal office hours either at or reasonably near the worksite. If these hours would require employee to take time off work, employer must provide another reasonable time for review.

Copying records: After reviewing files, employee may get a copy; employer may charge only actual cost of duplication. If employee is unable to view files at the worksite, employer, upon receipt of a written request, must mail employee a copy.

Employee's right to insert rebuttal: If employee disagrees with any information in personnel record and cannot reach an agreement with employer to remove or correct it, employee may submit a written statement explaining his or her position. Statement may be no longer than five 8½" by 11" pages.

Minnesota

Minn. Stat. §§ 181.960–181.966

Employers affected: Employers with 20 or more employees.

Employee access to records: Current employee may review files once per six-month period; former employee may have access to records once only during the first year after termination. Employer must comply with written request within seven working days (14 working days if personnel records kept out of state). Employer may not retaliate against an employee who asserts rights under these laws.

Written request required: Yes.

Conditions for viewing records: Current employee may view records during employer's normal business hours at worksite or a nearby location; does not have to take place during employee's working hours. Employer or employer's representative may be present.

Copying records: Employer must provide copy free of charge. Current employee must first review record and then submit written request for copies. Former employee must submit written request; providing former employee with a copy fulfills employer's obligation to allow access to records.

Employee's right to insert rebuttal: If employee disputes specific information in the personnel record, and cannot reach an agreement with employer to remove or revise it, employee may submit a written statement identifying the disputed information and explaining his or her position. Statement may be no longer than five pages and must be kept with personnel record as long as it is maintained.

Nevada

Nev. Rev. Stat. § 613.075

Employers affected: All.

Employee access to records: An employee who has worked at least 60 days, and a former employee, within 60 days of termination, must be given a reasonable opportunity to inspect personnel records.

Conditions for viewing records: Employee may view records during employer's normal business hours.

State Laws on Access to Personnel Records (continued)

Copying records: Employer may charge only actual cost of providing access and copies.

Employee's right to insert rebuttal: Employee may submit a reasonable written explanation in direct response to any entry in personnel record. Statement must be of reasonable length; employer may specify the format; employer must maintain statement in personnel records.

New Hampshire

N.H. Rev. Stat. § 275:56

Employers affected: All.

Employee access to records: Employer must provide employees with a reasonable opportunity to inspect records.

Copying records: Employer may charge a fee reasonably related to cost of supplying copies.

Employee's right to insert rebuttal: If employee disagrees with any of the information in personnel record and cannot reach an agreement with the employer to remove or correct it, employee may submit an explanatory written statement along with supporting evidence. Statement must be maintained as part of personnel file.

Oregon

Or. Rev. Stat. § 652.750

Employers affected: All.

Employee access to records: Within 45 days after receipt of request, employer must provide employee a reasonable opportunity to inspect payroll records and personnel records used to determine qualifications for employment, promotion, or additional compensation, termination, or other disciplinary action.

Conditions for viewing records: Employee may view records at worksite or place of work assignment.

Copying records: Within 45 days after receipt of request, employer must provide a certified copy of requested record to current or former employee (if request made within 60 days of termination). If employee makes request after 60 days from termination, employer shall provide a certified copy of requested records if employer has records at time of the request. May charge amount reasonably calculated to recover actual cost of providing copy.

Pennsylvania

43 Pa. Cons. Stat. §§ 1321–1324

Employers affected: All.

Employee access to records: Employer must allow employee to inspect personnel record at reasonable times. (Employee's agent, or employee who is laid off with reemployment rights or on leave of absence, must also be given access.) Unless there is reasonable cause, employer may limit review to once a year by employee and once a year by employee's agent.

Written request required: At employer's discretion. Employer may require the use of a form as well as a written indication of the parts of the record employee wants to inspect or the purpose of the inspection. For employee's agent: Employee must provide signed authorization designating agent; must be for a specific date and indicate the reason for the inspection or the parts of the record the agent is authorized to inspect.

Conditions for viewing records: Employee may view records during regular business hours at the office where records are maintained, when there is enough time for employee to complete the review. Employer may require that employee or agent view records on their own time and may also require that inspection take place on the premises and in the presence of employer's designated official.

Copying records: Employer not obligated to permit copying. Employee may take notes.

Employee's right to insert rebuttal: The Bureau of Labor Standards, after a petition and hearing, may allow employee to place a counterstatement in the personnel file, if employee claims that the file contains an error.

Rhode Island

R.I. Gen. Laws § 28-6.4-1

Employers affected: All.

Employee access to records: Employer must permit employee to inspect personnel file when given at least seven days' advance notice (excluding weekends and holidays). Employer may limit access to no more than three times a year.

Written request required: Yes.

Conditions for viewing records: Employee may view records at any reasonable time other than employee's work hours. Inspection must take place in presence of employer or employer's representative.

Copying records: Employee may not make copies or remove files from place of inspection. Employer may charge a fee reasonably related to cost of supplying copies.

State Drug and Alcohol Testing Laws (continued)

Testing applicants: Employer may require applicant to take a drug test only if offered employment or placed on an eligibility list.

Testing employees: Statute does not require or encourage testing. Employer may test based upon probable cause but may not base belief on a single accident, an anonymous informant, or off-duty possession or use (unless it occurs on the employer's premises or nearby, during or right before work hours); must document the facts and give employee a copy. May test randomly when there could be an unreasonable threat to the health and safety of coworkers or the public. Testing is also allowed when an employee returns to work following a positive test.

Employee rights: Employee who tests positive has three days to explain or contest results. Employee must be given an opportunity to participate in a rehabilitation program for up to six months; an employer with more than 20 full-time employees must pay for half of any out-of-pocket costs. After successfully completing the program, employee is entitled to return to previous job with full pay and benefits.

Notice and policy requirements: All employers must have a written policy, which includes the consequences of a positive result or refusing to submit to testing. Policy must be approved by the state department of labor. Policy must be distributed to each employee at least 30 days before it takes effect. Any changes to policy require 60 days' advance notice. An employer with more than 20 full-time employees must have an employee assistance program certified by the state office of substance abuse before implementing a testing program.

Maryland

Md. Code, Health-Gen. § 17-214

Employers affected: All employers.

Testing applicants: May use preliminary screening to test applicant. If initial result is positive, may make job offer conditional on confirmation of test results.

Testing employees: Employer may require substance abuse testing for legitimate business purposes only.

Employee rights: The sample must be tested by a certified laboratory; at the time of testing employee may request laboratory's name and address. An employee who tests positive must be given:

- a copy of the test results
- a copy of the employer's written drug and alcohol policy

- a written notice of any adverse action employer intends to take, and
- a statement of employee's right to an independent confirmation test at own expense.

Massachusetts

No statute on drug or alcohol testing, but court cases have defined some limitations *(Webster v. Motorola, Inc., 418 Mass. 425 (1994))*

Employers affected: All employers.

Testing employees: Random drug testing that doesn't distinguish between safety-sensitive positions and other positions is not allowed.

Minnesota

Minn. Stat. §§ 181.950–181.957

Employers affected: Employers with one or more employees.

Testing applicants: Employers may require applicants to submit to a drug or alcohol test only after they have been given a job offer and have seen a written notice of testing policy. May only test if required of all applicants for same position.

Testing employees: Employers are not required to test. Employers may require drug or alcohol testing only according to a written testing policy. Testing may be done if there is a reasonable suspicion that employee:

- is under the influence of drugs or alcohol
- has violated drug and alcohol policy
- has been involved in a work-related accident; or
- has sustained or caused another employee to sustain a personal injury.

Random tests permitted only for employees in safety-sensitive positions. With two weeks' notice, employers may also test as part of an annual routine physical exam. Employer may test, without notice, an employee referred by the employer for chemical dependency treatment or evaluation or participating in a chemical dependency treatment program under an employee benefit plan. Testing is allowed during and for two years following treatment.

Employee rights: If test is positive, employee has three days to explain the results; employee must notify employer within five days of intention to obtain a retest. Employer may not discharge employee for a first-time positive test without offering counseling or rehabilitation; employee who refuses or does not complete program successfully may be discharged.

State Drug and Alcohol Testing Laws (continued)

Notice and policy requirements: Employees must be given a written notice of testing policy that includes consequences of refusing to take test or having a positive test result. Two weeks' notice required before testing as part of an annual routine physical exam.

Mississippi

Miss. Code §§ 71-3-121, 71-3-205–71-3-225, 71-7-1–71-7-33

Employers affected: Employers with one or more full-time employees. Employers that establish a drug-free workplace program to qualify for a workers' compensation rate discount must implement testing procedures.

Testing applicants: May test all applicants as part of employment application process. Employer may request a signed statement that applicant has read and understands the drug and alcohol testing policy or notice.

Testing employees: May require drug and alcohol testing of all employees:

- upon reasonable suspicion
- as part of a routinely scheduled fitness-for-duty medical examination
- as a follow-up to a rehabilitation program, or
- if they have tested positive within the previous 12 months.

May also require drug and alcohol testing following an employee's work-related injury, for purposes of determining workers' compensation coverage. Testing is also allowed on a neutral selection basis.

Employee rights: Employer must inform an employee in writing within five working days of receipt of a positive confirmed test result; employee may request and receive a copy of the test result report. Employee has ten working days after receiving notice to explain the positive test results. Employer may not discharge or take any adverse personnel action on the basis of an initial positive test result that has not been verified by a confirmation test. Private employer who elects to establish a drug-free workplace program must have an employee assistance program or maintain a resource file of outside programs.

Notice and policy requirements: 30 days before implementing testing program employer must give employees written notice of drug and alcohol policy that includes consequences:

- of a positive confirmed result
- of refusing to take test, and
- of other violations of the policy.

Montana

Mont. Code §§ 39-2-205–39-2-211

Employers affected: Employers with one or more employees.

Testing applicants: May test as a condition of hire, but only for applicants who will work in a hazardous work environment; a security position; a position that affects public safety or health; a position with a fiduciary relationship to the employer; or a position that requires driving.

Testing employees: Same job restrictions apply to employees as to applicants. Employees in these positions may be tested:

- upon reasonable suspicion
- after involvement in an accident that causes personal injury or more than $1,500 property damage
- as a follow-up to a previous positive test, or
- as a follow-up to treatment or a rehabilitation program.

Employer may conduct random tests as long as there is an established date, all personnel are subject to testing, the employer has signed statements from each employee confirming receipt of a written description of the random selection process, and the random selection process is conducted by a scientifically valid method. Employer may require an employee who tests positive to undergo treatment as a condition of continued employment.

Employee rights: After a positive result, employee may request additional confirmation by an independent laboratory; if the results are negative, employer must pay the test costs. Employer may not take action or conduct follow-up testing if the employee presents a reasonable explanation or medical opinion that the original results were not caused by illegal drug use; employer must also remove results from employee's record.

Notice and policy requirements: Written policy must be available for review 60 days before testing. Policy must include consequences of a positive test result.

Nebraska

Neb. Rev. Stat. §§ 48-1901–48-1910

Employers affected: Employers with six or more full-time and part-time employees.

Testing employees: Employers are not required to test. Employer may require employees to submit to drug or alcohol testing and may discipline or discharge any employee who refuses, tests positive, or tampers with the test sample.

State Drug and Alcohol Testing Laws (continued)

Employee rights: Employer may not take adverse action on the basis of an initial positive result unless it is confirmed according to state and federal guidelines.

New Hampshire

N.H. Rev. Stat. § 275:3

Employers affected: All employers.

Testing applicants: May not require applicants to pay the costs of testing.

Testing employees: May not require employees to pay the costs of testing.

New Jersey

No statute on drug or alcohol testing, but court cases place some limitations *(Hennessey v. Coastal Eagle Point Oil Co., 129 N.J. 81 (1992); Vargo v. Nat'l Exch. Carriers Ass'n, Inc., 376 N.J. Super. 364 (App. Div. 2005))*

Employers affected: All employers.

Testing applicants: Employer may require applicants to undergo preemployment testing.

Testing employees: Random drug testing allowed for safety-sensitive positions.

North Carolina

N.C. Gen. Stat. §§ 95-230–95-235

Employers affected: All employers.

Testing applicants: May test as a condition of hire. Applicant has right to retest a confirmed positive sample at own expense. If first screening test produces a positive result, applicant may waive a second examination that is intended to confirm the results.

Testing employees: Employers may, but are not required to, test. Testing must be performed under reasonable, sanitary conditions, and must respect individual dignity to the extent possible. Employer must preserve samples for at least 90 days after confirmed test results are released.

Employee rights: Employee has right to retest a confirmed positive sample at own expense.

North Dakota

N.D. Cent. Code §§ 34-01-15, 65-01-11

Employers affected: All employers.

Testing applicants: May test as a condition of hire.

Testing employees: Employer may test following an accident or injury that will result in a workers' compensation claim,

if employer has a mandatory policy of testing under these circumstances, or if employer or physician has reasonable grounds to suspect injury was caused by impairment due to alcohol or drug use.

Employee rights: Employer that requires drug testing of any applicant or employee must pay for the test.

Ohio

Ohio Admin. Code § 4123-17-58

Employers affected: Employers that establish a drug-free safety program may qualify for a workers' compensation rate bonus.

Testing applicants: Must test all applicants and new hires.

Testing employees: Must test employees:
- upon reasonable suspicion
- following a return to work after a positive test, and
- after an accident that results in an injury requiring off-site medical attention or property damage.

Employers must test at random to meet requirements for greater discounts.

Employee rights: Employer must have an employee assistance plan. Employers who test at random to qualify for greater discount must not terminate employee who tests positive for the first time, comes forward voluntarily, or is referred by a supervisor. For these employees, employer must pay costs of substance abuse assessment.

Notice and policy requirements: Policy must state consequences for refusing to submit to testing or for violating guidelines. Policy must include a commitment to rehabilitation.

Oklahoma

Okla. Stat. tit. 40, §§ 551–565

Employers affected: Employers with one or more employees.

Testing applicants: May test applicants.

Testing employees: Statute does not require or encourage testing. Before requiring testing, employer must provide an employee assistance program. Random testing is allowed. May test employees:
- upon reasonable suspicion
- after an accident resulting in injury or property damage
- on a random selection basis
- as part of a routine fitness-for-duty examination, or
- as follow-up to a rehabilitation program.

State Drug and Alcohol Testing Laws (continued)

Employee rights: Employee has right to retest a positive result at own expense; if the confirmation test is negative, employer must reimburse costs.

Notice and policy requirements: Before requiring testing employer must: adopt a written policy; give a copy to each employee and to any applicant offered a job; and allow ten days' notice. Policy must state consequences of a positive test result or refusing to submit to testing.

Oregon

Or. Rev. Stat. §§ 438.435, 659.840, 659A.300

Employers affected: All employers.

Testing applicants: Unless there is reasonable suspicion that an applicant is under the influence of alcohol, no employer may require a breathalyzer test as a condition of employment. Employer is not prohibited from conducting a test if applicant consents.

Testing employees: Unless there is reasonable suspicion that an employee is under the influence of alcohol, no employer may require a breathalyzer or blood alcohol test as a condition of continuing employment. Employer is not prohibited from conducting a test if employee consents.

Employee rights: No action may be taken based on the results of an on-site drug test without a confirming test performed according to state health division regulations. Upon written request, test results will be reported to the employee.

Rhode Island

R.I. Gen. Laws §§ 28-6.5-1–28-6.5-2

Employers affected: All employers.

Testing applicants: May test as a condition of hire.

Testing employees: May require employee to submit to a drug test only if there are reasonable grounds, based on specific, documented observations, to believe employee may be under the influence of a controlled substance that is impairing job performance.

Employee rights: Employee must be allowed to provide sample in private, outside the presence of any person. Employee who tests positive may have the sample retested at employer's expense and must be given opportunity to explain or refute results. Employee may not be terminated on the basis of a positive result but must be referred to a licensed substance abuse professional. After referral, employer may require additional testing and may terminate employee if test results are positive.

South Carolina

S.C. Code §§ 38-73-500, 41-1-15

Employers affected: Employers that establish a drug-free workplace program to qualify for a workers' compensation rate discount.

Testing applicants: Employer is not required to test applicants to qualify for discount.

Testing employees: Must conduct random testing among all employees.

Employee rights: Employee must receive positive test results in writing within 24 hours.

Notice and policy requirements: Employer must notify all employees of the drug-free workplace program at the time it is established or at the time of hiring, whichever is earlier. Program must include a policy statement that balances respect for individuals with the need to maintain a safe, drug-free environment.

Tennessee

Tenn. Code §§ 50-9-101–50-9-114

Employers affected: Employers that establish a drug-free workplace program to qualify for a workers' compensation rate discount.

Testing applicants: Must test applicants for drugs upon conditional offer of employment. May test only those applying for certain positions, if based on reasonable job classifications. May test for alcohol after conditional offer of employment. Job ads must include notice that drug and alcohol testing is required.

Testing employees: Employer must test upon reasonable suspicion; must document behavior on which the suspicion is based within 24 hours or before test results are released, whichever is earlier; and must give a copy to the employee upon request. Employer must test employees:

- if required by employer policy as part of a routine fitness-for-duty medical exam
- after an accident that results in injury, or
- as a follow-up to a required rehabilitation program.

May test employees who are not in safety-sensitive positions for alcohol only if based on reasonable suspicion.

Employee rights: Employee has the right to explain or contest a positive result within five days. Employee may not be fired, disciplined, or discriminated against for voluntarily seeking treatment unless employee has previously tested positive or been in a rehabilitation program.

Harassment Will Not Be Tolerated

It is our policy and our responsibility to provide our employees with a workplace free from harassment. Harassment on the basis of

_____

_____

undermines our workplace morale and our commitment to treat each other with dignity and respect. Accordingly, harassment will not be tolerated at our Company.

Harassment can take many forms, including but not limited to touching or other unwanted physical contact, posting offensive cartoons or pictures, using slurs or other derogatory terms, telling offensive or lewd jokes and stories, and sending email messages with offensive content. Unwanted sexual advances, requests for sexual favors, and sexually suggestive gestures, jokes, propositions, email messages, or other communications all constitute harassment.

If you experience or witness any form of harassment in the workplace, please immediately notify the Company by following the steps outlined in our Complaint Policy (see Section _____ of this Handbook). We encourage you to come forward with complaints; the sooner we learn about the problem, the sooner we can take steps to resolve it. The Company will not retaliate, or allow retaliation, against anyone who complains of harassment, assists in a harassment investigation, or files an administrative charge or lawsuit alleging harassment. All managers are required to immediately report any incidents of harassment, as set forth in our Complaint Policy.

Complaints will be investigated quickly. Those who are found to have violated this policy will be subject to appropriate disciplinary action, up to and including termination.

How to Complete This Policy

Because harassment is legally considered to be a type of discrimination, a company's obligation to prevent and remedy harassment tracks its obligation not to discriminate. For example, if the law protects employees from discrimination on the basis of race, they are also protected from racial harassment. In the blank space, fill in the same prohibited bases for harassment that you included in your antidiscrimination policy.

Changes Due to #MeToo

Most of us first heard the phrase #MeToo in October of 2017, as part of the public airing of rape, sexual assault, and sexual harassment allegations against movie mogul Harvey Weinstein. (In fact, the phrase entered public usage as a way for survivors to show solidarity with each other more than a decade before.) What's now called the #MeToo Movement led to public allegations of harassment and assault against powerful men in many industries, followed by some high-profile terminations, disciplinary actions, and criminal prosecutions.

Much of the publicity around #MeToo has focused on celebrities: Many of those making accusations of harassment—and those accused of it—are household names. In fact, however, the #MeToo Movement has had wider effects. First and foremost, the public airing of so many personal stories has made clear that sexual harassment and assault are widespread, pervasive social problems. We have had a collective consciousness-raising about what harassment is, how it works, and why victims sometimes don't come forward. This can only help inform workplace efforts to properly and respectfully investigate and root out harassment.

Here are some other effects of #MeToo:

- The Equal Opportunity Employment Commission (EEOC) reported that sexual harassment charges filed with the agency increased by 12% in fiscal year (FY) 2018 over FY 2017. The agency also reported filing 66 lawsuits alleging sexual harassment in the same timeframe, a 50% increase over the prior year. In addition, the agency collected nearly $70 million for victims of sexual harassment in FY 2018 through its litigation and administrative enforcement efforts. The EEOC attributes all of these increases, in part, to the heightened awareness and demand created by #MeToo.

- Some states have passed laws requiring workplace sexual harassment training, prohibiting employers from including nondisclosure/confidentiality provisions in agreements to settle sexual harassment claims, and protecting more workers from sexual harassment.

- Large private employers have made changes in the way they handle sexual harassment. For example, Google, Facebook, and Microsoft have all announced that they will no longer require mandatory arbitration for sexual harassment claims—a change that will have the effect of making these claims more public and allowing them to be tried by a jury in court rather than an arbitrator in a confidential proceeding.

RESOURCE

For more information on federal antidiscrimination laws, see *The Essential Guide to Federal Employment Laws*, by Lisa Guerin and Sachi Barreiro (Nolo). This helpful resource devotes an entire chapter to each of the major federal employment laws, including the antidiscrimination laws listed above. You can also find helpful fact sheets, posters, compliance assistance, and more on the website of the Equal Employment Opportunity Commission—the federal agency that interprets and enforces federal antidiscrimination laws—at www.eeoc.gov.

State Laws Prohibiting Discrimination in Employment

Alabama

Ala. Code §§ 25-1-20, 25-1-21

Law applies to employers with: 20 or more employees

Private employers may not make employment decisions based on:

- Age (40 and older)

Alaska

Alaska Stat. §§ 18.80.220, 18.80.300, 39.20.520, 47.30.865

Law applies to employers with: One or more employees

Private employers may not make employment decisions based on:

- Age
- Ancestry or national origin
- Physical or mental disability
- Gender
- Marital status, including changes in status
- Pregnancy, childbirth, and related medical conditions, including parenthood (accommodations required)
- Race or color
- Religion or creed
- Mental illness

Arizona

Ariz. Rev. Stat. §§ 41-1461, 41-1463, 41-1465

Law applies to employers with: 15 or more employees

Private employers may not make employment decisions based on:

- Age (40 and older)
- Ancestry or national origin
- Physical or mental disability
- AIDS/HIV
- Gender
- Race or color
- Religion or creed
- Genetic testing information

Arkansas

Ark. Code §§ 11-4-601, 11-5-403, 16-123-102, 16-123-107

Law applies to employers with: Nine or more employees

Private employers may not make employment decisions based on:

- Ancestry or national origin
- Physical, mental, or sensory disability
- Gender
- Pregnancy, childbirth, and related medical conditions

- Race or color
- Religion or creed
- Genetic testing information

California

Cal. Gov't Code §§ 12920, 12926, 12926.1, 12940, 12941, 12945; Cal. Lab. Code § 1101

Law applies to employers with: Five or more employees

Private employers may not make employment decisions based on:

- Age (40 and older)
- Ancestry or national origin
- Physical or mental disability
- AIDS/HIV
- Gender
- Marital status
- Pregnancy, childbirth, and related medical conditions, including breast-feeding (accommodations required)
- Race or color
- Religion or creed
- Sexual orientation
- Genetic testing information
- Gender identity, gender expression
- Medical condition
- Political activities or affiliations
- Status as victim of domestic violence, sexual assault, or stalking
- Military and veteran status

Colorado

Colo. Rev. Stat. §§ 24-34-301, 24-34-401, 24-34-402, 24-34-402.5, 27-65-115; 3 Colo. Code Regs. §§ 708-1:60.1, 708-1:80.8

Law applies to employers with: One or more employees; 25 or more employees (marital status only)

Private employers may not make employment decisions based on:

- Age (40 and older)
- Ancestry or national origin
- Physical, mental, or learning disability
- AIDS/HIV
- Gender
- Marital status (only applies to marriage to a coworker or plans to marry a coworker)
- Pregnancy, childbirth, and related medical conditions (accommodations required)
- Race or color
- Religion or creed

State Laws Prohibiting Discrimination in Employment (continued)

- Sexual orientation, including perceived sexual orientation
- Lawful conduct outside of work
- Mental illness
- Transgender status

Connecticut

Conn. Gen. Stat. §§ 46a-51, 46a-60, 46a-81a, 46a-81c

Law applies to employers with: Three or more employees

Private employers may not make employment decisions based on:
- Age
- Ancestry or national origin
- Present or past physical, mental, learning, or intellectual disability
- Gender
- Marital status, including civil unions
- Pregnancy, childbirth, and related medical conditions (accommodations required)
- Race or color
- Religion or creed
- Sexual orientation, including having a history of such a preference or being identified with such a preference
- Genetic testing information
- Gender identity or expression
- Arrests or convictions that have been erased, pardoned, or rehabilitated
- Status as a veteran

Delaware

Del. Code tit. 19, §§ 710, 711, 724

Law applies to employers with: Four or more employees

Private employers may not make employment decisions based on:
- Age (40 and older)
- Ancestry or national origin
- Physical or mental disability
- AIDS/HIV
- Gender
- Marital status
- Pregnancy, childbirth, and related medical conditions including breast-feeding (accommodations required)
- Race or color
- Religion or creed
- Sexual orientation
- Genetic testing information
- Gender identity
- Family responsibilities

- Status as victim of domestic violence, sexual offense, or stalking
- "Reproductive health decisions"

District of Columbia

D.C. Code §§ 2-1401.02, 2-1401.05, 2-1402.82, 7-1703.03, 32-531.08

Law applies to employers with: One or more employees

Private employers may not make employment decisions based on:
- Age (18 and older)
- Ancestry or national origin
- Physical or mental disability
- Gender (includes reproductive health decisions)
- Marital status, including domestic partnership
- Pregnancy, childbirth, and related medical conditions, including parenthood and breast-feeding (accommodations required)
- Race or color
- Religion or creed
- Sexual orientation
- Genetic testing information
- Enrollment in vocational, professional, or college education
- Family duties
- Personal appearance
- Political affiliation
- Gender identity or expression
- Status as unemployed
- Tobacco use
- Credit information

Florida

Fla. Stat. §§ 448.075, 760.01, 760.02, 760.10, 760.50

Law applies to employers with: 15 or more employees

Private employers may not make employment decisions based on:
- Age
- Ancestry or national origin
- "Handicap"
- AIDS/HIV
- Gender
- Marital status
- Pregnancy, childbirth, and related medical conditions
- Race or color
- Religion or creed
- Sickle cell trait

State Laws Prohibiting Discrimination in Employment (continued)

Georgia

Ga. Code §§ 34-1-2, 34-5-1, 34-5-2, 34-6A-1 and following

Law applies to employers with: 15 or more employees (disability); ten or more employees (gender) (domestic and agricultural employees not protected); one or more employees (age)

Private employers may not make employment decisions based on:

- Age (40 to 70)
- Physical, mental, or learning disability
- Gender (wage discrimination only)

Hawaii

Haw. Rev. Stat. §§ 378-1 and following; Haw. Code §§ 12-46-107, 12-46-182,

Law applies to employers with: One or more employees

Private employers may not make employment decisions based on:

- Age
- Ancestry or national origin
- Physical or mental disability
- AIDS/HIV
- Gender
- Marital status
- Pregnancy, childbirth, and related medical conditions, including breast-feeding (accommodations required)
- Race or color
- Religion or creed
- Sexual orientation
- Genetic testing information
- Arrest and court record (unless there is a conviction directly related to job)
- Credit history or credit report, unless the information in the individual's credit history or credit report directly relates to a bona fide occupational qualification
- Gender identity and gender expression
- Status as a victim of domestic or sexual violence (if employer has knowledge or is notified of this status)

Idaho

Idaho Code §§ 39-8303, 67-5902, 67-5909, 67-5910

Law applies to employers with: Five or more employees

Private employers may not make employment decisions based on:

- Age (40 and older)
- Ancestry or national origin

- Physical or mental disability
- Gender
- Pregnancy, childbirth, and related medical conditions
- Race or color
- Religion or creed
- Genetic testing information

Illinois

410 Ill. Comp. Stat. § 513/25; 775 Ill. Comp. Stat. §§ 5/1-102, 5/1-103, 5/2-101, 5/2-102, 5/2-103; 820 Ill. Comp. Stat. §§ 105/4, 180/30; Ill. Admin. Code tit. 56, § 5210.110

Law applies to employers with: 15 or more employees; one or more employees (disability only)

Private employers may not make employment decisions based on:

- Age (40 and older)
- Ancestry or national origin
- Physical or mental disability
- Gender
- Marital status
- Pregnancy, childbirth, and related medical conditions (accommodations required)
- Race or color
- Religion or creed
- Sexual orientation
- Genetic testing information
- Citizenship status
- Military status
- Unfavorable military discharge
- Gender identity
- Arrest record
- Genetic information
- Victims of domestic violence
- Order of protection status
- Lack of permanent mailing address or having a mailing address of a shelter or social service provider

Indiana

Ind. Code §§ 22-9-1-2, 22-9-2-1, 22-9-2-2, 22-9-5-1 and following

Law applies to employers with: six or more employees; 1 or more employees (age only); 15 or more employees (disability only)

Private employers may not make employment decisions based on:

- Age (40 to 75—applies to employers with one or more employees)
- Ancestry or national origin

State Laws Prohibiting Discrimination in Employment (continued)

- Physical or mental disability (15 or more employees)
- Gender
- Race or color
- Religion or creed
- Status as a veteran
- Off-duty tobacco use
- Sealed or expunged arrest or conviction record

Iowa

Iowa Code §§ 216.2, 216.6, 216.6A, 729.6

Law applies to employers with: Four or more employees

Private employers may not make employment decisions based on:

- Age (18 or older)
- Ancestry or national origin
- Physical or mental disability
- AIDS/HIV
- Gender
- Pregnancy, childbirth, and related medical conditions
- Race or color
- Religion or creed
- Sexual orientation
- Genetic testing information
- Gender identity
- Wage discrimination

Kansas

Kan. Stat. §§ 44-1002, 44-1009, 44-1112, 44-1113, 44-1125, 44-1126, 65-6002(e)

Law applies to employers with: Four or more employees

Private employers may not make employment decisions based on:

- Age (40 or older)
- Ancestry or national origin
- Physical or mental disability
- AIDS/HIV
- Gender
- Race or color
- Religion or creed
- Genetic testing information
- Military service or status

Kentucky

Ky. Rev. Stat. §§ 207.130, 207.135, 207.150, 342.197, 344.010, 344.030, 344.040

Law applies to employers with: Eight or more employees

Private employers may not make employment decisions based on:

- Age (40 or older)
- Ancestry or national origin
- Physical or mental disability
- AIDS/HIV
- Gender
- Pregnancy, childbirth, and related medical conditions
- Race or color
- Religion or creed
- Occupational pneumoconiosis with no respiratory impairment resulting from exposure to coal dust
- Off-duty tobacco use

Louisiana

La. Rev. Stat. §§ 23:301 to 23:368

Law applies to employers with: 20 or more employees

Private employers may not make employment decisions based on:

- Age (40 or older)
- Ancestry or national origin
- Physical or mental disability
- Gender
- Pregnancy, childbirth, and related medical conditions (accommodations may be required) (applies to employers with 25 or more employees)
- Race or color
- Religion or creed
- Genetic testing information
- Sickle cell trait
- Being a smoker or nonsmoker

Maine

Me. Rev. Stat. Ann. tit. 5, §§ 19302, 4552, 4553, 4571 to 4576; tit. 26, § 833; tit. 39-A, § 353

Law applies to employers with: One or more employees

Private employers may not make employment decisions based on:

- Age
- Ancestry or national origin
- Physical or mental disability
- AIDS/HIV
- Gender
- Pregnancy, childbirth, and related medical conditions
- Race or color
- Religion or creed

State Laws Prohibiting Discrimination in Employment (continued)

- Sexual orientation, including perceived sexual orientation
- Genetic testing information
- Gender identity or expression
- Past workers' compensation claim
- Past whistle-blowing
- Medical support notice for child

Maryland

Md. Code, State Government, §§ 20-101, 20-601–20-608; Md. Code Regs. § 14.03.02.02

Law applies to employers with: 15 or more employees

Private employers may not make employment decisions based on:
- Age
- Ancestry or national origin
- Physical or mental disability
- AIDS/HIV
- Gender
- Marital status
- Pregnancy, childbirth, and related medical conditions (accommodations required)
- Race or color
- Religion or creed
- Sexual orientation
- Genetic testing information
- Civil Air Patrol membership
- Gender identity

Massachusetts

Mass. Gen. Laws ch. 149, §§ 24A, 105A; ch. 151B, §§ 1, 4; 804 Mass. Code 3.01

Law applies to employers with: Six or more employees

Private employers may not make employment decisions based on:
- Age (40 or older)
- Ancestry or national origin
- Physical or mental disability
- Gender
- Marital status
- Pregnancy, childbirth, and related medical conditions including breast-feeding (accommodations required)
- Race or color
- Religion or creed
- Sexual orientation
- Genetic testing information
- Military service
- Arrest record

- Gender identity
- Status as a veteran

Michigan

Mich. Comp. Laws §§ 37.1103, 37.1201, 37.1202, 37.2201, 37.2202, 37.2205a, 750.556

Law applies to employers with: One or more employees

Private employers may not make employment decisions based on:
- Age
- Ancestry or national origin
- Physical or mental disability
- AIDS/HIV
- Gender
- Marital status
- Pregnancy, childbirth, and related medical conditions
- Race or color
- Religion or creed
- Genetic testing information
- Height or weight
- Misdemeanor arrest record
- Civil Air Patrol membership

Minnesota

Minn. Stat. §§ 144.417, 181.81, 181.9414, 181.974, 363A.03, 363A.08

Law applies to employers with: One or more employees; 21 or more employees (pregnancy and childbirth accommodations)

Private employers may not make employment decisions based on:
- Age (18 to 70)
- Ancestry or national origin
- Physical, sensory, or mental disability
- Gender
- Marital status
- Pregnancy, childbirth, and related medical conditions (accommodations required)
- Race or color
- Religion or creed
- Sexual orientation, including perceived sexual orientation
- Genetic testing information
- Gender identity
- Member of local commission
- Receiving public assistance
- Familial status (protects parents or guardians living with a minor child)

State Laws Prohibiting Discrimination in Employment (continued)

Mississippi

Miss. Code § 33-1-15

Law applies to employers with: One or more employees

Private employers may not make employment decisions based on:

- Military status
- No other protected categories unless employer receives public funding

Missouri

Mo. Rev. Stat. §§ 191.665, 213.010, 213.055, 375.1306

Law applies to employers with: Six or more employees

Private employers may not make employment decisions based on:

- Age (40 to 70)
- Ancestry or national origin
- Physical or mental disability
- AIDS/HIV
- Gender
- Race or color
- Religion or creed
- Genetic testing information
- Off-duty use of alcohol or tobacco

Montana

Mont. Code Ann. §§ 49-2-101, 49-2-303, 49-2-310

Law applies to employers with: One or more employees

Private employers may not make employment decisions based on:

- Age
- Ancestry or national origin
- Physical or mental disability
- Gender
- Marital status
- Pregnancy, childbirth, and related medical conditions
- Race or color
- Religion or creed

Nebraska

Neb. Rev. Stat. §§ 20-168, 48-236, 48-1001–48-1010, 48-1102, 48-1104

Law applies to employers with: 15 or more employees

Private employers may not make employment decisions based on:

- Age (40 or older—applies to employers with 20 or more employees)

- Ancestry or national origin
- Physical or mental disability
- AIDS/HIV
- Gender
- Marital status
- Pregnancy, childbirth, and related medical conditions (accommodations required)
- Race or color
- Religion or creed
- Genetic testing information (applies to all employers)

Nevada

Nev. Rev. Stat. §§ 608.0193, 608.0198, 613.310 and following, 613.4353 and following

Law applies to employers with: 15 or more employees

Private employers may not make employment decisions based on:

- Age (40 or older)
- Ancestry or national origin
- Physical or mental disability
- AIDS/HIV
- Gender
- Pregnancy, childbirth, and related medical conditions, including breast-feeding (accommodations required)
- Race or color
- Religion or creed
- Sexual orientation, including perceived sexual orientation
- Genetic testing information
- Use of service animal
- Gender identity or expression
- Opposing unlawful employment practices
- Credit report or credit information (with some exceptions)
- Requesting leave or reasonable accommodation due to status as victim of domestic violence (applies to all employers)

New Hampshire

N.H. Rev. Stat. §§ 141-H:3, 354-A:2, 354-A:6, 354-A:7

Law applies to employers with: Six or more employees

Private employers may not make employment decisions based on:

- Age
- Ancestry or national origin
- Physical or mental disability
- Gender

State Laws Prohibiting Discrimination in Employment (continued)

- Marital status
- Pregnancy, childbirth, and related medical conditions
- Race or color
- Religion or creed
- Sexual orientation
- Genetic testing information
- Victims of domestic violence, harassment, sexual assault, or stalking
- Gender identity;
- Off-duty use of tobacco products

New Jersey

N.J. Stat. §§ 10:5-1, 10:5-4.1, 10:5-5, 10:5-12, 10:5-29.1, 34:6B-1, 43:21-49

Law applies to employers with: One or more employees

Private employers may not make employment decisions based on:

- Age (18 to 70)
- Ancestry or national origin
- Past or present physical or mental disability
- AIDS/HIV
- Gender
- Marital status, including civil union or domestic partnership status
- Pregnancy, childbirth, and related medical conditions, including breast-feeding (accommodations required)
- Race or color
- Religion or creed
- Sexual orientation, including affectional orientation and perceived sexual orientation
- Genetic testing information
- Atypical hereditary cellular or blood trait
- Accompanied by service or guide dog
- Military service
- Gender identity
- Unemployed status
- Liability for service in the U.S. Armed Forces
- Familial status

New Mexico

N.M. Stat. §§ 24-21-4, 28-1-2, 28-1-7, 50-4A-4; N.M. Code R. § 9.1.1

Law applies to employers with: Four or more employees

Private employers may not make employment decisions based on:

- Age (40 or older)
- Ancestry or national origin

- Physical or mental disability
- Gender
- Marital status (applies to employers with 50 or more employees)
- Pregnancy, childbirth, and related medical conditions
- Race or color
- Religion or creed
- Sexual orientation, including perceived sexual orientation (applies to employers with 15 or more employees)
- Genetic testing information
- Gender identity (employers with 15 or more employees)
- Serious medical condition
- Domestic abuse leave

New York

N.Y. Exec. Law §§ 292, 296; N.Y. Lab. Law § 201-d

Law applies to employers with: Four or more employees; all employers (sexual harassment only)

Private employers may not make employment decisions based on:

- Age (18 and over)
- Ancestry or national origin
- Physical or mental disability
- Gender
- Marital status
- Pregnancy, childbirth, and related medical conditions (accommodations required)
- Race or color
- Religion or creed
- Sexual orientation, including perceived sexual orientation
- Genetic testing information
- Lawful recreational activities when not at work
- Military status or service
- Observance of Sabbath
- Political activities
- Use of service dog
- Arrest or criminal accusation
- Domestic violence victim status
- Familial status
- Gender identity and transgender status

North Carolina

N.C. Gen. Stat. §§ 95-28.1, 95-28.1A, 127B-11, 130A-148, 143-422.2, 168A-5

Law applies to employers with: 15 or more employees

State Laws Prohibiting Discrimination in Employment (continued)

Private employers may not make employment decisions based on:

- Age
- Ancestry or national origin
- Physical or mental disability
- AIDS/HIV
- Gender
- Race or color
- Religion or creed
- Genetic testing information
- Military status or service
- Sickle cell or hemoglobin C trait
- Lawful use of lawful products off site and off duty

North Dakota

N.D. Cent. Code §§ 14-02.4-02, 14-02.4-03, 34-01-17

Law applies to employers with: One or more employees

Private employers may not make employment decisions based on:

- Age (40 or older)
- Ancestry or national origin
- Physical or mental disability
- Gender
- Marital status
- Pregnancy, childbirth, and related medical conditions (accommodations required)
- Race or color
- Religion or creed
- Lawful conduct outside of work
- Receiving public assistance
- Keeping and bearing arms (as long as firearm is never exhibited on company property except for lawful defensive purposes)
- Status as a volunteer emergency responder

Ohio

Ohio Rev. Code §§ 4111.17, 4112.01, 4112.02

Law applies to employers with: Four or more employees

Private employers may not make employment decisions based on:

- Age (40 or older)
- Ancestry or national origin
- Physical, mental, or learning disability
- AIDS/HIV
- Gender
- Pregnancy, childbirth, and related medical conditions
- Race or color

- Religion or creed
- Military status
- Caring for a sibling, child, parent, or spouse injured while in the armed services

Oklahoma

Okla. Stat. tit. 25, §§ 1301, 1302; tit. 36, § 3614.2; tit. 40, § 500; tit. 44, § 208

Law applies to employers with: One or more employees

Private employers may not make employment decisions based on:

- Age (40 or older)
- Ancestry or national origin
- Physical or mental disability
- Gender
- Pregnancy, childbirth, and related medical conditions (except abortions where the woman is not in "imminent danger of death")
- Race or color
- Religion or creed
- Genetic testing information
- Military service
- Being a smoker or nonsmoker or using tobacco off duty

Oregon

Or. Rev. Stat. §§ 659A.030, 659A.122 and following, 659A.303

Law applies to employers with: One or more employees

Private employers may not make employment decisions based on:

- Age (18 or older)
- Ancestry or national origin
- Physical or mental disability (applies to employers with six or more employees)
- Gender
- Marital status
- Pregnancy, childbirth, and related medical conditions
- Race or color
- Religion or creed
- Sexual orientation
- Genetic testing information
- Parent who has medical support order imposed by court
- Domestic violence victim status
- Refusal to attend an employer-sponsored meeting with the primary purpose of communicating the employer's opinion on religious or political matters
- Credit history

State Laws Prohibiting Discrimination in Employment (continued)

- Whistle-blowers
- Off-duty use of tobacco products

Pennsylvania

Pa. Stat. tit. 43, §§ 954 to 955

Law applies to employers with: Four or more employees

Private employers may not make employment decisions based on:

- Age (40 to 70)
- Ancestry or national origin
- Physical or mental disability
- Gender
- Pregnancy, childbirth, and related medical conditions
- Race or color
- Religion or creed
- Relationship or association with a person with a disability
- GED rather than high school diploma
- Use of service animal

Rhode Island

R.I. Gen. Laws §§ 12-28-10, 23-6.3-11, 28-5-6, 28-5-7, 28-6-18, 28-6.7-1

Law applies to employers with: Four or more employees; one or more employees (gender-based wage discrimination only)

Private employers may not make employment decisions based on:

- Age (40 or older)
- Ancestry or national origin
- Physical or mental disability
- AIDS/HIV
- Gender
- Pregnancy, childbirth, and related medical conditions, including breast-feeding (accommodations required)
- Race or color
- Religion or creed
- Sexual orientation, including perceived sexual orientation
- Genetic testing information
- Domestic abuse victim
- Gender identity or expression
- Homelessness

South Carolina

S.C. Code §§ 1-13-30, 1-13-80

Law applies to employers with: 15 or more employees

Private employers may not make employment decisions based on:

- Age (40 or older)
- Ancestry or national origin
- Physical or mental disability
- AIDS/HIV
- Gender
- Pregnancy, childbirth, and related medical conditions (accommodations required)
- Race or color
- Religion or creed

South Dakota

S.D. Codified Laws §§ 20-13-1, 20-13-10, 60-2-20, 60-12-15, 62-1-17

Law applies to employers with: One or more employees

Private employers may not make employment decisions based on:

- Ancestry or national origin
- Physical or mental disability
- Gender
- Race or color
- Religion or creed
- Genetic testing information
- Preexisting injury
- Off-duty use of tobacco products

Tennessee

Tenn. Code §§ 4-21-102, 4-21-401 and following, 8-50-103, 50-2-201, 50-2-202

Law applies to employers with: Eight or more employees; one or more employees (gender-based wage discrimination only)

Private employers may not make employment decisions based on:

- Age (40 or older)
- Ancestry or national origin
- Physical, mental, or visual disability
- Gender
- Pregnancy, childbirth, and related medical conditions (refer to chart on Family and Medical Leave)
- Race or color
- Religion or creed
- Use of guide dog
- Volunteer rescue squad worker responding to an emergency

State Laws Prohibiting Discrimination in Employment (continued)

Texas

Tex. Lab. Code §§ 21.002, 21.051, 21.101, 21.106, 21.402

Law applies to employers with: 15 or more employees

Private employers may not make employment decisions based on:
- Age (40 or older)
- Ancestry or national origin
- Physical or mental disability
- Gender
- Pregnancy, childbirth, and related medical conditions (accommodations required)
- Race or color
- Religion or creed
- Genetic testing information

Utah

Utah Code §§ 26-45-103, 34A-5-102, 34A-5-106

Law applies to employers with: 15 or more employees

Private employers may not make employment decisions based on:
- Age (40 or older)
- Ancestry or national origin
- Physical or mental disability
- AIDS/HIV
- Gender
- Pregnancy, childbirth, and related medical conditions, including breast-feeding (accommodations required)
- Race or color
- Religion or creed
- Sexual orientation
- Gender identity
- Genetic testing information

Vermont

Vt. Stat. tit. 18, § 9333; tit. 21, §§ 305, 495, 495d

Law applies to employers with: One or more employees

Private employers may not make employment decisions based on:
- Age (18 or older)
- Ancestry or national origin
- Physical, mental, or emotional disability
- AIDS/HIV
- Gender
- Pregnancy, childbirth, and related medical conditions (accommodations required)
- Race or color
- Religion or creed

- Sexual orientation
- Genetic testing information
- Gender identity
- Place of birth
- Credit report or credit history
- Status as crime victim.

Virginia

Va. Code Ann. §§ 2.2-3900, 2.2-3901, 40.1-28.6, 40.1-28.7:1, 51.5-41

Law applies to employers with: One or more employees

Private employers may not make employment decisions based on:
- Age
- Ancestry or national origin
- Physical or mental disability
- AIDS/HIV
- Gender
- Marital status
- Pregnancy, childbirth, and related medical conditions
- Race or color
- Religion or creed
- Genetic testing information

Washington

Wash. Rev. Code §§ 38.40.110, 49.002.011, 49.44.090, 49.44.180, 49.60.030, 49.60.040, 49.60.172, 49.60.180, 49.76.120; Wash. Admin. Code § 162-30-020

Law applies to employers with: Eight or more employees; one or more employees (gender-based wage discrimination only); 15 or more employees (pregnancy and childbirth accomodations)

Private employers may not make employment decisions based on:
- Age (40 or older)
- Ancestry or national origin
- Physical, mental, or sensory disability
- AIDS/HIV
- Gender
- Marital status
- Pregnancy, childbirth, and related medical conditions, including breast-feeding (accommodations required)
- Race or color
- Religion or creed
- Sexual orientation
- Genetic testing information
- Hepatitis C infection
- Member of state militia

State Laws Prohibiting Discrimination in Employment (continued)

- Use of service animal by a person with a disability
- Gender identity
- Domestic violence victim

West Virginia

W. Va. Code §§ 5-11-3, 5-11-9, 15–1K–4, 16-3C-3, 21-5B-1, 21-5B-3

Law applies to employers with: 12 or more employees; one or more employees (gender-based wage discrimination only)

Private employers may not make employment decisions based on:

- Age (40 or older)
- Ancestry or national origin
- Physical or mental disability, or blindness
- AIDS/HIV
- Gender
- Pregnancy, childbirth, and related medical conditions (accommodations required)
- Race or color
- Religion or creed
- Off-duty use of tobacco products
- Membership in the Civil Air Patrol (for employers with 16 or more employees)

Wisconsin

Wis. Stat. §§ 111.32 and following

Law applies to employers with: One or more employees

Private employers may not make employment decisions based on:

- Age (40 or older)
- Ancestry or national origin

- Physical or mental disability
- Gender
- Marital status
- Pregnancy, childbirth, and related medical conditions
- Race or color
- Religion or creed
- Sexual orientation, including having a history of or being identified with a preference
- Genetic testing information
- Arrest or conviction record
- Military service
- Declining to attend a meeting or to participate in any communication about religious matters or political matters
- Use or nonuse of lawful products off duty and off site

Wyoming

Wyo. Stat. §§ 27-9-102, 27-9-105, 19-11-104

Law applies to employers with: Two or more employees

Private employers may not make employment decisions based on:

- Age (40 or older)
- Ancestry or national origin
- Disability
- Gender
- Pregnancy, childbirth, and related medical conditions
- Race or color
- Religion or creed
- Military service or status

Complaint Policies

The purpose of a complaint policy is simple: to encourage employees to come forward with concerns and problems. If employees let managers know when trouble is brewing, the company will have an opportunity to resolve workplace difficulties right away, before morale suffers or workers start siding with or against each other. And a complaint policy helps managers and supervisors, by letting them know what their responsibilities are if they observe misconduct or receive a complaint.

As mentioned in Chapter 19 (on antidiscrimination and harassment policies), a complaint policy also offers companies an important legal bonus: some protection against harassment lawsuits brought by current or former employees. If your company has a clear complaint policy, and an employee who did not complain according to this policy later sues the company for harassment, the company can use the employee's failure to make a complaint as a legal defense in the harassment lawsuit. This might lead a court to decide that the employee cannot proceed with the lawsuit. The idea behind this is that an employee who fails to complain when a company has a clear complaint policy deprives the company of the chance to fix the problem.

However, these legal protections kick in only if your policy is user-friendly and genuinely encourages employees to make problems known and make a complaint. In this chapter, we'll show you how to put together policies that do just that.

CONTENTS

20:1 Complaint Procedures

File Name: 20_Complaints.rtf

Include This Policy?
- ☐ Yes
- ☐ No
- ☐ Use our existing policy
- ☐ Other _____

Alternate Modifications

None

Additional Clauses

Accounting Irregularities And
Shareholder Fraud

Insert?:   ☐ Yes   ☐ No

Related Policies

Chapter 19 includes policies against
discrimination and harassment
(often the subject of complaints).

Notes

_____
_____
_____
_____
_____
_____
_____
_____
_____
_____
_____
_____
_____
_____
_____
_____

20:1 Complaint Procedures

Your complaint policy should describe the conduct about which employees can complain, explain how to make a complaint, and let workers know what will happen once a complaint is filed.

Complaint Procedures

Our Company is committed to providing a safe and productive work environment, free of threats to the health, safety, and well-being of our workers. These threats include, but are not limited to, harassment, discrimination, violations of health and safety rules, and violence.

Any employee who witnesses or is subject to inappropriate conduct in the workplace may complain to _____ _____ or to any Company officer. Any supervisor, manager, or Company officer who receives a complaint about, hears of, or witnesses any inappropriate conduct is required to immediately notify _____ _____ . Inappropriate conduct includes any conduct prohibited by our policies about harassment, discrimination, discipline, workplace violence, health and safety, wages and hours, and drug and alcohol use. In addition, we encourage employees to come forward with any workplace complaint, even if the subject of the complaint is not explicitly covered by our written policies.

We encourage you to come forward with complaints immediately, so we can take whatever action is needed to handle the problem. Once a complaint has been made, _____ will determine how to handle it. For serious complaints, we will immediately conduct a complete and impartial investigation.

We expect all employees to cooperate fully in Company investigations by, for example, answering questions completely and honestly and giving the investigator all documents and other material that might be relevant. All complaints will be handled as confidentially as possible. When the investigation is complete, the Company will take corrective action, if appropriate.

We will not engage in or allow retaliation against any employee who makes a good-faith complaint or participates in an investigation. If you believe that you are being subjected to any kind of negative treatment because you made or were questioned about a complaint, report the conduct immediately to _____ _____ .

Who Needs This Policy

There are really no drawbacks to having a complaint policy, and plenty of good reasons to adopt one. From a legal standpoint, a complaint policy provides a possible legal defense against claims of harassment, as explained above. There are also many practical advantages of encouraging employees to make workplace problems known: The policy will give the company an opportunity to correct problems before they get out of hand, will promote communication and teamwork, and will let employees know that management cares about their concerns. Because of these benefits, we recommend that every employer adopt a complaint policy.

How to Complete This Policy

Our sample policy leaves you a space to designate the person or department that will be available to receive complaints. If your company has a human resource function, you can simply fill in all these blanks with "the human resources department."

If, like many smaller companies, your company doesn't have a dedicated human resources department, you will need to modify this policy to let employees know where to direct their complaints and who will deal with them. If you ask workers to complain to their direct supervisor or manager, make sure that employees can also complain to someone outside their chain of command, such as another supervisor or officer or even the head of the company. If an employee is being harassed or mistreated by his or her own supervisor, this allows the worker to bypass that person and complain to someone who isn't part of the problem. Even if the employee's direct supervisor is not the source of the complaint, some employees feel more comfortable talking to someone who won't be responsible for evaluating their performance and making decisions on promotions, raises, and assignments.

Because complaints—particularly complaints of harassment, discrimination, violence, or safety concerns—are a serious matter, many companies prefer to designate someone at the top of the company ladder, such as the president or CEO.

Make sure that the people whom you designate to take complaints are accessible to employees. For example, if the human resources department is located in a distant office or the company president spends most workdays traveling to promote the company, you should choose alternate people to accept complaints who are local and available.

! CAUTION

Confidentiality requirements are under scrutiny. Recently, both the National Labor Relations Board and the Equal Employment Opportunity Commission have challenged employers who imposed confidentiality requirements on employees who participate in investigations. Prohibiting employees from discussing workplace problems with each other could violate laws prohibiting employers from retaliating against their employees and from punishing workers for talking to each other about the terms and conditions of their employment. If you have this type of provision in your policies or you make an oral demand that employees keep investigations confidential, have the language you are using vetted by a lawyer who is up on the latest developments in this area.

Additional Clause Regarding Complaints of Accounting Irregularities and Shareholder Fraud

In the wake of corporate scandals involving WorldCom, Enron, and other large companies accused of defrauding shareholders, Congress passed the Sarbanes-Oxley Act of 2002 (SOX). The stated purpose of SOX is to protect investors in publicly traded companies by improving the accuracy and reliability of corporate disclosures, and the law seeks to further this goal by imposing strict rules for audits and auditors of publicly traded companies, preventing insider trading, requiring companies to adopt strict internal controls, and enhancing the penalties for white-collar crimes relating to investor fraud.

SOX also includes provisions intended to encourage employees to come forward with information about questionable accounting practices and potential shareholder fraud. These provisions do two things: They prohibit retaliation against employee whistle-blowers who complain of possible shareholder fraud to government agencies or company officials, and they require publicly traded companies to establish a system to allow employees to submit confidential, anonymous complaints about questionable accounting or auditing matters. Companies must also develop record-keeping procedures for handling and maintaining any complaints they receive.

If your company is publicly traded, you must include the clause below to alert employees to the rights created by SOX. Insert the clause immediately before the final paragraph of the policy. Complete the clause by describing your company's procedures for submitting anonymous, confidential complaints. For example, you might insert "calling our hotline at 800-555-1212, where you can submit your concerns confidentially," or "going to our

confidential complaint reporting website, which is operated
and maintained by an independent, third-party company, at
www.ourcompanyconfidentialcomplaint.com."

SEE AN EXPERT

Get some help with SOX compliance. SOX is a notoriously
complicated law that imposes significant burdens on the companies it
covers. Although the whistle-blowing and complaint mechanism provisions
are among the simpler passages in this lengthy statute, they also raise
a number of compliance questions, including what types of complaint
procedures are sufficiently anonymous and confidential, how complaints
should be handled once they are received, and exactly what type of
complaints qualify for SOX protection. We advise you to consult with a
lawyer to make sure your company meets its obligations under this law.

Additional Clause

We also encourage employees to come forward with complaints or
concerns regarding the Company's accounting, auditing, or internal
controls procedures, and complaints or concerns regarding possible
shareholder fraud. You may raise these issues through the complaint
procedures described in this policy, or you may do so anonymously
by _____
_____ .

20:2 Our Doors Are Open to You

File Name: 20_Complaints.rtf

Include This Policy?
- ☐ Yes
- ☐ No
- ☐ Use our existing policy
- ☐ Other _____

Alternate Modifications

None

Additional Clauses

None

Related Policies

None

Notes

_____
_____
_____
_____
_____
_____
_____
_____
_____
_____
_____
_____
_____
_____
_____
_____
_____

20:2 Open-Door Policy

Many employers choose to adopt an open-door policy in addition to a more formal complaint policy. While your complaint policy will encourage employees to come forward with big problems, such as serious misconduct and violations of company rules, an open-door policy serves a slightly different purpose. It encourages employees to keep in touch with their supervisors about day-to-day work issues. Employees probably wouldn't think of filing a formal complaint about, for example, personality conflicts with clients, creative ideas to boost profits, or concerns that their work group isn't coming together as a team. But an open-door policy will encourage employees to bring these issues to the attention of management, thereby giving the company a chance to make improvements by, for example, changing work assignments, adopting that good idea, or offering training to the team.

Our Doors Are Open to You

We want to maintain a positive and pleasant environment for all of our employees. To help us meet this goal, our Company has an open-door policy, by which employees are encouraged to report work-related concerns.

If something about your job is bothering you, or if you have a question, concern, idea, or problem related to your work, please discuss it with your immediate supervisor as soon as possible. If for any reason you don't feel comfortable bringing the matter to your supervisor, feel free to raise the issue with any company officer.

We encourage you to come forward and make your concerns known to the Company. We can't solve the problem if we don't know about it.

Who Needs This Policy

An open-door policy doesn't offer the legal benefit of a complaint policy, but its practical advantages are similar: It helps managers learn what's going on in the workplace, encourages communication, and promotes goodwill.

The potential disadvantage of an open-door policy is wasted time. If workers feel compelled to keep management apprised of their every thought and feeling, managers might soon be tempted to close their doors and lock them. However, this problem can usually be handled effectively through individual counseling. If necessary, tell the one or two employees who might abuse the policy that their enthusiasm is appreciated, but they need to use more discretion in deciding which matters are important enough to bring to a manager's attention.

In our opinion, the benefits of having an open-door policy outweigh this potential downside. However, this is a decision each company will have to make for itself, based on the character of its workforce and the amount of time managers can afford to spend listening to whoever comes through their open doors.

RESOURCE

For more information on investigating complaints and problems, see *The Essential Guide to Workplace Investigations,* by Lisa Guerin (Nolo), a step-by-step guide to investigating common workplace situations.

Ending Employment

Ending the employment relationship can be difficult for employer and employee alike. An employer's goals are to keep operations running smoothly as employees come and go, and to make sure that any employees who have to be fired or laid off don't decide to respond with a lawsuit.

If your company has adopted an at-will policy, discussed in Chapter 2, it has already gone a long way toward accomplishing this second goal. The company has warned workers that their employment can be terminated at any time and for any reason. And, for those workers who didn't hear it the first time, other policies throughout your handbook give them fair warning that they can expect to be disciplined or fired for taking part in certain types of prohibited conduct.

Policies about ending employment serve a slightly different purpose: to tell employees how the company will handle the practical concerns that may arise when an employee leaves, such as severance packages, references, and insurance coverage. Explaining these matters up front will help smooth the transition when employees leave: They'll know exactly what to expect and be able to plan accordingly. End-of-employment policies can also help you make sure that the company has met its legal obligations (to offer health insurance continuation and cut final paychecks on time, for example). By adopting uniform policies and applying them evenhandedly when employees leave, employers can also avoid claims of unfairness, as well as the lawsuits that these feelings sometimes fuel.

21:1 Resignation

File Name: 21_Ending Employment.rtf

Include This Policy?
- ☐ Yes
- ☐ No
- ☐ Use our existing policy
- ☐ Other _____

Alternate Modifications

None

Additional Clauses

None

Related Policies

None

Notes

_____
_____
_____
_____
_____
_____
_____
_____
_____
_____
_____
_____
_____
_____
_____
_____
_____
_____
_____
_____
_____
_____
_____

21:1 Resignation

No employment relationship lasts forever, and often it is the employee, not the employer, who decides that the time has come to move on. When that happens, you will no doubt want the employee to notify the right people and to give you plenty of notice. The policy below reminds employees that they must return company property and that they must continue to maintain the confidentiality of your company's trade secrets.

If You Resign

If you decide to leave our Company for another position, we wish you well. Please notify _____ in writing about your plans. If you can, please give us _____ weeks' notice. This will give us time to calculate your final paycheck and accrued overtime, vacation pay, and any other money that we owe you. Please see Section _____ of this handbook for more information about final paychecks.

You must return all company property in good condition. Please see Section _____ of this handbook for more about company property.

Even as you leave this Company and move on to future endeavors, you still have an obligation to keep confidential this Company's trade secrets and other protected proprietary and confidential information. Please see Section _____ of this handbook for more about this obligation.

21:2 Final Paychecks

Although no federal law requires employers to pay terminated employees by a particular date, the laws of most states impose fairly tight deadlines for final paychecks. Often, these deadlines vary depending on whether the employee quits or is fired. In some states, employers must pay a fired employee immediately. Other states allow employers to wait until the next payday.

Adopting a final paycheck policy that includes these deadlines will help ensure that your company complies with these laws. And employees will know when they can expect that check, especially if they don't have another job lined up right away.

Final Paychecks

Employees who resign from their job will receive their final paycheck
_____ . Employees whose employment
is terminated involuntarily will receive their final paycheck _____

_____ .

Final paychecks will include all compensation earned but not paid through the date of termination.

How to Complete This Policy

This policy includes two blanks for you to complete based on your state's law. The chart at the end of this chapter, "State Laws That Control Final Paychecks," lists employer requirements for final paychecks by state. In the first blank, insert the time limit for paying an employee who is fired (for example, within two weeks after termination). In the second blank, insert the time limit for paying an employee who quits.

Additional Clause to Specify Compensation Included in Final Paycheck

As you'll see from the chart at the end of this chapter, some states require employers to include unused vacation pay in an employee's final check. However, these laws apply only to vacation pay that has already been earned or accrued. For example, if employees accrue one day of vacation leave per month, and the company fires someone who has worked for a year without taking any vacation, that employee would be entitled to 12 additional days of pay in his or her final paycheck. But an employee who is fired after only two months gets only two days of vacation pay, assuming those days haven't been used.

21:2 Final Paychecks
File Name: 21_Ending Employment.rtf

Include This Policy?
☐ Yes
☐ No
☐ Use our existing policy
☐ Other _____

Alternate Modifications
None

Additional Clauses
Specify Compensation Included in Final Paycheck
Insert?: ☐ Yes ☐ No

Related Policies
Chapter 7 provides information and policies on pay.

Notes

In addition to vacation pay, some employers choose to pay out unused sick leave or personal leave, some portion of a discretionary bonus, or other forms of compensation. No law requires this. Employers who follow this route generally do so to maintain a good relationship with the departing employee and the workers who remain, and to create incentives for solid performance. By paying out unused sick time, for example, employers encourage their employees not to take sick leave unless it's absolutely necessary. And paying out a portion of a discretionary bonus encourages employees to do their best right up until their last day of work.

If your state requires employers to pay out unused vacation time, or if your company wants to pay this or other types of compensation even though it's not legally required, add the sentence below to the end of our sample policy. In the blank space, insert the type of additional compensation employees will receive (for example, all unused vacation time that the employee has earned as of the date of termination, or a pro rata share of any discretionary bonus for which the employee is eligible, based on the length of the employee's employment during the bonus period and the employee's performance).

Additional Clause

Final paychecks will also include _____ .

Seek Legal Advice for Layoffs and Layoff Policies

In a layoff, an employer generally terminates the employment of a group of employees for reasons related to business productivity, such as economic problems or shifts in the company's direction. When an employer lays workers off, it is legally required to provide them with a certain amount of notice and, in a few states, severance pay. If you wish to adopt a layoff policy, you'll have to consider a number of factors, such as how employees will be chosen for layoff, what benefits (if any) laid-off workers will receive, whether laid-off workers are eligible for rehire if circumstances turn around, and how employees will be informed of the layoff. Because these issues can get fairly complicated, we advise you to consult with a lawyer if you plan to adopt a layoff policy.

21:3 Severance Pay

Except for a few states that require severance pay when laying workers off, no law says that employers must give their employees severance pay. Unless the company promises severance pay or leads employees to believe they will receive it—for example, by saying so in a written contract or policy—there is no obligation to pay severance to terminated employees.

For many employers, that's all they need to know: If it isn't required, they aren't going to pay it. But before your company decides to join their ranks, consider the benefits of paying severance. For starters, it helps a fired worker get by until another job comes along, which sends the message that the company cares about its workers and wants to help out. This can go a long way not only toward building employee morale, but also toward nipping potential lawsuits in the bud. Studies have shown that the way in which employment terminations are handled plays a big role in determining whether a fired employee will sue the employer. Thus, a company will have to weigh these very tangible benefits against the eminently sensible desire not to pay out money unnecessarily.

Your severance policy should let employees know whether and under what circumstances the company offers severance pay. If your company will offer severance, the policy should tell employees who is eligible and how severance pay will be calculated.

We offer you several alternative sample policies below. Policy A is a simple no-severance policy. Policy B provides that a company will pay severance at its own discretion. Policy C is a severance policy with eligibility requirements and a formula for determining severance pay.

CAUTION

Severance plans can be tricky. If your company plans to adopt a policy to pay severance, whether according to a formula or other criteria, ask a lawyer to review it for you and to let you know whether your company has to follow the requirements of the federal law known as ERISA (the Employees Retirement Income Security Act, 29 U.S.C. §§ 1001 and following). This highly technical law imposes a number of requirements on employers who provide certain types of benefit plans to their employees. Severance plans may or may not be subject to these requirements, depending on the plan's features and the way courts in your state have interpreted the law.

21:3 Severance Pay

File Name: 21_Ending Employment.rtf

Include This Policy?

☐ Yes

Choose one: ☐ A ☐ B ☐ C

☐ No

☐ Use our existing policy

☐ Other _____

Alternate Modifications

None

Additional Clauses

None

Related Policies

None

Notes

_____
_____
_____
_____
_____
_____
_____
_____
_____
_____
_____
_____
_____
_____
_____
_____
_____
_____
_____
_____
_____

Alternate Policy A

No Severance Pay

Our Company does not pay severance to departing employees, whether they quit, are laid off, or are fired for any reason.

Alternate Policy B

Severance Pay Is Discretionary

Generally, our Company does not pay severance to departing employees, whether they quit, are laid off, or are fired for any reason. However, we reserve the right to pay severance. Decisions about severance pay will be made on a case-by-case basis and are entirely within the discretion of the Company. No employee has a right to severance pay, and you should not expect to receive it.

Alternate Policy C

Severance Pay

Employees may be eligible for severance pay upon the end of their employment. Employees must meet <u>all</u> of the following criteria to be eligible:

- They must have worked for the Company for at least 1 year prior to their termination.
- They must not have quit or resigned.
- Their employment must have been terminated for reasons other than misconduct or violation of Company rules.

Eligible employees will receive _____ of severance pay for every full year of employment with the Company.

How to Complete This Policy

If you adopt Sample Policy C, simply fill in the blank with the amount of severance the company plans to offer. Most employers offer one or two weeks of pay, at the employee's current rate, for every year of work. You can do the same by inserting "one week" or "two weeks" in the blank.

21:4 Continuing Your Health Insurance Coverage

If your company offers employees health insurance coverage under a group health plan, it may be required to offer them continued coverage under the circumstances outlined in the sample policy below. A federal law known as COBRA (the Consolidated Omnibus Budget Reconciliation Act) mandates that employees who quit, suffer a reduction in hours, or are fired for reasons other than serious misconduct are entitled to choose to continue on the employer's group health care plan for up to 18 months, and employees' dependents may continue their coverage for up to 36 months. COBRA applies only to employers with at least 20 employees.

Many states also have their own health insurance continuation laws. These laws generally apply to smaller employers. Some echo most of COBRA's provisions; others provide for shorter periods of insurance continuation and/or place limits on the types of benefits that must be provided. A chart of these state laws, entitled "State Health Insurance Continuation Laws," is included at the end of this chapter.

Your insurance continuation policy should tell employees:

- whether, and under what circumstances, they will be able to continue their insurance coverage after termination
- how long the continued coverage will last, and
- who will pay for the coverage.

How to Complete This Policy

In the blanks in this policy, insert the length of time for which employees and their dependents can continue their health insurance coverage. If your company is covered by COBRA, employees are entitled to continue their coverage for 18 months (insert this in the first blank), and dependents for 36 months (insert this in the second blank).

Smaller employers that are not covered by COBRA may nevertheless have to comply with a state insurance continuation law. Some of these laws also provide for 18 and 36 months of coverage; others provide for shorter periods of coverage. Consult the chart "State Health Insurance Continuation Laws," at the end of this chapter, to find out what your state requires.

21:4 Continuing Your Health Insurance Coverage

File Name: 21_Ending Employment.rtf

Include This Policy?
- ☐ Yes
- ☐ No
- ☐ Use our existing policy
- ☐ Other _____

Alternate Modifications
None

Additional Clauses
Include Eligibility Requirements
Insert?:   ☐ Yes   ☐ No

Related Policies
8:3 Health Care Benefits

Notes
_____
_____
_____
_____
_____
_____
_____
_____
_____
_____
_____
_____
_____
_____
_____
_____
_____

Continuing Your Health Insurance Coverage

Our Company offers employees group health insurance coverage as a benefit of employment. If you are no longer eligible for insurance coverage because of a reduction in hours, because you quit, or because your employment is terminated for reasons other than serious misconduct, you have the right to continue your health insurance coverage for up to _____ .
You will have to pay the cost of this coverage.

Others covered by your insurance (your spouse and children, for example) also have the right to continue coverage if they are no longer eligible for certain reasons. If you and your spouse divorce or legally separate, or if you die while in our employ, your spouse may continue coverage under our group health plan. And once your children lose their dependent status, they may continue their health care as well. In any of these situations, your family members are entitled to up to _____
of continued health care. They must pay the cost of this coverage.

You will receive an initial notice of your right to continued health insurance coverage when you first become eligible for health insurance under the Company's group plan. You will receive an additional notice when your hours are reduced, you quit, or your employment is terminated. This second notice will tell you how to choose continuation coverage, what your obligations will be, whether you are entitled to a partial subsidy, and how much you will have to pay for coverage. You must notify us if any of your family members become eligible for continued coverage due to divorce, separation, or reaching the age of majority.

Who Needs This Policy

If your company is covered by COBRA or a state health insurance continuation law, including this policy can alleviate a lot of anxiety for workers. One of the first questions a departing employee is likely to ask is, "What about my health insurance?" As the costs of medical care skyrocket, many employees cannot afford to go without health insurance until they find another job. Even if they line up new work quickly, their new employer might not offer insurance coverage or there may be a waiting period before coverage begins.

COBRA used to be the only (or at least, the least expensive) game in town for employees who lost their employer-provided health insurance coverage. It could be difficult for employees to qualify for or afford an individual policy on the open market. These days, however, the Affordable Care Act (Obamacare) gives everyone access to health insurance through the online health insurance exchange marketplace. Often, these plans are less expensive than continuing health insurance through COBRA. However, many employees still choose to use COBRA because their employer-based plan offers more generous benefits, allows the employee to continue to use familiar medical professionals, or otherwise is simply a better fit.

If your company is not covered by COBRA or a similar state law or doesn't offer health insurance coverage to your employees (see Chapter 8 for information on benefits policies), leave this policy out of the handbook.

Additional Clause to Include Eligibility Requirements

Some states require employers to offer continued coverage only to certain employees. Most commonly, employees are eligible only if they have worked for the employer and been covered by the employer's health insurance plan for at least three months. If your company is not covered by COBRA (which protects all employees who are covered by the employer's plan) but is covered by a state health insurance continuation law that protects only certain employees, modify our policy by adding the following language after the first sentence. In the blank, insert your state's eligibility requirements (for example, "have been covered continuously under our insurance policy for at least three months" or "work at least 25 hours a week").

Additional Clause

Only employees who _____ are entitled to continue their health insurance coverage under this policy.

21:5 Exit Interviews

File Name: 21_Ending Employment.rtf

Include This Policy?
☐ Yes
☐ No
☐ Use our existing policy
☐ Other _____

Alternate Modifications
None

Additional Clauses
None

Related Policies
None

Notes

_____
_____
_____
_____
_____
_____
_____
_____
_____
_____
_____
_____
_____
_____
_____
_____
_____
_____
_____

21:5 Exit Interviews

Exit interviews are a great way to learn valuable information about your company; they can also help diffuse the tension of an involuntary termination. Former employees can provide the lowdown on dozens of issues, from workplace morale and teamwork to how well (or poorly) managers and supervisors are doing their jobs. An employee on the way out the door is more likely to be candid in offering opinions, maybe brutally so. Although employers should certainly take these parting comments with a healthy dose of salt, they may get some helpful information about how the company is perceived by its workers and where it has room to improve.

The person who interviews employees who quit should try to find out why that employee is moving on: Did your company fail to offer opportunities to advance? Are the company's pay scales in line with those of other businesses in your industry? Are there problems in the company that management doesn't know about?

It can be equally valuable to interview employees you fire, although for a slightly different reason. These employees are probably somewhat upset about losing their jobs, and they may have a long list of negative comments about the company as a result. But they will have a chance to air these complaints during the interview, which allows the company to demonstrate that it cares about their concerns. If a fired employee feels that the company "gets it," that employee is less likely to seek a courtroom forum for his or her grievances. Adopting an exit interview policy tells these employees that there will be a time and a place for their voices to be heard.

Some employers hold exit interviews with every departing employee, while others schedule interviews only if the departing employee wants one. Adopting an optional interview policy has the benefit of drastically reducing the time spent conducting these interviews. Very few employees, other than those with a large ax to grind, will bother to take the time to share their opinions on the way out the door. The corresponding drawback is that a company that holds voluntary interviews won't be able to gather as much valuable information, because the interviewer will probably be hearing only from those whose employment experience was negative.

Exit Interviews

We will hold an exit interview with every employee who leaves the Company, for any reason. During the interview, you will have the opportunity to tell us about your employment experience here: what you liked, what you didn't like, and where you think we can improve. We greatly value these comments.

The exit interview also gives us a chance to handle some practical matters relating to the end of your employment. You will be expected to return all Company property at the interview. You will also have an opportunity to ask any questions you might have about insurance, benefits, final paychecks, references, or any other matter relating to your employment.

21:6 References

File Name: 21_Ending Employment.rtf

Include This Policy?

- ☐ Yes
  - *Choose one:* ☐ A ☐ B
- ☐ No
- ☐ Use our existing policy
- ☐ Other _____

Alternate Modifications

None

Additional Clauses

None

Related Policies

None

Notes

_____
_____
_____
_____
_____
_____
_____
_____
_____
_____
_____
_____
_____
_____
_____
_____
_____

21:6 References

Reference requests are fraught with legal and practical dangers for employers. If an employer criticizes a former employee unduly, or unfairly prevents that employee from getting a job, it could face a lawsuit for defamation or blacklisting. If an employer gives a reference that is too positive for an employee it knows to be dangerous or grossly unqualified, it risks legal trouble from the new employer if the truth comes out.

Given these risks, many employers choose to take a "name, rank, and serial number" approach, giving prospective new employers only the dates of employment, title, and salary of a former employee. If your company decides to go this route, our sample Policy A, below—a minimal reference policy to confirm dates of employment, salary, and positions held—will work for you.

But before deciding to adopt this type of policy, consider the purpose of a reference. Former employees count on them to find new work; and the sooner a fired employee finds new work, the less likely you are to face a wrongful termination claim. Prospective employers use references to figure out whom to hire and to read between the lines of carefully prepared résumés and interview responses. Both of these tasks are made a lot tougher by employers who adopt a minimal reference approach.

Employers can give an informative reference without undue risk of legal trouble if they insist on a written release from the employee, giving the former employer permission to talk to a prospective employer. And your company can protect itself further by insisting on written reference requests and responding to them only in writing. This gives the company a clear record of exactly what was said if a company representative is later accused of making a false statement. This approach also gives the person providing the reference time to craft a careful response. If your company decides to go this route, you can use our sample Policy B, below.

Alternate Policy A

References

When we are contacted by prospective employers seeking information about former employees, we will release the following data only: the position(s) the employee held, the dates the employee worked for our Company, and the employee's salary or rate of pay.

Alternate Policy B

References

When we are contacted by prospective employers seeking information about former employees, we will release the following data only:
the position(s) the employee held, the dates the employee worked for
our Company, and the employee's salary or rate of pay.

If you would like us to give a more detailed reference, you will have
to provide us with a written release—a consent form giving us your
permission to respond to a reference request. We will respond only to
written reference requests, and we will respond only in writing. Please
direct all reference requests to _____

_____ .

RESOURCE

For information on providing references, see *Dealing With
Problem Employees*, by Amy DelPo and Lisa Guerin (Nolo).

State Laws That Control Final Paychecks

Note: The states of Alabama, Florida, Georgia, and Mississippi are not included in this chart because they do not have laws specifically controlling final paychecks. Contact your state department of labor for more information. (See Appendix B for contact list.)

Alaska
Alaska Stat. § 23.05.140(b)

Paycheck due when employee is fired: Within three working days after termination.

Paycheck due when employee quits: Next regular payday at least three days after employee gives notice.

Unused vacation pay due: Only if agreed to by employer or required by company policy or practice.

Arizona
Ariz. Rev. Stat. §§ 23-350, 23-353

Paycheck due when employee is fired: Next payday or within seven working days, whichever is sooner.

Paycheck due when employee quits: Next regular payday or by mail at employee's request.

Unused vacation pay due: No provision.

Arkansas
Ark. Code § 11-4-405

Paycheck due when employee is fired: Upon request, within seven days of discharge; otherwise, next regular payday.

Paycheck due when employee quits: No provision.

Unused vacation pay due: No provision.

Special employment situations: Railroad or railroad construction: day of discharge.

California
Cal. Lab. Code §§ 201–202, 227.3

Paycheck due when employee is fired: Immediately.

Paycheck due when employee quits: Immediately if employee has given 72 hours' notice; otherwise, within 72 hours.

Unused vacation pay due: Yes.

Special employment situations: Motion picture business: next payday.

Oil drilling industry: within 24 hours (excluding weekends and holidays) of termination.

Seasonal agricultural workers: within 72 hours of termination.

Colorado
Colo. Rev. Stat. § 8-4-109

Paycheck due when employee is fired: Immediately. (Within six hours of start of next workday, if payroll unit is closed; 24 hours if unit is offsite.) When paycheck is not due immediately, employer may make the check available at the work site, the employer's local office, or the employee's last-known mailing address.

Paycheck due when employee quits: Next payday.

Unused vacation pay due: Yes.

Connecticut
Conn. Gen. Stat. §§ 31-71c, 31-76k

Paycheck due when employee is fired: Next business day after discharge.

Paycheck due when employee quits: Next payday.

Unused vacation pay due: Only if policy or collective bargaining agreement requires payment on termination.

Delaware
Del. Code tit. 19, § 1103

Paycheck due when employee is fired: Next payday.

Paycheck due when employee quits: Next payday.

Unused vacation pay due: Only if required by employer policy or agreement, in which case vacation must be paid within 30 days after it becomes due.

District of Columbia
D.C. Code §§ 32-1301, 32-1303

Paycheck due when employee is fired: Next business day unless employee handles money, in which case employer has four days.

Paycheck due when employee quits: Next payday or seven days after quitting, whichever is sooner.

Unused vacation pay due: Yes, unless there is an agreement to the contrary.

Hawaii
Haw. Rev. Stat. § 388-3

Paycheck due when employee is fired: Immediately or next business day, if timing or conditions prevent immediate payment.

Paycheck due when employee quits: Next payday or immediately, if employee gives one pay period's notice.

Unused vacation pay due: No.

State Laws That Control Final Paychecks (continued)

Idaho
Idaho Code §§ 45-606, 45-617

Paycheck due when employee is fired: Next payday or within ten days (excluding weekends and holidays), whichever is sooner. If employee makes written request for earlier payment, within 48 hours of receipt of request (excluding weekends and holidays).

Paycheck due when employee quits: Next payday or within ten days (excluding weekends and holidays), whichever is sooner. If employee makes written request for earlier payment, within 48 hours of receipt of request (excluding weekends and holidays).

Unused vacation pay due: No provision.

Illinois
820 Ill. Comp. Stat. § 115/5

Paycheck due when employee is fired: At time of separation if possible, but no later than next payday. Employer must comply with employee's written request to mail final paycheck.

Paycheck due when employee quits: At time of separation if possible, but no later than next payday. Employer must comply with employee's written request to mail final paycheck.

Unused vacation pay due: Yes.

Indiana
Ind. Code Ann. §§ 22-2-5-1, 22-2-9-1, 22-2-9-2

Paycheck due when employee is fired: Next payday.

Paycheck due when employee quits: Next payday. (If employee has not left address, (1) ten business days after employee demands wages or (2) when employee provides address where check may be mailed.)

Unused vacation pay due: If employer agrees to vacation pay, absent an agreement to the contrary, employer must pay out accrued unused vacation upon termination.

Special employment situations: Does not apply to railroad employees.

Iowa
Iowa Code §§ 91A.2(7)(b), 91A.4

Paycheck due when employee is fired: Next payday.

Paycheck due when employee quits: Next payday.

Unused vacation pay due: Yes.

Special employment situations: If employee is owed commission, employer has 30 days to pay.

Kansas
Kan. Stat. § 44-315

Paycheck due when employee is fired: Next payday.

Paycheck due when employee quits: Next payday.

Unused vacation pay due: Only if required by employer's policies or practice.

Kentucky
Ky. Rev. Stat. §§ 337.010, 337.055

Paycheck due when employee is fired: Next payday or within 14 days, whichever is later.

Paycheck due when employee quits: Next payday or within 14 days, whichever is later.

Unused vacation pay due: Yes.

Louisiana
La. Rev. Stat. § 23:631

Paycheck due when employee is fired: Next payday or within 15 days, whichever is earlier.

Paycheck due when employee quits: Next payday or within 15 days, whichever is earlier.

Unused vacation pay due: Yes.

Maine
Me. Rev. Stat. tit. 26, § 626

Paycheck due when employee is fired: Next payday.

Paycheck due when employee quits: Next payday.

Unused vacation pay due: Yes, accrued vacation is considered wages and must be paid out upon termination.

Special employment situations: Employer must pay employees all wages due within two weeks of the sale of a business.

Maryland
Md. Code, Lab. & Empl. § 3-505

Paycheck due when employee is fired: Next scheduled payday.

Paycheck due when employee quits: Next scheduled payday.

Unused vacation pay due: Yes.

State Laws That Control Final Paychecks (continued)

Massachusetts
Mass. Gen. Laws ch. 149, § 148

Paycheck due when employee is fired: Day of discharge.

Paycheck due when employee quits: Next payday. If no scheduled payday, then following Saturday.

Unused vacation pay due: Yes.

Michigan
Mich. Comp. Laws §§ 408.471–408.475; Mich. Admin. Code r. 408.9007

Paycheck due when employee is fired: Next payday.

Paycheck due when employee quits: Next payday.

Unused vacation pay due: Only if required by written policy or contract.

Special employment situations: Hand-harvesters of crops: within one working day of termination.

Minnesota
Minn. Stat. §§ 181.13, 181.14, 181.74

Paycheck due when employee is fired: Within 24 hours.

Paycheck due when employee quits: Next regular payday. If next payday is less than five days after employee's last day, employer may delay payment until payday after that. But in no event may payment exceed 20 days from employee's last day.

Unused vacation pay due: Only if required by written policy or contract.

Special employment situations: If employee was responsible for collecting or handling money or property, employer has ten days after termination or resignation to audit and adjust employee accounts before making payment.

Commissions must be paid to sales employees within three days if employee is fired or quits with at least five days' notice. Otherwise, commissions must be paid within six days.

Migrant agricultural workers who resign: within five days.

Missouri
Mo. Rev. Stat. § 290.110

Paycheck due when employee is fired: Day of discharge.

Paycheck due when employee quits: No provision.

Unused vacation pay due: No.

Special employment situations: Requirements do not apply if employee is paid primarily based on commission and an audit is necessary or customary to determine the amount due.

Montana
Mont. Code § 39-3-205; Mont. Admin. R. 24.16.7521

Paycheck due when employee is fired: Immediately if fired for cause or laid off (unless there is a written policy extending time to earlier of next payday or 15 days).

Paycheck due when employee quits: Next payday or within 15 days, whichever comes first.

Unused vacation pay due: Yes.

Nebraska
Neb. Rev. Stat. §§ 48-1229–48-1230

Paycheck due when employee is fired: Next payday or within two weeks, whichever is earlier.

Paycheck due when employee quits: Next payday or within two weeks, whichever is earlier.

Unused vacation pay due: Only if required by agreement.

Special employment situations: Commissions due on next payday following receipt.

Nevada
Nev. Rev. Stat. §§ 608.020, 608.030

Paycheck due when employee is fired: Immediately.

Paycheck due when employee quits: Next payday or within seven days, whichever is earlier.

Unused vacation pay due: No.

New Hampshire
N.H. Rev. Stat. §§ 275:43(V), 275:44

Paycheck due when employee is fired: Within 72 hours. If laid off, next payday.

Paycheck due when employee quits: Next payday, or within 72 hours if employee gives one pay period's notice.

Unused vacation pay due: Yes.

New Jersey
N.J. Stat. § 34:11-4.3

Paycheck due when employee is fired: Next payday.

Paycheck due when employee quits: Next payday.

Unused vacation pay due: Only if required by policy.

New Mexico
N.M. Stat. §§ 50-4-4, 50-4-5

Paycheck due when employee is fired: Within five days. ten days for commission or piece-based workers. § 50-4-4(A).

Paycheck due when employee quits: Next payday.

State Laws That Control Final Paychecks (continued)

Unused vacation pay due: No provision.

Special employment situations: If paid by task or commission, ten days after discharge.

New York
N.Y. Lab. Law §§ 191(3), 198-c(2)

Paycheck due when employee is fired: Next payday.

Paycheck due when employee quits: Next payday.

Unused vacation pay due: Yes, unless employer has a contrary policy.

North Carolina
N.C. Gen. Stat. §§ 95-25.7, 95-25.12

Paycheck due when employee is fired: Next payday.

Paycheck due when employee quits: Next payday.

Unused vacation pay due: Yes, unless employer has a contrary policy.

Special employment situations: If paid by commission or bonus, on next payday after amount calculated.

North Dakota
N.D. Cent. Code § 34-14-03; N.D. Admin. Code 46-02-07-02(12)

Paycheck due when employee is fired: Next payday.

Paycheck due when employee quits: Next payday.

Unused vacation pay due: Yes. However, if an employer provides written notice at the time of hire, employer need not pay out vacation that has been awarded, but not yet earned. And, if an employee quits with less than five days' notice, employer may withhold accrued vacation, as long as the employer gave written notice of the limitation at the time of hire and the employee was employed for less than one year.

Ohio
Ohio Rev. Code § 4113.15

Paycheck due when employee is fired: First of month for wages earned in first half of prior month; 15th of month for wages earned in second half of prior month.

Paycheck due when employee quits: First of month for wages earned in first half of prior month; 15th of month for wages earned in second half of prior month.

Unused vacation pay due: Yes, if company has policy or practice of making such payments.

Oklahoma
Okla. Stat. tit. 40, §§ 165.1(4), 165.3

Paycheck due when employee is fired: Next payday.

Paycheck due when employee quits: Next payday.

Unused vacation pay due: Yes.

Oregon
Or. Rev. Stat. §§ 652.140, 652.145

Paycheck due when employee is fired: End of first business day after termination.

Paycheck due when employee quits: Immediately, with 48 hours' notice (excluding weekends and holidays); without notice, within five business days or next payday, whichever comes first (must be within five days if employee submits time records to determine wages due).

Unused vacation pay due: Only if required by policy.

Special employment situations: Seasonal farmworkers: fired or quitting with 48 hours' notice, immediately; quitting without notice, within 48 hours or next payday, whichever comes first. If the termination occurs at the end of harvest season, the employer is a farmworker camp operator, and the farmworker is provided housing at no cost until wages are paid, employer must pay by noon on the day after termination.

Pennsylvania
43 Pa. Stat. §§ 260.2a, 260.5

Paycheck due when employee is fired: Next payday.

Paycheck due when employee quits: Next payday.

Unused vacation pay due: Only if required by policy or contract.

Rhode Island
R.I. Gen. Laws § 28-14-4

Paycheck due when employee is fired: Next payday. Paycheck is due within 24 hours if employer liquidates, merges, or disposes of the business, or moves it out of state.

Paycheck due when employee quits: Next payday.

Unused vacation pay due: Yes, if employee has worked for one full year and the company has verbally or in writing awarded vacation.

South Carolina
S.C. Code §§ 41-10-10(2), 41-10-50

Paycheck due when employee is fired: Within 48 hours or next payday, but not more than 30 days.

Paycheck due when employee quits: No provision.

Unused vacation pay due: Only if required by policy or contract.

State Laws That Control Final Paychecks (continued)

South Dakota
S.D. Codified Laws §§ 60-11-10, 60-11-11, 60-11-14

Paycheck due when employee is fired: Next payday (or until employee returns employer's property).

Paycheck due when employee quits: Next payday (or until employee returns employer's property).

Unused vacation pay due: No.

Tennessee
Tenn. Code § 50-2-103

Paycheck due when employee is fired: Next payday or within 21 days, whichever is later.

Paycheck due when employee quits: Next payday or within 21 days, whichever is later.

Unused vacation pay due: Only if required by policy or contract.

Special employment situations: Applies to employers with five or more employees.

Texas
Tex. Lab. Code §§ 61.001, 61.014

Paycheck due when employee is fired: Within six days.

Paycheck due when employee quits: Next payday.

Unused vacation pay due: Only if required by policy or contract.

Utah
Utah Code §§ 34-28-5; Utah Admin. Code r. 610-3

Paycheck due when employee is fired: Within 24 hours.

Paycheck due when employee quits: Next payday.

Unused vacation pay due: Only if required by policy or contract.

Special employment situations: Requirements do not apply to commission-based portion of sales employees' earnings if audit is necessary to determine the amount due.

Vermont
Vt. Stat. tit. 21, § 342(c)

Paycheck due when employee is fired: Within 72 hours.

Paycheck due when employee quits: Next regular payday or next Friday, if there is no regular payday.

Unused vacation pay due: No provision.

Virginia
Va. Code § 40.1-29(A.1)

Paycheck due when employee is fired: Next payday.

Paycheck due when employee quits: Next payday.

Unused vacation pay due: Only if agreed to in a written statement.

Washington
Wash. Rev. Code § 49.48.010

Paycheck due when employee is fired: End of pay period.

Paycheck due when employee quits: End of pay period.

Unused vacation pay due: No provision.

West Virginia
W. Va. Code §§ 21-5-1, 21-5-4

Paycheck due when employee is fired: Next regular payday (minus withheld amount for replacement cost of employer's unreturned property).

Paycheck due when employee quits: Next regular payday (minus withheld amount for replacement cost of employer's unreturned property).

Unused vacation pay due: Only if required by policy or contract.

Wisconsin
Wis. Stat. §§ 109.01(3), 109.03

Paycheck due when employee is fired: Next payday or within one month, whichever is earlier. If termination is due to merger, relocation, or liquidation of business, within 24 hours.

Paycheck due when employee quits: Next payday.

Unused vacation pay due: Yes.

Special employment situations: Does not apply to managers, executives, or sales agents working on commission basis.

Wyoming
Wyo. Stat. §§ 27-4-104, 27-4-501, 27-4-507(c)

Paycheck due when employee is fired: Next regular payday.

Paycheck due when employee quits: Next regular payday.

Unused vacation pay due: No, if employer's policies state that vacation is fortfeited upon termination of employment and the employee acknowledged the policy in writing.

Special employment situations: Requirements do not apply to commissioned sales employees if audit is necessary to determine the amount due.

State Health Insurance Continuation Laws

Alabama

Ala. Code § 27-55-3(a)(4)

Special Situations: 18 months for subjects of domestic abuse who have lost coverage they had under abuser's insurance and who do not qualify for COBRA.

Arizona

Ariz. Rev. Stat. §§ 20-1377, 20-1408, 20-2330

Employers affected: All employers that offer group disability insurance. Under § 20-2330, employers that offer group health insurance and have one to 20 employees.

Eligible employees: Employees covered under an employer's health benefits plan for at least three months before a qualifying event.

Length of coverage for employee: Under § 20-2330, 18 months (or less if the employee fails to make timely payments or becomes eligible for Medicare or Medicaid or obtains other health coverage, or if the employer terminates group coverage for all employees).

Length of coverage for dependents: Insurer must either continue coverage for dependents or convert to individual policy upon death or divorce of covered employee. Coverage must be the same unless the insured chooses a lesser plan.

Under § 20-2330, 18 months, or less if dependent becomes eligible for Medicare or Medicaid or obtains any other health coverage. Dependents with disabilities are eligible for an additional 11 months' coverage.

Qualifying event: Death of an employee; change in marital status; any other reason stated in policy (other than failure to pay premium).

Under § 20-2330, voluntary or involuntary termination of employment other than for gross misconduct; reduction of hours required to qualify for coverage under group plan; divorce or separation; employee's death or eligibility for Medicare; dependent child ceases to qualify as dependent under group plan; retired employees or their spouses or dependent children lose coverage within a year before or after employer files for bankruptcy.

Time employer has to notify employee: No provisions for employer. Insurance policy must include notice of conversion privilege. Clerk of court must provide notice to anyone filing for divorce that dependent spouse is entitled to convert health insurance coverage.

Under § 20-2330, 30 days after the qualifying event.

Time employee has to apply: 31 days after termination of existing coverage.

Under § 20-2330, 60 days after date of employer's notice.

Arkansas

Ariz. Code §§ 23-86-114–23-86-116

Employers affected: All employers that offer group health insurance.

Eligible employees: Employees continuously insured for previous three months.

Length of coverage for employee: 120 days.

Length of coverage for dependents: 120 days.

Qualifying event: Termination of employment; change in insured's marital status. Employer may—but is not required to—continue benefits on death of employee.

Time employee has to apply: Ten days.

California

Cal. Health & Safety Code §§ 1373.6, 1373.621; Cal. Ins. Code §§ 10128.50–10128.59

Employers affected: Employers that offer group health insurance and have two to 19 employees.

Eligible employees: All covered employees are eligible.

Length of coverage for employee: 36 months.

Length of coverage for dependents: 36 months.

Qualifying event: Termination of employment; reduction in hours; death of employee; change in marital status; loss of dependent status; covered employee's eligibility for Medicare (for dependents only).

Time employer has to notify employee: 15 days.

Time employee has to apply: 60 days.

Special situations: Employee who is at least 60 years old and has worked for employer for previous five years may continue benefits for self and spouse beyond COBRA or Cal-COBRA limits (also applies to COBRA employers). Employee who began receiving COBRA coverage on or after 1/1/03 and whose COBRA coverage is for less than 36 months may use Cal-COBRA to bring total coverage up to 36 months.

Colorado

Colo. Rev. Stat. § 10-16-108

Employers affected: All employers that offer group health insurance.

Eligible employees: Employees continuously insured for previous six months.

State Health Insurance Continuation Laws (continued)

Length of coverage for employee: 18 months.

Length of coverage for dependents: 18 months.

Qualifying event: Termination of employment; reduction in hours; death of employee; change in marital status.

Time employer has to notify employee: 60 days.

Time employee has to apply: 30 days after termination; 60 days if employer fails to give notice.

Connecticut

Conn. Gen. Stat. §§ 38a-512a, 31-51n, 31-51o

Employers affected: All employers that offer group health insurance.

Eligible employees: All covered employees are eligible.

Length of coverage for employee: 30 months, or until eligible for Medicare benefits.

Length of coverage for dependents: 30 months, or until eligible for Medicare benefits; 36 months in case of employee's death, divorce, or loss of dependent status.

Qualifying event: Layoff; reduction in hours; termination of employment; death of employee; change in marital status; loss of dependent status.

Special situations: When facility closes or relocates, employers with 100 or more employees must pay for insurance for employee and dependents for 120 days or until employee is eligible for other group coverage, whichever comes first (does not affect employee's right to conventional continuation coverage, which begins when 120-day period ends).

Delaware

18 Del. Code § 3571F

Employers affected: Employers that offer group health insurance and have one to 19 employees.

Eligible employees: Employees continuously insured for previous three months.

Length of coverage for employee: nine months.

Length of coverage for dependents: nine months.

Qualifying event: Employee's death; termination of employment; divorce or legal separation; employee's eligibility for Medicare; loss of dependent status.

Time employer has to notify employee: Within 30 days of the qualifying event.

Time employee has to apply: 30 days.

District of Columbia

D.C. Code Ann. §§ 32-731 to 32-732

Employers affected: Employers with fewer than 20 employees.

Eligible employees: All covered employees are eligible.

Length of coverage for employee: three months.

Length of coverage for dependents: three months.

Qualifying event: Any reason employee or dependent becomes ineligible for coverage, except employee's termination for gross misconduct.

Time employer has to notify employee: Within 15 days of termination of coverage.

Time employee has to apply: 45 days after termination of coverage.

Florida

Fla. Stat. § 627.6692

Employers affected: Employers with fewer than 20 employees.

Eligible employees: Full-time (25 or more hours per week) employees covered by employer's health insurance plan.

Length of coverage for employee: 18 months.

Length of coverage for dependents: 18 months.

Qualifying event: Layoff; reduction in hours; termination of employment; death of employee; change in marital status.

Time employer has to notify employee: Carrier notifies within 14 days of learning of qualifying event (beneficiary has 63 days to notify carrier of qualifying event).

Time employee has to apply: 30 days from receipt of carrier's notice.

Georgia

Ga. Code §§ 33-24-21.1–33-24-21.2

Employers affected: All employers that offer group health insurance.

Eligible employees: Employees continuously insured for previous six months.

Length of coverage for employee: three months plus any part of the month remaining at termination.

Length of coverage for dependents: three months plus any part of the month remaining at termination.

Qualifying event: Termination of employment (except for cause).

Special situations: Employee, spouse, or former spouse who is 60 years old and who has been covered for previous six months may continue coverage until eligible for Medicare. (Applies to companies with more than 20 employees; does not apply when employee quits for reasons other than health.)

State Health Insurance Continuation Laws (continued)

Hawaii

Haw. Rev. Stat. §§ 393-11, 393-15

Employers affected: All employers required to offer health insurance (those paying a regular employee a monthly wage at least 86.67 times state hourly minimum—about $542).

Length of coverage for employee: If employee is hospitalized or prevented from working by sickness, employer must pay insurance premiums for three months or for as long as employer continues to pay wages, whichever is longer.

Qualifying event: Employee is hospitalized or prevented by sickness from working.

Idaho

Idaho Code § 41-2213

Employers affected: All employers that offer group disability insurance.

Eligible employees: Employees or dependents who are totally disabled at the time the policy ends. (Applies to policies that provide benefits for loss of time during periods of hospitalization, benefits for hospital or medical expenses, or benefits for dismemberment.)

Length of coverage for employee: Must provide a reasonable extension of coverage (in the case of medical and hospital expenses, a reasonable extension is at least 12 months).

Length of coverage for dependents: Must provide a reasonable extension of coverage (in the case of medical and hospital expenses, a reasonable extension is at least 12 months).

Illinois

215 Ill. Comp. Stat. §§ 5/367e, 5/367.2, 5/367.2-5

Employers affected: All employers that offer group health insurance.

Eligible employees: Employees continuously insured for previous three months.

Length of coverage for employee: 12 months.

Length of coverage for dependents: Upon death or divorce, two years' coverage for spouse under 55 and eligible dependents who were on employee's plan; until eligible for Medicare or other group coverage for spouse over 55 and eligible dependents who were on employee's plan. A dependent child who has reached plan age limit or who was not already covered by plan, is also entitled to two years' continuation coverage.

Qualifying event: Termination of employment; reduction in hours; death of employee; divorce.

Time employer has to notify employee: Ten days.

Time employee has to apply: 30 days after termination or reduction in hours or receiving notice from employer, whichever is later, but not more than 60 days from termination or reduction in hours.

Iowa

Iowa Code §§ 509B.3, 509B.5

Employers affected: All employers that offer group health insurance.

Eligible employees: Employees continuously insured for previous three months.

Length of coverage for employee: Nine months.

Length of coverage for dependents: Nine months.

Qualifying event: Any reason employee or dependent becomes ineligible for coverage.

Time employer has to notify employee: Ten days after termination of coverage.

Time employee has to apply: Ten days after termination of coverage or receiving notice from employer, whichever is later, but not more than 31 days from termination of coverage.

Kansas

Kan. Stat. § 40-2209(i)

Employers affected: All employers that offer group health insurance.

Eligible employees: Employees continuously insured for previous three months.

Length of coverage for employee: 18 months.

Length of coverage for dependents: 18 months.

Qualifying event: Any reason employee or dependent becomes ineligible for coverage.

Time employer has to notify employee: Reasonable notice.

Kentucky

Ky. Rev. Stat. § 304.18-110

Employers affected: All employers that offer group health insurance.

Eligible employees: Employees continuously insured for previous three months.

Length of coverage for employee: 18 months.

Length of coverage for dependents: 18 months.

Qualifying event: Any reason employee or dependent becomes ineligible for coverage.

State Health Insurance Continuation Laws (continued)

Time employer has to notify employee: Employer must notify insurer as soon as employee's coverage ends; insurer then notifies employee.

Time employee has to apply: 31 days from receipt of insurer's notice, but not more than 90 days after termination of group coverage.

Louisiana

La. Rev. Stat. §§ 22:1045, 22:1046

Employers affected: All employers that offer group health insurance and have fewer than 20 employees.

Eligible employees: Employees continuously insured for previous three months.

Length of coverage for employee: 12 months.

Length of coverage for dependents: 12 months.

Qualifying event: Termination of employment; death of insured; divorce.

Time employee has to apply: By the end of the month following the month in which the qualifying event occurred.

Special situations: Surviving spouse who is 50 or older may have coverage until remarriage or eligibility for Medicare or other insurance.

Maine

Me. Rev. Stat. tit. 24-A, § 2809-A

Employers affected: All employers that offer group health insurance and are not subject to COBRA.

Eligible employees: Employees employed for at least six months.

Length of coverage for employee: One year.

Length of coverage for dependents: One year.

Qualifying event: Temporary layoff; permanent layoff if employee is eligible for federal premium assistance for laid-off employees who continue coverage; loss of employment because of a work-related injury or disease.

Time employee has to apply: 31 days from termination of coverage.

Maryland

Md. Code, Ins. §§ 15-407–15-409

Employers affected: All employers that offer group health insurance.

Eligible employees: Employees continuously insured for previous three months.

Length of coverage for employee: 18 months.

Length of coverage for dependents: 18 months upon death of employee; upon change in marital status, 18 months or until spouse remarries or becomes eligible for other coverage.

Qualifying event: Termination of employment; death of employee; change in marital status.

Time employer has to notify employee: Must notify insurer within 14 days of receiving employee's continuation request.

Time employee has to apply: 45 days from termination of coverage. Employee begins application process by requesting an election of continuation notification form from employer.

Massachusetts

Mass. Gen. Laws ch. 175, §§ 110G, 110I; ch. 176J, § 9

Employers affected: All employers that offer group health insurance and have fewer than 20 employees.

Eligible employees: All covered employees are eligible.

Length of coverage for employee: 18 months; 29 months if disabled.

Length of coverage for dependents: 18 months upon termination or reduction in hours; 29 months if disabled; 36 months on divorce, death of employee, employee's eligibility for Medicare, or employer's bankruptcy.

Qualifying event: Involuntary layoff; death of insured employee; change in marital status.

Time employer has to notify employee: Carrier must notify beneficiary within 14 days of learning of qualifying event.

Time employee has to apply: 60 days.

Special situations: Termination due to plant closing: 90 days' coverage for employee and dependents, at the same payment terms as before closing.

Minnesota

Minn. Stat. §§ 62A.17, 62A.20, 62A.21

Employers affected: All employers that offer group health insurance and have two or more employees.

Eligible employees: All covered employees are eligible.

Length of coverage for employee: 18 months; indefinitely if employee becomes totally disabled while employed.

Length of coverage for dependents: 18 months for current spouse or child after termination of employment; divorced or widowed spouse can continue until eligible for Medicare or other group health insurance. Upon divorce or death of employee, dependent children can continue until they no longer qualify as dependents under plan.

State Health Insurance Continuation Laws (continued)

Qualifying event: Termination of employment; reduction in hours.

Time employer has to notify employee: Within 14 days of termination of coverage.

Time employee has to apply: 60 days from termination of coverage or receipt of employer's notice, whichever is later.

Mississippi

Miss. Code § 83-9-51

Employers affected: All employers that offer group health insurance and have fewer than 20 employees.

Eligible employees: Employees continuously insured for previous three months.

Length of coverage for employee: 12 months.

Length of coverage for dependents: 12 months.

Qualifying event: Termination of employment; divorce; employee's death; employee's eligibility for Medicare; loss of dependent status.

Time employer has to notify employee: Insurer must notify former or deceased employee's dependent child or divorced spouse of option to continue insurance within 14 days of their becoming ineligible for coverage on employee's policy.

Time employee has to apply: Employee must apply and submit payment before group coverage ends; dependents or former spouse must elect continuation coverage within 30 days of receiving insurer's notice.

Missouri

Mo. Rev. Stat. § 376.428

Employers affected: All employers that offer group health insurance and are not subject to COBRA.

Eligible employees: All employees.

Length of coverage for employee: 18 months.

Length of coverage for dependents: 18 months if eligible due to termination or reduction in hours; 36 months if eligible due to death or divorce.

Qualifying event: Termination of employment; death of employee; divorce; reduction in hours; employee's eligibility for Medicare; loss of dependent status.

Time employer has to notify employee: Same rules as COBRA.

Time employee has to apply: Same rules as COBRA.

Montana

Mont. Code §§ 33-22-506–33-22-507

Employers affected: All employers that offer group disability insurance.

Eligible employees: All employees.

Length of coverage for employee: One year (with employer's consent).

Qualifying event: Reduction in hours.

Special situations: Insurer may not discontinue benefits to child with a disability after child exceeds age limit for dependent status.

Nebraska

Neb. Rev. Stat. §§ 44-1640 and following, 44-7406

Employers affected: Employers not subject to federal COBRA laws.

Eligible employees: All covered employees.

Length of coverage for employee: Six months.

Length of coverage for dependents: One year upon death of insured employee. Subjects of domestic abuse who have lost coverage under abuser's plan and who do not qualify for COBRA may have 18 months' coverage (applies to all employers).

Qualifying event: Involuntary termination of employment (layoff due to labor dispute not considered involuntary).

Time employer has to notify employee: Within ten days of termination of employment must send notice by certified mail.

Time employee has to apply: Ten days from receipt of employer's notice.

Nevada

Nev. Rev. Stat. § 689B.0345

Employers affected: All employers that offer group health insurance.

Eligible employees: Employees who are on unpaid leave due to total disability.

Length of coverage for employee: Coverage must continue for 12 months, unless one of the following events occurs sooner: the employee is terminated, the employee obtains another health insurance policy, or the group health insurance policy is terminated.

Length of coverage for dependents: Coverage must continue for 12 months, unless one of the following events occurs sooner: the employee is terminated, the employee obtains another health insurance policy, or the group health insurance policy is terminated.

State Health Insurance Continuation Laws (continued)

New Hampshire

N.H. Rev. Stat. §§ 415:18

Employers affected: All employers that offer group health insurance.

Eligible employees: All insured employees are eligible.

Length of coverage for employee: 18 months; 29 months if disabled at termination or during first 60 days of continuation coverage.

Length of coverage for dependents: 18 months; 29 months if disabled at termination or during first 60 days of continuation coverage; 36 months upon death of employee, divorce or legal separation, loss of dependent status, or employee's eligibility for Medicare.

Qualifying event: Any reason employee or dependent becomes ineligible for coverage.

Time employer has to notify employee: Carrier must notify beneficiary within 30 days of receiving notice of loss of coverage.

Time employee has to apply: Within 45 days of receipt of notice.

Special situations: Layoff or termination due to strike: six months' coverage with option to extend for an additional 12 months. Surviving, divorced, or legally separated spouse who is 55 or older may continue benefits available until eligible for Medicare or another employer-based group insurance.

New Jersey

N.J. Stat. §§ 17B:27-51.12, 17B:27A-27

Employers affected: Employers with two to 50 employees.

Eligible employees: Employed full time (25 or more hours).

Length of coverage for employee: 18 months; 29 months if disabled at termination or during first 60 days of continuation coverage.

Length of coverage for dependents: 18 months; 36 months upon death of employee, divorce or legal separation, loss of dependent status, or employee's eligibility for Medicare.

Qualifying event: Termination of employment; reduction in hours; change in marital status; death.

Time employer has to notify employee: At time of qualifying event.

Time employee has to apply: Within 30 days of qualifying event.

Special benefits: Coverage must be identical to that offered to current employees.

Special situations: Total disability: employee who has been insured for previous three months and employee's dependents entitled to continuation coverage that includes all benefits offered by group policy (applies to all employers).

New Mexico

N.M. Stat. § 59A-18-16

Employers affected: All employers that offer group health insurance.

Eligible employees: All insured employees are eligible.

Length of coverage for employee: Six months.

Length of coverage for dependents: Six months for termination of employment; may continue group coverage or convert to individual policies upon death of covered employee or divorce or legal separation.

Qualifying event: Termination of employment.

Time employer has to notify employee: Insurer or employer must give written notice at time of termination.

Time employee has to apply: 30 days after receiving notice.

New York

N.Y. Ins. Law § 3221(m)

Employers affected: All employers that offer group health insurance.

Eligible employees: All covered employees are eligible.

Length of coverage for employee: 36 months.

Length of coverage for dependents: 36 months.

Qualifying event: Termination of employment; death of employee; divorce or legal separation; loss of dependent status; employee's eligibility for Medicare.

Time employee has to apply: 60 days after termination or receipt of notice, whichever is later.

North Carolina

N.C. Gen. Stat. §§ 58-53-5–58-53-40

Employers affected: All employers that offer group health insurance.

Eligible employees: Employees continuously insured for previous three months.

Length of coverage for employee: 18 months.

Length of coverage for dependents: 18 months.

Qualifying event: Termination of employment.

Time employer has to notify employee: Employer has option of notifying employee as part of the exit process.

Time employee has to apply: 60 days.

State Health Insurance Continuation Laws (continued)

North Dakota

N.D. Cent. Code §§ 26.1-36-23, 26.1-36-23.1

Employers affected: All employers that offer group health insurance.

Eligible employees: Employees continuously insured for previous three months.

Length of coverage for employee: 39 weeks.

Length of coverage for dependents: 39 weeks; 36 months if required by divorce or annulment decree.

Qualifying event: Termination of employment; change in marital status, if divorce or annulment decree requires employee to continue coverage.

Time employee has to apply: Within ten days of termination or of receiving notice of continuation rights, whichever is later, but not more than 31 days from termination.

Ohio

Ohio Rev. Code §§ 1751.53, 3923.38

Employers affected: All employers that offer group health insurance.

Eligible employees: Employees continuously insured for previous three months who were involuntarily terminated for reasons other than gross misconduct on the part of the employee.

Length of coverage for employee: 12 months.

Length of coverage for dependents: 12 months.

Qualifying event: Involuntary termination of employment.

Time employer has to notify employee: At termination of employment.

Time employee has to apply: Whichever is earlier: 31 days after coverage terminates; ten days after coverage terminates if employer notified employee of continuation rights prior to termination; ten days after employer notified employee of continuation rights, if notice was given after coverage terminated.

Oklahoma

Okla. Stat. tit. 36, § 4509

Employers affected: All employers that offer group health insurance.

Eligible employees: Employees insured for at least six months (all other employees and their dependents entitled to 30 days' continuation coverage).

Length of coverage for employee: 63 days for basic coverage; six months for major medical at the same

premium rate prior to termination of coverage (only for losses or conditions that began while group policy in effect).

Length of coverage for dependents: 63 days for basic coverage; six months for major medical at the same premium rate prior to termination of coverage (only for losses or conditions that began while group policy in effect).

Qualifying event: Any reason coverage terminates (except employment termination for gross misconduct).

Time employer has to notify employee: Carrier must notify employee in writing within 30 days of receiving notice of termination of employee's coverage.

Time employee has to apply: 31 days after receipt of notice.

Special benefits: Includes maternity care for pregnancy begun while group policy was in effect.

Oregon

Or. Rev. Stat. §§ 743B.343–743B.347

Employers affected: Employers not subject to federal COBRA laws.

Eligible employees: Employees continuously insured for previous three months.

Length of coverage for employee: Nine months.

Length of coverage for dependents: Nine months.

Qualifying event: Termination of employment; reduction in hours; employee's eligibility for Medicare; loss of dependent status; termination of membership in group covered by policy; death of employee.

Time employer has to notify employee: Ten days after qualifying event.

Time employee has to apply: Within the time limit determined by the insurer, which must be at least ten days after the qualifying event or employee's receipt of notice, whichever is later.

Special situations: Surviving, divorced, or legally separated spouse who is 55 or older and dependent children entitled to continuation coverage until spouse remarries or is eligible for other coverage; must include dental, vision, or prescription drug benefits, if they were offered in original plan (applies to employers with 20 or more employees).

Pennsylvania

40 Pa. Stat. § 764j

Employers affected: Employers that offer group health insurance and have two to 19 employees.

State Health Insurance Continuation Laws (continued)

Eligible employees: Employees continuously insured for at least three months.

Length of coverage for employee: Nine months.

Length of coverage for dependents: Nine months.

Qualifying event: Termination of employment; reduction in hours; death of employee; change in marital status; employer's bankruptcy.

Time employer has to notify employee: 30 days after qualifying event.

Time employee has to apply: 30 days after receiving notice.

Rhode Island

R.I. Gen. Laws §§ 27-19.1-1, 27-20.4-1–27-20.4-2

Employers affected: All employers that offer group health insurance.

Eligible employees: All insured employees are eligible.

Length of coverage for employee: 18 months (but not longer than continuous employment); cannot be required to pay more than one month premium at a time.

Length of coverage for dependents: 18 months (but not longer than continuous employment); cannot be required to pay more than one month premium at a time.

Qualifying event: Involuntary termination of employment; death of employee; change in marital status; permanent reduction in workforce; employer's going out of business.

Time employer has to notify employee: Employers must post a conspicuous notice of employee continuation rights.

Time employee has to apply: 30 days from termination of coverage.

Special situations: If right to receiving continuing health insurance is stated in the divorce judgment, divorced spouse has right to continue coverage as long as employee remains covered or until divorced spouse remarries or becomes eligible for other group insurance.

South Carolina

S.C. Code § 38-71-770

Employers affected: All employers that offer group health insurance.

Eligible employees: Employees continuously insured for previous six months.

Length of coverage for employee: Six months (in addition to part of month remaining at termination).

Length of coverage for dependents: Six months (in addition to part of month remaining at termination).

Qualifying event: Any reason employee or dependent becomes ineligible for coverage.

Time employer has to notify employee: At time of termination, employer must clearly and meaningfully advise employee of continuation rights.

South Dakota

S.D. Codified Laws §§ 58-18-7.5, 58-18-7.12; 58-18C-1

Employers affected: All employers that offer group health insurance.

Eligible employees: All covered employees.

Length of coverage for employee: 18 months; 29 months if disabled at termination or during first 60 days of continuation coverage.

Length of coverage for dependents: 18 months; 29 months if disabled at termination or during first 60 days of continuation coverage; 36 months upon death of employee, divorce or legal separation, loss of dependent status, or employee's eligibility for Medicare.

Qualifying event: Termination of employment; death of employee; divorce or legal separation; loss of dependent status; employee's eligibility for Medicare.

Special situations: When employer goes out of business: 12 months' continuation coverage available to all employees. Employer must notify employees within ten days of termination of benefits; employees must apply within 60 days of receipt of employer's notice or within 90 days of termination of benefits if no notice given.

Tennessee

Tenn. Code § 56-7-2312

Employers affected: All employers that offer group health insurance.

Eligible employees: Employees continuously insured for previous three months.

Length of coverage for employee: Three months (in addition to part of month remaining at termination).

Length of coverage for dependents: Three months (in addition to part of month remaining at termination); 15 months upon death of employee or divorce (in addition to part of month remaining at termination).

Qualifying event: Termination of employment; death of employee; change in marital status.

Special situations: Employee or dependent who is pregnant at time of termination entitled to continuation benefits for six months following the end of pregnancy.

State Health Insurance Continuation Laws (continued)

Texas

Tex. Ins. Code §§ 1251.252–1251.255; 1251.301–1251.310

Employers affected: All employers that offer group health insurance.

Eligible employees: Employees continuously insured for previous three months.

Length of coverage for employee: Nine months; for employees eligible for COBRA, six months after COBRA coverage ends.

Length of coverage for dependents: Nine months; for employees eligible for COBRA, six months after COBRA coverage ends. Three years for dependents with coverage due to the death or retirement of employee or severance of the family relationship.

Qualifying event: Termination of employment (except for cause); employee leaves for health reasons; severance of family relationship; retirement or death of employee.

Time employee has to apply: 60 days from termination of coverage or receiving notice of continuation rights from employer or insurer, whichever is later. Must give notice within 15 days of severance of family relationship. Within 60 days of death or retirement of family member or severance of family relationship, dependent must give notice of intent to continue coverage.

Utah

Utah Code § 31A-22-722

Employers affected: All employers that offer group health insurance.

Eligible employees: Employees continuously insured for previous 3 months.

Length of coverage for employee: 12 months.

Length of coverage for dependents: 12 months.

Qualifying event: Termination of employment; retirement; death; divorce; reduction in hours; sabbatical; disability; loss of dependent status.

Time employer has to notify employee: In writing within 30 days of termination of coverage.

Time employee has to apply: Within 60 days of qualifying event.

Vermont

Vt. Stat. tit. 8, §§ 4090a–4090c

Employers affected: All employers that offer group health insurance.

Eligible employees: All covered employees are eligible.

Length of coverage for employee: 18 months.

Length of coverage for dependents: 18 months.

Qualifying event: Termination of employment; reduction in hours; death of employee; change of marital status; loss of dependent status.

Time employer has to notify employee: Within 30 days of qualifying event.

Time employee has to apply: Within 60 days of receiving notice following the occurrence of a qualifying event.

Virginia

Va. Code §§ 38.2-3541–38.2-3542

Employers affected: All employers that offer group health insurance.

Eligible employees: Employees continuously insured for previous three months.

Length of coverage for employee: 12 months.

Length of coverage for dependents: 12 months.

Qualifying event: Any reason employee or dependent becomes ineligible for coverage.

Time employer has to notify employee: 14 days from termination of coverage.

Time employee has to apply: Within 31 days of receiving notice of eligibility, but no more than 60 days following termination.

Special situations: Employee may convert to an individual policy instead of applying for continuation coverage (must apply within 31 days of termination of coverage).

Washington

Wash. Rev. Code § 48.21.075

Employers affected: All employers that offer disability insurance.

Eligible employees: Insured employees on strike.

Length of coverage for employee: Six months if employee goes on strike.

Length of coverage for dependents: Six months if employee goes on strike.

Qualifying event: If employee goes on strike.

Special situations: All employers have option of offering continued group health benefits.

State Health Insurance Continuation Laws (continued)

West Virginia

W. Va. Code §§ 33-16-2, 33-16-3(e); W. Va. Code R. § 114-93-3

Employers affected: Employers providing insurance for between two and 20 employees.

Eligible employees: All employees are eligible.

Length of coverage for employee: 18 months in case of involuntary layoff.

Qualifying event: Involuntary layoff.

Time employer has to notify employee: Carrier must notify beneficiaries within 15 days of receiving notice from beneficiary of intent to apply.

Time employee has to apply: 20 days to send notice of intention to apply; 30 days to apply after receiving election and premium notice.

Wisconsin

Wis. Stat. § 632.897

Employers affected: All employers that offer group health insurance.

Eligible employees: Employees continuously insured for previous three months.

Length of coverage for employee: 18 months (or longer at insurer's option).

Length of coverage for dependents: 18 months (or longer at insurer's option).

Qualifying event: Any reason employee or dependent becomes ineligible for coverage (except employment termination due to misconduct).

Time employer has to notify employee: Five days from termination of coverage.

Time employee has to apply: 30 days after receiving employer's notice.

Wyoming

Wyo. Stat. § 26-19-113

Employers affected: Employers not subject to federal COBRA laws.

Eligible employees: Employees continuously insured for previous three months.

Length of coverage for employee: 12 months.

Length of coverage for dependents: 12 months.

Time employee has to apply: 31 days from termination of coverage.

Revolution and Urban Politics
in Provincial France

CHAPTER I

Introduction: Politics and the French Revolution

꙳

POLITICS IS A much abused word. In our time people deny their interest in politics as if it were an illegitimate child, an unpleasant reminder of the less inspiring facts of life. Politics is "dirty," corrupt, or, worse yet, meaningless. At the same time politics has become a loose word. There are sexual politics, the politics of liberation, the politics of health care, the politics of sport. Politics means nothing and everything.

Politics is also out of fashion among historians—historians of France in particular. This is true for both of the dominant schools of French historiography: the so-called "Annales" school and the Marxists. The "Annalistes" regard politics as evanescent; they liken it to the foam on the sea, a mere surface agitation produced by the more profound movements of history. The "Annales" school draws attention to the virtually unchanging geography of a region, the rising and ebbing movements of the economy, or the rhythmic repetitions in social relations—i.e., to the "longue durée" of history— rather than to those fleeting events we call political.[1] No one will deny that our notion and practice of history have been greatly enriched by the work of historians such as Fernand Braudel, Emmanuel Le Roy Ladurie, and Pierre Goubert, and I do not intend to argue for a return to a more narrative, more "political," or "straighter" history of the French Revolution of 1789.[2] Rather, I hope to demonstrate that politics is a form of social activity and hence amenable to the kind of rigorous analysis developed by social historians. Like birth- and deathrates, marriage customs, or harvest and factory records, local patterns of political activity tell us much about the organization and development of society.

I

The denigration of politics did not begin with the "Annales" school. Marx's use of the metaphor "superstructure" encouraged the view that political activity simply reflected or expressed "deeper" conflicts and contradictions in the economy and class structure. Just as the "Annales" school transformed the study of the Old Regime in France, so did Marxism recast the historiography of the French Revolution. Jean Jaurès, Albert Mathiez, and Georges Lefebvre emphasized the importance of food shortages, class interests, and changes in property relations, and in doing so opened up whole new areas for investigation. Unfortunately, the Marxist interpretation remains mired in disputes over the Revolution's role in the transition from feudalism to capitalism. Political changes are attributed to underlying economic causes: the bourgeoisie grabs power in order to liberate the growth of capital from the shackles of a feudal social system. As a consequence, politics plays no role of its own: the new ideology and the new state only appear as handmaidens to the magnates of the marketplace. This has happened despite the fact that since Gramsci and Lukács Marxist theory has moved toward the rehabilitation of politics, seeing political activity and organization as the expression of consciousness, i.e., as a sphere of activity in its own right, not unrelated to economic and social forces, but capable of exercising a decisive or mediating influence on social relations.

This essay is an attempt to salvage politics by applying the methods and insights of those whose work has contributed so much to the sinking of its reputation. The methods of social historians can be applied because politics is a social practice: it is the activity of making decisions about community issues. Politics has rules, and every society has a political system insofar as it has a discernible code governing political activities. The political system can be studied over time to determine its patterns and its directions of change.

A study of the political system is essential to the interpretation of the French Revolution. In 1789 the French people made a radical break with their political past. They demolished the political system of the Old Regime and on its ruins began to build a new political structure. France did not emerge from the years of constitutional experiment and dictatorship, both revolutionary and military, with a dominant capitalist mode of production; France did emerge with a transformed political system. In 1786 the political system of France was hidden in the folds of tradition, and kinship relations informed politics more than did class, legal status, or ideology. During the Revolution the French discovered the many uses of politics: they learned how to formulate their grievances; they organized themselves along political lines to achieve political goals; and they forged new political instruments such as committees and clubs, the prototypes of the political party. In the process they established a revolutionary tradition that continues to haunt France and Europe today.

For the political system, the first year of the Revolution was, in many respects, the "crucial year."[3] Within the space of a few weeks the Old Regime disintegrated. It had been weakened by previous strains, and it fell apart virtually all at once. In the ensuing turmoil, many new political alternatives were advanced; some were suppressed after a brief trial, but others became the cornerstones of a new political structure, the rules of a new way of conducting politics. In this first year the French definitively ruptured their political continuity.

The new politics of 1789 was not the creation of Paris alone. Local uprisings toppled town governments all over France, and revolutionary committees sprang up everywhere to lead the "municipal revolution."[4] This urban revolution was the mainstay of the national revolution: the peasantry could regulate the pace of change, accelerating it by revolt as it did in 1789, obstructing it by disinterest or hostility as it did in 1793–94. But without the Parisian revolution the National Assembly would have been stillborn, and without the urban revolution in the provinces the national revolution would have died in infancy as it did in 1848 and 1870.

At the heart of the urban revolution, both in Paris and in the provinces, were the municipal "committees" of 1789. By introducing them, the townspeople announced their intention to participate in the revolution taking shape in Paris and Versailles. The committees took charge of local militias and directed local efforts to supply food and work. By their very existence the committees promoted local political education: they provided a forum for the discussion of political issues and for the dissemination of revolutionary propaganda. Not infrequently, the committees polarized local political opinion. But whether beleaguered or acclaimed, the extraordinary, extralegal committees dominated local political life until the spring of 1790; and by the time the constitutional government was installed, they had successfully consolidated the local, and thereby the national, revolution.

All but two of the 30 largest towns and cities in France set up municipal committees to meet with or to supplant their town councils.[5] Most towns hastily organized committees in the days following the fall of the Bastille in Paris, and a number of them replaced the early committees with elected ones in August or September. In about half of the large towns the committees shared control with the town councils; in the other half the committees spearheaded local efforts to drive out the Old Regime altogether. As might be expected, conflicts over political authority often engendered violence. In the summer months of grain shortages, high prices, and quickening political agitation, almost every town experienced some sort of collective violence, ranging from demonstrations for lower bread prices or for arms to wild riots, pillaging, and killing. Crowds in Strasbourg, for example, sacked the city hall; a mob in Paris killed the intendant.

Studying in depth all the large towns and cities in France during this chaotic and decisive period is clearly impossible. I have chosen to focus on two quite ordinary towns in order to determine the meaning of the Revolution for local people. I picked Reims and Troyes, the two leading towns in Champagne, because they seemed to enjoy similar economic, social, and administrative positions yet witnessed very different political events in 1789. Reims, with its majestic cathedral and storehouses of renowned wines, and Troyes, with its intricate grid of canals for bleaching cloth, were both a day or two's ride (depending on the means of transport) to the east of Paris. Although they were within reach of the capital city's demanding grasp, Reims and Troyes resembled many other medium-size French towns. They housed the major judicial, administrative, and ecclesiastical institutions of their region and were, like many towns, centers for the manufacture of textiles. In terms of their social and economic structure, we might expect Troyes and Reims to have been similar to Caen, Amiens, Tours, Lille, Orléans, Montpellier, or Montauban, all of them manufacturing towns of the hinterland.[6]

Politically, a comparison of Troyes and Reims covers much of the variety of the municipal revolution. Both established committees less than a week after the fall of the Bastille, and both replaced them with elected committees by the end of August. The Reims committee's reign was uneventful and relatively long: the elected committee met jointly with the town council, and the two bodies cooperated in repressing food riots and maintaining a comparatively placid political atmosphere during the entire first year of the Revolution. The Troyes committee, by contrast, led a brief and tempestuous life: it usurped the functions of the town council, which had firmly resisted its election, as well as of the chief police magistrate. Less than two weeks after the committee's election a vengeful crowd rioted during a public hearing, killed and mutilated the mayor in a horrifying outburst of popular rage, and ended the day in a frenzy of pillaging directed against the foremost representatives of the Old Regime in Troyes. In response to these singular events, the national government reinforced the local army garrison, nervous property owners formed their own countermilitia, and the *bailliage* court declared the committee illegal. Like Marseille, Troyes experienced one of the earliest counterrevolutions of the Revolution.

The chapters that follow aim to explain the differences between Troyes and Reims and at the same time show how the two towns, for all their differences, resembled the other medium- and large-size towns of France. Essential to both purposes is a comparison of the political system of the Old Regime with the political system emerging in 1789. Who held political office? Which institutions and groups exercised political power? How were political decisions made? What was the relationship between politics and other aspects of social life? And how did all these change in 1789? Answers to these questions will show both the common characteristics and the variants of local politics under the Old Regime; in addition, the comparison of the two towns will help clarify what was peculiarly local and what was more generally national about the Revolution of 1789.

CHAPTER 2

Urban Politics at the End
of the Old Regime

~~✒~~

ONE OF THE DEFINING characteristics of the Old Regime was its lack of clearly circumscribed political institutions. France had no House of Commons, no national elections, and consequently no independent political organizations. Political allegiance was no longer symbolized by an act of homage uniting lord and vassal, but neither was it yet determined by affiliation with a political party. Politics—in the sense of the professional conduct of political affairs—scarcely existed under the Old Regime; there were no professional politicians until the Revolution created the channels (elections) and arenas (local and national assemblies) for organized political activity.

Political life, such as it was, found expression in family networks. The courts, most administrative posts, the town councils, and the guilds all were controlled by coalitions of families; hence the chief principle animating Old Regime institutions was the preservation of patrimony. Reformers constantly came up against the stone wall formed by the interpenetration of family, property, and office. In the sixteenth century, the monarchy had sacrificed a good part of its prerogative of naming officials in order to secure the loyalty of its servants; but once it had recognized the right of families to pass on the offices they purchased, the crown never completely recovered its freedom of maneuver. Every administrative innovation was designed to counter the overweening influence of kinship in politics, but each such endeavor was eventually undermined. To some extent the intendants were exceptions to this rule, but even the post of subdelegate, the intendant's deputy, soon succumbed to family domination. Since family alliance was the basis of the entire social system, it could not be circumvented for long.

Although the crown was forced to work within the framework of kinship, it did manage to reduce the political competence of most institutions. In a sense this was part of the historic bargain between the monarchy and its bureaucracy: families received assurance that their offices could be bequeathed in exchange for bureaucratic obedience. Government consequently became more patrimonial and less susceptible to political challenge at the same time. This fostered the trend in the Old Regime toward government by administration.

On the national level, only the sovereign courts managed to maintain a modicum of independence in the face of the crown's drive to extend its administrative dominion. Yet though the *parlements* periodically organized resistance to royal programs, their function remained essentially judicial rather than political; they could register and interpret laws, but they could not make them. Local governments were better able to preserve their initiative. Provincial Estates still met in a few provinces (the *pays d'états*), and many towns and cities retained some form of local elections despite the crown's efforts to convert all local offices into salable and hence hereditary possessions. In the absence of viable national political institutions, the people of the provinces learned what they knew about politics in their hometowns.

Troyes and Reims housed the regional institutions characteristic of the *pays d'élections*, the large, centrally controlled, inner core of France. Each town had a subdelegate (a deputy of the intendant, who supervised the *généralité* of Champagne from Châlons-sur-Marne), a civil and criminal court (the *bailliage*), a tax court (the *élection*), a *maîtrise des eaux et forêts* with jurisdiction over forests and waterways in the king's domain, and a contingent of mounted highway police (the *maréchaussée*). (See Figure 1.) There were no provincial Estates in Champagne and no sovereign courts in Troyes or Reims; appeals went directly from local jurisdictions to Paris. Thus before 1787 there were no specifically provincial institutions in Champagne mediating local and national politics besides the intendant.*

* In 1787 the crown established provincial assemblies in the *pays d'élections*. This is discussed in Chapter 3.

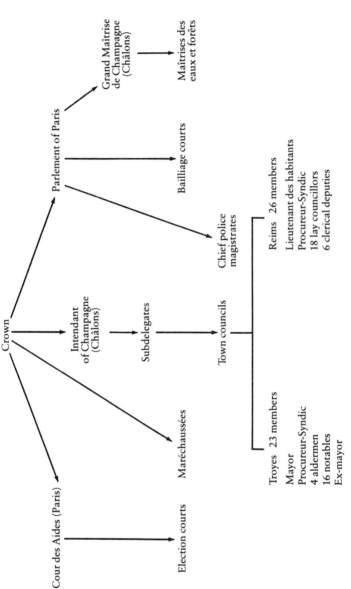

Fig. 1. The Structure of Government at the End of the Old Regime. The arrows show direction of flow of authority down to the local level in Champagne.

The actual operation of local institutions and the character of local politics everywhere in France varied according to social context. Economic and social structures did not mechanically determine the form and content of local politics, yet they did limit political options. Towns with numerous merchants and thousands of textile workers, for example, had different kinds of political strategies and choices available than towns with many magistrates and lawyers but few textile workers. Since both Troyes and Reims were manufacturing centers, they resembled each other in some fundamental ways. Nonetheless, there were differences between them that had significant ramifications for urban politics not only under the Old Regime but also during the Revolution. Let us begin, then, by describing the more salient of these differences.

I

Troyes and Reims shared economic preeminence in Champagne, a province rich in sparkling wines but relatively poor in wheat. Both towns had been solid, and at times splendid, religious and commercial centers since the Middle Ages, thanks to their felicitous locations at intersections of major trade routes connecting Germany and Switzerland with Paris, Flanders, and Great Britain.[1] The manufacture of woolens in Reims and cottons in Troyes had long contributed to the prosperity of each, but by the middle of the eighteenth century textiles had come to assume paramount importance in the economies of both towns. In the last decades of the Old Regime textile production boomed and the populations of Troyes and Reims swelled as a result, with Troyes reaching 28,000 and Reims 32,000 inhabitants by 1789 (see Figure 2).[2]

Reims enjoyed the fruits of a diverse economy. The town was surrounded by the gentle, rolling hills of northern Champagne, the wine-producing region of the province. The combination of wine and woolen industries gave Reims an air of well-being noticed by travelers such as Arthur Young, who found the streets "broad, straight, and well-built," his inn "large and well-served," and the gates of the town "superb and elegant."[3] According to Young, the Reims region produced 9,814,600 livres worth of cloth and four to

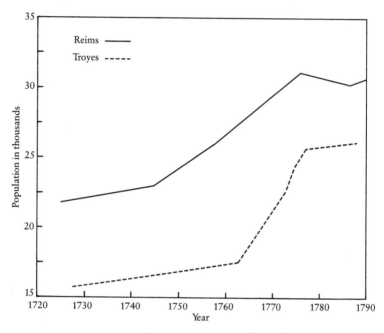

Fig. 2. Population Growth of Troyes and Reims in the Eighteenth Century. The figures for Reims are from Jean-Noël Biraben, "La Population de Reims et de son arrondissement," *Population*, 16 (1961), pp. 722–30. For Troyes I have converted the figures for *feux*, or households, given in Albert Babeau, *La Population de Troyes au dix-huitième siècle* (Troyes, 1873), p. 9, taking one *feux* as roughly equivalent to four people.

five million livres worth of wine in 1782; this contrasted with the 4,572,400 livres worth of cloth produced in the Troyes region.[4]

Reims society was animated by the presence of many nobles and a powerful church establishment. Two to three times as many members of the privileged orders resided in Reims as in Troyes.[5] The disparity was due in large measure to the attraction of the Reims church, which offered honorable and lucrative positions to the younger children of noble families. Since the time of Clovis and Saint Remi the kings of France had journeyed to Reims to receive their crowns in an elaborate religious ceremony, and successive monarchs had shown their appreciation by showering many favors upon the city. Her archbishop was a peer of the realm, and her local chapters were among the richest and most powerful in the country.[6] The presence of a renowned university faculty fortified the Reims church's intellectual reputation and claim to political as well as moral leadership in the local community.

With its rich mixture of champagne, fine woolens, a cathedral, and a university, Reims offered many avenues to social advancement—apparently many more than did Troyes. Between 1760 and 1789, for instance, the Bureau des Finances in Châlons-sur-Marne recorded letters of nobility for six *rémois* as opposed to only three *troyens*.[7] Although in itself this difference cannot explain the inequality in number of nobles, it is indicative of the greater opportunity for upward mobility in Reims. *Roturiers* who made their mark in the worlds of industry, commerce, or letters in Reims could reasonably aspire to join the world of their social betters.

Because it had a relatively homogeneous economy, Troyes anticipated many of the social traits of a nineteenth-century industrial town. It was the market and manufacturing center for the southern half of Champagne, the *Champagne pouilleuse*. The chalky soil of the region yielded miserably little sustenance to the inhabitants, and agricultural laborers relied on off-season spinning and carding to make ends meet. In the Middle Ages, Troyes had been an artistic, religious, and commercial center of great repute, but other towns progressively took over her religious and artistic leadership as her fairs decayed. Yet the cotton industry continued to expand right up until the years immediately preceding the Revolution. Troyes merchants bought raw cotton from Santo Domingo, Martinique, and Guadeloupe and exported the finished cloth to southern France, Italy, or Spain. Nearly two-thirds of the town's population was employed in the manufacture of cotton, making Troyes in essence a single-industry town.[8] In the absence of a powerful church hierarchy and numerous resident nobles, the bourgeoisie of Troyes, her merchants and nonnoble royal officials, dominated the local social and political scene.

The differences between the manufacture of cottons and woolens had important social and political consequences. The manufacture of cotton cloth required a great investment in raw material, since cotton had to be imported, but involved no risk in equipment for the merchant, since the weavers usually owned their handlooms. About 50 merchants (*négoçiants*) were involved in the production of cotton cloth in Troyes, but a few families actually controlled the local business.[9] Originally, clothiers (*fabricants*) played a vital role in the production process; they bought the thread from the spinners and controlled its warping and weaving. By the 1780's, however, the merchants no longer needed them to organize local production: the spinners bought the raw cotton from the merchants; the weavers bought the thread from the spinners; and the merchants bought the woven cloth back from the weavers, had it bleached, and then exported it. As might be expected, there were few clothiers who occupied positions of community leadership in Troyes.[10]

In the Reims economy, on the other hand, the clothiers maintained their function because the manufacture of woolen cloth was much more delicate and complicated, and hence less mechanized, than the production of cotton cloth. Merchants dealing in woolens entered the process only after the cloth was woven; the clothiers purchased the spun wool and supervised its weaving. There were 380 to 400 clothiers in Reims, and the more entrepreneurial among them owned looms, so that weavers were forced to work directly for them. A handful of Reims clothiers established large enterprises employing hundreds of workers each.[11] The intermediary role of the clothiers in Reims became especially noteworthy during the textile depression of the late 1780's: though the woolen merchants cut back their purchases of cloth, the clothiers continued to employ as many workers as possible in the hope that the market would improve. In Troyes, cotton workers suffered immediately when merchants refused to buy because there was no one buffering them from the effects of a depressed market. The result was that in 1789 the textile workers in Troyes were much more desperate than their Reims comrades.

The organizational possibilities among cotton workers were much more limited than among woolen workers. Most cotton weavers worked with their families in their own cellars and had few regular occasions for contact with fellow weavers. By the 1780's the guild structure in Troyes had begun to disintegrate under the combined impact of the influx of new laborers and the rapid extension of the putting-out system into the nearby countryside.[12] As cotton cloth-manufacturing became mechanized, illiterate peasants and even or-phaned children learned to weave, thereby enabling the merchants to keep piece rates low and to circumvent the regulations of the guild.[13] As a result, only those master weavers who were able to maintain several handlooms were able to retain a position superior to that of journeymen weavers. The others found themselves increasingly as-similated to a virtually homogeneous mass of textile workers.

In Reims, the guild structure maintained itself against the pres-sures of textile industry expansion because woolen cloth-manu-facturing required more skills than did cotton cloth-manufacturing. Although the carders and spinners in Reims had been reduced to an undifferentiated pool of laborers, the weavers, dyers, and fullers were still distinguished by their skills and hence able to sustain the guild tradition of master, journeyman, and apprentice. Conse-quently, the work force in Reims was relatively more cohesive than that in Troyes—a difference that was to have striking repercussions in 1789. Despite the fact that they were less desperate than the workers in Troyes, the Reims textile workers effectively manifested their solidarity even before the Revolution: in March 1789 they demonstrated for greater political participation in the electoral meetings held in preparation for the Estates General. By contrast, the Troyes textile workers were politically as well as economically isolated from each other.

II

Despite their economic differences, Troyes and Reims were di-vided along similar political lines. Local society was ranged into three basic groups: those who were entirely excluded from regular political participation; those who had some voice in community af-fairs but could never hold positions of community leadership; and those who held office or were considered eligible for positions of leadership in the community. One's place in this scheme depended primarily on economic position, though social status became important at the upper range of the scale. People were excluded from "regular" political participation (they might riot) if they did not meet minimal property qualifications. This customarily affected all women, at least for communitywide decisions, and most unskilled or semiskilled workers. Men who held some property—and this included guild masterships—could vote, but if they worked with their hands they could not expect to be chosen as leaders of the whole community. Nonetheless, master artisans and shopkeepers might be leaders of their own "communities," i.e., their guilds. Only men of property and leisure were eligible for town office. They might work, they might even trade; but they never worked with their hands.[14]

Although a man could cross the boundaries separating these three urban groups, the distinctions between them were apparent to contemporaries. The greatest chasm was that dividing the propertyless day laborers and textile workers from the rest of the population. The contrast between their lives and those of other townspeople was succinctly described by a doctor in Troyes. In 1786, Dr. Picard described the health and hygiene problems he observed in the town.

There is a great difference in the life-style of the different classes of citizens depending on their status and their wealth. The rich here, like the rich everywhere, cover their tables with the finest foods and wines imported from other provinces or foreign countries. They digest while playing cards or games and spend the rest of the day in soft indolence. Prosperous people content themselves with what one calls ordinary, bourgeois repast, which consists of boiled beef, vegetables cooked in butter, or various sorts of meats in stews or roasts. Quite often they add pork sausage, which is excellent in Troyes. They drink *pinot* wine which they make themselves.

Life is very different for the majority of the population, who suffer because food supplies are very expensive. The nourishment of the people consists of a dark bread, rarely made with pure wheat, most often mixed with rye or barley, sometimes dipped in water to which they add a little rancid oil and vegetables such as cabbage, turnips, beans, and dried peas to make a simple soup. They drink water from the wells and a crude wine of which they obviously make a habit more immoderate than regulated. The people in the countryside live less badly; around their thatched cottages they find resources which the poor artisans of the towns lack. Here the people do not drink cider or beer regularly, but all of the workers take eau-de-vie before beginning their day; many of them die at a young age, victims of their abuse of this liquor whose pernicious effects would be even more common except for the humid constitution of our atmosphere.

. . . The weavers spend most of their time in the cellars that serve as their workshops; at night they retire to dirty, poorly ventilated rooms where the entire family eats and sleeps. The outside air that penetrates into these rooms is permeated with deleterious vapors. Since time immemorial the artisans, who all live in the same quarter, have had the right to dump their sewage in front of their doors. No police ordinance has yet been able to change this situation. The difficulty of digging privies in their houses (their workshops are located underneath) contributes as much as their lack of cleanliness and the example of their ancestors (the latter has great force for them) to maintain this abuse. They all have a bluish, livid complexion. Their most common maladies are "putrid fevers," chronic rheumatism, "cold tumors," scurvy, and intermittent fevers that end with obstruction of the viscera, dropsy, and finally death. Circulating the air in their workshops, maintaining greater cleanliness in their houses and their quarter, and changing their manner of clothing themselves, which does not protect them enough against the humidity of their cellars, would save the artisans from many of their troubles. Their wives and an infinity of other women who work as cotton spinners are exposed to all the maladies occasioned by the sedentary arts. In addition, the coarse and unhealthy food and bad well water make goiter very common among them. Caught in time it can be cured; left to develop it acquires a great size and becomes incurable. The violent and repeated motions used by the stockingmakers to run their looms cause malfunctions in the lung and problems with the circulation of the blood. From there develop the pains in the side, the feeling of suffocation, the spitting of blood, and other lung diseases that carry away most of these artisans in the prime of life. Lucky are those who complain only of frequent fatigue in the arms and the legs, pains produced by the effort of vigorous beings! [15]

The majority of the population clearly lived in the "realm of necessity," and this disqualified them from regular politics.[16] They did not appear on the property-tax rolls: less than a third of the adult male population of Reims was included in the *contribution foncière* for the year 1792, for example.[17] Some of them made marriage contracts, yet even those textile workers, servants, and poor artisans who did were much poorer than the "average" man. (See Tables 1 and 2.)

TABLE 1
The Position of Socioeconomic Groups in Reims

Occupation	Average tax (livres)	Percent of males with identified occupations
Nobles[a]	1,940	0.3%
Clergy[a]	249	1
Wholesale merchants	527	10
Clothiers	322	6
Members of the liberal professions	269	8
Advocates	202	
Physicians	295	
"Bourgeois"	—	0
Small merchants	342	4
Hotel and transport personnel	234	8
Luxury craftsmen	125	1
Food tradesmen	264	15
Dry goods merchants	339	
Bakers	216	
Butchers	162	
Construction trades artisans	260	8
Clothing trades artisans	272	8
Rural[b]	254	13
Textile workers	229	15
Skilled textile workers	414	
Weavers	112	
Carders	186	
Service workers[c]	142	3
TOTAL		100.3%
Occupations unknown (N = 370 males)	276	
Occupations known (N = 577 males)	290	
Women (N = 141)	314	
TOTAL SAMPLE (N = 1,088)	285	

NOTE: This table is based on information in the entries for the 1,088 names beginning with the letters "A" through "J" in the rolls of the *contribution foncière* of 1792 (A.C. Reims, registre 194). Occupations for 34 percent of the sample were not listed; many of these entries probably represented "bourgeois," i.e., men without professions who lived off investments of various sorts.

[a] The figures for identified nobles and clergymen are given for comparison. Nobles are underrepresented because many had emigrated, left town, or concealed their identities. The clergy as a group was much smaller and less wealthy in 1792 than it had been before the Revolution.

[b] "Rural" includes gardeners and farmers living in town.

[c] "Service workers" include *domestiques, manouvriers,* and other day laborers.

TABLE 2

The Position of Socioeconomic Groups in Troyes

Occupation	Average contract (livres)	Percent of contracts with evaluations given
Nobles[a]	67,633	2%
Wholesale merchants	26,018	6
Clothiers	5,019	< 1
Members of the liberal professions	24,185	7
Advocates	24,221	
Physicians	13,952	
"Bourgeois"[b]	14,238	< 1
Small merchants	6,449	3
Hotel and transport personnel	5,147	2
Luxury craftsmen	11,075	1
Food tradesmen	6,174	8
Dry good merchants	16,282	
Bakers	4,353	
Butchers	3,651	
Construction trades artisans	3,805	10
Clothing trades artisans	3,824	7
Rural[c]	3,246	11
Textile workers	3,824	16
Skilled textile workers	5,019	
Stocking-makers	4,284	
Weavers	3,214	
Service workers[d]	2,014	21
Occupations unknown	13,151	6
TOTAL SAMPLE	8,884	

NOTE: This table is based on the 1,361 marriage contracts made between 1770 and 1789 with evaluations given (out of a total of 1,592 contracts listed in the "Table alphabétique des contrats de mariage," A.D. Aube, IIC Supplement 36. These 1,361 marriage contracts represent about one third of all the marriages celebrated during the period (according to the *Almanach de la ville et du diocèse de Troyes*, which states that 4,073 marriages were celebrated in Troyes between 1775 and 1789). Of those town councillors who married between 1754 and 1789, the contracts of only 35 percent are represented in the "Table alphabétique"; thus this source does not seem overly biased in favor of upper-class marriages. Nonetheless, the lower classes, and especially the textile workers, are undoubtedly somewhat underrepresented in this sample. For a much more detailed analysis, see Lynn A. Hunt, "The Municipal Revolution of 1789 in Troyes and Reims" (Ph.D. dissertation, Stanford University, 1973), Appendix 2.

[a] The figures for nobles are given for comparison.

[b] "Bourgeois" includes those listing themselves as "*bourgeois, rentiers,* or *propriétaires.*"

[c] "Rural" includes gardeners and farmers living in town.

[d] "Service workers" include *domestiques, manouvriers,* and other day laborers.

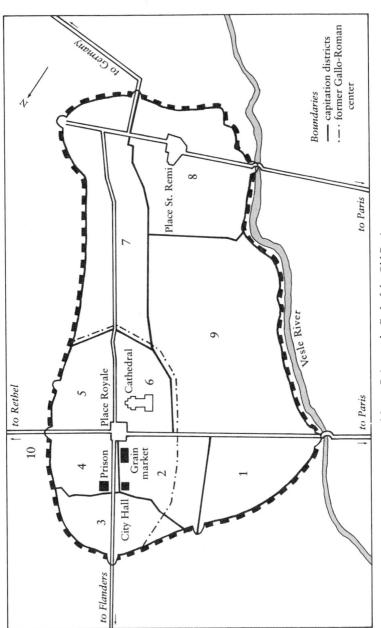

Map 1. Reims at the End of the Old Regime

The working poor were not only excluded from politics, they were also pushed out of the town's center. In the larger French towns and cities this segregation of the poor became increasingly evident in the eighteenth century.[18] The waves of migrants seeking employment were forced to settle in the outlying quarters, and consequently urban space polarized into an inner zone of the rich and prosperous and an outer zone inhabited primarily by the impoverished. This can be seen in Reims by using the *capitation* roll, which was based on rent.[19] For the purpose of assessment, the town was divided into nine districts within the walls and a tenth suburban district (see Map 1). Districts 2–6 were located in what had been the Roman and medieval core of the town, and in the eighteenth century these were the wealthiest districts in Reims. The capitation rolls show that in 1770, districts 2, 3, 4, and 5 alone paid 59.4 percent of the town's tax bill.[20] In 1789, these same four districts paid 57.4 percent of the capitation taxes, yet included only 35.7 percent of the taxpayers.[21] In the remaining districts within the walls, about 80 percent of the taxpayers paid less than five livres, and none paid more than 100 livres (the highest tax category). As Table 3 shows, a far smaller percentage of poor townspeople lived in districts 2–5 than in any of the other urban districts, and almost all of the richest men in Reims lived there.

TABLE 3
The Distribution of Wealth by District in Reims, 1789

	Percentage assessed a capitation tax of				
District	Less than 5 l.	5– 10 l.	11– 50 l.	51– 100 l.	More than 100 l.
1	79%	11%	10%	–	–
2	52	24	20	3%	1%
3	60	16	19	4	1
4	50	19	26	4	1
5	54	18	21	4	2
6	77	12	11	1	–
7	73	14	13	1	–
8	83	12	5	–	–
9	79	13	7	1	–
10	67	17	15	1	–

SOURCE: A.C. Reims, registre 679, fonds anciens, "Capitation de 1789."

TABLE 4

The Distribution of Domestic Help and Textile Workers by District in Reims, 1789

District	Domestic help per 100 taxpayers[a]	Textile workers[b] per 100 taxpayers
1	6.1	27.9
2	35.8	15.3
3	19.3	17.0
4	35.3	5.5
5	44.4	4.7
6	9.9	38.2
7	8.3	38.6
8	3.6	62.5
9	8.4	40.2
10	13.3	13.7

SOURCE: A.C. Reims, registre 679, fonds anciens, "Capitation de 1789."

[a] "Taxpayers" includes textile workers but excludes domestic workers.

[b] "Textile workers" includes weavers, carders, and spinners (both male and female).

The wealthier sections also had more domestic servants per taxpayer and fewer textile workers (see Table 4). Yet the proportion of women taxpayers per district did not seem to reflect economic differences.[22]

The consequences of residential polarization became most apparent during the food riots of the Old Regime and the demonstrations and riots of the Revolution. Food riots almost always began either in the marketplaces or at the town gates when grain-laden wagons tried to leave for other destinations. Since most markets and grain storehouses (owned by merchants, religious houses, or the towns themselves) were located in the central sections, food rioters tended to converge there. The city hall and other official buildings also being centrally located, demonstrations with political objects usually ended there, too. The demonstration by Reims textile workers in March 1789 is a good example. The workers gathered in their home districts (chiefly 7 and 8 on Map 1) in response to the rousing speeches of a notorious local political maverick. From there the surging ranks of political outcasts fell on the city hall (district 2), where they invaded the meeting of "bourgeois" citizens without corporate affiliation. In this way the unemployed and propertyless made their political voices heard. (A full description of this demonstration is given in Chapter 3.)

In "normal" times, when most urban-dwellers managed to stay within the margins of subsistence, the artisans and shopkeepers mediated between the town's center and its periphery. They provided food, supplies, and services to rich and poor alike. They were the "average" taxpayers and they made the "average" marriages. For example, artisans and shopkeepers made up over half the taxpayers assessed for the *contribution foncière* of 1792 in Reims.[23] Moreover, they could be found in almost all of the different districts in Reims: in contrast to the merchants and professionals, who resided in the central districts, and the textile workers, who lived in the outer districts, artisans and shopkeepers were spread relatively evenly across town except for the areas most removed from the center.[24] The same was true of Troyes.[25]

If a concentration of artisans and shopkeepers could be said to have existed anywhere in Reims, parish records suggest that it was in the zone between the rich and the very poor. In response to a 1774 questionnaire sent by the archbishop of Reims to all the parishes under his jurisdiction, only the priest for the parish of Saint Michel (district 6) reported a large number of shopkeepers among his flock. This parish was located on the boundary between the town's medieval center and the peripheral areas built up in later centuries.[26]

Artisans and shopkeepers were also political intermediaries in both Troyes and Reims. In times of crisis they formed the backbone of the urban militia, protecting property-owners (like themselves) from the often very real menace of violent retribution at the hands of the unemployed and hungry textile workers. The skilled craftsmen and petty traders were the last bulwark in the defense of kinship ties; they fought tenaciously to maintain family monopolies in the guilds in order to resist the encroaching disintegration brought by the expanding textile industry. Their guilds gave them enormous organizational advantages in comparison to the hapless textile workers; in the community of the guild they learned how to organize themselves collectively to achieve their goals. The guilds gave the butchers, bakers, and candlestickmakers a voice in community affairs. With this kind of political experience behind them, artisans and shopkeepers were able to demand an even greater role in 1789.

At the top of the political ladder were the local elites, the men of property and leisure who controlled the local political system. They exercised this control primarily through three key institutions that made most of the immediate decisions affecting public life in Troyes and Reims: the office of the subdelegate, the town council, and the office of the chief police magistrate.[27] The subdelegate (*subdélégué*) held his post by commission from the intendant in Châlons-sur-Marne. Although theoretically his commission could be revoked at any time, in practice a few local families monopolized the office for long periods. The subdelegate was the king's deputy in local affairs; he was the link between national and local government.[28] The town council controlled town finances, public works, and what remained of the local militia.[29] Although the councils were elected by the townsmen, they were directly responsible to the subdelegate. The chief police magistrate sat on the town council either as an adviser (Troyes) or as a voting member (Reims). He regulated bread prices and quality, supervised public places (e.g., markets and inns), and enforced ordinances covering public hygiene, local publications, and religious observances. In addition, he presided in his own court over trials involving infractions against his ordinances.[30] This important urban office was venal, and, like all venal offices, its sale had to be approved by the crown.

Despite the crown's occasional and usually opportunistic efforts at reform, access to these institutions remained closed to all except a few "notables."[31] This was most obviously true for the subdelegates, since they were handpicked by the intendant at Châlons-sur-Marne from local magistrate families noted for their loyalty and long service to the crown.[32] But it was also true of the town councils, even though many townsmen could vote in the elections for councilmen. Local notables monopolized council seats by manipulating a two-stage election process. In Troyes, 61 socioprofessional "corporations" first chose 140 delegates, who then met to elect town councillors according to a weighted method of voting prescribed by royal edict in 1773.[33] Prior to this edict, merchants and royal officials had alternated in a seesaw battle for hegemony: merchants had controlled the council until the introduction of the royal edicts of 1764–65 known as the Laverdy reforms, after which the officials of the bailliage court predominated until the reform edicts were withdrawn, whereupon members of both groups requested a royal decree to resolve their increasingly acrimonious conflicts. The king's edict of 1773 divided the most important municipal offices equally between merchants and royal officials: of the four aldermen (*échevins*), who controlled most day-to-day town business, no more than two could be merchants and no more than two could be royal officials.[34]

The election procedure in Reims was also indirect. The adult, tax-paying males chose delegates ("electors") by districts, rather than by corporations as in Troyes, and the electors in turn picked the town councillors. Through a system of patronage and clientage, a select group of leading merchants, nobles, and royal officials had maintained an exclusive hold on the lay municipal offices for 150 years. A handful of families became known as the "Nous-ferons" because they could do as they pleased in local politics.[35] Unlike their Troyes counterparts, however, the lay notables of Reims were forced to share their power with local clergymen, for the crown had given the Reims church the right to name six clerical deputies to the town council.

Despite these variations in manner of selection and composition, the councils of Troyes and Reims shared one telling feature: the lower classes were almost entirely excluded. The guilds chose one or two token councillors, but the textile workers had no representatives and only rarely had the right to vote.[36]

The powerful office of chief police magistrate had been established at the end of the seventeenth century, and in introducing it the crown exacerbated previously existing tensions within local ruling circles and in some places markedly altered the local balance of power.[37] This occurred because the new office included in its jurisdiction much of the judicial authority formerly held by the town council. Moreover, in Champagne, appeals from the new jurisdiction went directly to the Parlement of Paris over the head of the local bailliage courts. In Troyes, the members of the bailliage court got around this latter difficulty and at the same time upstaged the merchant-dominated council by buying the office of chief police magistrate and sharing its prerogatives and responsibilities as a group. In 1781, however, the crown finally separated the office from the court and sold it to one man, himself a former bailliage magistrate.

In Reims, by contrast, the sale of the new office drove a wedge between the lay notables and the church because the king sold it to the archbishop rather than to the bailliage court. This gave the church the most extensive legal jurisdiction in the town, but it also aggravated local resentment of the church since the archbishop already enjoyed the right to tax all grain coming into the Reims market (the *droit de stellage*)[38] and to name clerical deputies to the town council. A perennial sense of grievance against these special privileges united the various groups of lay notables in Reims to an extent uncommon in most French towns, with the result that during the Revolution the church rather than the lay notables became the focus of local hostility toward the Old Regime. In 1789 most lay notables in Reims successfully accommodated themselves to the Revolution.

Closer examination of the men who held the key offices in Troyes and Reims in 1789 will show that they occupied similar social positions in the local community: they were the most prestigious members of the highest-ranking urban social groups. Pierre-Jean Paillot had been the subdelegate of Troyes since 1742.[39] His son and assistant, Louis-Nicolas Paillot, was the *lieutenant-général* of the bailliage court, and Pierre-Jean himself previously had held the office of king's proctor in the élection court. In 1718 the Paillot family had recovered its noble status by letters patent, a step that had been made necessary by their ancestors' decision to engage in commercial activity.[40] The subdelegate of Reims, Nicolas Polonceau, was apparently not noble, but he, too, was a royal official. The intendant of Champagne chose him in 1768 over the other candidate, Patouillart de Chevrières, the king's proctor in the élection court of Reims.[41] Polon-

ceau was a councillor in the bailliage court, and in 1779 he was allowed to make his son his assistant.

The chief police magistrates in the two towns also began their
careers as royal officials. François-Nicolas Sourdat, the police magistrate in Troyes after 1781, formerly held the office of king's advocate
in the bailliage court. His father had been the *lieutenant-criminel* of
the same court.[42] Gérard Jacob, the archbishop's choice for the post
in Reims, was a recently ennobled royal official, who had held various local offices for over 30 years.[43] Sourdat alone of these four
major officials was a relatively young man at the age of 44 in 1789.
The subdelegates were both over 70 and Jacob was probably in his
late 50's or early 60's.

Although the town councillors were drawn from a wider variety of
urban groups than the subdelegates or the police magistrates, they,
too, won office because they were prestigious members of the local
community. The mayor or *lieutenant des habitants* of Reims in 1789,
Souyn, was a nobleman from a sword family.[44] The *procureur-
syndic* (a kind of city manager who generally organized council business and had enormous power), Dessain de Chevrières, had been the
king's proctor in the élection court since 1774 and a councillor in the
bailliage court since 1785. He was 39 in 1789. The clergymen on the
council were among the highest-ranking members of the Reims
church hierarchy, and the eight merchants and clothiers on the
council included the town's largest employer of textile workers,
Ponsardin, and a rich wine merchant, Ruinart de Brimont, who had
purchased the ennobling office of *secrétaire du roi*. Of the Reims
council's 26 members in 1789, four were nobles and two were *secrétaires du roi*.[45]

Compared to the Reims council, resplendent with Old Regime
luminaries, the Troyes council appeared solidly representative of the
Third Estate. In 1788–89, five of every six Troyes councilmen were
members of the Third Estate, as opposed to only about one of every
two in Reims. Rival groups of nonnoble magistrates and merchants
overshadowed all others on the Troyes council. The mayor was
Claude Huez, the senior councillor in the Troyes bailliage court. He

had succeeded his father on the court in 1743.[46] Three other bailliage magistrates and two officials in the élection court also sat on the Troyes council. They were joined by eight merchants, including the two wealthiest textile merchants in the region, Fromageot and Berthelin. Berthelin, a nobleman, had been the mayor before Huez. His business partner and brother-in-law Fromageot had been the *procureur-syndic* for fifteen years prior to 1788.[47]

Whether noble or bourgeois, merchant or official, town councillors possessed considerably more property than most of their fellow townsmen. The Reims councillors paid three times the average property tax (*contribution foncière*), which was more than the tax paid by any social group except the nobles.[48] The marriage contracts made by the Troyes councillors were evaluated at nine times the value of the average marriage contract,[49] and three-fourths of the Troyes councillors were listed among the town's 340 highest taxpayers in 1791.[50] Thus we can describe the councilmen of Reims and Troyes as members of an economic elite.

In its composition each council reflected the alignment of forces in town. The Reims council reproduced a local society dominated by typically Old Regime groups: clerics from a rich and powerful local church; nobles of ancient vintage; and bourgeois, both merchants and officials, persistently and successfully buying their way into the ranks of the nobility. The Troyes council, on the other hand, resembled the governing bodies of nineteenth-century towns with their *grands notables* of merchants, landowners, and officials.[51]

Differences in the configurations of local politics can also be seen in the regional institutions headquartered in Reims and Troyes, the most prominent of which were the bailliage courts.[52] Although the bailliage courts of both towns had the same kinds of jurisdictions and judicial functions, i.e., the same place in the national bureaucracy, their places within the local communities differed greatly. In 1789 there were fewer officeholders in the Reims court (9) than in the Troyes court (16); however, more of the Reims magistrates held offices above the rank of "councillor" and more of them were nobles than was the case in Troyes. At least a third of the Reims magistrates were noble, as opposed to only an eighth of the Troyes magistrates.[53]

The Reims court had close ties with the law faculty of the university (two members were on the faculty),[54] and it is possible that the presence of a prestigious university law faculty was in part responsible for the aristocratic makeup of the Reims court, for its fame drew students and faculty from many parts of France. Whatever the reason, the Reims court attracted many nobles to local judicial office, whereas the Troyes court remained the bailiwick of local *roturier* families for whom judicial office was the crowning glory of their careers.

This fundamental difference between the courts in Reims and Troyes was not new in 1789. During the period 1750–89 only seven men bought the office of councillor in Reims whereas fifteen did so in Troyes.[55] The disparity is significant because the office of councillor was the one most accessible to local nonnoble families. It was not the result of lower price for office in Troyes, since the buyers there paid a higher finance charge than the buyers in Reims.[56] Apparently, the Reims bailliage court was less attractive as an investment in status for nonnobles than its Troyes counterpart because the Reims church courts had jurisdiction over most of the town and much of the region. Nonnobles in Reims bought offices elsewhere, leaving many of the councillorships in the bailliage court vacant for years at a time. The higher bailliage court offices of lieutenant and president, on the other hand, never lacked interested buyers and were traditionally considered by the Reims nobility as suitable places for their sons.[57] Despite the example of local noble families, bourgeois families in Reims did not establish as strong a tradition of judicial officeholding as did their Troyes counterparts.

The pattern of social mobility in the Reims court consequently differed markedly from that in the Troyes court. Nonnobles in Reims, if they bought office in the bailliage court at all, usually did so after service in some other capacity; bailliage office gave added luster to an already distinguished career. Among the seven *rémois* buying the office of councillor between 1750 and 1789 were a law professor, a lieutenant of the maréchaussée, a king's proctor in the élection court, and a president of the *grenier à sel*. As a result of the pattern of late purchase, most of the new councillors were relatively old when they took up office—their median age was 46. And not one of the seven Reims magistrates succeeded a relative in office or had relatives on the court. This was in marked contrast to Troyes, where two of the fifteen new councillors in the period 1750–89 succeeded their fathers, and two others had uncles on the court. Moreover, the median age of the Troyes councillors upon taking office was 29.

Neither court served as an escalator for social mobility, however. In Troyes, the same nonnoble families dominated the court for generations if not centuries, and they did not readily admit newcomers to their ranks. The Comparots, the Corrards, the Huez, and the Sourdats all had provided at least two generations of magistrates, and together they formed a tight-knit group that not only controlled the bailliage and élection courts but also aimed to dominate town affairs through the council. Merchants did not find the doors to judicial office easy to open in either town, and I have found only one magistrate whose father was a merchant. Merchants in Troyes and Reims turned elsewhere for recognition; those who were wealthy enough bought ennobling offices in Paris or in other regional courts.[58]

Although office in the bailliage court represented the highest regional status for a nonnoble, it rarely served as a stepping-stone to the satisfaction of nationally oriented ambitions prior to the Revolution. Only one officeholder, a *troyen*, was ennobled during his years of service on the court,[59] and few men moved on to more prestigious positions. Despite some differences, membership in the bailliage courts in towns with sovereign courts was also quite stable. Montpellier, for example, had a *cour des comptes, aides et finances*, so the *sénéchaussée* court (the southern equivalent of the bailliage) was not the apex of the local officeholding hierarchy. Instead, the sénéchaussée served as the consolation prize for the younger sons of families holding office in the Cour des Comptes: of the 22 men who purchased the office of councillor in the sénéchaussée between 1750 and 1789, at least nine came from families of the Cour des Comptes.[60] Yet as in Troyes and Reims, the Montpellier councillors rarely graduated to office in more important courts: only one councillor in the last half of the eighteenth century moved up to the Cour des

Comptes. Although more offices were sold in the Montpellier court in this period than in either Troyes or Reims, the buyers held them just about as long in Montpellier as in Reims.[61]

Since offices in the bailliage courts of Troyes and Reims were the plums of the local judicial hierarchy, their owners were considered and certainly considered themselves natural leaders of the community. Their numbers on both town councils reflected this shared perception of their high social status. But because the courts differed in their social function within the community, the magistrates as a group related differently to other prominent urban groups. Noble and nonnoble officials mixed well on the bailliage court of Reims, and together they joined the wholesale merchants and a few high-ranking members of the liberal professions to form a relatively cohesive though heterogeneous group of lay notables on the town council. The magistrates of Troyes, on the other hand, formed a more separate and distinct group than did their Reims colleagues, precisely because they were more exclusively bourgeois. In Troyes, nobles, officeholders, merchants, doctors, and lawyers did share control of the town council, but as a group they were not as socially coherent as their counterparts in Reims. Residential patterns indicate this difference.

As an indicator of the residential patterns of the local political rulers, I have determined the addresses of men holding office in the town councils, the bailliage and élection courts, and the maréchaussée, as well as the addresses of the chief police magistrates and the subdelegates.[62] Other men might qualify as "rulers," but the officeholders considered here were certainly the most powerful. In both towns, the rulers congregated in the medieval center: the parishes of Sainte Madeleine and Saint Jean in Troyes, and the parishes of Saint Hilaire and Saint Pierre in Reims. Of the 40 rulers whose addresses are known in Reims (87 percent of the total of 46 rulers), 36 lived in the four center parishes, 26 of these in either Saint Hilaire or Saint Pierre (districts 2, 3, and 4 on Map 1). Of the 40 Troyes rulers whose addresses are known (77 percent of the total of 52 rulers), all but three lived in the parishes of Sainte Madeleine or of Saint Jean (one of the three lived out of town). Within the medieval

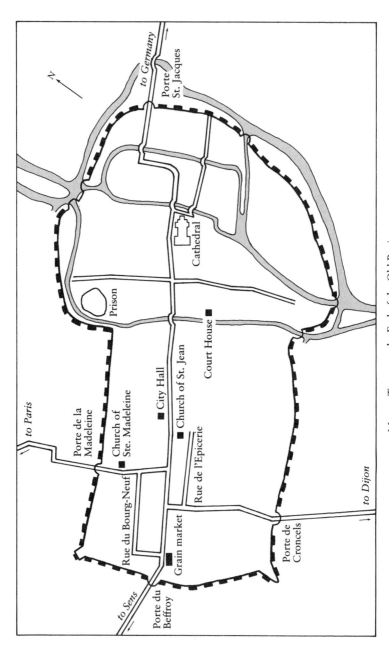

Map 2. Troyes at the End of the Old Regime

N

to Germany

Porte
St. Jacques

Cathedral

Prison

to Paris

Porte de la
Madeleine

Church of
Ste. Madeleine

City Hall

Church of St. Jean

Court House

Rue de l'Epicerie

Rue du Bourg-Neuf

to Dijon

Grain market

Porte de
Croncels

to Sens

Porte du
Beffroy

heart of Troyes, however, social groups were more segregated than in Reims. Ten royal officials lived on the rue du Bourg-Neuf in the parish of Sainte Madeleine in Troyes. Their social hub was the salon of Madame Comparot de Longsols, the wife of a bailliage magistrate and town council member. At her soirées, magistrates associated with nobles and clergymen; in 1787 they met there with the exiled members of the Parlement of Paris.[63] A few blocks away on the rue de l'Epicerie in the parish of Saint Jean, wealthy textile merchants held their own salons in the homes of mesdames Berthelin and Fromageot. (See Map 2.) These two adjoining but separate social centers were evidence of the division of the Troyes rules into parallel dynasties of magistrates and merchants.

There were no two streets in Reims comparable to the rue du Bourg-Neuf and the rue de l'Epicerie in Troyes. Nobles, magistrates, and merchants lived next door to each other in Reims: for example, the cloth manufacturer Ponsardin, the salt-tax collector Bourgogne, and the élection magistrate Folliet all resided on the rue de Cérès just around the corner from Cocquebert de Crouy, a noble member of the town council. When combined with the alluring presence of many resident nobles and upwardly mobile bourgeois, this social proximity made emulation of the nobility a powerful social glue in Reims. In Troyes, on the other hand, the conspicuous social cleavage within the living space of the bourgeoisie fostered the potential for intrabourgeois conflict.

Intermarriage helped close the gap somewhat between merchants and magistrates in Troyes. The most noteworthy examples of the links forged in this way were the marriages made by the subdelegate Pierre-Jean Paillot and his son, Louis-Nicolas. Old Paillot had married the sister of Berthelin, the noble textile merchant and mayor of Troyes before Huez. Louis-Nicolas Paillot, the child of this union, married Marie Harlan, whose father was a local tax official and whose mother was a Guérard (a Guérard was president of the élection court in Troyes). One of Marie's sisters married the noble commander of the local army garrison, and among Marie's cousins who signed the marriage contract were Comparot de Longsols, the influential bailliage magistrate, and two textile merchants, one of whom sat on the town council in the late 1770's and early 1780's.[64] Thus despite the history of competition between merchants and magistrates for hegemony in Troyes, merchant, official, and noble families were joined through marriage. In this instance we have seen how the subdelegate and his son were firmly tied through the dense web of marriage relations to local ruling family interests.

If intermarriage did not break down the rival dynasties of merchants and officials, it did at least prevent their differences from widening into an irreparable breach. Most merchants in the ruling group in fact married into other merchant families: five of the eight merchants on the 1788–89 Troyes council were sons of merchants (there is no information on the other three), and all but one had married daughters of merchants. These five merchants were related to at least one other merchant sitting on the council, yet four were also related through marriage to magistrate families. Similarly, most of the sixteen bailliage magistrates were the sons of royal officials, and ten were related to at least one other bailliage magistrate. At least one of the magistrates (Comparot de Longsols) had married the daughter of a merchant, however; and at least six others were related through marriage to ruling merchant families. In all, the marriage contracts affirm that at least 27 of the 52 rulers of Troyes in 1788–89 were related to each other through marriage. Marriage bonds cut across and therefore transcended economic and socioprofessional differences to unify the ruling group.[65]

As men of wealth, education, and leisure, the rulers of Troyes and Reims shared many social interests. Most of them owned luxurious town houses as well as country estates.[66] They attended salons; they prided themselves on their philanthropic endeavors; and some of them joined Masonic lodges. There were two Masonic lodges in Reims and one in Troyes before the Revolution. In Troyes participation seems to have been limited to a group of minor functionaries and members of the liberal professions. The Reims rulers were evidently more attracted to the fellowship provided by Masonry: included on the membership roles of the Triple Union lodge for 1787–88 were the subdelegate's son, two members of the town council (a doctor and a merchant), an official of the *maîtrise des eaux et forêts*, and two noble judges of the bailliage court. Most of the Reims rulers who joined lodges were young; only one was over 50 years old. Whereas fewer than a third of the members of the Troyes Union of Sincerity lodge were merchants, in Reims nearly half of the members of the Triple Union lodge and some two-thirds of the members of the Perfect Friendship lodge represented commerce and industry. Thus, like residential patterns, the Masonic lodges reflected many of the critical differences between the ruling groups of Reims and Troyes: the Reims lodges brought nobles, officials, and merchants together, thereby giving the ruling group another element of cohesion; at the same time they offered individual rulers a way of identifying themselves with "progressive ideas." A local opposition faction was hardly likely to take shape in lodges frequented by such preeminent families as the Mopinots, the Sutaines, the Tronssons, or the Clicquots. The Troyes rulers, by contrast, showed little interest in Masonry; they held themselves aloof from any newfangled notions and, as a consequence, left the field open to their potential opponents. Five of the 32 Masons listed on the rolls of the Union of Sincerity lodge for 1787 later became members either of the revolutionary committee of 1789 or of the new government of 1790.[67]

The scanty information available suggests that the rulers of Troyes and Reims read the same books—whatever their particular political opinions. The departmental archives in Troyes contain library catalogs for three bailliage magistrates drawn up by local officials as part of the investigation of suspects, *émigrés*, and condemned men in the year II (1793–94).[68] Although few in number, the catalogs are interesting because the three magistrates took dramatically different political paths in 1789. Jean-Baptiste Comparot de Longsols, 48 years old in 1789, was the recognized social leader of the prerevolutionary ruling group. During the opening months of the Revolution, Comparot evaded making political choices by leaving town during the weeks of greatest tumult. Jacques Truelle de Chambouzon, who was 60 years old in 1789, became president of the revolutionary committee in Troyes. Nicolas Parent, the youngest of the three at 34, became the leading apologist of the counterrevolution in Troyes. Despite their different political orientations, their reading tastes were much alike.

None of the three magistrates showed much interest in theology or devotional literature; all possessed relatively large collections of dictionaries, grammars, plays, novels, and periodical literature (belles-lettres). In both these ways, the provincial libraries echoed a trend toward the desacralization of society that others have detected on the national level.[69] These Troyes magistrates manifested interests somewhat different from those of national professional groups, however (see Table 5). They had fewer titles in history and in sciences and arts than the magistrates in the Parlement of Paris or the Farmers-General, and more in what might be termed "entertainment literature." With some exceptions, the catalogs show the Troyes magistrates to have been distinctly "provincial" in their tastes: they were not abreast of the new publications on political economy, agricultural improvements, or the problems created by manufacturing. They collected books of professional interest (law) and literature for amusement.

The three Troyes magistrates did show an interest in Enlightenment authors. Comparot, the most politically "traditional," possessed only Rousseau's *Confessions*. Parent had several titles: *De l'esprit* of Helvétius; Voltaire's *Annales de l'Empire*; Montesquieu's *Esprit des lois*; Rousseau's *Émile* and *Lettres de la montagne*; and Diderot's *Entretiens sur le fils naturel*. Truelle de Chambouzon, the only magistrate in the Troyes court who actively supported the Revolution in 1789, owned the largest and most systematic collection of works by the *philosophes*: three volumes of the works of Montesquieu; 68 volumes of the works of Voltaire; nineteen volumes of the works of Rousseau, including five of the *Confessions*; 39 volumes of the *Encyclopédie*; and four volumes of Bayle's *Dictionnaire historique*. Nevertheless, interest in the Enlightenment did not necessarily correlate with support for the Revolution, since representatives of both sides in 1789 (Parent on one, Truelle on the other) demonstrated Enlightenment tastes in their library collections. Moreover, all three became suspect during the Terror, including the hero of

TABLE 5

A Comparison of the Libraries of Three Troyes Magistrates, the
Magistrates of the Parlement of Paris, and the Farmers-General
at the End of the Old Regime

(In percentages of five types of books)

	Types of books					
Library owner	Theology	Law	History	Sciences and Arts	Belles-Lettres	Total
Troyes magistrates	4%	17%	26%	10%	43%	100%
Comparot (N = 333)	4	10	37	8	42	101
Parent (N = 167)	6	26	25	7	37	101
Truelle (N = 233)	3	21	11	16	49	100
Members of the Parlement of Paris	12	22	32	20	14	100
Farmers-General	6	7	35	27	34	109

SOURCES: For the Troyes libraries, library catalogs or inventories located in the dossiers for Comparot de Longsols (4Q/14), Parent (4Q/105), and Truelle de Chambouzon (4Q/79) in A.D. Aube, série 4Q, "dossiers des émigrés." For the *parlementaires*, François Bluche, *Les Magistrats du Parlement de Paris au XVIIIe siècle, 1715–1771* (Besançon, 1960), p. 291. For the Farmers-General, Yves Durand, *Les Fermiers généraux au XVIIIe siècle* (Paris, 1971), p. 562.

NOTE: The five types of books are categories developed by François Furet and expounded in "La 'Librairie' du royaume de France au 18e siècle," *Livre et société dans la France du XVIIIe siècle*, vol. 1 (Paris, 1965), pp. 3–33. The figure of 109 percent at the base of the last column apparently stems from Durand's having included some books in more than one category.

1789, Truelle. However, we can conjecture that a predilection for Enlightenment authors accompanied a strong interest in politics per se.

In their daily lives the rulers of Troyes and Reims had almost nothing in common with the toiling masses of their towns. The rulers lived in well-appointed houses whose value might run as high as 15,000 livres or more.[70] The average journeyman weaver, on the other hand, inhabited a ramshackle dwelling with perhaps two rooms and a cellar, where he kept his loom and worked every day. One of the two rooms upstairs would serve as a kitchen, and the other would serve as a common room for the rest of the family's activities. A master artisan might have a grain storage area (*grenier*) in addition, but the basic living unit was much the same. In the best of times, textile workers earned from five to ten sous (a quarter to a half livre) a day. Most artisans earned no more than two livres a day. The income of Claude Huez, the mayor of Troyes in 1789, was estimated at 6,000 to 7,000 livres a year—or 40 times the yearly income of a textile worker. Berthelin, the noble textile merchant, withdrew an average of 26,000 livres a year from his business for his personal use.[71] Although there was a range of wealth within the ruling circles, all of them knew the comforts and pleasures of the good life.

The ruling groups were neither homogeneous nor monolithic— except perhaps in their attitudes toward the lower classes. Their social harmony could be disturbed by discordant economic forces and social values. The merchants depended more exclusively on liquid capital than did the landowning nobles and bourgeois officials,[72] and their social status thus flowed from a different source: the merchants gained access to the ruling group in the end because they had wealth to offer. Supposedly the most divisive social distinction under the Old Regime was the legal boundary dividing nobles and bourgeois, for it cut across merchants and officials. Yet this line was not fixed, and it does not appear to have become inflexible in the 1780's. Bourgeois merchants and officials regularly entered the Second Estate, even in Troyes. As we have seen, between 1760 and 1789 the Bureau des Finances in Châlons-sur-Marne recorded letters of nobility for nine men (three per decade, as it happened): two royal officials, two merchants, one militia captain, and one writer in Reims; and two merchants and one royal official in Troyes.

Although political conflict did on occasion endanger the ruling group's unity, conflict was always regulated, either by the rulers themselves or, in extreme cases, by the central government. Factional strife between merchants and officials abated whenever the rulers were threatened from the outside. When the monarchy created new offices, the rulers pooled their resources, and those of their fellow townspeople, to buy them up. And when the townspeople rioted in reaction to high prices and unemployment, the rulers organized emergency committees to find food and to direct local repressive efforts.[73] External threats such as government intervention and food riots intensified and reinforced ruling group solidarity and cooperation, for it was in response to such threats that the rulers became conscious of themselves and their interests as a group. This happened periodically during the Old Regime, but the rulers emerged most clearly as a group, both in the minds of the rulers and the ruled, in the years of crisis preceding the Revolution. This will be the subject of the next chapter.

IV

For all their differences, we can characterize the rulers of Troyes and Reims as political elites composed of local notables. They were elites—i.e., narrow and powerful cliques—because admission to their circle, though not closed, was carefully circumscribed. By the middle of the eighteenth century, wholesale merchants, lawyers, and doctors had been integrated into the ruling circle of royal officials and noblemen. Wealth and professional affiliation were not magic passwords, however; only family connection could definitively open the door to political position. Once a merchant became wealthy or a doctor prestigious, he could marry his way into the ruling circle if the other rulers found him acceptable. Town elections did not occasion the arbitrary rotation of elites; the members of the political elite themselves chose their partners and successors, and they "naturally" chose the men who shared their family interests.

I call the rulers local notables because they included nobles and nonnobles. Once selected for office, local rulers developed a community of interest based on the demands of ruling: ruling linked noble and bourgeois, landowner and merchant; and their social alliances buttressed this pragmatic understanding.[74] Political interests overshadowed underlying economic and status distinctions.

Thus, though quarrels between nobles and nonnobles, old nobles and new nobles might plague national institutions such as the army and the sovereign courts, local rulers had learned to adapt to the new social values nurtured by capitalism and urbanization. Nobles and nonnobles learned how to rule in tandem on the local level in order to defend a social system based on property and family. This accommodation was not possible everywhere. In the towns with sovereign courts, and especially in those towns with parlements, there were too many nobles and there was too much vested interest in noble-dominated institutions for such a political merger between nobles and nonnobles to take place. Consequently, towns such as Dijon and Rennes had to await the Revolution and its destruction of the parlements before local elites could fashion a society of notables. But in Reims and Troyes and towns like them, the political style usually associated with nineteenth-century French politics first took shape in the final decades of the Old Regime. In this, as in the Revolution itself, the towns took the lead.

Although Troyes and Reims were not uniform cogs in some kind of efficient national political machine, the rules governing their political structures at the end of the Old Regime were quite clear. There was a local political "system" whereby certain groups controlled local politics through kinship alliances and cooptation. The local political code differed from that on the national level, in part because there was no evident locus of national politics. Consequently, each town developed its own characteristic political amalgam, whose constitution depended on the alignment of local economic and social forces. Local political systems did not take form in a vacuum, nor were they in any sense independent of social structures. They grew out of specific historical conditions such as the structure of the economy, the implantation of privileged groups, and the evolution of patterns of officeholding. Some of these factors were of the "longue durée"; others were the result of monarchical whim. What matters is that they eventually contributed to the molding of coherent, distinct political structures that were at once a part of and the regulators of local society. Thus the rulers of Troyes and Reims could face the difficult years after 1787 with the confidence conferred by long-standing, though hardly immutable, organization.

CHAPTER 3

Local Mobilization of Discontent

~~~~

ALTHOUGH IT WAS neither predicted nor plotted, the Revolution of 1789 did not come without warning, for signs of imminent upheaval began to accumulate after 1787. First the textile market collapsed, leaving thousands of men, women, and children unemployed. Then in 1788 the price of grain began to climb inexorably. At the same time, the national government was experimenting with a hodgepodge of administrative and political reforms designed to avert impending national bankruptcy. Taken together, the economic crisis and political tinkering bred an atmosphere of urgency. Many people began to sense the shakiness of the Old Regime months before it actually fell apart, and in the midst of emergency efforts to hold the crumbling regime together they gained invaluable political experience. Without the multiple crisis and the resulting political education, the Revolution would not have occurred.

The crisis of 1787–89 was national, even though some regions suffered more than others and certain regions took the lead in opposing crown reforms. It was national because the regime's dysfunction originated in the national fiscal machinery: all else followed from the realization that the crown could not pay the interest on its debts. With its increasingly desperate attempts to develop new sources of revenue, with its revival of some nearly extinct institutions and its invention of a few new ones, the crown eventually drew all the regions of France into its orbit of crisis. However unsuccessful the regime's improvisations were, they awakened local interest in national politics; and when they failed, the crown finally agreed to convoke the Estates General and invited all Frenchmen to air their grievances.

In its eleventh hour the crown thus nationalized awareness of the constitutional breakdown.

Like the constitutional crisis, the economic crisis was national in scope. Although the economic pinch hurt the northern half of France more than the southern half, the textile market declined everywhere and the price of grain rose, for the marketplace was in some sense national. Champagne experienced the crisis of 1787–89 in much the same way the other provinces in northern France did—especially the other provinces of the *pays d'élections*. Local economies in northern textile towns such as Rouen, Amiens, Orléans, and Caen were crippled by declining demand; and the same new institutions were introduced in all of them to direct local economic and political recovery efforts.

I

The earliest and most serious long-term economic problem facing local leaders in Troyes and Reims was the depression in the textile market, which began in 1787. The causes of the depression remain subject to dispute, but overproduction combined with English competition seem the most likely ones.[1] In 1779, the national government had given in to merchant pressure and relaxed restrictions on the production of cloth in the countryside (i.e., outside the guild structure). As a result, greater and greater quantities of lower-quality cloth were produced by virtually unskilled rural laborers, and prices and wages were kept low. Nonetheless, when in 1786 France signed a free trade treaty with England that allowed English textiles to enter the French market without restraint, French cloth could not compete with the even more cheaply manufactured English cloth because the French industry was not as mechanized as the English industry. Demand consequently ebbed rapidly after the high-water mark of 1786.[2] Merchants in Troyes and Reims refused to buy the cloth being produced, and the textile workers were left without a livelihood.

The effects were immediately catastrophic in Troyes: by the middle of 1788, only 1,117 handlooms were in operation (a reduction to just over 40 percent of capacity); by October, more than 10,200 textile workers were without work.[3] Some 6,000 of these unemployed workers eventually left Troyes to return to their homes in the countryside, but the remainder stayed in the town, starving. The crisis enhanced the contradictions between the interests of the merchants and those of the workers, and it sharpened the workers' perception of those contradictions. The intendant of Champagne, Rouillé d'Orfeuil, described the situation to the comptroller-general of finances on August 17, 1788:

My subdelegate in Troyes has just informed me that the position of manufacturing in that town is becoming more critical than ever; the journeymen and workers are beginning to grumble, and they are even putting up placards in which they threaten to burn down the merchants who refuse to buy. The latter find themselves in great difficulty because of the recent bankruptcy in England of a company that bought our best cottons last year. . . . The result is that the merchants of Troyes, whose warehouses are full and who do not wish to sell their cottons at a loss—in three weeks, they say, the price has declined by 30 to 40 percent—hardly buy any more. On his side the clothier, who sells only to live, is obliged to sell his merchandise at a loss and to lay off the workers that he can no longer employ.

You can imagine how alarming the situation is in Troyes; we fear with some reason that next winter will be stormy. . . . We must establish public workshops where each worker will be assured of finding work and a resource against misery. This would be, in fact, the most sure means of quieting spirits, and it could not be put into effect too soon in order to remove any pretext for complaint and discontent.

But while waiting for some disposition of this subject, the municipal officials of Troyes have believed it necessary to establish day and night patrols in order to overawe the evil-minded and to keep all of the workers within the just limits of Duty and Subordination.[4]

Despite official efforts, the tension and antagonism continued unabated in Troyes for more than a year.

The crisis in Reims was less disastrous, for though in mid-1788, 300 handlooms were silent and 3,000 workers were unemployed, all but 600 of the workers returned to their home villages. The inspector of manufactures, Taillardat de Sainte-Gemme, noted that the clothiers of Reims continued to provide work despite the slump in demand: "Production has not diminished as much as one might have thought; the clothiers of this town, who are generally prosperous, have mustered all of their means in order to support the greatest

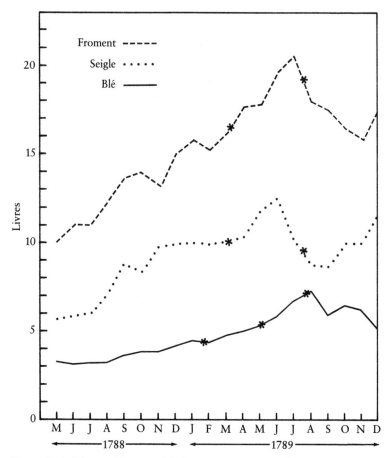

Fig. 3. Grain Prices at Troyes and Reims, May 1788–December 1789. Prices are given per *septier* for Reims (*froment* and *seigle*) and per *boisseau* for Troyes (*blé*). Asterisks mark the occurrences of food riots in 1789: at Reims on March 11 and July 22; at Troyes on January 25, May 4, and July 18–20. The figures for Reims are from Walter Elliott Schaap, "Etude du mouvement des prix des céréales dans quelques villes de la généralité de Champagne pendant les années qui précèdent la Révolution," *Assemblée générale de la Commission centrale et des comités départementaux*, 1939 (Besançon and Paris, 1942–45), vol. 2, pp. 37–71, table 7. The figures for Troyes are from Julien Ricommard, *La Lieutenance générale de police à Troyes au XVIIIᵉ siècle* (Paris, 1934), graph 3.

number of their workers."[5] The clothiers had invested in hand-looms, and that made withdrawal from the market difficult. They and their workers were able to weather the crisis because the market for wool improved in 1788 and 1789. The cotton industry in Troyes, on the other hand, never regained its position of the early 1780's: Troyes calicoes lost out to Lancashire cottons, and after the Revolution *bonneterie* became the dominant industry in Troyes. English competition did not menace the woolen industry in Champagne because mechanization advanced slowly and fitfully in the production of woolen cloth.

Textile slumps often provoked food riots. In 1770, for example, a major food riot had erupted in Reims during a period of depression in the textile industry. Food riots intensified in number and gravity in 1789, when inflated bread prices were added to the already dire manufacturing crisis. Three food riots shook Troyes between January and July of 1789; Reims had two during the same period. The extent of the price rise feeding discontent can be seen in Figure 3. Between May 1788 and the second half of June 1789, the price of *froment* (first-quality wheat) in Reims rose 112 percent from 10 livres per *septier* to 21.2 livres per *septier*. The price increase for rye (*seigle*) was even greater—141 percent—over the same period. In Troyes, the cost of first- and second-quality bread rose by 28 percent and 41 percent, respectively, between the late summer of 1788 and late June 1789. What was worse, the price of raw wheat—*blé*— jumped by 230 percent between June 1788 and July 1789.* For textile workers and poor artisans, who were barely able to subsist in normal times, these price rises were calamitous. Coupled with un-employment, they meant starvation for thousands.[6]

The effects of the economic crisis can also be seen in demographic records. As workers left town and future prospects dimmed, fewer people married and fewer had children (see Table 6).[7] The decline in Reims came later than in Troyes—probably because the economic squeeze in Reims was less tight. Yet in both towns people reacted quickly to their reduced circumstances.

*Bread prices did not rise as rapidly as grain prices because the chief police magistrate officially controlled bread prices.

TABLE 6

*Marriages, Births, and Deaths in Troyes and Reims
in the Last Decade of the Old Regime*

Year	Marriages		Births		Deaths	
	Troyes	Reims	Troyes	Reims	Troyes	Reims
1780	190	282	1,284	1,521	1,099	1,257
1781	229	288	1,194	1,437	937	1,263
1782	232	327	1,215	1,532	1,109	1,181
1783	214	316	1,181	1,592	1,125	1,240
1784	273	267	1,176	1,474	1,501	1,179
1785	305	285	1,224	1,481	1,517	1,152
1786	420	328	1,340	1,568	979	1,078
1787	308	337	1,409	1,588	1,054	1,001
1788	228	287	1,355	1,625	1,156	1,159
1789	175	243	1,201	1,389	1,061	1,231

SOURCES: For Troyes, the marriage figures are from the *Almanach de Troyes* for the years 1780–89, and the birth and death figures are from Albert Babeau, *La Population de Troyes au dix-huitième siècle* (Troyes, 1873), p. 23; for Reims, all figures are from A.C. Reims, *états civils*.

NOTE: The parish of Saint Denis in Reims did not have records for the years 1783–85, so I estimated the numbers for that parish on the basis of earlier records. I also estimated the number of deaths for those parishes recording deaths only for boys and girls over ten; in this case I used the ratio of infant deaths to total mortality in parishes that had records for both.

Food shortages and textile depressions did not necessarily precipitate revolutions. Revolution did not occur in June 1789, when prices were higher than ever before. When the mixture of textile crisis and high bread prices exploded in July, it did so because it had been detonated by the national constitutional crisis. Food riots in July threatened the structure of government, not just the houses of grain merchants; and they had that political effect in July because the atmosphere in the towns was not only tense but politicized. The timing of the Revolution cannot be explained without this background of spreading political consciousness.

II

The crown's reforms of the late 1770's and 1780's chiefly concerned those segments of the urban population most closely connected to the local ruling elites. The most important innovation was the establishment of provincial assemblies, begun as an experiment in Berry in 1778, in Haute-Guyenne and Dauphiné in 1779, and in the Bourbonnais in 1781, and extended throughout most of the *pays d'élections* in 1787. There were three levels of assemblies within each province: assemblies for the parishes, for the élections (tax districts), and for the province as a whole. In all of these assemblies, the Third Estate had as many deputies as the first two estates combined ("doubling of the third"), and voting was by head rather than by order. Each estate met separately, however. The Assembly of Notables approved this potentially sweeping reform with enthusiasm because it gave them an institutionalized participation in regional and local politics and an effective base of opposition to the intendants. Moreover, the notables and the ministers expected that many Third Estate deputies would in fact be chosen from the clergy and the nobility. Although elections were to be scheduled in 1790, in 1787 the king himself named half of the members of the provincial assemblies, and they then chose the other half themselves.[8]

The provincial assemblies were designed to be responsible for the assessment and collection of the *taille*, the *vingtième*, and the *capitation*, and for the distribution of funds for public works and poor relief. They were introduced to counter the powers of the intendants and of the parlements in the provinces, but they never became viable political alternatives because they met only once, in the late fall of 1787.[9] The special commissions (*commissions intermédiaires*) that were set up to carry on the business of the provincial assemblies continued to meet, as did the assemblies at the élection level, but their authority remained limited and ill-defined.

The provincial assembly of Champagne began meeting in Châlons-sur-Marne on November 17, 1787, under the presidency of the archbishop of Reims, Alexandre-Angélique de Talleyrand-Périgord. The assembly included twelve clergymen, twelve nobles, and 24 "propriétaires des villes et campagnes."[10] The three deputies for the Third Estate from Troyes and Reims were all members of the ruling elite: Souyn, the noble *lieutenant des habitants* (or mayor) of Reims; Huez, the mayor of Troyes; and Fromageot, the wealthy Troyes textile merchant who had been *procureur-syndic* for several years. It is likely that the deputies from the other towns were equally influential; seven of them were mayors or former mayors.

The élection assemblies in Champagne, which met in large towns such as Troyes and Reims, were responsible for taxation and public works on the local level. The selection procedure for them paralleled that for the provincial assembly itself: for each élection, the provincial assembly chose three clergymen, three nobles, and six deputies for the Third Estate, and these twelve then named an equal number to join them. Six of the twelve Third Estate deputies for the élection headquartered at Troyes were members of the 1788–89 Troyes ruling elite; most of the others were probably rurally based landowners.[11] Only three of the twelve Third Estate deputies in the Reims assembly were residents of Reims: the chief police magistrate (a noble) and two merchants who were former town council members. The others were landowners from nearby villages.[12] Like the provincial assembly, the élection assemblies were dominated by the local social elites.

Despite their limitations, the assemblies did provide the local elites with new political experience. This was especially true at the parish level, where assemblies were established in those villages that did not already have municipalities. At the élection and provincial levels, commissions gathered information on local agricultural and industrial problems and conditions, and as a consequence the members of these new bodies became familiar with a wide range of economic and social questions. In addition, the deputies became involved in debates over taxation and in conflicts between rural and urban areas. But the operation of the assemblies did not deviate from the principles and values of the established social hierarchy.[13] Those who manned the new organizations did not intend to open up politics to other groups. Given their brief time of operation and their restrictions on membership, the new local assemblies could not significantly alter the political system of the Old Regime.

Local responses to the other national administrative reforms were also limited in scope. The calling of the Assembly of Notables in 1787 rejuvenated the national political aspirations of local elites, and interest in national politics expanded with each new development in Paris. Yet, for the most part political interest was confined to those members of local elites who had some tie to either the national administration or the judicial bureaucracy. In all the parlementary towns, the crown's struggle with the local parlement stimulated great excitement; elsewhere, though, attention was riveted on the great parlement, the Parlement of Paris. The leaders of the movement in support of the Parlement of Paris were local judicial officeholders, usually magistrates in the bailliage courts. The same men led resistance to the local judicial innovations of 1788, and in both instances they were defending their own corporate interests.[14] Other townspeople followed the ups and downs of the contest, but in non-parlementary towns such as Troyes and Reims they watched from the sidelines. Although none of the government's reforms took root, they nevertheless accomplished one thing: they made many people aware of the need for, and the possibility of, change.

III

Revolution came only after most of the population had been politicized, i.e., after people everywhere started to feel directly concerned with the resolution of political issues. This process began in earnest when the king decided to summon the Estates General to confer with him about the nation's finances. Within a few months, the stopgap reforms and limited politicization of 1787–88 gave way to a deluge of political agitation. In the early months of 1789, Frenchmen rightly saw themselves entering a new era in which their voices would be heard and recognized. Michelet grasped the essence of the situation when he claimed that "la convocation des Etats-Généraux de 1789 est l'ère véritable de la naissance du peuple. Elle appela le peuple tout entier à l'exercice de ses droits."[15]

The method for selecting deputies to the Estates General was set out in the royal "Règlement," or rule for convocation, published on January 24, 1789. Members of the First and Second Estates were to assemble in the chief town of their bailliage (or sénéchaussée), formulate their grievance lists, and select delegates to travel to Versailles.[16] The situation with regard to the Third Estate was somewhat more complicated. In the large towns, such as Troyes and Reims, preliminary meetings were held in two stages. First the corporations met. There were 45 of them in Troyes and 41 in Reims, and each one drew up a list of grievances and chose delegates to attend the town meeting, the second stage. At the town meeting, new lists of grievances were drawn up and delegates were selected to attend the bailliage meeting of the Third Estate. Since both Troyes and Reims were bailliage seats, they hosted the assemblies of clergy, nobility, and Third Estate for their respective regions. It was at these latter meetings that the actual delegates to the Estates General were chosen and the general grievance lists of each order formulated. Yet at all of the meetings, from the corporate to the bailliage level, grievance lists were written and deputies elected. Frenchmen thus enjoyed an unusual series of opportunities to meet together and to express and discuss their opinions.

Excitement, anticipation, and tension filled the air by the spring of 1789. For over 150 years the Estates General had not been convoked by the kings of France. Now, almost overnight, scores of frankly political meetings were to take place in towns such as Troyes and Reims. As Table 7 shows, the month of March was filled with constant political activity.

Beset by economic dislocation, the residents of Troyes and Reims gathered to fulfill the tasks assigned by the king: the formulation of lists of grievances and the selection of deputies to carry the lists to the next meeting in the process. Both the lists and the elections give some indication of each group's analysis of current problems, but none of the lists includes either comprehensive criticism of the regime or plans for revolution. Nevertheless, the grievance lists can serve as a concrete basis for comparison of the different views and attitudes of the various social groups *in March of 1789*. Similarly, the election of deputies indicates which men were considered appropriate representatives of group opinion.

The grievance lists were not explicit ideological documents; therefore, political awareness or consciousness can only be inferred from the language, the order, and/or the number and kinds of demands made.[17] Here political awareness will be defined as the manifested perception of the need for political solutions to recognized problems.

The lists of the corporate groups in Troyes and Reims varied enormously. Some were long and detailed; others were very short. The kinds and numbers of demands also differed. Corporations al-

TABLE 7
Schedule of Electoral Meetings in Troyes and Reims

Event	Troyes	Reims
Delivery of the "Règlement" (rule for convocation) of January 24, 1789	February 13	February 17
Preliminary meetings of the Third Estate		
Corporation meetings	March 8–11	March 5–8
Town meetings	March 12–18	March 11–14
Meetings of the clergy, nobility, and Third Estate of the bailliage[a]	March 26–April 8	March 16–April 3

[a] The regular clergy, the chapters, and ecclesiastics not holding an office held preliminary assemblies to choose delegates to the general assembly of the clergy of the bailliage. The secular clergy met only on the bailliage level. See note 16.

most never made specific demands for changes in the local political system, except for demands concerned with taxation or the venality of offices. National government and taxation were the foci of attention since the lists were meant to serve as guidelines for the Estates General, which was to begin meeting in May.

Table 8 provides a short list of demands made by one or more corporate groups in Troyes and Reims that had political implications, i.e., their implementation would have significantly modified or even transformed the political system of the Old Regime. "National" demands were those addressed to the operation of the Estates General and the central government; they were explicitly political, but they did not concern local political (town) issues. Demands for changes in taxation, on the other hand, were very important on the local level since taxes were one of the most visible local signs of the presence of government. "General" demands concerned the operation of society, both nationally and locally. The twelve demands in Table 8 were deliberately chosen to reflect different levels and kinds of problems: some were abstract and principled; others were concrete and specific to a particular issue; all required fundamental constitutional and/or legislative changes. Demands pertaining to education, to religion, or to other areas not distinctly political have been excluded from the table—despite the fact that one could argue that

TABLE 8

Political Demands Made by Corporate Groups
in Troyes and Reims, 1789

National:
　　The Estates General should write a Constitution
　　Voting in the Estates General should be by head and not by order
　　The Estates General should meet periodically
　　The consent of the Estates General should be required for taxation
　　The king's ministers should be responsible to the Estates General
　　Provincial estates should be established in Champagne
　　Intendancies should be abolished

Taxation:
　　All three estates should be taxed in proportion to their income
　　The *aides* and the *gabelle* should be abolished

General:
　　Venal offices should be abolished
　　Seigneurial dues should be abolished
　　Members of the Third Estate should be allowed access to all offices

such demands had political implications insofar as their satisfaction would have required changes in the law. What I have tried to do in Table 8 is to construct a short list of demands whose political significance is clearly articulated. In the interest of brevity and clarity, I have chosen not to do a more complicated analysis, e.g., one with more demands, one with a more sophisticated measure of political significance, or one in which the order or rhetoric of the demands is considered.[18]

Though the number of political demands a group made does not necessarily indicate its desire for change, it may denote the range of questions on which that group deemed it necessary or legitimate to comment. In general, few corporations made a large number of political demands; they had been authorized to write grievance lists as corporate groups and consequently preferred to speak to issues directly affecting their group. The average for the 45 corporate grievance lists of Troyes was 3.2 political demands;* for the 41 corporate lists of Reims, 3.3 political demands. (For a corporation by corpora-

---

*The grievance list for the Prêtres de l'Oratoire has been excluded from the calculations for Troyes because they were not an officially recognized corporate group.

tion list, see Table 9.) Those groups with the largest numbers of political demands (7 to 10) usually also had the largest absolute numbers of demands (27 to 55). The length of their lists expressed a desire to be heard; the number of explicit political demands expressed an awareness of and an interest in general political problems.

In Table 10 I have grouped the corporations into four social and occupational categories, and I have then listed the percentage of each category making different numbers of the specifically political demands identified in Table 8. It is noteworthy that royal officials, members of the liberal professions, and small merchants and artisans all wrote lists with about the same average number of articles, even though the first two groups were much better educated than the third. Moreover, the royal officials demonstrated no more eagerness for political change than did the small merchants and artisans: two-thirds of the grievance lists of both the royal officials and the small merchants and artisans made three demands or less for political changes. Members of the liberal professions showed more interest in political change than did royal officials and artisans, but not nearly so much as the merchants and clothiers. The latter wrote much longer grievance lists and made many more political demands than any of the other groups. This evidence suggests that the merchants and clothiers were the least "defensive" social group in both towns.*
They were not dependent on their corporate status; they even benefited from the disintegration of the guild structure. Unlike the royal officials, they did not depend on the ownership of an office for status. And though the merchants and clothiers gained economically under the Old Regime, their social status and economic well-being did not rest on the continuation of that regime. Consequently, the merchants and clothiers were in a good position to criticize the existing order without fear.

As might be expected, the four social and occupational groups did not give the same weight to the three types of political demands set

---

*The merchants and clothiers in Troyes did not see eye to eye on everything. The merchants defended manufacturing in the countryside, whereas the clothiers bitterly opposed it. Nevertheless, the merchants and clothiers expressed similar views on the broader social and political problems confronting them and the nation.

TABLE 9

The Corporations of Troyes and Reims Arranged by the Number of Political Demands in Their Grievance Lists and by Social Group

Corporation	Total demands	Corporation	Total demands
7–10 POLITICAL DEMANDS		Maçons, torcheurs (T)	12
Royal officials		Menuisiers, tourneurs (R)	19
Election (R)	47	Tâpissiers, miroitiers (T)	5
Liberal professions		**2–3 POLITICAL DEMANDS**	
Notaires (R)	40	*Royal officials*	
Notaires (T)	28	Grenier à sel (R)	5
Libraires-Imprimeurs (R)	36	Maîtrise des eaux	
Merchants & clothiers		et forêts (T)	15
Marchands (T)	46	*Liberal professions*	
Fabricants (R)	55	Maîtres en pharmacie (R)	9
Fabricants (T)	35	Commissaires (T)	6
Négoçiants, mds.		Avocats (R)	20
drapiers (R)	48	*Small merchants & artisans*	
Small merchants & artisans		Bouchers (T)	13
Cordonniers (T)	27	Cordonniers (R)	21
Boulangers (T)	27	Perruquiers (T)	8
Tailleurs (T)	33	Maçons, couvreurs (R)	18
Epiciers (R)	51	Serruriers, ferblantiers (R)	27
4–6 POLITICAL DEMANDS		Cordiers (T)	10
Royal officials		Perruquiers, barbiers (R)	10
Bailliage royal (R)	39	Tanneurs, corroyeurs (R)	17
Traites-Foraines (R)	12	Orfèvres, joailliers (T)	12
Liberal professions		Fondeurs,	
Procureurs (R)	22	chaudronniers (R)	11
Procureurs (T)	8	Tailleurs, fripiers (R)	17
Faculté de Droit (R)	16	Teinturiers (T)	3
Apothicaires (T)	10	Tondeurs (T)	12
Libraires-Imprimeurs (T)	15	Laboureurs (R)	16
Avocats (T)	18	Aubergistes, cafetiers (T)	3
Huissiers (R)	15	Boulangers (R)	14
Small merchants & artisans		Tanneurs, mégissiers (T)	4
Serruriers, taillandiers (T)	42	*Other*[a]	
Miroitiers, tâpissiers (R)	22	Prêtres de l'Oratoire (T)	11
Bonnetiers (R)	55	Habitants libres (R)	15
Bouchers (R)	10	Habitants libres (T)	8
Bonnetiers (T)	25	**1 POLITICAL DEMAND OR NONE**	
Couteliers, armuriers (R)	11	*Royal officials*	
Charpentiers (T)	13	Maîtrise des eaux	
Fondeurs,		et forêts (R)	9
chaudronniers (T)	17	Juridiction de	
Menuisiers, ébénistes (T)	16	Monnaies (R)	3

TABLE 9 (continued)

Corporation	Total demands	Corporation	Total demands
Maréchaussée (T)	2	Selliers, bourreliers (R)	7
Maréchaussée (R)	23	Cuisiniers-traiteurs (R)	3
Liberal professions		Charpentiers (R)	13
Juré-priseurs (T)	16	Compagnons des arts et	
Médecins (T)	6	métiers (T)	23
Médecins (R)	16	Couteliers, armuriers (T)	4
Chirurgiens (T)	4	Traiteurs, rotisseurs (T)	5
Chirurgiens (R)	1	Marchands vinaigriers (T)	2
Merchants & clothiers		Ouvriers charpentiers (R)	5
Négoçiants en gros (T)	9	Compagnons	
Juridiction consulaire (T)	6	bonnetiers (T)	2
Juridiction consulaire (R)	8	Encordeurs,	
Small merchants & artisans		charbonniers (T)	1
Orfèvres, horlogers (R)	15	Cartiers, papetiers (T)	4
Epiciers, ciriers (T)	19	*Other*[a]	
Aubergistes,		Bourgeois vivant	
cabaretiers (R)	4	noblement (T)	4
Selliers, bourreliers (T)	4		

SOURCES: For Reims, *Cahiers de doléances . . . Département de la Marne*, vol. 4, pp. 13–203; for Troyes, *Cahiers de doléances du bailliage de Troyes . . .* , vol. 1, pp. 1–197.

[a] Under the heading "Other" I have listed the four corporations that did not fit into the sociopolitical categories I devised for the present analysis.

TABLE 10

Percent of Corporations Making Different Numbers of Political Demands, by Social Group, Troyes and Reims, 1789

Social group	Percent of corporations making				Average no. of articles	No. of corporations
	7–10 political demands	4–6 political demands	2–3 political demands	1 political demand or none		
Royal officials	11%	22%	22%	45%	17	9
Liberal professions	17	39	17	27	16	18
Merchants & clothiers	80	–	–	20	39	5[a]
Small merchants & artisans	8	25	36	31	15	48

SOURCES: same as for Table 9.

[a] The grievance lists for the *Juridictions consulaires* have been eliminated because the men in these groups were both merchants and officials.

TABLE 11
Types and Average Numbers of Political Demands Made by
Social Groups, Troyes and Reims, 1789

Social group	Type of political demand			Ave. no. of political demands		
	National	Taxation	General	Reims	Troyes	Both towns
Royal officials	65%	17.5%	17.5%	2.8	1.5	2.6
Liberal professions	61	27	12	3.8	3.3	3.6
Merchants & clothiers	52	26	22	7.5	5.3	6.0
Small merchants & artisans	43	36	21	3.0	2.9	3.0

out in Table 8 (national, taxational, and general). Table 11 presents the percentages of each type of demand made by the four groups. From this table we can see that royal officials and members of the liberal professions concentrated on national political issues, whereas the small merchants and artisans showed the least interest in national issues and the most interest in taxation. It is important to note, however, that an interest in national political questions did not necessarily go hand in hand with a great desire for change: the high percentage of national political demands made by the royal officials, for instance, should not blind us to the fact that they made by far the fewest political demands of any kind (see the last three columns of Table 11).

Comparison of the average number of political demands made by the social groups in the two towns shows that despite some differences their rank order is the same. Corporate groups in Troyes and Reims generally manifested the same interests; noticeable variations often reflected concrete political or economic differences between the towns. For example, five of the artisanal corporations in Troyes demanded the abolition of the spinning jenny because its use led to unemployment.* None of the Reims corporations made this demand

*All five were artisanal groups of low status: tailors, shoemakers, joiners, journeymen of the arts and crafts, and journeymen stocking-makers. Nine corporate groups demanded the suppression of manufacturing in the countryside: the clothiers, the advocates, the notaries, the stocking-makers, the grocers, the tailors, the shoemakers, the locksmiths, and the smelters.

since the spinning jenny could not yet be used in the woolen industry.

None of the corporations writing grievance lists envisaged the transformation that was to come in the summer and fall of 1789. Yet everyone perceived the need for some kind of change, and the process of formulating grievances and electing deputies fostered the development of political awareness. Political consciousness burgeoned in the multiple meetings involving thousands of townspeople, and voices rarely heard in the town elections of the Old Regime now resounded through the local meeting halls.

Everyone was not included, however. Women were excluded, and a few corporations were not authorized to meet. Textile workers had little part in the proceedings. The rule for convocation divided the corporations into two groups: the corporations of the "liberal arts" (royal officials, legal professions, wholesale merchants, and manufacturers); and the "arts and crafts" corporations (the guilds of artisans and small merchants). The former were allotted two deputies for every hundred members; the latter, one per hundred. As a result, royal officials, members of the liberal professions, merchants, and manufacturers were disproportionately represented in the town meetings that followed.

Troyes and Reims each scheduled one meeting where those who had no corporate affiliation, the so-called *habitants libres*, were to elect one delegate to the full town meeting for every hundred men present. The assembly of *habitants libres* in Reims on March 6, 1789, attracted the first major political demonstration of the Revolution in Champagne. When the meeting began, only a few minor functionaries and "bourgeois" (property-owners with no profession) were present. But the meeting was soon invaded by a buzzing multitude of some 2,000 textile workers led by Hédoin de Pons Ludon, a notorious local crackpot.[19] For years Hédoin had been fighting legal battles with just about every court and official in Reims, and at one point he was even imprisoned for slandering a tribunal. He and his confederates asserted their right as inhabitants without corporate affiliation to join in the discussion of grievances and the election of delegates. After a grueling (and one might imagine tumultuous) session that lasted into the evening, the meeting was adjourned until March 9. Undeterred by the delay, Hédoin once more appeared at the head of hundreds of workers, and voting for delegates began. Although the textile workers outnumbered all the other interest groups in this assembly of 2,400, they only succeeded in electing Hédoin and one textile worker as deputies. Most of the other 22 deputies were solidly middle-class: three *rentiers*, two wood merchants, five wine merchants, two former merchants, one former official, two writers, one former lawyer (*procureur*), one retired military man (a *chevalier de Saint Louis*), a grocer, a military supplier, a glassmaker, and two cloth finishers (the aristocrats of the woolen artisanate). The textile workers did not possess the political know-how or discipline to turn their numbers to account and simply drifted away from the meeting once they had succeeded in electing Hédoin.[20] As a result, the grievance list of the *habitants libres* did not represent the interests of the Reims workers. It made only two of the political demands in Table 8: that provincial estates should be established in Champagne, and that all three estates should be taxed in proportion to their income. On their own the 24 deputies drew up a somewhat more radical list containing six political demands. The second (and later) grievance list showed greater interest in regional and national issues, and reflected the more highly developed political interests of the deputies.

The textile workers of Troyes made no attempt to force their way into the meeting of the local *habitants libres*, perhaps because they had two other opportunities to express their grievances: at the meeting of the "arts and crafts" journeymen, and at the meeting of the journeymen stocking-makers. Fewer than 400 men appeared at each of these two meetings, and the grievance lists compiled demonstrated little interest in issues other than those directly affecting the journeymen. The only political demand made by either group was for the suppression of the *aides* and the *gabelle*, the most limited of all the demands in Table 8. As we have seen, however, both groups joined the tailors, shoemakers, and joiners in requesting the abolition of the spinning jenny.

The corporate meetings in early March 1789 presented the textile workers of Troyes and Reims with their first opportunity for collective political activity, an opportunity they proved unable to make much of for lack of political organization and discipline. When the town meeting of the Third Estate opened in Reims on March 11, food riots broke out in the eastern districts of the city (districts 7 and 8 on Map 1). Thus the energy that only days before had been channeled into the meeting of the *habitants libres* now reverted to the more traditional form of poor people's protest. That these food riots were clearly political as well as economic was obvious from their timing; but a food riot could not deliver the direct political power that would enable the workers to secure redress for their grievances.

After the arrival of an army regiment from nearby Laon, the town meeting in Reims resumed. At the same time (March 12) meetings of the Third Estate began in Troyes under the presidency of the mayor, Claude Huez. The delegates (100 in Reims, 92 in Troyes), assembled in each town to select representatives for the bailliage meetings and to write a grievance list for the town. Table 12 shows the percentage of delegates from each of the four social and occupational groups set out in Tables 10 and 11. The most striking feature of Table 12 is the large percentage of delegates in both towns representing the small merchants and artisans. The representatives of this group had much more say in the town proceedings than they had ever had before, and this educated them for their role in the months to come. Nevertheless, when the delegates began by picking committees to draft grievance lists, they chose local notables: seven of the ten chosen in Troyes had held an office in the Old Regime ruling institutions, as had nine of the twelve in Reims. The Troyes committee comprised five merchants or clothiers and five officials or magistrates. Of the twelve committeemen in Reims, six were officials or magistrates and four were merchants or clothiers. All the men chosen to draw up the town grievance lists were subsequently elected as deputies to the bailliage meeting. Most of the others elected had also had political experience under the Old Regime. Few artisans and shopkeepers were chosen. Thus though the town meetings opened political office to some new faces (at least one-third of the town deputies never occupied posi-

TABLE 12

*Deputies to the Town Meetings Elected by the
Corporations in Troyes and Reims*

Social group	Percent elected in Reims (N = 100)	Percent elected in Troyes (N = 92)
Royal officials	14%	11%
Liberal professions	23	22
Merchants & clothiers	15	13
Small merchants & artisans	45	32
SUBTOTAL	97%	78%
Bourgeois	3%	2%
Occupations not ascertained	0	21
TOTAL	100%	101%

SOURCES: For Reims, *Cahiers de doléances . . . Département de la Marne*, vol. 4, pp. 204–6; for Troyes, *Cahiers de doléances du bailliage de Troyes . . .* , vol. 1, pp. 7–209.

NOTE: 73 of the 92 Troyes deputies were listed at the end of the individual *procès-verbal* of each corporate group. Almost all those not listed were delegates for corporations of artisans or shopkeepers.

tions in the Old Regime), there was no radical replacement of the local political leadership. Merchants, lawyers, and officials continued to dominate local politics (see Table 13, and compare Table 12).

Both town grievance lists were very long since the authors attempted to state every urban interest possible.[21] Both made the "national" political demands of voting by head, periodic meetings of the Estates General, taxation only with the consent of the nation, ministerial responsibility, and provincial estates for Champagne. Troyes demanded the abolition of the post of intendant as well. In taxation, both requested the abolition of the *aides* and the *gabelle* and the establishment of a proportional tax on all fortunes without exception. Likewise, both wanted reform of the civil and criminal codes, suppression of the *lettres de cachet*, and guarantees for freedom of the press. The Third Estate was to have access to all titles and offices. Only the Troyes list asked for the elimination of some seigneurial rights and dues.

In tone and spirit, however, the Reims list was more progressive, less pretentious, and certainly more to the point than the verbose and legalistically convoluted Troyes list. The Troyes list contained twice as many articles as the Reims list, not so much because its authors

TABLE 13

Deputies to the Bailliage-level Meetings Elected by the Town Meetings in Troyes and Reims

Social group	Percent elected in Reims (N = 30)	Percent elected in Troyes (N = 24)
Royal officials	20%	21%
Liberal professions	27	21
Merchants & clothiers	33	33
Small merchants & artisans	17	21
SUBTOTAL	97%	96%
Bourgeois	3%	4%
TOTAL	100%	100%

SOURCES: Same as for Table 12.

NOTE: 60 percent of the deputies elected from Reims, and 67 percent of those elected from Troyes, had held office under the Old Regime.

had more grievances to state but because its rhetoric was so labyrinthine. The difference in style is forcefully exemplified by the opening articles of the two lists. The first article of the Reims list minced no words: "Pénétré du respect le plus profond pour Sa Majesté Royale, le Tiers Etat demande que la distinction humiliante de ne parler au Roi qu'à genoux, soit supprimée." No translation could convey the character of the Troyes list's opening:

Que tout ce qui aura été statué, arrêté, consenti par les Etats généraux sur leur convocation, leur composition, le nombre des députés de chaque Ordre, la forme des délibérations (qu'elle entend être demandée par ses représentants par tête et non par ordre dans toutes les délibérations essentielles, particulièrement en matière d'impôts), la permanence au moins ou le retour périodique des Etats généraux, l'intervalle qui sera fixé entre les époques de ce retour dans le cas où la Nation ne jugerait pas à propos d'en fixer la permanence, et généralement tout ce qui a été reconnu par les ministres du roi et avoué en son nom comme droits incontestables de la Nation par le résultat de son Conseil du 27 décembre 1788, dont les dispositions sont rapportées ci-dessus, sera suivi et observé à perpétuité comme loi de l'Etat stable et inviolable. A l'effet de quoi, en vertu de l'autorité de Sa Majesté et du consentement libre desdits Etats généraux, le tout sera lu, publié, et registré dans toutes les cours et tribunaux, sans que lesdites cours et tribunaux puissent admettre et reconnaître aucuns édits, lettres patentes, et lois quelconques qui y seraient contraires.

This was hardly the introduction to a fiery manifesto; throughout, the Troyes list insistently emphasized legal procedures and the defense of legal prerogatives. One-third (62 articles) of the Troyes list was devoted to the "administration of justice," as opposed to less than one-fifth (17 articles) of the Reims list.[22] Neither list demanded the abolition of venality of office, yet only the Troyes list explicitly defended judicial offices.

The Reims list critized local government and consistently took the side of local merchants. One of its last articles repeated the demand of many corporations for modification of the local rule that only natives of the town were eligible for the town council and suggested that any citizen who lived in Reims fifteen years be considered eligible for municipal office. The town council added a disclaimer to the list stating their disapproval of this demand.[23] On questions of commerce and manufacturing, the Troyes list merely reiterated the claims on both sides—those of the artisans against manufacturing in the countryside and those of the merchants for its unhindered extension. In contrast, the Reims list almost always made the argument for commercial interest.

The most telling, though also the most subtle, difference between the two town lists was in language. The language of the Troyes list was traditional: the deputies of the three "orders" were all members of the same "family," and the king was their "father." The Reims list, too, was flavored by traditional concepts, but its discourse anticipated a new constitutional order in which the nation would be *re-established* as an equal partner with the king, and all citizens would share the burdens and responsibilities of government. The Reims list distinguished between king, state, Estates General, nation, and citizens—distinctions that were blurred in the Troyes list. Only legal concepts, not political ones, were clearly articulated by the Troyes authors.

Contrasts in language can be simply demonstrated by using three pairs of key words for comparison (see Table 14). Although the number of instances is small, the pattern is relatively plain. In every case, the Reims authors chose the "modern" (politically conscious, constitutional, or forward-looking) word more often than their

TABLE 14

Key Words in the Grievance Lists of Troyes and Reims

Key word pairs ("modern" word second)	Occurrences in Reims		Occurrences in Troyes	
	No.	Pct.	No.	Pct.
King (*Roi, Souverain*, etc.)	8	42%	32	67%
Nation (or *Nation assemblée*)	11	58	16	33
Subject	1	11	2	18
Citizen (or *Français*)	8	89	9	82
Orders (in reference to society of orders)	4	67	11	73
People	2	33	4	27

SOURCES: *Cahiers de doléances . . . Département de la Marne*, vol. 4, pp. 204–25; *Cahiers de doléances du bailliage de Troyes . . .* , vol. 1, pp. 210–88.

NOTE: This table is constructed on the basis of the kinds of techniques used—much more extensively— by André Burguière in "Société et culture à Reims à la fin du XVIIIe siècle: la diffusion des 'Lumières' analysée à travers les cahiers de doléances," *Annales: E.S.C.*, 22 (1967), pp. 303–39; and by Régine Robin, *La Société française en 1789: Semur-en-Auxois* (Paris, 1970).

Troyes counterparts did. Thus, though the authors of the two town grievance lists came from the same high-ranking social groups, their writing revealed disparate political orientations.

The social and professional affiliation of the authors obviously only tells part of the story. Though there is no direct contemporary evidence of the political differences between the town deputies of Troyes and Reims during this period other than the lists, the deputies' later political fortunes are illuminating. Twenty-one of the 30 Reims town deputies (70 percent) sat on the revolutionary committee of August 1789; a few more entered the constitutional government of 1790. Only nine of the 24 Troyes deputies (38 percent) were picked for the August revolutionary committee, and only five were elected to the constitutional government that followed. Thus, even though virtually the same proportion of deputies elected in March had held Old Regime offices in each town, their political behavior was viewed very differently by the townspeople. With their relatively aggressive and forthright grievance list, the Reims town deputies won the approval of their fellow citizens. Undoubtedly the eruption of a violent food riot at the outset of their deliberations propelled them in the direction of political reform, or at least openness to discussion. In the calmer atmosphere of Troyes, on the other hand, the town deputies proved to be as rigid, pedantic, and jealous of their privileges as ever. The people of Troyes consequently approached the summer of 1789 feeling restive and frustrated with their habitual political leaders.[24]

In the subsequent regional (bailliage) meetings, attention was diverted from the municipal arena and focused instead on conflicts between town and country and between the three orders or estates. Like the previous assemblies, these meetings took place in Troyes and Reims; but at this level few residents felt directly involved. Each of the three orders met separately and wrote its own grievance list for the Estates General and elected its delegates to Versailles. Originally, the crown had allotted four deputations to Reims and only one to Troyes. But on the complaint of the Troyes town council, each bailliage received instead two deputations and hence chose two deputies for the clergy, two for the nobility, and four for the Third Estate.[25]

The meetings of the clergy (the First Estate) occasioned political conflict all over France by bringing forth the long-standing antagonism between parish priests and the upper clergy. The parish clergy were more numerous and united in the Troyes meetings than in the Reims ones. Three-quarters of the votes (including *procurations*, or proxy votes) in Troyes belonged to parish priests; 107 of the 154 clergy present were parish priests. Parish priests controlled only 57 percent of the Reims votes; but, more important, the parish priests of the Reims region split when it came to selecting deputies. The clergy of the Troyes bailliage elected two parish priests to represent them, passing over the bishop of the Troyes diocese. The clergy of the Reims region picked the archbishop of Reims and a parish priest. When the parish priest resigned to accept election from another bailliage, he was replaced by the first alternate, a canon from Reims who sat on the 1788–89 town council. The contrast between the choices of the two regions could not have been more striking.[26]

The grievance lists give concrete evidence of the differences between the two regional clerical gatherings. This was most apparent in the sections devoted to ecclesiastical questions. The clergy of the Troyes region demanded the restitution of the tithe to the parish priests (article 54), the amelioration of the situation of rural parish priests (article 55), and, most notably, the right to assemble as a group to deal with their affairs (article 60). In addition, the Troyes parish priests claimed precedence in rank over the other clergy, with only the bishop to have superior rank. They also proposed many reforms in the organization of the regular clergy.[27]

The Reims clergy showed little conern for the problems of parish priests. Instead, they concentrated on relations between church and state and between the French church and the pope—issues that characteristically interested the clerical establishment. The Reims list championed the claims of the regular clergy: it requested that the chapters and universities be given larger representation at future meetings of the Estates General. The language of the Reims list was more "enlightened" than that of the shorter and simpler Troyes list. Frequent references were made by the Reims authors to the "lumières de notre siècle," to the need for clarity and precision in fixing the fundamental laws of the constitution and guarantees for personal liberties. Despite its enlightened formulas, the clergy of Reims stopped far short of requesting basic reforms in the ecclesiastical establishment. In contrast, the Troyes clergy indicated with unadorned and direct phrases their willingness to consider changes in the political and social system as well as in the ecclesiastical structure of France. For example, the Reims clergy unambiguously asserted that voting in the Estates General should be by order and not by head, whereas the clergy of Troyes wanted voting by head on questions of taxation. Similarly, the Troyes list left open the possibility that the Estates General might abolish venality of offices and permit the suppression with compensation of seigneurial dues.

The clerical elections and grievance lists undoubtedly influenced townspeople's perceptions of their clergymen. People in Troyes noted that their parish priests had broken with the church hierarchy, and later they rewarded them with election to the revolutionary committee and to the government of 1790. Not one cleric was elected to either of these new bodies in Reims. Resentment of the Reims clergy finally boiled over into violence in 1792 in the local counterpart to the September massacres in Paris; as foreign armies began their invasion of the region, a panic-stricken crowd in Reims murdered ten suspected agents, six of whom were priests.[28]

In contrast to the clerical meetings, the regional convocations of the nobility inspired little discord. The nobles resolved their political differences by picking deputies to represent both poles of aristocratic opinion. The 90 nobles meeting in Reims chose the marquis d'Ambly, an intransigent supporter of the Old Regime, and the marquis de Sillery, a liberal partisan of the duc d'Orléans. The 84 nobles gathered in Troyes elected the marquis de Mesgrigny, the scion of a family long-involved in Troyes affairs, and the marquis de Crillon, an ardent proponent of reform.

Neither of the noble grievance lists was very reform-minded.[29] Like the clergy of both bailliages, the nobles asked for periodic meetings of the Estates General and the establishment of provincial estates. Both noble groups proved willing to give up their fiscal privileges, but neither would part with their seigneurial rights. As might be expected, neither list expressed a desire to grant the Third Estate access to all titles and offices. The nobles intended to retain their special position in French society.

While the clergy and nobility of the bailliages met nearby, hundreds of regional deputies crowded into the assemblies of the Third Estate in Troyes and Reims. To facilitate discussion and the conduct of business, the deputies began by reducing their numbers from 676 for the bailliage of Troyes to 169, and from 624 for the bailliage of Reims to 200.[30] The town deputations for Troyes and Reims were not required to participate in these reductions, so they retained their original numbers of 24 in Troyes and 30 in Reims. Although they were both mere islands in the sea of regional deputations, the deputies from Reims exerted a commanding influence on the proceedings whereas those of Troyes were swamped.

In the selection of deputies for the Estates General, Reims succeeded in imposing two of its men upon the regional conclave. The deputies elected by the bailliage of Reims were Raux, a *maître de forges* from Hurtault; Viellart, the chief judge of the ducal (archbishop's) court and a professor in the law faculty of Reims; Labest, a bourgeois from Lumières; and Baron, an *avocat en Parlement* and official of the Reims *maîtrise des eaux et forêts*. Merchants did better in Troyes than in Reims. The four deputies chosen by the Troyes meeting were Camusat de Belombre, a merchant from Troyes; Baillot, an *avocat en Parlement* from Evry; Jeannet, an *avocat en Parlement* from Saint-Florentin; and Jeannet-Jeannet, a merchant from Arcis-sur-Aube (and an uncle of Danton). No magistrates were selected by the Troyes meeting.

The 30 Reims deputies apparently monopolized the preparation of the grievance list for the bailliage, which incorporated all the articles in the town list with only minor changes in their order.[31] The Troyes bailliage list reproduced many of the demands of the Troyes town list but was written in much simpler and shorter sentences. The preface to the Troyes town list was dropped, as were all of the long explicatory passages preceding particular demands. Where the town list had hedged or hesitated, the bailliage list vigorously insisted. Where the two lists differed in actual demands made, the bailliage list took the more consistently liberal, free-trade line. For example, on the question of corporate organization, the Troyes town list repeated the request of many corporate groups that the guild structure be maintained (article 144). The bailliage list recognized this demand, but stated nevertheless that most of the Third Estate of the bailliage favored the suppression of the guilds (article 108).[32] Thus, both in their selection of deputies and in their formulation of a grievance list the deputies of the Troyes region rebuffed the lead offered by the Troyes town deputies. Implicit in their denial was a repudiation of the magistrates' domination of the town proceedings, a domination most clearly reflected in the legalistic and defensive town list of grievances. The Reims regional delegates, on the other hand, heartily endorsed the conduct of the Reims town deputies, who advocated a spirited, reform-minded list of demands.

IV

The grievance lists put together on the bailliage level expressed the opinions of very select groups. Since few townspeople from Troyes and Reims participated directly in the regional meetings, there is no point in analyzing the regional lists in great detail. What did matter is that the townspeople got some notion of the political divisions between clergy, nobles, and Third Estate—divisions that were to sharpen dramatically once the Estates General itself opened. All three orders in Troyes and Reims shared certain grievances: they all wanted a constitution, periodic meetings of the Estates General, the establishment of provincial estates in Champagne, and the guarantee of a free press. All accepted in principle the need for more equitable taxation. None of them required the immediate abolition of seigneurial dues or a ban on buying and selling government offices. Nevertheless, certain key issues separated the three orders. Neither the clergy nor the nobility agreed to voting by head in the Estates General, and in this they anticipated the chief split within the Estates General itself.* On the question of Third Estate access to all offices, the nobles of both bailliages remained silent. Piecemeal reform they could accept, but fundamental transformation of the social system was inconceivable to them. Thus even though the authors of the grievance lists (except the clergy of Troyes) spoke the rhetoric of the Enlightenment and shared the culture of literate elites, incontrovertible political differences came between them.†

The unity of the regional elite broke up on the rocks of political privilege. The Parlement of Paris had initiated the breakup when it argued in September 1788 for the revival of the 1614 procedures for the Estates General (voting by order, orders meeting separately). As Colin Lucas asserts, "The decision to separate the nobility from the Third Estate pushed the central and lower echelons of the elite down into the Third Estate. It rent asunder what was essentially now a homogeneous social unit." [33] The grievance lists show, however, that it was not just the Parlement of Paris that clung to obsolete social visions; the nobles of Troyes and Reims and the clergy of Reims aligned themselves behind the society of orders, too. The regime could not end without a fight.

---

*As mentioned earlier, the clergy of Troyes wanted voting by head on matters of taxation only.

†This is a point that recent exclusive emphasis on the rhetoric of the Enlightenment obscures. See the article by André Burguière cited in note 18.

In nonparlementary manufacturing towns such as Troyes and Reims, nobles and bourgeois (nonnobles) managed to resolve *local* political problems without much conflict since nobles and nonnobles had long been integrated into one effective ruling elite on the local level. In Troyes and Reims nonnobles held most positions of local power; there was no division by orders; voting in town affairs had always been by head. The bailliage meetings of the three estates demonstrated that the local modus vivendi did not hold for national politics. The major cleavages of 1789 split national or regional elites (I call them regional since there were no national political institutions), and the divisive issues were those of national politics. Thanks to the lengthy preliminaries to the Estates General, the people of Troyes and Reims learned firsthand about those national issues.

Once the lists were approved and the deputies elected, the delegates went home. By the end of the first week in April, the meetings had ended and the townspeople of Troyes and Reims returned to life as usual. But they went back to their looms, their shops, their law offices, or their countinghouses with the memory of their recent political discussions freshly etched on their minds. The March meetings had created a new local political arena whose gates were thrown open to men long accustomed to their exclusion from Old Regime politics. The "little man" of the towns had his chance to enter the contest, to speak up, and to vote. Nonetheless, those most familiar with the rules of the game had the advantage at the outset, and so the traditional local elites retained their hold on power. Still the process, not the results, counted most. The redrawing of lines on local political maps had begun.

CHAPTER 4

The Towns Revolt

THE ESTATES GENERAL was to open officially on May 5, 1789. To commemorate this auspicious occasion, the king and the deputies of the three estates heard mass together on May 4 in the church of Saint Louis in Versailles. The representatives of the kingdom marched to the church in solemn procession, with the deputies of the Third, clothed in sober black, at their head. Following them were the nobles with their white-plumed hats, their laces and gold ornaments. The deputies of the First Estate came next in two clearly distinct groups: the prelates in violet robes, and the mass of parish priests in their black soutanes. At the end of this "gothic ceremonial," as Michelet called it, came the king, the queen, and the royal entourage. Everyone held a candle. When the impressive assemblage reached the church, the deputies began crowding into the available seats. A representative of the Third Estate from Brittany was seen quarreling with the marquis de Brézé about the seating arrangement:

"Monsieur," said de Brézé, "it is the order of 1614."

"Monsieur, we are no longer in 1614, and it is a very long way from us to the men of that time."

"Monsieur, the king himself has determined the order."

"I respect the order of the king; he has the advantage of force, and his orders must be followed for now. But the Estates will decide the question." [1]

Eventually the deputies sat wherever they could find room. Tempers were already on edge, and the lines of battle were being drawn. In Michelet's words, "Thus this grand festival of peace and union showed symptoms of war."[2] The sacrament of May 4 turned out to be the last rites of the regime.

After the king and his ministers delivered their initial addresses on May 5, procedure became the order of the day. Would the estates meet separately? Would they vote by order or by head? How were the mandates of the deputies to be verified? For weeks the Estates General was stymied by irreconcilable differences, until finally on June 17 the deputies of the Third Estate voted to declare themselves, and whoever would join them, the National Assembly. Ten days later, after his efforts to stem the rising tide failed, the king acquiesced and ordered the reluctant clerical and noble deputies to join the common deliberations. By then, many parish priests had already enlisted in the revolutionary cause. The national revolution took its first giant step forward.

The people of the provinces followed the events in Versailles with a mixture of excitement and concern. There were few newspapers published during the months of May and June, even in Paris. The papers in Troyes and Reims came out only once a week, and though their political content increased markedly in 1788 and 1789 they were not published frequently enough to keep up with the rapidly developing political crisis.[3] Townspeople relied on letters from their deputies in Versailles for up-to-date news of national politics. Many deputies wrote almost every day, and when the mail coach or special courier arrived with the precious epistles, the news moved by word of mouth with lightning speed from café to café, from drawing room to marketplace. The deputies were kept abreast of local news by return post.

It is not hard to imagine the electric effect of letters such as those written by the merchant deputy from Troyes, Camusat de Belombre.[4] In May and early June, his letters described how the Third Estate painstakingly turned over every stone in its search for a way to bring the other two orders over to its side. As each endeavor successively came to nought, Camusat's letters expressed growing exasperation: "C'est par de pareilles manoeuvres, par les insinuations artificieuses de tous ceux qui craignent les Etats généraux que nous

nous trouvons ainsi arreté à chaque pas."[5] Then, on June 18, he conveyed "the happy news" of the Third Estate's resolution to constitute itself as the National Assembly.[6] Camusat suspected that this would be greeted enthusiastically at home: "J'espère que ma précédente aura fait dans Troyes la plus vive sensation."[7]

The next days were critical, and Camusat dashed off almost hourly reports of developments in Versailles. Would the king use force to dissolve the infant Assembly? In his letter of June 24, Camusat despairingly detailed the *lit de justice* of the day before: "On entering the chamber . . . I found myself seized by a feeling of sadness. Everything seemed to announce something sinister." On leaving, the deputies found a huge crowd waiting; these people swore "they were ready to sacrifice their lives to support us. The worry, the sadness, the fury, all the diverse sensations created a lugubrious spectacle." There were rumors of a "sinister revolution" in the capital plotted by the reactionary court faction. Camusat would not sign his letter because he feared that all the mail from Versailles was opened.[8]

After giving a sigh of relief when the king relented on the 27th of June, Camusat redoubled his alarms. Talk of cabals against the Assembly raised Paris to a fever heat, and now the deputies found themselves surrounded by royal troops: "All of the places near Versailles and the capital are filled with soldiers; all of the passages, all means of communication are guarded. Convoys of artillery are arriving from all parts; ten to twelve regiments are expected in eight days [this on July 9], and altogether these different troops will form a body of 50,000 men." The deputies were "horrified and indignant."[9] "Everyone is convinced that the approach of the troops covers some violent design."[10] Tension saturated the atmosphere in Paris and Versailles, and people all over France waited in suspense for the denouement.

At home the price of grain was on everyone's mind.* Figure 2 in Chapter 3 traced the implacable rise in grain prices between the summer of 1788 and the summer of 1789 and showed that the most

*No political events of importance had occurred in Troyes and Reims between mid-April and July. Elections for the town councils had been held in Reims on March 8 and in Troyes on April 14, but they did not significantly change the composition of

critical months were those of late spring and summer, 1789: between March and July of 1789 the price of first-quality wheat (*froment*) in Reims rose 37 percent, that of first-quality bread in Troyes 24 percent, and that of *blé* in Troyes 44 percent.[11] Townspeople readily imagined a conspiratorial connection between soaring prices and the menace of aristocratic counterattack in Paris. They believed that local officials were in collusion with grain merchants and anonymous hoarders. On July 4 the son of Comparot de Longsols wrote to his father, the bailliage magistrate, with a dire warning about the mood in Troyes. "Today someone planted a gibbet in the wheat market with a printed notice conceived in these terms: 'If in three days the price of wheat is not lowered, Sourdat [the chief police magistrate] will be hung and dragged through town by all those who are dying of hunger.'"[12] Troyes officials were thus forewarned of the fate in store for those suspected of starving the revolution.

The price of bread reached its highest point in many markets in the first two weeks of July, and this added fuel to the political fire about to rage through France. The spark that touched it off was the dismissal of Necker on July 11. At 9 A.M. on July 12, Camusat scrawled a brief, distressed note to his friends in Troyes; he had just then heard about the overturn of the ministry. "It is clear today that they invested Paris and Versailles with cannons and soldiers in order to contain the populace at the moment when they would find out about the disgrace of the only man who still had credit."[13] As Camusat and his fellow deputies sounded the alarm in the provinces, the people of Paris swung into motion. At the end of the afternoon of July 12, a large impatient crowd invaded the Paris city hall and demanded arms for the defense of Paris. The court intrigues would not go unchallenged; the revolution had moved its headquarters to Paris.

During the next three days of constant commotion, the deputies found themselves on tenterhooks in Versailles, cut off from the scene of action in Paris. On July 13 Camusat painted a foreboding picture

---

town government since the terms of only a few councillors expired in 1789. The outgoing councillors were replaced by men from the same socioprofessional groups. The method of selection remained the same as it had been during the preceding decades, and the elections aroused no more interest than usual.

of the situation: "Today all of the evils overwhelm France, and we are between despotism, carnage, and famine. . . . All Paris has risen up. . . . If this fire spreads to the provinces, I dare not say what revolution menaces us; it cannot but be fatal to the Sovereign." [14] His prediction was uncannily accurate, though the following day Camusat believed that order had been restored in Paris. In his letter of July 15 he admitted his mistake; France seemed on the verge of civil war. [15]

As might be expected, Camusat found the hurly-burly of events in Paris bewildering. He knew only that the people had armed themselves, that they had taken the Bastille and that the provost of merchants, the "mayor," had been brutally killed. Any semblance of order apparently depended upon the newly formed "troupes bourgeoises." The municipal bureau and a handful of city "electors" had set up a special committee (the *comité permanent*) on July 13 to take charge of Paris under arms, and though the committee's control seemed illusory at first, within two or three days it managed to get the upper hand and establish itself as the command center of the Parisian revolution. [16] On July 18 the Paris committee called elections, and one week later 120 elected delegates (two per district) declared themselves the "Assembly of the Representatives of the Commune of Paris."

The people of Paris mobilized quickly to defend the infant national revolution by buttressing the hesitant National Assembly with an urban revolution of support. This was much more than a Parisian movement, however. On July 12 riots erupted in Rouen, and town officials there felt compelled to create a committee that turned out to be remarkably similar to the one set up in Paris at the same time. [17] When word arrived of Necker's dismissal and of the Parisian revolution, provincial ferment flared up into full-scale revolt. Demonstrations and riots seared the body politic at Alençon, Caen, Le Havre, Nantes, Strasbourg, Grenoble, Lille, and other places. Troyes and Reims followed the dominant pattern of urban insurrection: within a few days of the fall of the Bastille, local rebellions challenged the municipal regimes. [18]

I

Food riots broke out in Troyes on July 18 and continued un-
checked for three days. On July 20 the mayor and aldermen wrote a
frantic letter to the intendant in Châlons-sur-Marne.

Yesterday we experienced the greatest alarms and we saw ourselves several times on the verge of being subjected to all the horrors of the most
terrifying revolt.

For some time we had known that there was grumbling among the people,
and we had been told of vague threats that could not but worry us even
though we had no details or certain knowledge. Accordingly, we believed it
necessary to take precautions, and in the fear that the people would seize the
arms of the militia, whose storehouse was not at all secure, M. de Saint-
Georges [commander of the army garrison] had all the arms transferred to
the city hall.

The day before yesterday (Saturday) there was much talk in the marketplace on the subject of wheat prices, and there were threats of pillaging
the arms that everyone knew had been transferred to the city hall. We invited
the upright citizens [*citoyens honnêtes*] to gather at the city hall for its defense; it was fortunate that they spent the night there, for a considerable
crowd appeared which we spent all night fending off.

Yesterday (Sunday) afternoon more than seven or eight thousand people,
men and women, assembled in front of the two gates to the city hall and
could have massacred all those inside; we were forced to negotiate with them
and to promise to give them wheat at 100 sous per *boisseau* and to reduce
[the price of] bread to 14 sous per six pounds.

We hoped that after that the people would withdraw, but despite our invi-
tations, only darkness separated them.

This morning (Monday) the noise and the sedition are beginning again;
we are obliged to cut short this letter in order to see to our defense.[19]

Confronted with persistent demands for arms and lower bread
prices, the town council of Troyes decided on July 20 to set up an
emergency committee to regulate the formation of a militia and organize the distribution of grain. This committee had 25 members, 22
of whose occupations we know: there were three army officers, the
chief police magistrate, seven town councillors (four of whom were
also bailliage magistrates), eight bailliage magistrates, and three
maréchaussée officers.

In Reims on the same day (July 20), the *lieutenant des habitants* reported to the town council that seditious talk made the formation of an emergency committee necessary.[20] An army regiment was sent to reinforce the one hundred soldiers who had been in garrison in Reims since the troubles of March. The "permanent committee" began meeting at the city hall on July 22, the day that rioting began. But grain prices were holding steady in Reims, and the turmoil subsided quickly. By decision of the town council, the Reims committee included about 60 men—the town councillors, former town officers, police officials, the 30 town deputies chosen in March, and the four chief officers of the newly formed militia—some four-fifths of whom were Old Regime officials.

Where Troyes and Reims differed was in the fact that the Troyes town council did not invite the 24 town deputies to join the committee; this differentiated Troyes not only from Reims but also from Paris and most of the other large towns and cities that established committees. The Troyes officials saw their committee as a creature of circumstance, an ad hoc formalization of the cooperation developed in the months of crisis between the leading officials of the local Old Regime institutions.* The Troyes committee was meant not to transform local politics but rather to direct the protection of property against popular disorders.†

Even though Troyes was jolted by much greater violence in mid-July than Reims, Troyes officials seemed reluctant to join the revolution in progress. The Reims councilmen diligently organized a committee that actively and immediately intervened in all matters of public security. The Reims "permanent committee" kept precise minutes of its meetings; the Troyes committee met in secret, like the municipal council of the Old Regime. The only minutes kept in

---

*This is explained in an apology for the Old Regime in Troyes written late in 1789. "Comme elle [the committee of July 20] n'était que l'effet des circonstances, elle cessa avec elles." Edme Alexis Gillet and Nicolas Parent, *A Nosseigneurs de l'Assemblée Nationale* (Troyes, 1789), p. 5. Gillet was a medical doctor who had been a town councillor for two years. Parent had been king's advocate in the bailliage court for six years.

†The town council described its new militia to the marquis de Mesgrigny, a deputy from the nobility of Troyes to the Estates General: "cette Bourgeoisie . . . a senti la nécessité de se réunir afin de pouvoir veiller par elle-même à sa défense et à la conserva-

Troyes were for the infrequent full meetings of the town council, which regularly approved the decisions made by the mayor and aldermen. The Reims committee divided itself into *bureaux* so that it would be able to meet every day ("en permanence"), and its authority was clearly defined in regulations published on July 22. At the same time, the rules governing the formation of the Reims *Garde bourgeoise* were also printed: 1,200 men were to form eight militia companies; officers were picked by the committee; and each company was to be commanded by two military officers resident in Reims.[21] The president of the committee was the *lieutenant des habitants* and presiding over each bureau was a councilman. No regulations governing the committee were issued in Troyes.

Neither in Troyes nor in Reims did the committees supplant the town councils, and Old Regime officials continued to control local decisions. In these hectic July days politics was subordinated to the more urgent problem of public order. A semblance of calm was more easily restored in Reims, in part because the food shortage and unemployment there were less critical than in Troyes, in part because the Reims committee acted quickly to regularize the militia. Within a few days of their arrival in Reims, the additional troops requested left for other more unsettled towns. The garrison at Troyes received 220 dragoons on July 29; they stayed to prevent a recurrence of the rioting of July 18–20, which had so terrified the town council.

The mood in Troyes after the riots was ugly. The bailliage court and town council passed new ordinances against "attroupements," and the leaders of the "sedition" were arrested. On July 23, the court condemned one man to immediate hanging and sentenced two others to the galleys in perpetuity as examples to the rest of the populace. Only the presence of a loyal army garrison made the execution possible.* In Reims no one was tried for participation in the food riot of July 22.

---

tion de ses propriétés; elle a en conséquence conçu le projet de l'établissement d'une milice." A. C. Troyes, AA carton 55, "Correspondance, 1789," letter of July 24, 1789.

*Troyes had quartered a permanent garrison of at least 150 soldiers since the 1750's. In May 1789, 50 dragoons were sent from Vitry to reinforce the garrison. The arrival of 220 additional dragoons on July 29 gave the Old Regime even more protection.

The hasty judgment of the bailliage court polarized opinion in Troyes. Opposition to the town council and its puppet committee mounted, not only among the already embittered workers, but also among some of the educated professionals. Truelle de Chambouzon, one of the magistrates on the court, opened an investigation on behalf of the widow of the man hanged. Truelle and Lalobe, a local merchant, had distinguished themselves earlier by attempting to mediate between the town council and the aroused crowd on July 19. After their intervention, the people arrested on July 18 were released and the price of grain was lowered. Two other men, the Chaperon brothers, also made names for themselves as friends of the people and now began mobilizing opposition to the regime in Troyes.[22]

Internal urban politics were complicated by the appearance of the Great Fear in Champagne. Once again Reims seems to have been spared the worst; the hysteria produced by rumors of marauding gangs of thugs and robbers convulsed the southern half of Champagne, the region near Troyes, but it left the Reims region relatively untouched.[23] The officials of Troyes took the lead in urging villagers to remain calm, but the *troyens* had direct contact with the Fear on July 29 when residents of the suburbs streamed into the city to escape the brigands thought to be approaching. By the end of July the textile workers and poor people of Troyes were overloaded with anxieties and real suffering. Thousands were still unemployed. Bread prices hovered above the ceiling of endurance. Rural panic reverberated off the town walls, and news filtered in fitfully of revolts all over the country. Paris was a political maelstrom, and the National Assembly had yet to take effective direction of the country. Still the officials of Troyes continued peevishly on their twofold course of resistance to all innovation and spiteful repression of any collective protest.

In August the committees appointed by the town councils came under fire almost everywhere in France for being unrepresentative. New elections were held in Paris on August 1, but the lead of Paris was no longer necessary. If towns set up new committees, their decisions to do so depended more on local politics than on the example of Paris. With the price of grain and bread declining even in the penurious north in August, with charity workshops occupying some of the unemployed, and thus with economic stress lessening its grip on the towns, townspeople were gradually able to redirect their energies to questions of political organization. In August, as in July, the Reims rulers greeted demands for political change with flexibility and finesse, while the Troyes authorities maintained their adamantine attitude.

II

In late July and early August, the Reims council and committee worked night and day seeking grain, requesting arms, and arranging public works projects. On August 12, in reaction to growing political agitation, the council again asked the government to send troops (this time a hundred dragoons) and requested more rifles for the militia.[24] Five days later, in response to a report by the procureur-syndic that many citizens did not consider the committee established on July 20 legitimate because its members had not been elected by the "commune," the town council voted to call elections for a new committee.[25] Just as in the National Assembly and in Paris, in Reims legitimacy was to rest upon election to office.

The new committee was selected by the same procedure used in electing town councillors: on August 18 each of Reims's nine districts chose ten electors; on August 21 these 90 electors then chose 49 deputies to sit with the town council as a committee. The big winners in the August 18–21 elections were the merchants and clothiers (see Table 15). Half the members of the new committee were merchants or clothiers, whereas less than a third of the town councillors had come from this group. Their increase in representation came largely at the expense of the Reims clergy: no clergymen were chosen either as electors or as committee members. The elections of August 18–21 did not open government to the town's lower classes, even though a substantial number of artisans and shopkeepers were picked by their districts to serve as electors; the skilled craftsmen and shopkeepers continued to rely on their social betters for leadership. Nevertheless, the election of a committee did change the balance of power within the ruling group; nobles, royal officials, doctors, and lawyers found themselves reduced to minor partnership in the ruling coalition.

TABLE 15

Reims: The Social Composition of the Committee of August 21, 1789

Social group	Men elected August 18–21		26 town councillors as of March 8
	90 electors	49 deputies	
Nobles[a]	8%	22%	19%
Clergy	0	0	23
Royal officials	8	12	15
Liberal professions	12	10	12
Merchants & clothiers	31	49	27
Small merchants & artisans	34	2	0
Bourgeois	3	0	0
Laboureurs	6	4	0
Occupation unknown	1	0	4
TOTAL	99%	99%	100%

SOURCES: For the electors and deputies, A. C. Reims, registre 226, fonds moderns, "Délibérations du Comité permanent," August 21, 1789; for the town council, A. C. Reims, registre 116, fonds anciens, "Conclusions du Conseil de Ville," March 8, 1789.

[a] Nobles include *secrétaires du roi* and all those royal officials and merchants who were nobles.

Socially, the newly elected committeemen did not represent a great break with the past. As a group they appear to have been wealthier than the ruling group of 1788–89 analyzed in Chapter 2: the committee members paid an average *contribution foncière* in 1792 of 1,095 livres, as compared to an average of 765 livres for the Old Regime notables.[26] Like the Old Regime rulers, most of the men elected to the August committee lived in the wealthy central parishes. Twenty-five of the 40 committeemen with known addresses lived in either Saint Hilaire or Saint Pierre parish; 26 of the 40 rulers of 1788–89 with known addresses lived in the same parishes. All but three of the committee members lived in the parishes of the old medieval center of Reims. The new partners in local authority often resembled the Old Regime oligarchs.

Yet despite the continuity in the social base of leadership, 51 percent (25) of the elected committee members had never held an office under the Old Regime. Ten of these 25 newcomers had been chosen as corporate delegates during the March meetings, and eight had also been elected as deputies for the town of Reims to the bailliage meeting of the Third Estate. The effect of the March meetings now became apparent: of the committee members elected in August, nearly half (49 percent) had been delegates for their "corporations," and over one-third (37 percent) had represented the town at the bailliage meetings.

On August 28, the 49 deputies met with the members of the town council in a general assembly to establish a joint government. By the terms approved at this meeting, the council was to continue to have sole responsibility in certain areas: it would still receive reports on grain supply and public works, approve appropriations of funds, and function as the official link to the national government. Hence it was the town council alone that collected the "patriotic contribution" of 1789 and prepared the tax rolls for 1790.[27] Nevertheless, the hub of activity shifted from the town council alone to the general assembly of council and committee, which met once a week. The assembly was divided into seven bureaus, one for each day of the week. Precise minutes were kept of each bureau's meetings, as well as of meetings of the general assembly. The seven bureaus did most of the assembly's work: all of them met every week from August until mid-February 1790; some of them met into March; and two meetings were recorded for April 1790.[28] In the first weeks of their tenure, the bureaus concentrated on organizing grain supply. After the beginning of October, attention focused primarily on public order, i.e., passport control and guard discipline. The committee's concern with food supply declined as prices stabilized: the price of wheat reached a high in July of 23 livres, 10 sous, but between September and January it hovered around 16–17 livres.[29]

Control of the National Guard was the general assembly's chief responsibility and its main claim to local authority. The assembly raised money for the Guard, approved expenditures on arms, and enforced Guard regulations. Although the assembly itself did not pass ordinances, it requested them from the chief police magistrate. At its very first meeting on August 28, the assembly established the regulations for the National Guard, which resembled in many respects the rules issued by the earlier emergency committee for the *Garde bourgeoise*: there were to be eight companies, each commanded by two resident army officers; several dragoons from the army garrison were attached to each militia patrol; and arms for the militia were to be kept in the city hall.[30] All adult males who paid a capitation of four livres or more were eligible for service. The assembly clearly intended to keep control of the new local armed force away from the lower classes: only 40 percent of the men on the capitation roll of 1789 paid four livres or more in tax.[31] Textile workers and artisans were excluded in favor of respectable, property-owning citizens. The army's authority was upheld by the presence of army officers and enlisted men on guard patrols. As might be expected, conflicts between the regular military and the National Guard preoccupied the assembly throughout the fall and winter.

The town council members exerted considerable influence within the assembly. A councilman presided over each bureau's meetings, and council members were frequently more zealous in their attendance than the elected deputies.[32] When the assembly sent envoys to other organizations in Reims, to other towns, or to Paris, town council members were often picked for the job. Yet the most active members of the assembly were merchants and clothiers. Sixteen members attended their bureau meetings more than ten times: twelve were elected deputies; four were councilmen. Ten of the sixteen were merchants or clothiers; they were joined by two royal officials, one clergyman (a town councillor), one farmer, one medical doctor, and one finisher. Moreover, in every bureau except the Wednesday one (and it was attended least often in general), either a merchant or a clothier appeared most frequently for meetings. The mercantile elite did not intend to let their great opportunity pass by for want of effort or application.

The leaders of the Reims assembly were successful businessmen with established reputations in the commercial community. Typical of the "new" leadership was Mathieu Assy-Guérin, a clothier who attended his bureau meetings more often than any other assembly member (eighteen times). His assessed property tax (*contribution foncière*) of 1,116 livres put him in the top 3 percent of clothiers and the top 4 percent of the tax-paying population in general. He lived on the rue de Vesle, a broad street radiating out from the town center. Near him resided Lévesque de Pouilly, one of the town's most esteemed aristocrats; Oudin-Paul, a town council member and officer in the *maîtrise des eaux et forêts*; and Pinchart, a wealthy merchant member of the assembly. Assy-Guérin had made his local political debut in March when he was first elected as a delegate by his fellow clothiers and then chosen to represent Reims at the bailliage meetings. By 1790, his enthusiastic participation in the assembly was to be rewarded with election to the post of municipal officer, and in 1792 he was to become president of the departmental directory.

The keen, new faces elected on August 21 worked in partnership with veterans such as Pierre Louis Mopinot-Pinchart, a 66-year-old merchant and former alderman also elected on that day. Mopinot had been chosen to represent the Third Estate in the élection assembly at Reims in 1787–88, and in 1789 he served as a delegate for the merchant drapers and later as a town deputy to the bailliage meeting. He lived just down the street from Assy-Guérin on the central Place Royale. His property tax of 1,900 livres made him one of the richest men in town; only three other elected deputies to the assembly paid higher taxes. His capitation tax of 108 livres put him in the top 1 percent of the town's taxpayers in 1789. Mopinot demonstrated his interest in the Revolution by attending his bureau a respectable ten times, and in 1790 his fellow citizens were to elect him president of the new district government. Like six other elected deputies, Mopinot was a Mason; in fact, his name appears on one of the earliest extant membership rolls for the Triple Union lodge (1778). In general, the political veterans elected in August were men who had built reputations for "progressive" thinking; their prior political experience did not stigmatize them as intractable defenders of the Old Regime.

The elected committee in Reims did not replace the Old Regime town council in local affairs, and in this sense it failed to effect a complete local revolution. Yet it did enlarge the base of local rule; more men attained positions of authority as new instruments of political and social control were fashioned. The old rulers were not thrown out; they were joined by new men. The newcomers, most of them merchants and manufacturers, brought with them the principles of good business: orderly accounts and strict discipline of the working classes. The joint assembly of committee and council reflected these principles in its bureaucratic structure—with a clear division of labor and meticulous minutes—and in its tightly controlled bourgeois militia.

Reims entered the Revolution in orderly fashion, carefully guided by an effective, "rationalized" government that merged merchant and noble, manufacturer and professional in the interest of the preservation of order and property. The transition was facilitated by recovery in the woolen industry and by the steadying of grain prices. Yet equally important was politically shrewd management on the part of the ruling group, which met each crisis with a united front, gave in where discretion was the better part of valor, and enlarged the political arena rather than relinquish control of it. In this the rulers were blessed by the peculiar balance of power within Reims; the church with its overweening archbishop took the blame for the ills of the Old Regime, and the lay notables used the occasion to consolidate their position. With the language of accommodation and quick action, they kept hold of the reins of power.

III

Troyes, on the other hand, was a hotbed of revolution. By systematically either refusing or ignoring growing demands for an elected committee, the rulers of Troyes blindly created an impossible situation. In response to the obdurate conduct of the town council, the opposition leaders succeeded in mobilizing the townspeople much faster and more extensively than was the case in most provincial towns. The committee that emerged in Troyes was much more radical in its composition and orientation than most of the committees elected in 1789. But the forces of resistance to revolution did not accept this challenge passively; radical revolution and counter-revolution developed dialectically.

There had been little public political activity in Troyes after the July riots because gatherings were forbidden by police ordinance. Nevertheless, on August 8 a meeting was held in a cemetery just outside town, away from the eyes of the army and the police. It was a market day and a Saturday. Prices had declined, but they were still high enough to provoke outrage. After assembling in the cemetery, the crowd marched to the courthouse (Place du Palais) in the center of Troyes, where they took over a large hall. There they demanded the immediate reassignment of the regiment of Royal Dragoons that had arrived on July 29. Commander Saint-Georges presented himself to the meeting, put on the revolutionary cockade, and agreed to send the troops away. According to Gillet and Parent, the regiment did in fact leave town that very day. Emboldened by their easy victory, the crowd then demanded lower bread prices and the release of the people arrested for the July riots. When Saint-Georges refused on the grounds that he lacked the necessary authority, a part of the assembled group went off to find Cadot, the lieutenant of the maréchaussée. Faced unexpectedly with a hostile crowd while walking across town, Cadot acceded and gave his written consent to the release of the prisoners. According to observers, one of the crowd's leaders was Truelle de Chambouzon.[33]

In the following days, the town council heard repeated demands for a new committee, and in response the mayor and the four aldermen met on August 13 with the 24 town deputies, who had been excluded from the committee established on July 20. Since the deputies proved unwilling to take responsibility for acting on the question, the full town council met the next day with delegates from the clergy and nobility as well as the town deputies. Not surprisingly, this group declared that the leadership of the town council was entirely adequate. In the end, however, these efforts at procrastination broke down when the need to organize a militia became inescapable. The situation could not be contained without additional armed force.

On August 16, the mayor and aldermen called elections for militia officers. The opposition won a sweeping victory. Camusat de Belombre, the merchant deputy from the bailliage of Troyes to the Estates General, was elected commandant over Saint-Georges, the army commander.[34] When the new officers met on August 25, they unanimously resigned and demanded new, more democratic elections. They insisted that all heads of households, "even widows and unmarried women who headed households," be enfranchised.[35] By resigning, they hoped to force the hand of the town council.

As the town fathers dawdled, another mass meeting began on the afternoon of August 27. Again the crowd gathered in front of the courthouse; in response, the mayor and the four aldermen met at the Hôtel de Ville and called out the soldiers in garrison. In the early evening a deputation from the meeting in the Place du Palais arrived at the city hall to demand arms and immediate elections for new militia officers. The mayor replied that it was too late to deliver arms and impossible to arrange elections so quickly, but that elections would be held on Sunday, August 30. The deputation, led by the Chaperon brothers, returned to the Place du Palais to announce the agreement. Unsatisfied, the crowd surged toward the city hall to demand that the people be armed on the spot.

When the crowd arrived, it found the building guarded by soldiers. Nevertheless, the mob forced its way past the sentries at the gates and started to rush the building where the militia arms were stored. The accounts differ on what happened next. According to some reports, Saint-Georges was about to give the order to fire on the crowd when one of the Chaperon brothers raised his pistol and shouted that Saint-Georges would be the first to die if he gave the order; the mayor then armed himself with a saber and exhorted the soldiers to "sabrons cette canaille."[36] Other accounts state that both Saint-Georges and the mayor gave the order to fire. Regardless of who did or did not give the order, the troops withheld their fire. At this point Saint-Georges withdrew hastily while the mayor led the way to the arms cache. Then the mayor, too, slipped away and hid in a neighboring house, where he heard the crowd plotting to cut off Saint-George's head.[37] The latter decamped for his country estate as effigies of him appeared around town with placards threatening his life.[38] The next day, August 28, the mayor and the aldermen called immediate elections for militia officers and for a "General Committee" that would organize the Citizens' Guard of Troyes.

That afternoon the inhabitants of the sixteen "companies" (the district divisions for militia service) voted for militia officers and for deputies to the committee.[39] District One suggested that the committee assist the town council in administering town affairs, and all but one of the other districts concurred. The council's vexing endeavors to prevent or postpone the election of a committee had finally been foiled. On August 29, the 64 elected deputies met with the full council at the Hôtel de Ville and declared themselves the "Provisional General Committee." In concert with the mayor and the aldermen, they announced, the committee would control the Citizens' Guard and take charge of the municipal administration.[40] In response to this pronouncement, the other members of the town council, the "notables," walked out of the meeting; only when the deputies agreed to their inclusion in the new ruling body did they return to the session. The mayor and the aldermen proclaimed that "they never had the intention of making a mystery of their administration," and they accepted the formation of a committee composed of the 64 deputies and all 23 councillors (the mayor, the four aldermen, the procureur-syndic, and the seventeen notables).

Organization of the committee began on August 31 with the establishment of eleven bureaus for daily control of town affairs and eight bureaus for specific problems such as grain supply.[41] Six to eight elected deputies sat on each bureau along with two or three town council members. On September 1, Truelle de Chambouzon was elected president of the full committee. His selection over the mayor symbolized the domination of the opposition within the new body. The council was absorbed and outnumbered, and it was not allowed to meet separately. As a result, most of the town councillors decided to withdraw from town affairs rather than associate with the committee.[42] Despite their defection, bitter divisions continued to plague the committee. Grain prices rose again in September, and many townspeople were convinced that the Old Regime officials were conspiring against the lower classes and the new committee. As the situation heated up, leading officials began to leave town to wait out events in the tranquillity of their country estates. During these days of nearly constant uproar, the committee did not have time to establish regular procedures: the bureaus did not take minutes, and many bureaus never had a chance to meet at all.

The committee tried to master the situation by making "popular" decisions. It promised to lower bread prices and the price of salt. Committee members personally inspected the marketplace and fined bakers if they sold bread at too high a price.* On September 10 the committee suspended use of the spinning jenny and forbade tanners to use grain products of any sort in their work.† But these frantic efforts never caught up with events, which were rapidly careening out of control. The committee assumed responsibility for town affairs, but it found itself caught between the former rulers and their adherents, who withheld their support for the new regime, and the turbulent mass of workers and artisans, who demanded quick solutions to the problems of food and work.

In the opinion of the former rulers, the committee was the monstrous creature of the guild masters. Individuals "without quality, without titles or mission" had erected themselves into a tribunal that illegitimately usurped the functions of the town council.[43] The conception of this impudent innovation had been made possible by the seduction of the people, who were led astray by the lies and calumnies directed at the municipality. The committee, on the other hand, considered itself the embodiment of the commune, the rightful representative of the townspeople.[44]

The overlords of the Old Regime might well have felt threatened by these brash new men who differed so conspicuously from them in their social origins and orientation. The committee elections resulted in a coalition of merchants, professionals, artisans, and shopkeepers (see Table 16) and the repudiation of the nonnoble royal officials

---

*The committee took over all police powers when the chief police magistrate, Sourdat, left town. The committee's president, Truelle, had already established a reputation as defender of the people in 1786 and 1787, when he wrote lengthy pamphlets accusing Sourdat of collusion with the bakers against the interests of the populace. A. C. Troyes, Fonds François Carteron, vol. 38, "Observations sur le tarif et la boulangerie de Troyes, 1786" and "Suites des observations sur le tarif et la boulangerie de Troyes, 1787."

†This was alleged by Gillet and Parent, *A Nosseigneurs*, p. 27. Although the ordinances were not recorded in the minutes of the committee meetings, the committee's apologists admitted that the committee had in fact passed such ordinances. The committee members maintained, however, that it was not Truelle alone who acted in this matter, as alleged, but the committee as a whole. *Réplique au mémoire des sieurs Parent et Gillet*, p. 4.

TABLE 16

*Troyes: The Social Composition of the Committee
of August 28, 1789*

Social group	64 men elected August 28	23 town councillors as of April 14
Nobles	5%	13%
Clergy	8	4
Royal officials	3	30
Liberal professions	14	13
Merchants & clothiers	30	30
Small merchants & artisans	30	4
Bourgeois	3	4
Occupation unknown	8	0
TOTAL	101%	98%

SOURCES: For the 64 men elected in August, names and occupations are given in A.C. Troyes, A registre 54, August 29, 1789; for the 23 town councillors, names are given in A.C. Troyes, A registre 54, April 14, 1789.

who had controlled town politics in the past. Only two royal officials were named to the committee, and one of them was Truelle de Chambouzon, the renegade court magistrate. The people of Troyes did not overlook the nobles (three) or clergymen (five), but by and large butchers, tanners, grocers, and masons replaced the magistrates of 1788–89.

Animating the Troyes committee were the men who mediated between the enraged crowd and the town authorities during the riots of July and August. Truelle de Chambouzon was a natural choice for committee president. Although he was related to other rulers (Truelle-Balbedat was a merchant member of the 1789 town council; Truelle-Rambourg was an élection magistrate and also a town councillor in 1789), Truelle de Chambouzon apparently always had been the black sheep in the family. He started his judicial career innocuously, becoming an élection magistrate at the age of 27 and moving up to the bailliage court a decade later in 1766. In 1770–71, Truelle first set himself apart from his colleagues by supporting the crown's efforts to reform the judiciary (the Maupeou reforms); in a tightly knit town such as Troyes, betrayal of local solidarity was neither forgotten nor forgiven. Moreover, Truelle did not marry into the ruling group, and his son did not become a judge; instead, the young man went to Spain and became an officer in the Spanish army.* Truelle's daughter married an engineer. This social and political distance from the town rulers was reinforced by the fact that Truelle lived several blocks away from the city center near the town prison. In the late 1780's Truelle gained popular acclaim for his outspoken attacks on the chief police magistrate, Sourdat (another relative by marriage), whom he accused of collusion with the bakers who wanted to raise prices. Thus it is not surprising that the 60-year-old Truelle stepped forward in the summer of 1789 to speak for the crowd and that he was immediately embraced as the chief of the opposition.[45]

Truelle's lieutenants were the brothers Jean-François and Benoît Chaperon. These two were ideally situated to be familiar with crowd grievances; Jean-François was a police bailiff (*huissier*), and Benoît was a bailiff in the bailliage court. They were in daily contact with the town rulers, but in a subordinate position, and they were certainly not rich men. Jean-François married the daughter of a vinegar-maker in 1787 and made a marriage contract evaluated at the very modest sum of 2,400 livres. The Chaperons were ambitious minor functionaries with enough education to set them apart from the lower classes but without enough wealth to work their way beyond the edges of power. The Revolution offered them their chance.[46]

The elections in Troyes brought about a radical change in the social base of political leadership, for behind the notorious leaders of the committee were a core of merchants and professionals and a rank and file of shopkeepers and artisans. The prototypes of the *sans-culottes* pushed forward to the center stage of local politics for the first time as families prominent in the guilds or in their *quartiers* superseded the ruling families.† These new people occupied an intermediate position between the former rulers and the bulk of the

---

* Ironically, in 1793 Truelle was charged as the father of an émigré because his son was in Spain.

† This happened because the elections for deputies took place in the districts, thus foreshadowing the sectional elections of 1793–94. In Reims this did not happen because the district electors met to choose deputies on a townwide basis.

working population: they spoke for the poor though they were not themselves poor. They headed a political opposition based on respectability, but not high status, and on tight district networks of affiliation rather than townwide patterns of intermarriage. Although the committeemen at marriage were twice as rich as the average townsman, their election did mark a shift downward on the urban social scale: the new rulers made marriage contracts that were evaluated at only one-third the value of the contracts made by the former town councillors.[47] A few committeemen were related by marriage or friendship to the town's former rulers, but most of the new men represented families clearly outside the old ruling group.[48]

The election of a committee by districts decentralized the local power structure. Clusters of families from various trades and quarters took over from a single, cohesive ruling group that had been concentrated in one or two parishes in the town's medieval core. There was considerable intermarriage within the committee, but almost all of it linked families within the same trades.* The Lalobe, Dusaussay, Cousin, Terrillon, Huot, and Roblot families intermarried; they were all merchants and clothiers in the cotton business. The Chaperon brothers were the focal point for the minor functionaries and lesser professionals on the committee, and the Clignys formed the nucleus for the shopkeeping families. The two Clignys were butchers, and they were joined by Edme Dereins, a scion of the town's other big butcher family. Kinship had not been eliminated as a factor in the formation of political alliances, but in the committee kinship informed a multipolar political structure rather than a bipolar one of merchants and magistrates.

In fact, the Troyes committee can only loosely be called a political "structure," for its fluid operation never crystallized. Nevertheless, the rules governing local politics had changed. Kinship did not guarantee access to the committee, nor did it cement the committee members into a single cohesive group. Wealth and status no longer sufficed as qualifications for local office. The committee members were men with political reputations; they spoke for the crowd and

---

*At least sixteen of the 64 committee members were related by marriage.

they mobilized the crowd for collective action with political goals. They used popular pressure in the form of demonstrations and riots to attain positions of political control. As a consequence, their continuing authority rested in large measure on their responsiveness to popular demands. All efforts at internal bureaucratization of the committee shriveled in the feverish dialogue between committee and crowd. The committee remained amorphous because it could not afford to distance itself from its initial base of support.

Since the committee was composed of bunches of disparate families, its source of unity was not social but political—the deputies had organized the opposition to the former rulers. Only six members of the committee had ever held an office in the ruling institutions of the Old Regime. Few of them had been elected deputies during the meetings preliminary to the Estates General: ten had been chosen as delegates by their corporations, and four had been picked to represent the town at the bailliage meetings. Most of the committeemen were unknown outside their districts before the summer of 1789. They were truly new men, and their election ruptured the local political system. Yet their newness and their negative identity also hampered their attempts to govern. They lacked the support of the big property owners, and they had been elected because they opposed the Old Regime rather than because they carried with them concrete plans for a new one. They needed time to consolidate their position, and time was running out.

The installation of a committee in Troyes did not calm the seething spirits in the town. One objective had been attained, but people were still hungry and unemployed, and mobilization once in gear was hard to brake. Paris and the provincial towns weathered a stormy period in September, and Troyes and Reims were no exceptions. Everywhere the committees confronted ominous problems of public order. The committees had been established to cope with local emergencies and to coordinate local participation in the revolution; yet their legitimacy was questionable, and their mandate uncertain. In the absence of effective direction from the embryonic national government, they had sole responsibility for the direction of the new National Guard, which as yet was national only in name.

The committees' relation to the new militias was the key issue of the fall and winter of 1789. Where the committee kept a firm grip on the militia, it usually also managed to retain control of town politics. But where the militia broke away from the grasp of the committee, the urban revolution changed course. In September the differences between Troyes and Reims became starkly apparent.

CHAPTER 5

Consolidation or Counterrevolution?

꽃

AFTER THE SPONTANEOUS, general outburst of mid-July, the urban revolution developed at varying paces. In August and September, the National Assembly began preparing a constitution while town leaders in the provinces worked to reestablish local order and harmony by coordinating food supplies, directing public works projects, and organizing the militia or National Guard. Though ostensibly similar, the local tasks proved grossly unequal in Troyes and Reims. In Reims, the committee and council jointly kept the upper hand despite occasional flare-ups of acrimonious opposition from the lower classes. In this, Reims conformed to the predominant pattern taking shape in the towns of France, whereby the committees controlled the local militias and—with or without the cooperation of the former town councils—watched over municipal affairs until the elections of 1790. Just a few miles from Reims, however, the Revolution came to an abrupt halt: the Troyes committee succumbed to counterrevolution after it lost control of the forces of revolution. In this Troyes prefigured the politics of 1793–94, with its concurrent radicalism and reaction.

I

From the time of its embattled inauguration at the end of August and beginning of September, the Troyes committee constantly found itself in a critical situation. The Old Regime rulers had only acquiesced unwillingly to the committee's establishment, and they showed no inclination to second the committee's efforts. The militia that had taken shape in August was spearheaded by local militants who had forced the installation of a committee. Understandably, the committee was reluctant to anger its supporters in the militia by drawing up restrictive regulations for membership and discipline that might eliminate artisanal and working-class guardsmen. But this reluctance also meant that the committee had to contend with a virtually autonomous armed force.

In addition to being caught between these two incompatible political blocs, the committee also had to answer to the crowd. But scrambling endeavors to organize the supply of food and work failed to pacify the crowd, because just as the committee's tenure commenced the price of grain shot up again after weeks of steady decline. A believable explanation for the rise had to be found and, barring that, a scapegoat.

The Troyes committee apprehensively struggled to establish its authority. On Sunday, September 5, the committee passed an ordinance forbidding the posting of placards that threatened farmers and grain merchants.[1] During its deliberations that day, the committee received a hastily scribbled note from the president of the state salt monopoly (*grenier à sel*), who reported that a "prodigious mob" of men, women, and children were at that moment besieging the salt warehouse and demanding an immediate price reduction. The note requested armed assistance. The committee replied that "considering the state of effervescence of the people at this time, it is appropriate to act in such a way as to avoid embittering spirits." It begged the salt monopoly officials "to be persuaded that we wish infinitely [that we could] stop the violence, but that it is perhaps prudent to dissemble, except for eventually taking the necessary precautions."[2] The crowd dispersed when promised lower prices.

Two days later 80 guild masters assembled at the courthouse. Some proposed that the mayor and aldermen be removed from office; others wanted the army troops withdrawn from town and bread sold at two sous a pound.[3] After a noisy session of incessant talk lasting into the night, they adjourned until two days later— Thursday, September 9. According to Gillet and Parent, Truelle de Chambouzon refused to order this meeting broken up on the grounds that "these are our friends, our brothers, and they work for us."[4] The day after the guild masters' meeting, Wednesday, people "de tous les sexes" were seen running through the streets of town urging workers and artisans to gather at the courthouse: "'It's today that we are going to kill M. Huez.' 'No,' replied the others, 'it's set for Thursday.'"[5] The chief police magistrate, Sourdat, and many of the bailliage officials had already left town, but Mayor Huez, a 65-year-old bachelor, adamantly refused to abandon his post. Many townspeople believed that the departed army commander, the mayor and aldermen, and the grain merchants were plotting to starve the town into submission in order to eliminate the new committee.[6] Any incident could touch off disaster.

September 9, Thursday, was a market day, always a dangerous time when prices were high and tempers on edge. Early in the morning the National Guard convoyed two wagons loaded with precious sacks of imported rice flour to city hall. From there the sacks were quickly transported to the grocer who had ordered them. At 8 A.M. the committee received word that something was wrong with the flour.[7] By 10:30 A.M. a large crowd had invested city hall; incensed, they claimed that the flour was rotten and that someone was trying to poison the townspeople.[8] The unfortunate grocer anxiously requested an official investigation. The committee called in doctors and apothecaries to sample, analyze, and report on the flour to a special session of the police court scheduled for that afternoon. Since the chief police magistrate was one of those who had departed in panic, Mayor Huez was to preside.

The mayor opened the fateful hearing in a courtroom bulging with irate spectators. In the midst of growing commotion, scores of voices loudly insisted that Truelle de Chambouzon take the president's chair. Eventually Huez, Truelle de Chambouzon, and Truelle-Rambourg, an alderman and élection court judge, shared the rostrum and the disagreeable responsibility of passing judgment on the case. On the evidence of the investigators that the flour was not fit for consumption, they ordered it burned. As the magistrates stepped down from their places, someone in the gallery yanked at Huez's judicial robes and tripped him. Truelle de Chambouzon melodramatically described the ensuing melee:

He fell into my arms, I clasped him with all my soul, but despite my efforts, my urgent prayers, my tears, and my humiliated posture, this old man was taken away from me and dragged into the hall, stumbling and bloodied. There in the council chamber I was on my knees before the people, whose footsteps I watered with my tears. I saw this respectable old man stretch out his arms to me and just as I was flying to him, someone came to tear me away by carrying me off; someone kissed my hands and while pressing me tenderly with one arm assassinated my dear colleague with the other.[9]

With the assistance of the Chaperon brothers, Truelle made a last futile effort to save Huez by spiriting him into an adjoining ante-chamber; but the clamoring mob broke down the door, ruthlessly pulled Huez away, and beat, stabbed, and stoned him to death. Then the mob capped their merciless revenge by mutilating the mayor's corpse, after which the women and children took charge of the gro-tesquely disfigured remains and towed the body by a noose through the town's poor districts. When their trophy had been adequately displayed, they dumped it in front of city hall. Meanwhile, the men in the crowd moved on to the houses of those local notables they had marked out for retaliation. In a blurred fury, gangs of long-suffering and now inflamed men pillaged the townhouses of Saint-Georges, Huez, Cadot (chief officer of the mounted highway police), and Guyot (one of the town's leading grain merchants). The crowd's rage fixed on those responsible for repression or high prices, the two sides of the vise that was inexorably crushing them. Throughout the long night bands of desperate men roamed the streets of Troyes.[10]

II

The committee's position in these hours of pandemonium was, to say the least, embarrassing. Truelle endeavored to explain the committee's impotence to the national government.

You will ask me no doubt, Your Grace [Saint-Priest, Minister of the Interior], how it could happen that in a large and very populous town we were unable to find the means to stop the madmen in their madness and contain the hundred unfortunates who formed the seditious band. One word will be my answer, and I bemoan it still. The companies of the Citizen's Guard who were then on service refused to march and would not permit us to call out the dragoons. As a result we were forced by this unheard-of insurrection to watch all these horrors without being able to improve the situation. We were again constrained by our Citizen's Guard to release 30 wretches, all drunk and exhausted with pillage, whom several worthy men had had the decency to arrest themselves and bring into the guardhouse.[11]

Quiet reappeared in the streets of Troyes at 2 A.M. after regular army troops at last were allowed to take up positions around the town. The wild rampage completed the polarization of Troyes and showed that the committee could not control the Guard or, through it, the crowd. In the crisis the Guard had refused to act against the crowd; this confirmed many property owners' suspicions about the Guard and the committee, and on the night of September 9 these men of property armed themselves and organized patrols to protect their houses and their families. The committee's position was crumbling.

On one side was the crowd. Nearly 200 men and women were eventually arrested in connection with the events of September 9. The most complete list gives the names of 95 men and twelve women (see Table 17).[12] Their average age was 33; the youngest was sixteen, the oldest 60. As might be expected, most were either artisans (22 percent) or textile workers (57 percent). The vast majority of the latter were weavers rather than skilled artisans (finishers, bleachers) or unskilled workers (carders, spinners): a full 38 percent of all those arrested were master weavers or journeymen weavers. The active core of the crowd did not come from the town's riffraff—the professional beggars, pickpockets, and thieves. Nor was it composed of the characteristically most indigent, hapless workers—the spinners, carders, and service workers. Most of those arrested were respectable though poor men with semiskilled occupations. In prosperous times, the weavers and artisans held more secure positions than the spinners and menial laborers, who wandered restlessly from village to town in search of work. The weavers and artisans were tied to the town by their occupations, and in 1788 and 1789 they could not escape the economic squeeze that tormented Troyes. They stayed, they starved, and finally they exploded in exasperation.

On the other side were the determined adversaries of the committee, the Old Regime officials and their propertied supporters. Those

TABLE 17
Occupations of 107 Suspects in the Killing of the Mayor of Troyes

Occupations of the suspects	No.	Pct. of total	Occupations of the suspects	No.	Pct. of total
WOMEN		11%	Journeyman mason	1	
			Carpenter	1	
Spinners	7		Master shoemakers	2	
Shoemaker's daughter	1		Journeyman		
Carpenter's daughter	1		shoemakers	4	
Tailor's wife	1		Apprentice shoemaker	1	
Roofer's wife	1		Master tailors	2	
Occupation unknown	1				
			Textile workers		51%
MEN		89%	Master weavers	12	
"Bourgeois"	1	1%	Journeyman weavers	29	
			Master		
Members of the minor			stockingmakers	2	
liberal professions		4%	Journeyman		
Bailiffs	2		stockingmaker	1	
Apprentice printer	1		Drapers	3	
Student	1		Journeyman drapers	2	
			Journeyman bleacher	1	
Small merchants	4	4%	Carder	1	
			Spinners	2	
Artisans		22%	Woolworker	1	
Tavernkeepers	2				
Carter	1		*Service workers*		5%
Pewterer	1		Gardeners	2	
Plasterer	1		Menial laborers	2	
Journeyman plasterers	2		Day laborer	1	
Journeyman roofer	1				
Wood supplier	1		*Occupation unknown*	2	2%
Smith	1				
Journeyman joiner	1		TOTAL	107	100%
Journeyman					
locksmiths	2				

SOURCE: A.D. Aube, Nouvelles Acquisitions 6201, "Procès des assassins de Claude Huez."

who rallied to the defense of order on the night of September 9 speedily formed companies of armed volunteers called *grenadiers* and *chasseurs*. On September 11, Berthelin, the former mayor, told the committee that "several young men of family" wanted to create separate militia companies in order to restore order and public tranquillity in town, and asked the committee to officially recognize the new companies.[13] The committee, perhaps in the hope that the creation of these new units would frighten the existing Guard into recognition of its authority, agreed. The battalions of reaction were falling into line.

The views of the propertied were expressed most forcefully in a letter written to the National Assembly in early 1790. The letter was signed by over 120 property owners, who argued for the continued presence of the army troops stationed in Troyes. In no uncertain terms it gives their assessment of the balance of forces in Troyes.

The voting citizens and property owners of Troyes, . . . filled with love for the public good and eager to see tranquillity rule, believe it necessary to set forth to the August Representatives of the Nation their anxieties about the new misfortunes with which this town appears to be menaced.

The excruciating outrages committed in this town during the day of last September 9, whose horrible memory will never be erased, have made clear the necessity for the presence of troops of the line.

The utility of these troops was generally recognized during the entire trial concerning these atrocities, and since then for the maintenance of order and especially for the collection of taxes.

The divisions prevailing in this town as a result of the hatred inspired in the people against the good and respectable citizens is the first [reason for the need of] the troops of the line, especially if one considers that this town is composed of 28,000 souls, that of this number there are at least 18,000 who are workers employed in spinning and in the production of cloth, among whom one would find hardly 200 voting citizens, whereas the citizens signing below, although much inferior in number, pay between them four-fifths of the bulk of taxes.

A second proof of this necessity is the little concert that prevails in the different companies of the National Guard, of which the greatest part is composed of artisans and nonvoting workers. As a result, if there were an insurrection among the people, the citizens would run the greatest risk because they would not be able to contain the multitude without finding themselves reduced to repulsing violence by means that could not accord with the spirit of humanity and brotherhood that characterizes them.[14]

In the opinion of the property owners, the committee had created an atmosphere of "license without limits, contempt for order, cabals, and menacing plots" that took the place of "sound liberty."

Of those who signed the letter, 106 gave their occupations or titles: four were nobles, including the former subdelegate Pierre-Jean Paillot and his son; seventeen were royal officials; 31 were merchants;

nineteen were members of the liberal professions; 26 were clergymen; four were bourgeois; and five were small merchants or artisans.[15] Most of the clergy who signed were canons (21) rather than
parish priests. The artisans were watchmakers and goldsmiths rather
than tailors and shoemakers. Twenty-three signers had held offices in
local Old Regime institutions in 1788–89. Seven signers were committee members who evidently found the committee's policies re-
pugnant: four were merchants, one was a notary, one a nobleman,
and one a clergyman. This was the antipode to the crowd.

After September 9 the committee tried vainly to steer a course between these two poles. Deputies were dispatched to the countryside
to seek grain supplies, and it was on September 10 that the committee
prohibited the use of the spinning jenny. At about the same time,
Truelle de Chambouzon, acting for the committee, secretly approached the government and requested military assistance.

> We are redoubling our efforts to feed the town and contain the populace. . . .
> Given the limited resources at our disposal, we envisage a horrible future and
> we believe it necessary to notify Your Grace that we need a battalion of
> infantry as much for impressing the people and forestalling the unfortunates
> as for aiding us in case of need. . . . Our plan is first to lodge a battalion in
> bourgeois homes, as is customary for troops passing through; then we will
> make discreet arrangements to garrison the soldiers and give them their
> officers' orders in such a way that they will communicate as little as possible
> in front of the people.[16]

On September 13 the committee declared all gatherings illegal and
ordered their dispersal by the Guard. Merchants were forbidden to
sell powder without the permission of the committee. Two days later
the committee received word that the central government planned to
transfer some of the troops in garrison on the 20th; in response, it
voted to send Gillet and Poterat to Paris to solicit the revocation of
the orders. There was some opposition to this decision, but it received the majority of votes.[17] By voting to send a town councillor
and a retired noble army officer to Paris, the committee demonstrated its fear of the crowd and its distrust of its own militia. The
committee was trying to dissociate itself from the crowd.

The committee's agonized attempt to placate both sides was fatal.
Those initially well disposed to the committee who now doubted its

chances of survival began to question its legitimacy and sever their connections with it. The first public blow to the committee's prestige was the abrupt resignation of Camusat de Belombre as colonel of the National Guard. His wife wrote to the committee on September 13 requesting that her husband be allowed to resign so that someone from within the town could take the post.[18] Camusat was a deputy in the National Assembly, and heretofore he had taken sides with neither the town council nor the committee. In fact, he had written to the town council on August 31 warning them that resistance to a properly elected committee would only infuriate the populace: "Dear sirs, do not try to elude the object of [the people's] demand. Otherwise you will risk animating them all the more and perhaps pushing them to take by force what you would not give them willingly."[19] Now, in a self-serving maneuver, Camusat separated himself from the ill-starred committee.

After September 14 the Old Regime officials who had retired to their country estates began to return. They were confident that the tide was turning rapidly in their favor. The committee seemed trapped in an impossible bind: it could not satisfy the national government or the town's property owners without turning its back on the crowd that had carried it to power. The committee started, however halfheartedly, to round up suspects in the killing of the mayor. On September 14, Jacquinot, a prominent Troyes property owner, wrote to his friend Comparot de Longsols, who was still biding his time in the country: "It appears that the party of respectable men (*honnêtes gens*) is superior. Truelle de Chambouzon no longer enjoys the same confidence. The Committee received a letter from the Ministry which M. Parent brought back yesterday; the Ministry is complaining bitterly about the assassination of M. Huez."[20]

The committee's position rapidly deteriorated as initiative passed to its opponents. The new companies of the Guard led the way in tracking down suspects. On September 19, Sourdat, the chief police magistrate, reappeared in Troyes; on the spot he ordered the arrest of the Chaperon brothers, one of whom was his subordinate on the police force. Sourdat originally had ordered their arrest on August 31, but at that time he could find no one to execute his command.

After September 21 the Chaperon brothers languished in prison, and the committee was stripped of two of its most active leaders. The bailliage judges, now all back in Troyes, met on September 23 for the first time since their homecoming. Two days later they excommunicated their maverick colleague, Truelle de Chambouzon, and secretly ordered the suppression of the troublesome committee. The latter decision they wisely refrained from publishing until September 29, by which date the troops requested of the national government finally had arrived. On September 26 the committee wrote to the national government to request the opening of the trial of the suspects, 120 of whom had been arrested and imprisoned by then. This letter proved to be the committee's last public act. On September 29, committee members arrived at city hall to find their way barred by 1,200 soldiers, most of whom were reliable Swiss guards.

The bailliage court's judgment to suppress the committee, made public the same day, was of uncertain legality since the court's very existence was in question by this point in 1789. The committee vociferously complained to all who would listen that the court did not have jurisdiction in the matter. Yet the court had the armed force necessary to enforce its decision. The magistrates claimed in a letter to the authorities in Paris that "the conduct of the committee was detrimental to the security and life of the citizens. The committee had exceeded not only the powers conferred on it by the commune, but even the most simple notions. It was the duty and the competence [of the court] to suppress these excesses of the committee." [21] In his official report to the court, Parent, king's advocate, argued that the committee had not restricted itself to its proper consultative role, but had illegally absorbed the jurisdiction and authority of the municipal officers. By ridiculing the municipality, the committee had incited the people to "excesses of ferocity." [22] On the basis of affidavits presented by Parent, Gillet, and Sourdat, the court declared that "all of the bourgeois and inhabitants of this town are forbidden to recognize or obey any other judges than their legitimate judges mandated with powers and authority from the King." [23]

The Old Regime reasserted itself quickly. On September 30 the town council resumed its functions, with Comparot de Longsols taking Huez's place as mayor. Preparations for a trial of the suspects accelerated. The Troyes bailliage court requested that a different court hear the case, and the court of Chaumont was assigned to do so. As Noché, a court magistrate and the procureur-syndic of the town council, wrote to Comparot de Longsols on September 24: "The people is now something quite different from what it was a year ago; its customs have been changed by examples, it senses its influence; some abuse this strangely. . . . Punishment will appear to be vengeance; the trial will appear to be animated by a spirit of party and of war, from which our descendants will gather bitter fruits."[24]

Once restored, the town council took measures to reinforce its position. The day of its reinstallation, the council voted to establish a prize for the largest shipment of wheat brought to the Troyes market. On October 6 the council met with the officers of the bailliage court, the maréchaussée, and the police to develop new security procedures. The result was an order for a house-by-house search for arms, which was promptly conducted by army troops in conjunction with the National Guard.[25] According to Abbé Trémet, arms were confiscated in order to prevent a new riot when news arrived of the march of the Paris crowd to Versailles and the removal of the royal family to Paris.[26] According to Gillet and Parent, however, the timing of the search was purely fortuitous; the search was made in order to recover the rifles taken August 27 and to look for suspects.[27] On October 17 the town council approved regulations for the National Guard that officially recognized the grenadiers and chasseurs as separate companies.[28]

The bailliage court and the town council both tried to counteract the influence of the committee members on the townspeople. On October 21 the court cited Truelle de Chambouzon and two other former committee members for passing out leaflets calling for a meeting of the commune. Truelle was not arrested, but his arrest did appear imminent, so he and three other former members of the committee left for Paris to plead the committee's case. On October 22 the town council sent Parent and Gillet to Paris to solicit a decree against the publication of divisive pamphlets—those written by former committee members. At the end of October the National Assembly's decree of martial law for France was read aloud in the town's major public centers.

Despite these measures, the town council and the bailliage court feared a reversal of their fortunes. Only the trial of those suspected of killing the mayor promised them more restful nights. This can be seen in the town council's letters. On October 19 they wrote to army commander Saint-Georges and asked him to stay away from Troyes until the judgment was rendered: "We hope that a month from now you can return to our town without ill-disposed people being able to misinterpret your return." On October 25 the council wrote to the court in Chaumont asking them to hasten to Troyes: "Your presence, dear sirs, is absolutely necessary in Troyes. It is important not only for good order, for public tranquillity, for the security of the inhabitants, but also for their Existence; in a word, we believe we can assure you that there is not a moment to lose." [29]

With a largely unreliable Guard and a town torn in two by rapid shifts in the locus of authority, the restored regime depended on the army to buttress its shaky control. On November 4 the town council described the situation to Gillet, who was still in Paris: "We regard as indispensable that we retain 400 Swiss and 100 hussars or all of the hussars and 100 Swiss. That is all the more essential since it is only too true that the fermentation is still very considerable. Everything indicates that it prevails less among the masses than in a slightly more elevated order. It is manifested by posters and placards which indicate that it is very necessary that the spirit of sedition be stifled." [30] The council's position was weak because the national government had not yet clearly taken a side. Most towns still had their committees, and the bailliage courts had been largely discredited along with all the other venal institutions. On November 5, Gillet and Parent wrote to Comparot de Longsols with a suggestion:

Between you see if it would not be expedient in order to quiet the people to announce by a poster that they have been misled; that someone has been trying to prejudice them against the respectable citizens ready to sacrifice everything for their subsistence; that if the spirit of revolt . . . continues, these citizens, in order to take shelter from all insults, will be forced to abandon the town; that in that case the charities will cease and that, left to themselves and without work, they will be exposed to dying from starvation. In vain will they hope to find help from the people who guide them at this time.[31]

There is no evidence that the town council took up the suggestion to threaten the townspeople with starvation, but it is apparent that the town council and its deputies in Paris feared the renewal of overt agitation. Moreover, since the Paris committee soon decided to defend the cause of its sibling in Troyes, the Old Regime officials in Troyes had good reason to wonder if the national government would turn against them.* A quick judgment in the trial of the suspects was their one hope, for it would serve as an example to the rest of the townspeople and at the same time fortify the restored regime's claim to legitimacy. Justice—the justice of the Chaumont magistrates—was bound to be on their side.

The judgment of the court was not made public until November 27, 1789. By that time hundreds of witnesses had been heard and scores of suspects were being formally detained. The mounted highway police tracked down suspects in villages and towns all over the region in what became one of the largest manhunts of the epoch. In the eighteenth century prisons were used primarily for the detention of vagabonds, beggars, or suspects awaiting trial. Prison sentences were not often used as a form of punishment, and the prisons in Champagne were consequently not equipped to hold large numbers of prisoners. Up until the end of the Old Regime, the largest number of people ever held in the Troyes prison at one time had been 110.[32] Yet between the beginning of June 1789 and the end of December, 239 people were incarcerated, some for only a few days, others for long periods.[33] As a result, overcrowding and disease became a great problem during the trial, and at least two suspects died in prison. The prisoners had to pay the jailers if they wished to receive their pound and a half of bread daily. In this period of high prices and unemployment, few suspects could pay the two sous a day required for

*On November 11, while Gillet and Parent were in Paris, four deputies from the Paris committee appeared at the bar of the National Assembly to speak on behalf of the Troyes committee. Gillet and Parent scolded the Paris committee for its attempts to dictate to the other towns. Gillet and Parent, *Réflexions ultérieures* (Paris, 1789).

bread; hence the prisoners barely survived in a state of near starvation.

After the arrival of the court magistrates from Chaumont at the end of October, the pace of the interrogations quickened. Most of the questioning was conducted by Parent and Lucot d'Hauterive, the noble commanding officer of the maréchaussée of Champagne. They grilled most suspects two or three times, though some, such as the Chaperon brothers, faced as many as six interrogations. The families of the Chaperon brothers wrote to the National Assembly complaining that the new criminal laws were not being followed, and the national government reminded the officials of their obligations.[34]

The court's final judgment, rendered on November 27, was harsh. Five were condemned to die, one on the wheel and four by hanging. All were to "make amends" first: they were to march with ropes around their necks and torches in their hands to the gates of the cathedral, the courthouse, and the city hall, and at each site to declare their repentance and ask the forgiveness of God, the Nation, the king, and justice. Three men were sentenced to be branded with a hot iron and then sent to the galleys for life. Two men were to stand in the marketplace wearing placards reading "Seditious" and "Insolent and Seditious Beggar." Both were then to be sent to the galleys, one for nine years, the other for three years. Two men were banished from the province and the généralité for nine years; two more were sent to prison, for five years and for three years, respectively.[35] At the same time, the court ordered more arrests and requested additional information about several suspects, including the Chaperon brothers. The continuation of the *procès* over the next two months maintained fears of reprisal among the townspeople; retribution had not had its final word yet.

The people condemned by the court were typical of those arrested by the police forces. The man sentenced to be broken on the wheel was a 22-year-old unskilled workman (*manouvrier*). Of the four sentenced to hang, one was a woman, the 35-year-old wife of a journeyman carpenter; the others were two journeyman weavers and a smith, aged 24, 26, and 32. Most of the other nine sentenced were textile workers: three were journeyman weavers, two were master weavers, and one was a spinner. An apprentice printer, a gardener, and a 52-year-old man from the suburbs who called himself a "bourgeois" formed the rest. The average age of those sentenced was 35, with a range from eighteen to 60.[36] The people convicted by the court were for the most part not reckless, shiftless youths; they came from the same poor but previously respectable groups that formed the backbone of the crowd.

The severity of the judgment was just as unusual as the large-scale imprisonments that preceded it. In the fifteen years from 1751 to 1765, 663 serious crimes had been reported in all of Champagne for an average of 44 crimes a year.[37] In the judgments of 601 closed cases, 49 people had been sentenced to death, 40 had been condemned to the galleys for life, and 73 had been sent to the galleys for some specific period. The courts of Champagne were much less harsh after 1770. The Cour Souveraine of Reims, for instance, sentenced 70 people to hang between 1740 and 1765 but ordered only one hanging after 1766.[38] Even during the years of sternest repression, an average of only three or four people a year were sentenced to death in all of Champagne. Reims suffered two riots in 1789, but only two men received sentences; both were condemned to the galleys for life. Apparently, the Chaumont magistrates felt that the killing of the mayor of Troyes far exceeded the limits of thinkable violence even in those violent times.

The executions were carried out the day after the sentences were read as a warning to a still restive populace. The scaffold was set up in the square in front of the courthouse where most of the confrontations between the crowd and the officials of the Old Regime had taken place. Ten of the fourteen sentences included public displays of penance that were to be offered at the town's most central and most public places, including the marketplace, the origin of most of the riots. All of the punishments were administered in the presence of troops. The officials designed this chastening and lugubrious spectacle for crowd consumption, and its effect, reinforced in various gruesome ways, could not have failed to impress even a population long inured to daily violence.

That the court's decision was a political as well as a criminal judgment was revealed in the report it issued with the second sentencing on February 9, 1790:

The multitude, misled by the false precepts of a misunderstood doctrine on the equality of men, attacked the rich, the men in place.

. . .

The trumpet of discord announced everywhere that the Communes had risen against the Municipalities, whose regime they censured; everywhere people plotted their fall by undermining them with new establishments under the name of Committee, to which they turned over the public administration. Love of novelty no doubt strengthened this work of the citizens of all the orders.

. . .

Men tormented by the desire to command others, to raise themselves to the places they believed they merited, used the circumstances to their profit.[39]

In their statement, the Chaumont magistrates echoed many of the assertions of the Troyes magistrates: they attributed the creation of the committee to the power-grabbing ambitions of those who manipulated the crowd, and they blamed the atmosphere created by the committee for the tragic death of the mayor.

The deliberations that led to the second sentencing moved at a leisurely pace throughout December and January. In the second and final decision of February 9, 1790, several others were sentenced and two were condemned to death, but this time the sentences were carried out in effigy, the eighteenth-century version of a suspended sentence. By then, the political climate had altered; nonetheless, it was not until March 9, 1790, that the Chaperon brothers were finally released from prison.

The town council celebrated its restoration with a memorial service for Huez on December 3, just a few days after the public executions. A week later, the Troyes committee failed to get the support of the National Assembly; the Committee of Reports entered a resolution on the floor against the judgment of the bailliage court, but it was withdrawn in the face of many protests.[40] The renascent Old Regime could breathe more easily now, and when the national government offered 19,000 livres to help supply the town, the council appropriated 5,000 livres to repair the houses of Saint-Georges and

Cadot.[41] The former committee members withdrew to the shadows of public life, and the people of the once awesome crowd stayed home. Winter promised to be bitter.

Although the trial successfully frightened the population into submission, it also exacerbated the divisions in Troyes. Abbé Trémet, an observer sympathetic to the Old Regime, described the atmosphere of rancor and discord.

Everything that we saw up to now was more than sufficient to afflict the inhabitants of the town of Troyes, but what followed capped the scandal. The demon of discord sowed division in all bodies and completed the affliction of the respectable people [*gens de bien*]. The division that began in the clergy soon spread among the people and into the different bodies of which it is composed. It even reached the tribunals, which fought one against the other: the bailliage, the municipal officers, the former members of the committee, the officers of the maréchaussée, the bourgeois militia, finally the people. Everyone was divided. Every day memoirs and printed and handwritten pamphlets appeared. . . . Friends no longer spoke to each other.[42]

Undercurrents of virulent animosity menaced the town council as it tensely performed its functions. Food prices declined somewhat, but unemployment continued at high levels. Only the army provided a thin margin of security. The town recovered a semblance of normality, but no one had forgotten or forgiven.

III

While violence and political turnabouts kept Troyes in constant turmoil, the Reims alliance of council and committee functioned smoothly. Although the crowd had rioted in Reims in mid-July, its manifestations of anger were never as ferociously desperate as the rampages of the Troyes crowd. No one was killed in Reims, either by the crowd or by the authorities. There was division in Reims, but not extreme polarization; ideologies clashed, but only rarely in a conscious or explicit way. The lower classes chafed against the joint rule of the Reims committee and council, but the remnants of the Old Regime never became the symbols of starvation and political conniving as they did in Troyes. Moreover, the Old Regime rulers never provoked the formation of a determined bourgeois opposition willing and able to use the grievances of the lower classes for political leverage. In Troyes, the bourgeoisie fragmented and thus opened the door to both radical revolution and counterrevolution. In Reims, propertied groups coalesced to assert their newly won political rights. In their endeavors, the rulers of Reims enjoyed the invaluable aids of steady—albeit not declining—bread prices and growing employment.

The chief issue in Reims during the fall months was the presence of army troops. As in Troyes, the National Guard wanted the soldiers removed so that the militia would be the sole armed force in the town. Even as the voters gathered in their districts to elect a committee on August 18, the Reims town council was writing to Necker to explain the delicacy of the situation: "It is essential that we keep for a few months yet the 100 dragoons that we have here in garrison, but it would be dangerous to send us any more soldiers, as much for the expense they cause us, which we bear with difficulty, as for the fermentation that prevails among the people and among the bourgeois. There have been several quarrels between members of the bourgeois militia and the dragoons, and these cause us to desire the conservation of the soldiers we have here only until that time when our markets are reestablished in the state in which they ought to be." [43] More soldiers were garrisoned in Troyes than in Reims, but the presence of regular army troops was relatively new to Reims. As we have seen, Troyes had had a garrison since 1740, but Reims was garrisoned only after the food riots of March 1789. In both towns the burden of feeding and lodging the soldiers fell upon the townspeople, and this vexed a population already ground down by a ruined local economy. In many towns throughout France during 1789, the residents felt affronted by the presence of army troops—for by sending them the national government indicated its distrust of the local armed forces. The confrontations between townspeople and soldiers quickly developed a persistent pattern. Militiamen on patrol would accuse the dragoons of insulting the nation either by refusing to wear the revolutionary tricolor cockade or by sporting a black one instead. Fistfights and free-swinging brawls followed, and it was left to the committees to mediate.

The Reims council and committee chose to stress the need for discipline within the National Guard. The oath prescribed for Guard members reminded them of their high purpose and required their dedication to the nation. The procureur-syndic described the carefully prepared ceremony of September 1, in which all the Reims Guardsmen pledged a collective oath of loyalty and obedience: "It [the Guard] has for its goal the maintenance of legitimate authority and the respect due the laws. . . . Those therefore who have abandoned their duties will again become good citizens of the Nation and loyal Subjects of the King; the reform of abuses will take place peacefully and tranquilly and will no longer be marked by disastrous events. Each will contribute what he can to the reestablishment of order, peace, union, and tranquillity."[44] Reims officials feared the Guard's potential to organize itself and relied on the officers to maintain discipline and keep them informed of any threatening developments. De la Salle, the commander of the Reims National Guard, made this clear in a speech to the officers on September 27, 1789:

Equally essential is the daily surveillance of licentious or seditious talk, . . . which it is very important to stop. You inhabit all parts of the town, sirs; pay the greatest attention to this, listen to everything of this sort and please, on the spot, if you hear anything, inform me of it. Be assured of my discretion; you will not be compromised, I give you my word.

I have learned, sirs (not without being surprised), that you have been sent notices of convocation asking you to assemble today at the Cordeliers; I do not know who sent them, this is an irregularity. . . . I repeat to you, sirs, when any of you has something to communicate to me that has escaped me and would be for the public good, I will always make it my duty to listen with gratitude; but no assemblies of individuals—I must prohibit them and I do prohibit them.[45]

The people of Reims did not riot after mid-July, but neither did they passively yield to the recent minimal realignment in the ruling circle.

The loyalty of the National Guard worried the Reims committee and council throughout the fall. On October 23 the Friday bureau of the committee received word that members of one of the patrols intended to keep their arms after completing their rounds.[46] A week later the same bureau learned that a wagonload of gunpowder had just been delivered to a merchant in one of the suburbs. The council and committee ordered the confiscation of the powder and interrogated several of those thought involved. This was the only incident during its long tenure that the committee considered significant enough to report to the National Assembly.[47] Again on November 2 rumors were reported of vague plans for armed gatherings.[48] The committee and council reacted quickly to each of these incidents, and they never allowed Guard members to take their arms home. Every episode remained isolated, and an opposition movement failed to form. The Reims committee showed no interest in allying itself with dissidents in the Guard in order to take power from the town council.

After November even the occasional threats to public order diminished and nearly disappeared. On January 15, 1790, the town council wrote to the minister of war to request the withdrawal of the soldiers. Antagonism between the Guard and the troops still flared up from time to time, and now the council felt it could safely remove this source of irritation.[49] The National Guard was sufficiently well disciplined and numerous to keep order by itself. The townspeople no longer hoped to effect changes through the committee; instead, they looked forward to the elections ordered by the National Assembly, the first elections to be held under a constitutional government.

IV

In both Troyes and Reims, the final weeks of 1789 and the first weeks of 1790 were relatively quiet. It was an uneasy peace that was often enforced by soldiers from other lands and residents of the upper classes. There were no riots during this period. From Paris came a rapid stream of new laws that aimed to reorganize the country and its provinces. Both Troyes and Reims wanted to be named headquarters of their respective new departments, and both town councils zealously lobbied in Paris.[50] The National Assembly designated Troyes the capital of the Department of the Aube, but Reims remained subordinate to its longtime administrative rival, Châlons-sur-Marne. Although the Reims rulers lost out in this competition between towns, they did not consequently lose control of politics at home.

The voters of Troyes and Reims went to the polls in 1790 with very different political experiences behind them. The collapse of the Old

Regime had opened contests for power everywhere, and new contenders for positions of authority appeared in most French towns. Yet the nature of the struggle, as well as its outcome, varied depending on several factors: the alignment of power before 1789; the gravity of the local economic situation in 1788 and 1789; the attitudes of the prerevolutionary ruling elites; and the capabilities of the bourgeois opposition. The ruling elite of Troyes had fostered the growth of a determined opposition by obstinately resisting local demands for political renovation. In turn, the combination of rising prices and protracted unemployment had enabled the opposition leaders to use crowd pressure, either actual or threatened, as a springboard to power. Yet the Troyes committee's failure to solve the economic problems of its supporters doomed it; it ran aground while trying to negotiate a treacherous course between the recalcitrant former rulers and the unappeased crowd. The revolution in Troyes brought reaction in its wake.

The resilient Reims elite weathered every political confrontation. Agilely sidestepping, yielding ground when necessary, the Reims rulers dexterously either anticipated or outlasted their opponents. The elite was able to do this because it was strengthened by diversity, and nobles and bourgeois continued to cooperate during the first year of the Revolution just as they had so successfully during the last decades of the Old Regime. In 1789 it was the merchants and manufacturers of Reims who emerged most fortified by the contest, and it was the clergy who suffered the decisive defeat. The townspeople blamed the Reims church for the evils of the Old Regime, and the lay notables came away relatively unscathed. In the process the political arena expanded in Reims, and new men tried out their political skills. As yet, however, the rules of the game had not much changed.

CHAPTER 6

The Inauguration of a New Regime

꿕

THE URBAN REVOLUTION of July forced the National Assembly to consider the question of municipal government. Debates began as early as July 23, 1789, when Mirabeau and Mounier disagreed on the virtues of local autonomy.[1] Initially, the Assembly gave most attention to Paris, where the administration changed several times in 1789. In August both the National Assembly and the Paris committee began to formulate plans for a new official administrative structure in the capital. By the end of September the National Assembly's Committee on the Constitution was ready to present its proposal for the reorganization of all municipal governments. The Committee's project was extensively debated in November. Everywhere confusion and uncertainty plagued local governments: some town councils had been overthrown, and others had resigned; the position of the committees in local affairs was equivocal. A growing chorus of town governments implored the National Assembly to regularize their situations. Finally, on December 14, 1789, the Assembly approved the plan that had been submitted by its Committee on the Constitution.

In reordering municipal government, the National Assembly established the pattern for all of its subsequent administrative legislation: the new constitutional government was to be uniform, elected, and relatively decentralized. The law of December 14, 1789, provided for a municipal structure as follows: at the head of each municipality were a mayor and a *procureur* (who exercised nearly the same functions as the *procureur-syndic* of the Old Regime council), both elected for two-year terms; next came an elected *corps municipal* of town officers; and then came a "General Council of the Commune" composed of separately elected notables plus the municipal officers. The size of the General Council depended upon the population of the town. Both Troyes and Reims were to elect fifteen municipal officers (including the procureur) and 30 notables, for a 45-member Council. Large towns and cities were divided into sections, which were to hold elections in general assemblies called "primary assemblies." Troyes was divided into seven sections, Reims into eight. The General Council was elected for a two-year term, and half of its members were up for election each year.[2]

The National Assembly invested the new municipal governments with more extensive authority than the former town councils had ever had. Though administratively subordinate to the new district and department councils, municipalities were now to take over the functions previously associated with the office of chief police magistrate. This new police power also encompassed control of the National Guard, and eventually included the power to regulate the prices of bread and meat (laws of July 19–22, 1791). Thus the town governments of 1790–91 incorporated the administrative domains of both the Old Regime councils and the revolutionary committees. With the law of December 14, 1789, the National Assembly recognized the urban contribution to the Revolution and confirmed the changes that had taken place in the preceding six months.

The criteria to determine eligibility to vote and to stand for election were also prescribed by the new municipal legislation. The primary assembly of each section of the commune was open to all "active citizens," defined as men 25 and over who had lived at least one year in the town, were not servants, were enrolled in the National Guard, had taken the civic oath, and had paid a direct tax equal to at least three days' wages at the local rate.[3] At first, the value of three days' wages was left to each locality to define, but after many disputes the National Assembly decreed on January 15, 1790, that the estimation of one day's wages should not exceed twenty sous (one livre). Consequently, an adult male usually had to pay a minimum of three livres direct tax a year in order to qualify to vote. Not all those who qualified to vote were eligible to stand for office, however. To be eligible for municipal office, a voting citizen had to pay a direct tax equal to at least ten days' wages, or ten livres in most places.*

The new local election procedures called for direct election of all municipal officials, which vitiated the control formerly exercised by the Old Regime elite in Reims and Troyes by eliminating the two-stage electoral process. When there were only 90 "electors," as had been the case in Reims, it was relatively easy for local notables to manipulate elections through patronage. Direct elections made such intervention much more difficult. At the same time, the Reims church lost its privilege of selecting six clerical deputies, and the corporate quotas in Troyes and many other provincial towns were eliminated.

Though according to R. R. Palmer poverty kept about one-quarter of the adult males in France from enjoying the franchise, for him this does not lessen the "democratic" character of the Constitution of 1790–91.[4] The national figures, however, mask great local variations.[5] Although Troyes and Reims had about the same size populations, they had very different numbers of "active citizens": Troyes had only 2,760 eligible to vote, whereas Reims had 5,539. The Troyes figure represented about 10 percent of the total population and less than 50 percent of the adult males. In Reims the figure represented about two-thirds of the adult males.[6] Since both Troyes and Reims had large populations of poor textile workers, the proportion of voting citizens in the two towns fell short of Palmer's national average. And since the textile depression of the late 1780's hit Troyes harder than Reims, fewer textile workers qualified for the vote in the former than in the latter. Yet despite the exclusion of thousands of poor males, the "lower classes" were well represented among voters. In Reims, for example, 75 percent of the voters came from the lower classes: 40 percent were textile workers, 26 percent were small merchants or artisans, and 9 percent were service workers.[7]

The social composition of those eligible for *office* was quite another story, however. In Reims only 1,547 voters (28 percent) could meet the required "ten livres" in direct tax to be able to stand

---

*Ten days' wages were originally set at fifteen livres in Troyes, and at nine livres, ten sous in Reims. Troyes had to reduce its evaluation to ten livres by decision of the National Assembly.

for election.[8] And as we might expect, the requirement worked in favor of the upper classes. One-fourth of the eligible citizens were nobles, clergymen, royal officials, bourgeois, or professionals, and another 17 percent were merchants or clothiers; this contrasted with about 40 percent who were artisans or small merchants, and fewer than 10 percent who were textile or service workers. Of the remaining 8 percent, who did not list occupations, most were probably nobles or property owners without professions.

Comparable information on Troyes could not be found in the local archives. But the number of eligible citizens there (1,142) was about the same as the number in Reims (1,547), which reinforces the impression of greater poverty among the textile workers in Troyes than among those in Reims. Few textile workers in either town were eligible for office; but more textile workers met the voting criteria in Reims than in Troyes.

I

Voting began at the end of January in Troyes and at the beginning of February in Reims. Three weeks were required in each town for the completion of these first elections under the new constitution. The prospect of lengthy meetings in the sectional assemblies worried town officials, and in Reims the town council put the maréchaussée on the alert.[9] Quarrels and fistfights disrupted the elections in Troyes, where the balloting promised a final resolution to the contest between the committee and the Old Regime town council.[10]

The municipal elections dragged on because the voting procedures were complicated and an absolute majority was required for election. In the event that no one received a clear majority on the first ballot, a second ballot had to be ordered. If after the second ballot no one had received a majority, then a third ballot was necessary and the person receiving the plurality on that one was declared the winner. In the elections for mayor this system worked relatively efficiently because only one person was to be chosen and each voter chose only one candidate. If a third ballot was required in the mayoral election, only the two candidates with the highest totals on the second ballot were eligible. Balloting for municipal officers and notables, however, was more involved because each voter selected two candidates for every slot (30 officers and 60 notables) in each of the necessary ballots. Even if only 1,000–1,500 voters turned out, the paperwork was prodigious and time-consuming. The second ballot, when one was needed, was often delayed several days while officials laboriously tabulated the results of the first.

The complexity and unfamiliarity of the electoral procedures undoubtedly contributed to voter absenteeism. In Troyes, only 59 percent of the "active citizens" (1,627) voted in the mayoral elections of January 23, and participation declined steadily thereafter. A week later 1,500 voted in the elections for municipal officers, and on February 3 this dropped to 1,112 (40 percent). Two days later, less than one-third of the voters (899) turned out.[11] The Reims elections showed the same decline in interest. Fifty-six percent (3,066) of the voters turned out on February 7 for the mayoral elections, but only 1,316 voted in the elections for municipal officers. By February 22 only 1,232 (22 percent) showed up for the election of town notables.[12]

The municipal elections in Troyes resulted in almost a clean sweep for the partisans of the committee. Only the office of mayor escaped them, for Camusat de Belombre, Troyes' deputy to the National Assembly, was elected to that post on the first ballot with nearly 80 percent of the votes cast. Camusat enjoyed a reputation for impartiality—owing in large measure to his absence from town during the devastating months of the municipal revolution—and was thus acceptable to most people, whatever their local political loyalties. He had served on the town council in the early 1770's, but he was not linked with the Old Regime in the minds of his fellow townspeople. His letters from Versailles had expressed his enthusiastic support for the Revolution being made by the National Assembly, and he had consistently distanced himself from both the town council and the committee.[13] Hence he was an ideal candidate for a town racked by division.

Eleven of the fifteen municipal officers chosen had been members

of the committee, and at least one other, Prignot, was a known supporter of the committee's position.* Only three of the fifteen had
held office under the Old Regime: one was an architect who had sat
on the town council in the early 1780's; the second was an officer of
the maréchaussée; and the third was Truelle de Chambouzon, who
as president of the former committee can hardly be considered an
Old Regime "notable." Four of those elected were merchants (as was
the mayor), seven were members of the liberal professions, two were
royal officials, one was a clergyman, and one was an artisan.[14]

The committee's adherents also did well in the elections for town
notables. Thirteen of the 30 notables had been members of the committee; only two had held offices in the Old Regime. One of the two
was a merchant town councillor, and the other was an official in the
maîtrise des eaux et forêts. Not one prominent opponent of the
committee was elected to municipal office in Troyes in 1790. Ten of
the notables were merchants or clothiers, and fourteen were shopkeepers or artisans. They were joined by two clergymen, two gardeners, one royal official, and one "bourgeois."[15] No noble was elected.

The Reims committee also did well in the municipal elections, but
this did not mean that the former ruling group was excluded as it was
in Troyes. In the Reims mayoral elections Pierret, king's proctor in
the *maîtrise des eaux et forêts*, was chosen on the third ballot over
Savoye, a wealthy textile merchant and former town councillor. The
mayor-elect had served on the committee, as had nine of the fifteen
municipal officers. Yet three of the new municipal officers had been
town councillors under the Old Regime, and two others were royal
officials, including the new procureur, who had been the procureur-
syndic for the former town council.[16] Nine of the fifteen municipal
officers were merchants or clothiers; the municipal elections thus
confirmed the political preponderance of the mercantile groups,
which had been established earlier in the committee elections. These
nine were joined by the two royal officials, one notary, one farmer,

---

*Prignot edited the *Patriote troyen*, a new journal established to combat the
influence of the *Patriote français cadet*, the journal supporting the Old Regime rulers
in Troyes.

one building contractor (*entrepreneur*), and one finisher. No clergy-man or noble was elected as a municipal officer in Reims.

A large number of new men were elected as notables in Reims. Six members of the committee and four Old Regime officeholders were picked, but the other twenty notables had never held office before. Five of these new men had served as deputies for their corporations during the meetings preliminary to the Estates General; the other fifteen were political unknowns. Merchants and clothiers predominated among the notables as they had in the earlier elections: fourteen of the notables were merchants or clothiers, nine were artisans or shopkeepers, five came from the liberal professions, and two were farmers.[17] The only noble selected for a new municipal position was Louis Sutaine, the son of a former subdelegate, who was chosen as assistant to the procureur of the new municipality. The former rulers did not lose out altogether, but the most privileged groups, the nobles and clergymen, were dislodged from their places in local government. The revolution that the committee failed to push was completed now.

All over France, according to Jacques Godechot, "[the elections] confirmed in a tangible manner the success of the revolution. In the great majority of communes in France, the 'patriots' triumphed."[18] Despite the denial of the vote to thousands of textile workers in Troyes and Reims, the local revolution surged forward. Apparently, it was not the "patriots" who stayed home on election days. In Troyes, the townspeople avenged the revolutionary committee by turning out its adversaries, the Old Regime rulers. In Reims, the voters ratified the committee's leadership and with it the now dominant position of the mercantile groups; at the same time they cut a path for new political leaders by electing notables previously untried in the political arena. The meaning of the elections did not escape contemporaries. Abbé Trémet expressed the dismay of the former rulers in Troyes in his journal: "Those who were the most ambitious were precisely those who composed the former committee, . . . and by their schemings, their intrigues, and their cabals, they attained positions in the municipality. People murmur much about it in Troyes because they were individuals who were hardly worthy to fill such positions." [19] An anonymous author in Reims uttered a similar opinion of the men elected in 1790: "What a difference today. Every sort of class votes for or holds positions, whereas in the old days it was the foremost people [*les premiers*] of the town or the place who controlled the positions and who named people to them." [20] The old order had passed away.

There were some noteworthy differences between the municipal elections in Troyes and Reims. Although nobles were passed over in both towns, the clergy fared much better in Troyes than in Reims. A canon was elected as a municipal officer (he had been a committee member), and two other clergymen were elected as notables. The exclusion of the clergy in Reims demonstrated once again how low the credit of the church was in that cathedral town. In Troyes, the royal officials and town councillors were perceived as the enemies of the Revolution. Merchants and clothiers came off best in the Reims elections, even though they failed to capture the mayoralty. The same groups did reasonably well in Troyes, but fell far short of outright command. The municipal officers elected in Troyes were a varied lot of merchants, notaries, doctors, and lawyers brought together by their political stance rather than by their professional affiliations. This happened for two reasons: the merchants had been discredited by the severe depression in Troyes, and the violently alternating fortunes of the committee had divided the town's highest-ranking social groups along political lines. Hence it was the enthusiastic politicians who won election in Troyes rather than the patrons of industry. *

II

Elections for the district and department governments took place in the spring of 1790. These elections had less immediate or telling effect on town politics than the municipal elections of the winter. The district and department elections took place in two stages, and the

---

*Included among the new municipal officers were three of the four committee members who wrote memoirs justifying the committee and spoke on behalf of the committee in Paris, the editor of the "patriot" paper, and the lawyer-writer who defended the Chaperon brothers actively in print.

councils elected included men from the surrounding regions as well as from Troyes and Reims. Since the district and department governments were regional administrations, they are of interest here only insofar as they affected town politics.

Electors for the department elections were assigned on the basis of one for every hundred voters, so that Troyes was allotted 28 electors and Reims 55. The primary assemblies met and picked their quota of electors, and then the town electors met with those chosen by other towns and villages in the department. Nearly half of the Troyes electors (45 percent) were merchants or clothiers (17 percent) or artisans or shopkeepers (28 percent). Half of the Reims electors likewise fell into the commercial category: 47 percent were merchants or clothiers, and 7 percent were artisans or shopkeepers.[21] At the department level, however, the town electors were completely outnumbered: in the Aube department there were 386 electors in addition to the paltry 28 delegates from Troyes. The big industrial towns were not to tyrannize the regional proceedings.

Two social groups outweighed all others among the department electors and, consequently, in the new department administrations: men with legal training (either lawyers or royal officials), and rural landowners. Merchants and tradesmen, who dominated town politics in Troyes and Reims, made up only 18 percent of the Aube electors from outside Troyes. Nearly half of the Aube electors were either royal officials or members of the liberal professions, and nearly a third were rural landowners.[22] The electors in the Marne department chose ten royal officials, seven men of the law, one doctor, eight landowners, five local mayors or procureurs (most of them also landowners), two "bourgeois," and only three merchants to sit on the new General Council of the department.[23] Three of these were men from Reims—one merchant and two royal officials. Likewise, three men from Troyes were elected to the General Council of the Aube department—one merchant, one royal official, and one clergyman.

The men from Troyes and Reims who were elected to the new district and department councils formed, with the men elected in the new municipalities, the new ruling group. Comparison of them with

TABLE 18
*Troyes: The Social Composition of the 52 New Rulers
Elected in 1790, the Committee of August 28, 1789, and the
Old Regime Town Council*

Social group	52 new rulers[a]	64 men elected to the committee	23 Old Regime town councillors
Nobles	2%	5%	13%
Clergy	8	8	4
Royal officials	8	3	30
Liberal professions	19	14	13
Merchants & clothiers	29	30	30
Small merchants & artisans	33[b]	30	4
Bourgeois	2	3	4
Occupation unknown	0	8	0
TOTAL	101%	101%	98%

[a] Includes district and department officials from Troyes as well as the newly elected municipal officials.
[b] Includes two gardeners.

the Old Regime town councils and the 1789 committees shows how the Revolution transformed local political leadership. In Troyes, where the committee represented a radical break with the Old Regime, the 1790 rulers strongly resembled the committee; nearly half of the new rulers had been committee members. The nobles and royal officials were replaced in the ruling coalition by artisans and small merchants (see Table 18). The Revolution did not open the political arena to the poorest and most numerous of the urban groups, the textile workers, but it did broaden the social base of local power to include the *petite bourgeoisie*.

Typical of this new class of political leaders in Troyes were Pierre Bréon and Edme Herluison-Cornet. Bréon, a merchant tanner, was elected a municipal officer in 1790 after having served on the committee. His father was also a tanner, as were his uncles and his brother. In 1758 Bréon had married a joiner's daughter, and with a marriage contract evaluated at a modest 3,800 livres he commenced a hardworking, respectable career as an "average" artisan (see Table 1).[24] After three decades as a local shopkeeper, Bréon had undoubtedly forged the close ties to other trade families in his neighborhood that were a prerequisite for attaining political leadership in revolutionary Troyes. In 1790 Bréon lived, appropriately enough, on the rue de la Petite-Tannerie near many of his confreres.

Joining Bréon on both the committee and the new municipal council was Edme Herluison-Cornet, a sculptor and professor at the local school of design. His father had been a sculptor (which in the eighteenth century was more a building trade than a fine art); his brother Louis was a master joiner; and he had a close cousin who was a goldsmith. Herluison had married the daughter of a local farmer in 1774 and had made a rather average marriage contract for 7,700 livres.[25] He lived on the Grande Rue, a main street linking the town center to the poorer eastern quarters. Down the street lived Paupe, a barber-surgeon, who had also sat on the committee and who in 1790 was elected to the new district government. Like Bréon, Herluison came to local office without any previous political experience; but both men had behind them years of contact with their neighbors and fellow tradesmen.

Artisans and small merchants were represented chiefly in the new municipal government in Troyes, and even there their strength was largely confined to the lower echelon, i.e., the 30 notables. On the district and department levels, royal officials, merchants, and members of the liberal professions prevailed. The district government included from Troyes one noble (the brother of Berthelin, the former mayor), one royal official (Truelle de Chambouzon), two advocates, one notary, one barber-surgeon, and one merchant. Of the ten district and department officials from Troyes, three had held offices under the Old Regime. Two of the three sat on the department council. Thus only at the highest regional level of government was the Old Regime ruling group able to recover any of its former influence.

The new rulers of Troyes were men who came to political prominence only in 1789. Only seven of them (13 percent) had held an office under the Old Regime. Two had served in the élection assembly of 1788–89; one became a district official, the other a member of the department council. Nine (17 percent) had been chosen as deputies for either their corporation, the town, or the bailliage during the meetings preceding the Estates General. The committee elected in late August had marked the entry into local politics of 24 of the 52 new rulers (46 percent). For nineteen other new rulers (including six merchants or clothiers and nine artisans or shopkeepers) the elections of 1790 marked their entry into local politics. Yet it is worth noting that fourteen of the nineteen neophytes won positions as town notables; the 1790 elections opened local government to new men, but most of those who won offices of prime importance had already gained distinction by serving on the committee.

Like the committeemen, the new rulers were much less wealthy than the former ruling group. The median marriage contract among seventeen new rulers was 8,000 livres; this compared to a median of 7,700 livres for the committee members and 30,000 livres for the former town councillors.[26] Three-quarters of the former ruling group of Troyes were located on the list of the town's 340 highest taxpayers in 1791, as opposed to 41 percent of the committee members and 48 percent of the new rulers.[27] The elections of 1790 also confirmed the committee's displacement of political leadership from the town's former ruling center. Few of the new rulers lived in the Beffroy quarter (the northwest section of town that included Sainte-Madeleine parish); only one new official lived on the rue du Bourg-Neuf, and he had been a royal official under the Old Regime. Many new rulers resided in the merchant quarter of Croncels (the southwest section that included the parish of Saint-Jean), and several others lived in the districts previously peripheral to town politics.[28]

Although the evidence is far from complete, it does seem that kinship relations had been outweighed, however temporarily, by political opinion. Some of the new rulers were related to each other through marriage—nine according to the marriage contracts—but the number of interrelationships was too small to give the new ruling group a clear identity based on kinship. Moreover, by 1790 political opinion had divided families in Troyes. One of the new district administrators was Nicolas Truelle-Sourdat, a rich young lawyer. He sat on the district council with his uncle, Truelle de Chambouzon, the president of the revolutionary committee. Less than a decade before, however, he had married the sister of the chief police magistrate, François Sourdat.[29] Would family loyalties put him on the "patriot"

TABLE 19

Reims: The Social Composition of the 50 New Rulers
Elected in 1790, the Committee of August 21, 1789,
and the Old Regime Town Council

Social group	50 new rulers[a]	49 men elected to the committee	26 Old Regime town councillors
Nobles[b]	2%	22%	19%
Clergy	0	0	23
Royal officials	10	12	15
Liberal professions	14	10	12
Merchants & clothiers	46	49	27
Small merchants & artisans	22	2	0
Laboureurs	6	4	0
Occupation unknown	0	0	4
TOTAL	100%	99%	100%

[a] Includes district and department officials from Reims as well as the newly elected municipal officials.
[b] Includes *secrétaires du roi* and noble royal officials.

side with his uncle, or would they place him next to his brother-in-law, one of the most vociferous opponents of the committee? Given his election in 1790, it appears that Truelle-Sourdat, like his uncle, chose to cast his lot with the Revolution. For the educated classes, the Revolution offered and required this kind of political choice. Yet choosing the side of the Revolution meant aligning oneself with a movement propelled forward by the lower classes. Thus, though the choice was individual for some, its meaning was distinctly social.

In Troyes, the elections of 1790 acknowledged the 1789 urban revolution by returning its leaders to power. The committee stamped the mold for the constitutional leaders of Troyes. Since the Reims committee shrank from out-and-out revolution, the elections of 1790 did much more there than endorse changes already made; the townspeople repudiated the previously preponderant privileged groups (see Table 19). The clergy had already been disowned, and now the nobles, too, were discarded as political leaders. One nobleman was picked for a district office: Nicolas-Louis Jouvant became procureur-syndic of the district. Though he had held office in the bailliage court for nearly three decades (in 1789 he was 59 years old),

Jouvant had shown his interest in new ideas by joining the Triple Union lodge of Masons. It seems likely that this identification helped make him an acceptable candidate for the new constitutional post.[30]

In general, the merchants and clothiers of Reims retained their commanding position in local politics, but they were joined by artisans and shopkeepers rather than by more privileged groups. Yet, as in Troyes, the gains of the craftsmen and *boutiquiers* failed to extend beyond the municipal level. Of the eight men elected to district or department office from Reims, three were royal officials (one noble), four were merchants or clothiers, and one was a lawyer (the younger brother of Baron, one of the deputies from the bailliage of Reims to the Estates General). Six of the eight had held offices during the Old Regime. Here again the former ruling group exerted most influence on the regional as opposed to the municipal level. One important contrast with Troyes should be noted: the Reims mercantile groups obtained more positions of regional political power than did their Troyes counterparts. One-half of the Reims regional officials were merchants or clothiers, as compared to only one-fifth of the Troyes ones. On all administrative levels, merchants and manufacturers wielded considerably more authority in Reims than in Troyes.

In the elections of 1790 Reims moved much further away from the Old Regime than it had in the earlier elections for its committee. Only thirteen of its 50 new rulers (26 percent) had held office under the Old Regime, whereas nearly half of the committee members had done so. Almost half (24) of the new rulers had been chosen as delegates for their corporations or for the town during the preliminaries to the Estates General, but all but five of the 24 had also been picked for the committee or had held office under the Old Regime. Only eighteen of the new rulers had served on the committee; however, nine of them were now municipal officers. The townspeople appreciated the committee's role in 1789, but in 1790 they selected many new men to complement the committee: nineteen of the 50 new rulers neither held an Old Regime office, nor represented their corporations or the town in the spring of 1789, nor sat on the committee. The new men came from the social groups most recently admitted to the political arena: six were artisans or shopkeepers, seven were clothiers, three were merchants, two were members of the liberal professions, and one was a farmer.

A few of the new *petit-bourgeois* rulers in Reims resembled their Troyes counterparts: the grocer Gervais and the brewer Hourelle, for example, were completely new faces. Neither was wealthy—Gervais paid 444 livres in property tax; Hourelle paid only 150 livres in tax—and both lived in the predominantly working-class east side of town. However, like most of the new rulers who were tradesmen, Gervais and Hourelle were elected as town "notables" rather than as officers. The new officers, in contrast, were generally rich. Merchant Marc Guittard, for instance, paid 1,009 livres in property tax and 72 livres in capitation, and he lived on the rue de Cérès right in the center of town. Guittard was a Mason, as were six other new rulers. The contractor Ponce Barbier, another new municipal officer, paid a higher property tax than any other new ruler—3,094 livres. Barbier resided on one of the broad boulevards leading into the center of Reims.[31]

Because of the large number of merchants in their ranks, the new rulers of Reims were on the whole a wealthy group: they paid an average *contribution foncière* (property tax) of 1,005 livres, which was slightly less than the committee's average of 1,095 and considerably more than the former ruling group's average of 765. The merchants paid an average tax of 1,145 livres, the clothiers, 972 livres. A few of the tradesmen were exceptionally rich: a miller paid 2,151 livres, and a finisher paid 3,025. The other artisans and shopkeepers averaged only 713 livres in tax.

Though they were just as well-off as the committee members, the new rulers were more residentially dispersed than either the committeemen or the former rulers. Over a third of them (15 of the 43 with known addresses) lived outside the central parishes of the medieval core of Reims. The election of men from the outlying districts weakened the hegemony of the town's center and brought the outer districts into the local polity. As it did in Troyes, this decentralization of the locus of political power in Reims presaged the sectionalization of politics in the year II. With this diffusion of the local power base, with this extension of participation and positions to social groups formerly excluded and residential quarters previously ignored, the elections of 1790 marked a decisive shift in the local political structure in Reims.

III

From strikingly different experiences in 1789, Troyes and Reims emerged with remarkably similar ruling groups in 1790. The coalition of privileged groups and wealthy merchants disintegrated. Those merchants and clergymen who joined the revolutionary fraternity were rewarded with election to new constitutional offices. But the revolutionary coalition that included them was different: merchants allied themselves now with skilled artisans and tradesmen, with doctors and lawyers. The balance of power tipped down toward the lower end of the urban social scale.[32]

The new coalition was composed of men who made their political names in 1789. They were the men who had the political education and political organization to seize control when the Old Regime was discredited. Though unaccustomed to the demands and prerogatives of municipal or regional authority, the new rulers had learned the ways of political power in their guilds or corporations and their local districts. They had behind them the discipline of "corporate" life; they were not just individual politicians, but representatives of local organizations. They may not have been habitués of municipal politics, but they were prepared to use lower-class support to attain positions of control. Because they represented social groups previously barred from local politics and because they came to power on the shoulders of the crowd, the new rulers' election signaled a major innovation in the rules of local politics. The social boundaries of the local political arena expanded, and the means to, and hence the responsibilities of, power were transformed. However inarticulate, the crowd was now a recognized force in local politics.

There were some differences between the new rulers of Troyes and Reims. The Reims group was dominated by the merchants and clothiers of the textile industry; in Troyes, the proportions of merchants, tradesmen, and members of the liberal professions were more nearly equal. There were two sources for this important difference:

the industrial structures of the towns, and their political experiences in 1789. As we saw in Chapter 2, the clothiers retained a vital position in the Reims economy but declined in importance as a group in Troyes. In 1790, clothiers accounted for one-quarter of the new rulers in Reims, as compared with less than one-tenth of the new rulers in Troyes. In addition, the manufacturing magnates of Troyes lost favor as the textile depression continued, whereas in Reims the clothiers won acclaim and then votes for their efforts to provide employment for the workers dependent on them. Lawyers and journalists played a larger role in politics in Troyes because the seesawing power struggles there in 1789 offered them manifold opportunities to display their talents as pamphleteers and political rhetoricians. The difference in clerical representation merely reproduced a distinction that developed in 1789: the Reims church established a reputation as the town's foremost enemy of the Revolution, whereas the Troyes church was neutral or even favorable to the "patriot" party.

The results of the 1790 elections augured well for the National Assembly's constitutional aims; local differences were largely effaced. If the results in Troyes and Reims are any indication, then it appears that the standardized election procedures produced relatively similar groups of local rulers. Members of low-status groups were allowed to participate in elections, but the propertyless were excluded. Venality of office was abolished, thereby eliminating both a major support of entrenched local interests and the chief means for perpetuating the local dominance of privileged social groups. The towns were to have equal status in the nation, and most of the male citizens were to enjoy equal political rights in their community.[33]

In exchange for uniformity, the towns had to sacrifice some of their initiative. Though no longer subject to the odious intendants, the towns now found themselves inserted into a clearly defined hierarchy of authority linking town, district, department, and national government. The departments and districts were created explicitly to destroy the provincial obstructionism of the Old Regime and to circumscribe the autonomy of the towns.[34] At the same time, however, the National Assembly wanted to protect the departments against ministerial despotism. During 1790 and 1791, as a result, the relations between the departments and the national government and between the departments and the municipal governments were ambiguous. Centralizing and decentralizing impulses coexisted ambivalently in the new governmental structure, providing a source for continuous quarrels.

The National Assembly tried to define and delimit clearly the major areas of decision-making by dividing responsibilities and jurisdictions between the various governmental levels. Police power was divided between the municipal and department governments. The new town councils controlled the National Guard; the departments took command of the *gendarmerie nationale* (the former maréchaussée). The Old Regime's palimpsest of conflicting police jurisdictions was erased and replaced with a uniform administration. Elected lay officials supplanted the motley congeries of royal and seigneurial courts, venal royal officers, and church establishments that had previously haggled over local police power.

Judicial and administrative functions were separated by the laws of August 16–24, 1790, which reorganized the judicial system. Judicial officials were forbidden to hold administrative offices (December 14, 1789, and August 24, 1790) or to interfere in legislative affairs. Here the Assembly aimed to eliminate the preponderance of court officials on many town councils (as in Troyes). Justice was to be free and judges were to be elected. All of the special jurisdictions, such as seigneurial courts, were abolished. A municipal police tribunal composed of three municipal officers heard those cases formerly assigned to the chief police magistrate. Two new categories of elected judges were introduced on the local level: justices of the peace for the canton, who were elected for two-year terms; and judges of the district tribunals, who were elected for six-year terms.

Old Regime officials recouped some of their losses by winning election to local courts. Four of the six men elected to the Reims district tribunal were Old Regime officeholders; two of them were former bailliage magistrates. Three of the six men elected to the Troyes district tribunal were Old Regime officeholders, but only one of them was a former bailliage magistrate. None of the justices of the peace for Troyes had been a bailliage councillor, and only one had been an officeholder in the Old Regime (an élection court magistrate).[35] The Reims magistrates fared better than their Troyes counterparts because they were less associated with the evils of the Old Regime. The Reims magistrates did not actively oppose the Revolution, and in the past they often had led the fight against the archbishop's judicial pretensions.

In the delimitation and definition of governmental authority some features of the Old Regime were retained. Chief among these was the centralized hierarchy of the administrative structure. The municipality controlled town affairs. The district council apportioned taxes among the communes, established lists of active citizens (voters), directed public works projects, and, most important, controlled the sale of *biens nationaux*. The department council acquired most of the functions previously performed by the intendant or the provincial assembly: apportionment of taxation among the districts, upkeep of bridges and roads, control of the national domain (formerly the jurisdiction of the *maîtrise des eaux et forêts*), command of regional police, and direction of hospitals and prisons and of public welfare and public instruction. Administrators depended upon the voters for their jobs, and in this the new regime was less "despotic" than the old. Yet the systematizing and standardizing of governmental structures did not curtail the long reach of government; on the contrary, the bureaucratic reorganization and rationalization of government justified the expansion of the dominion and prerogatives of government. Thus, as Tocqueville argued, the revolutionary government pushed forward on the path first blazed by the Old Regime.[36]

The committees of 1789 had broken through the pattern of increasing definition, division, and stratification of authority. They invaded the jurisdiction of many of the local ruling institutions of the Old Regime: they handed down judicial decisions, passed ordinances, policed the markets, and controlled the new National Guard. The committees had been practically independent of central authority—though they sought the approval of the national government, and especially of the National Assembly. Because they originated in an atmosphere of intense political discussion and mobilization, the committees functioned on the basis of continual debate and constant surveillance of town affairs. Decisions were not made according to precedent, since there was none; decisions were made in response to local and immediate demands. The legitimacy of a committee's authority was derived from its election and maintained by its responsiveness to local problems.

The legitimacy of the municipalities of 1790 was also based on election, but election within the framework of a national constitution. The national government made the political and legislative decisions; the local governments administered. The National Assembly swept away the extraordinary powers of the judiciary and the intendants under the Old Regime, but they filled the vacuum on the local level with districts and departments rather than with local initiative. Moreover, the Constitution of 1790–91 sharply restricted public opportunities for political mobilization. It guaranteed the right of assembly and the right to petition against the municipal government (Articles 61 and 62 of the law of December 14, 1789), but the conditions for these public gestures were carefully delineated. Voters could denounce their municipality if they presented their complaints to the directory of the department first. Voters could meet to draw up petitions only if they advised the municipal officers of the time and place of their meetings in advance. Armed meetings were prohibited.[37]

In 1789 the local political arrangement was questioned, and the committees offered a novel response to the problems at hand. Their extraordinary size and procedures encouraged incessant political dialogue; this made them truly *comités permanents*. As a result, political mobilization widened under the committees' rule: new journals were published and pamphlets proliferated; individuals and groups besieged committee meetings; corporations held their own public gatherings; and the crowd seemed always ready to move into action. The Constitution of 1790–91 closed the question again by clearly defining the authority of government and by limiting the possibility of citizens' initiative. It was not until 1792–93 that the political system was challenged again. Until then, political discussion was channeled into extragovernmental organizations such as the Jacobin Clubs. Revolutionary fervor was diverted away from local government into these new local coteries where political education for the middle classes of the towns continued. The political structure recovered its revolutionary animus when political discussion moved back into government, for example, when sectional revolutionary committees were set up in 1793. During the year II, politics became revolutionary again, not just because new lower-class groups participated in the government, but also because government itself became political and politicizing.

CHAPTER 7

The Revolutionary Commune

POLITICS BECAME A revolutionary activity for the people of France in 1789. For centuries the French kings had persistently and often successfully tried to circumscribe and even to replace local and national political forums with centralized administrations and judicial bureaucracies. Intendants imposed the king's will on the towns, and the initiative of the few remaining provincial estates was progressively curtailed. When the crown found itself on the verge of bankruptcy in the 1780's, however, its governmental legitimacy began to deteriorate. First the nobles and clergy, and then the Third Estate as well, demanded greater participation in political affairs in exchange for financial support of the state. In the subsequent struggles with the vacillating crown government and then with the increasingly reactionary sectors of the aristocracy, the French people learned how to formulate their interests, organize to demand changes, and mobilize to achieve their goals. The wellsprings of political activity, so long obstructed by royal design, now gushed forth and deluged the Old Regime.

Politicization, i.e., the expansion and sharpening of political awareness and the consequent generation of new political organizations, was most intense in the towns because it was there that people met most frequently to confront the constitutional issues posed by the bankruptcy of the crown. Widespread political education began in earnest in the spring of 1789 when the townspeople gathered to elect deputies and draft grievance lists for the meeting of the Estates General. Crowds rioted during the local meetings in some towns (Reims, Toulon), and in Marseille townsmen seized the opportunity to create the first municipal committee of the Revolution. When the king surrounded Paris and Versailles with soldiers in July, the urban movement flashed to almost all of France's large towns and cities. Political education was translated into political practice.

Troyes and Reims were part of the municipal movement, and in many respects their experiences resembled those of the other big manufacturing towns. All of the thirteen largest textile-manufacturing towns set up committees in 1789 (the committee in Lille, however, lasted only a week).[1] In general, the municipal revolutions in the towns specializing in textile production, naval construction, or frontier defense were more thoroughgoing than the movements in the commercial and administrative towns (see Map 3).* Among the 30 largest towns in France, all of those with large military garrisons (Strasbourg, Metz, Nancy, and Besançon) and naval construction works (Bordeaux, Marseille, Nantes, Brest, and Toulon) introduced committees, half of which claimed sole authority over town affairs. On the other hand, three of the four towns that either did not install a committee or established one for only a few days were administrative towns: Grenoble, Toulouse, and Clermont-Ferrand. Most commercial cities instituted committees, but few of them were powerful; only the committees of Strasbourg and Nantes—towns that were both commercial and military or naval centers—exercised complete and continuous control of town affairs. Thus the towns with large manufacturing or military populations proved most likely to install new local regimes. These were the towns with huge restive lower classes that were ready to swing into action in times of high bread prices and, in the case of manufacturing towns, soaring industrial unemployment.

In the manufacturing towns, merchants most often formed the vanguard of the local revolution. Yet their strength varied according to the different kinds of textiles their towns produced. Merchants of the silk-producing towns shared committee positions with professionals and royal officials in part because most of the silk towns (Lyon, Montpellier, Nîmes) were also important administrative cen-

---

*Most of the largest towns and cities had more than one economic function. Only the most general trends are indicated here.

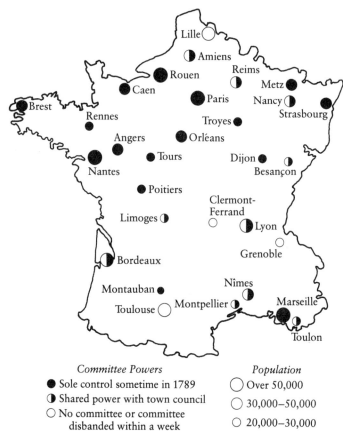

Committee Powers

● Sole control sometime in 1789
◗ Shared power with town council
○ No committee or committee
   disbanded within a week

Population

○ Over 50,000
○ 30,000–50,000
○ 20,000–30,000

Map 3. The Thirty Largest Towns in France, 1789:
Committee Powers and Town Population

ters.[2] Moreover, silk towns did not have concentrations of unskilled
and semiskilled laborers as large as those in the woolen- and cotton-
producing towns; hence the silk merchants lacked the extensive
political clientele available to other kinds of textile merchants. Merchants dominated the committees elected in the wool towns such as
Reims and Orléans; in the latter, for example, eleven of the twenty
committee members elected on July 19 were merchants.[3] If Troyes
was at all typical of cotton towns, then it would seem that cotton

merchants were considerably less successful than woolen merchants; the catastrophic drop in demand for cotton cloth and resulting unemployment weakened the appeal cotton merchants might have had as political leaders. The influence of merchants, even in manufacturing towns, apparently depended to a great extent upon the structure of the local industry and its fortunes in the years just preceding the Revolution.

Despite their differences, the textile towns, as might be expected, offered more political opportunities to their merchant communities than did the administrative centers. In Paris, the committees of July 25 and September 18 both included over 50 percent members of the liberal professions and barely over 10 percent merchants.[4] The merchants' position improved only slightly in the elections of 1790: 42 percent of the members of the new municipal government were members of the liberal professions; 20 percent were merchants. Eleven of the twelve men elected to the first committee in Dijon were members of the liberal professions. Though this dropped to only 28 percent in the elections of 1790, the slack was not taken up by the Dijon merchants—they made up a mere 6 percent of the rulers of the new municipality.[5] Royal officials and professionals also predominated in parlementary towns such as Metz: one-half of the noble deputies and one-third of the Third Estate deputies to the committee were royal officials or professionals there, whereas only 12 percent of the Third Estate deputies were merchants.[6] Although the evidence about committee formation in the 30 largest French towns remains spotty, it appears that local political alliances were determined more by local economic and social structures than by some national dividing line such as noble versus bourgeois or landowner versus capitalist entrepreneur.

The comparison of Troyes and Reims makes this even clearer. Insofar as they were alike in 1789, they resembled the other large manufacturing towns: they installed committees that offered local merchants relatively great opportunities for political participation. But Troyes and Reims differed in several significant ways. The committee in Reims shared power with the town council, whereas the Troyes committee first captured sole authority and then fell victim to a local counterrevolution. The merchants gained most in Reims—at the church's expense. In Troyes, on the other hand, the benefits of the first year of revolution were shared by a coalition of merchants, professionals, artisans, and shopkeepers—at the expense of the royal officials. The explanation of these differences rests on a conjunction of long- and short-term factors: economic and social structures that limited political options; political traditions that grew out of the social structure; and differential effects of the economic crisis of 1787–89.

All these factors were expressed in terms of political organization and political options. In Reims, the local Old Regime was dominated by a rich and powerful church establishment, by a nobility holding royal offices, and by a bourgeoisie of merchants and lesser officials who were successfully buying their way into coveted noble status. Since the Reims church quickly opposed the Revolution, the lay notables of the town were able to capitalize on the church's unpopularity and secure for themselves the benefits of the Revolution—at least until 1790. The tenor of the Revolution of 1789 in Reims is shown by the composition and actions of the town's committee: it meekly cooperated with the town council, but exercised firm control over the new militia. The merchants and clothiers who ran the committee were deferential to the councillors and had no intention of allowing the rank and file of their supporters to get out of hand. The growing hegemony of the mercantile groups and the success of their politics in 1789 were made possible by the structure of the local woolen industry. and by its partial economic recovery in 1788–89. With the expansion of political participation, the merchants and especially the clothiers gained great influence in Reims politics because they closely regulated an industry with relatively large concentrations of workers. The clothiers who owned handlooms and continued to employ their hapless workers in 1787–88 at their own expense won in exchange a large clientele and consequently many votes. There was more potential for collective action in the concentrated woolen industry than in the highly dispersed and relatively unskilled cotton industry; as early as March 1789 the woolen workers of Reims demonstrated for political as well as economic ends. Yet, the woolen workers were apparently also more easily kept in line (once the price of bread stabilized in Reims) by their employer-clothiers, who served as officers in the new National Guard, and sometimes even resided in the same districts as their workers. These protocaptains of industry could make a revolution in their own image—orderly and bureaucratic—and at their own pace.

The possibilities for political organization were quite different in Troyes. The privileged groups there, i.e., the clerical and aristocratic establishments, were relatively small in size and hence in political influence. As a result, most local political conflicts took place within and divided the upper strata of the Third Estate, the nonnoble royal officials and merchants. Because the textile depression and the inflation of bread prices were both so extreme in Troyes, the leaders of the opposition to the Old Regime were able to mobilize and manipulate crowd pressure to topple the obdurate town council. But the new leaders proved unable to control the crowd of angry textile workers they had set in motion, so that when an enraged mob brutally killed the mayor, the Troyes committee found itself helpless before a counteroffensive by the former rulers backed by both the town's property owners and hundreds of soldiers dispatched by the central government.

The opposition leaders in Troyes came to power through their use of rhetorical skills rather than through their positions in the process of textile production, as was the case in Reims. This happened for two reasons. First, the action of the Troyes town council created a situation of overt political conflict that brought into play such political skills as the ability to write pamphlets, speak before mass meetings, and organize groups. Consequently lawyers, with practice in public argument, and guild masters, with practice in running their own communities, stood as much chance of becoming political leaders as merchants did under these conditions. Second, the cotton industry provided less political leverage for merchants and clothiers than the woolen industry did. The Troyes clothiers did not do so well politically as their counterparts in Reims because they no longer occupied a mediating role between merchants and textile workers; moreover, since the weavers owned their own handlooms in Troyes, the clothiers could not use their economic position to exercise political influence during elections. The Troyes merchants were unable to capitalize on the opportunity presented by the municipal revolution because the textile depression had vitiated their usually strong position as political leaders. Hence merchants and clothiers were compelled to seek alliance with aspiring politicians from the liberal professions and even with small merchants and artisans.

The structure of cotton production and its vicissitudes in 1787–89 also shaped the possibilities for collective action on the part of the textile workers in Troyes. Isolated from each other in their cellars, the textile workers were unable to mobilize themselves for explicit political ends. However, when they believed that they were being deliberately starved, they rioted against the regime they thought to blame. In the dire economic circumstances of 1788–89, the textile workers of Troyes were more than ready to respond to the leadership offered by the bourgeois opposition. But because the textile workers were not concentrated in workshops and thus were not under employer supervision, they were virtually unmanageable. The conditions that made radical revolution possible in Troyes also made it difficult to contain.

The social base of political control changed in both Troyes and Reims during 1789, but in neither town did the conflict simply pit aristocrats or privileged groups in general against a unified bourgeoisie. In both towns nobles were virtually eliminated from local political office by 1790, but in neither town was the nobility perceived as the immediate enemy of the Revolution: the August committees in Troyes and Reims included several nobles, and it was not until the elections of 1790 that the nobility was for the most part repudiated. This is the one sense in which Troyes and Reims conformed to a national pattern. The nobility gradually lost favor during 1789 because its deputies to the Estates General and then the National Assembly only reluctantly acquiesced to the revolution made by the Third Estate, and because many aristocrats emigrated to foment counterrevolution abroad. By 1790 the nobles were suspect.

The groups that first lost power in the local revolutions were those townspeople identified most closely with the Old Regime—the church in Reims, and the royal officials in Troyes. The Reims church was the biggest property owner in the town; its archbishop enjoyed the fruits of a tax on all grain sold in the market and also owned the office of chief police magistrate; the ecclesiastical chapters named six clerical deputies to the town council; and the various church organizations exercised seigneurial jurisdiction over much of the town. It is not surprising, then, that the merchants and clothiers gained at the expense of the clergy, and that not one clergyman was elected to either the August committee or the 1790 municipal government in Reims. The church in Troyes did not suffer a comparable loss in influence or authority in 1789 because it was neither as powerful nor as reluctant to accept the Revolution as its Reims counterpart. The royal officials stood for the Old Regime in Troyes, and consequently were the first to be overthrown by the townspeople. In the absence of numerous nobles or a potent church, the men who held positions in the local courts and jurisdictions had become the "foremost" men, the rulers of Troyes. Through intermarriage, a handful of magistrate families established powerful dynasties whose members dominated the various courts, the office of chief police magistrate, and the town council. Although almost entirely nonnoble, this tight-knit group was resented by the people of Troyes as much as the clerical establishment was resented by the people of Reims.

Though the objects of the municipal revolutions varied across France, as they did in Troyes and Reims, the means of revolution were national: the committee was the revolutionary political alternative of 1789. Some committees were originally convoked by town councils as temporary emergency measures, based on precedents established in the past whenever food shortages and their attendant food riots had threatened to overwhelm the limited capacities of local police forces. Nevertheless, when the townspeople elected committees in 1789 the structure of power was everywhere transformed. The basis of legitimacy, the functions of government, and the relationship of governors to governed all changed dramatically.

Under the Old Regime most townspeople could not compete for control of community resources, i.e., could not participate directly in local politics. The monarchy had progressively centralized and bureaucratized the lines of authority linking national and local power centers until very little scope for initiative was left at the local level. At the same time, the social boundaries of the local polity contracted as access to positions of local power was closed to all but a small elite. Whether town councils were appointed or elected, the mechanism of succession to the ruling elite was similar everywhere: the town notables in effect co-opted men from their own ranks to rule. Legitimacy stemmed from tradition and recognition by the monarchy: the notables and the king agreed that the notables were the natural leaders of the community by virtue of their high social status. The mass of the townspeople was to be controlled and contained, not represented.

All this changed when the committees were elected. The functions of government and the boundaries of the polity expanded, and the key to both was the shift in the basis of legitimacy. The committees were elected in order to represent the commune. They were not created by the national government, and they did not derive their legitimacy from being part of a national framework—except insofar as they symbolized the communes' participation in the national revolution. Though local elections were not in themselves novel, the results most often were: the stranglehold of the notables was broken, and many new political groups appeared in the local arena. The presence of new men was virtually assured by the election everywhere of very large committees. The 49 elected deputies in Reims and the 64 in Troyes were not unusual—the Paris committee of September 18 had 300 members.

All over France the committees extended the functions of local government beyond the limits set under the Old Regime by acting wherever a community interest was in question. The committees politicized their fellow townspeople by intervening in their daily lives: government was to be present in the marketplace and at the town gates, as well as in the city hall. And by recording their minutes regularly, the committees eliminated the secrecy surrounding most Old Regime institutions.

The committees in both Troyes and Reims tried to follow the lead of the National Assembly by setting up subcommittees for discussing and carrying out various tasks. In Reims these "bureaus" worked successfully because the committee was not overwhelmed by popular pressure but instead was able to discourage and obstruct mobilization of the working populace through control of the militia. Although the boundaries of the local polity expanded when the Reims committee was elected in August, the committee thereafter carefully circumscribed political activities. With its concurrent bureaucratization and demobilization of politics, the new political style developed by the committee in Reims during 1789 resembled the one laid out by the National Assembly for 1790–91.

In Troyes, however, politics became a daily activity for almost everyone. The committee there, which came to power by mobilizing the populace against the Old Regime, was immediately confronted by a dire economic situation with explosive political possibilities. The Troyes committee met daily in some semblance of a general session, and intense dialogue took place both within the committee and between the committee and the townspeople. The customary distance between government and the people was effaced; politics took place everywhere. In part the continuing mobilization that characterized Troyes was a result of the committee's inability to control its militia; but it was also the result of the committee's relatively extensive social base. The men elected to the Troyes committee represented not only the mercantile interests and professional groups in town but also the guilds. More important, they represented all of the town's various quarters. Hence the Troyes committee was more intimately connected to the townspeople, less bureaucratic, and less representative of the interests of the property owners than the Reims committee was. The style of politics in Troyes was therefore less "bourgeois" than in Reims.

The new constitutional government of 1790–91 reinstalled local government in a national network so that it was part once again of a centralized, hierarchical arrangement of power. Town government no longer derived its legitimacy solely from its relationship to the commune. The municipal regulations of 1790 were designed to control the political mobilization that had developed in 1789: government again was clearly delimited, relatively closed, and depoliticized; bureaucratic administration replaced discussion; citizenship was restrictively defined; mass meetings without specific authorization were prohibited; and the press, elections, and offices were all controlled by the patriot *bourgeoisie*. In this way the new government repressed popular political activity. Not until 1792 did the committees reappear as the hallmark of revolutionary politics.

The committees of 1789 were revolutionary because they revived the archetypal notion of the "commune"—the urban space where freedom, i.e., the right to engage in politics, was possible. The committees never defined what they meant by the "commune," and indeed it was the very ambiguity of the concept that made it so powerful: as long as government's boundaries were not precisely defined, as long as authority rested in some sense with the commune, dialogue continued, conflict continued, revolution continued. The National Assembly closed off the revolutionary ambiguity of the notion of the commune by precisely defining its boundaries, making its structure hierarchical, and limiting access to it.

Although the committees politicized most of the townspeople, they did not affect all social groups equally. Merchants and lawyers were the first to step forward to reconstruct the local political arena because they had had experience regulating community affairs in the marketplace and in the courts. Artisans and shopkeepers could demand a voice because they had practice in guild affairs. But the textile workers had no political voice: illiterate, politically uneducated, incompletely urbanized, they were a heterogeneous social group largely isolated from one another by the conditions of production. They lived in the realm of necessity, outside politics. Their wants and their actions affected the alignment of power, but they could not participate in the act of sovereignty themselves. Hence the commune of 1789 excluded them, as it excluded women. It excluded everyone who did not have the freedom, i.e., the education and the leisure time, to be political.[7]

Consequently, the committees were, for the most part, the creatures of those literate, lay urban dwellers with the leisure time necessary for discussion and argument about public questions. The revolutionaries in 1789 were merchants and lawyers (and, more rarely, shopkeepers), and it was their aim to create both a local and a national political system that would serve their interests. They wanted a government that would be more responsive to them and more rational, one open to talent rather than closed to all but the privileged few. In short, they wanted a society ruled by men like themselves—educated, property-owning, but not formerly privileged under the social system of the Old Regime.

During the first year of the Revolution the people of France transformed the structure of politics. While the National Assembly was creating a bureaucratic state at the center based on national, popular sovereignty, the people of the towns were independently developing their own bureaucratic organization of government in the committees. The election of representatives and the regular, open operation of government were first worked out in the towns. Thus while the new national state was being outlined on paper in Paris, the provincial townspeople were learning new political habits on their own. The ultimate solidity of the Revolution's achievement depended not so much on the foresight of the French constitutional fathers as on the practical experience of local leaders all over the country.

The townspeople lived with three different local political structures in the short space of a year: the first had the weight of tradition (and the burden of bankruptcy) behind it; the second was an experiment of their own creation; and the third was fashioned by their deputies in Paris. By 1790 the bureaucratic form had been firmly established on the national as well as the local level. But government's capacity to check the mobilization of the population was only temporarily successful. In 1792–94, 1848, and 1870–71, the revolutionary heritage burst forth anew in France; the commune was revived; the political arena opened up again. Each time, those formerly excluded from politics demanded access to it, and in the ensuing struggles sharpened their image of themselves as political actors. Each time, the revolutionary political system was characterized by the proliferation of new political organizations and the politicization of government itself.

In times of revolution, such as 1789, the emergent political system was much more than a faint reflection of the social structure; the bourgeoisie did not simply spring to power in a reflex reaction to the recognition that it wielded considerable economic power. At the heart of the revolutionary process was the elaboration of new political structures: new kinds of coalitions, novel forms of organization, and consequently remodeled governments. It was within and by means of these new structures that social groups and classes confronted each other and struggled for hegemony. The political systems that issued from the contest were not just instruments of class rule; they were the locus of social conflict and the sphere in which consciousness of group interests matured. Hence the political structure—the space in which politics "took place"—was crucial to the development of new social structures, new alignments of the social system. Politics, the field of mediation of social conflict, was also the site of social change.

Reference Matter

Notes

The following abbreviations are used in the Notes:

Chapter 1

1. See for example Fernand Braudel's preface to *La Méditerranée et le monde méditerranéen à l'époque de Philippe II* (Paris, 1949). The "Annales" school is the name given to those historians associated with the journal *Annales: Economies, Sociétés, Civilisations.* Although the "Annales" school de-emphasized political history, they would not oppose the systematic approach to politics I advocate here. To my knowledge, however, none of them has shown interest in applying their techniques to the study of politics.

2. On the question of "straight" history, see Betty Behrens, " 'Straight History' and 'History in Depth': The Experience of Writers on Eighteenth-Century France," *Historical Journal*, 8 (1965), pp. 117–26.

3. I borrow the term from Frédéric Braesch, *1789: Année cruciale* (Paris, 1941).

4. The importance of this period was emphasized by Daniel Ligou, "A propos de la révolution municipale," *Revue d'histoire économique et sociale*, 38 (1960), pp. 146–77.

5. Toulouse and Clermont-Ferrand were the two exceptions: they did not establish committees. For a comparative discussion of the municipal revolution in the 30 largest French towns, see Lynn A. Hunt, "Committees and Communes: Local Politics and National Revolution in 1789," *Comparative Studies in Society and History*, 18 (1976), pp. 321–46.

6. Edward Whiting Fox argues that there was a difference between port towns and towns of the hinterland in *History in Geographic Perspective: The Other France* (New York, 1971).

Chapter 2

1. Roads passed through Reims from Burgundy, Champagne, and Lorraine to Flanders and the Channel ports. Emile Chantriot, *La Champagne, étude de géographie régionale* (Paris, 1906), p. 149. Several major royal highways intersected at Troyes: #19 from Paris to Basel, #60 from Orléans to Nancy, #77 from Nevers to Sedan, and #71 from Paris to Dijon. (These were the numbers of the highways in 1789.) Théophile Boutiot and Emile Socard, *Dictionnaire topographique du département de l'Aube* (Paris, 1874).

2. For Reims, see Henri Jadart, "La Population de Reims à l'époque de la Révolution," *T.A.N. Reims*, 96 (1893–94), pp. 57–70. For Troyes, see Albert Babeau, *La Population de Troyes au dix-huitième siècle* (Troyes, 1873), p. 16.

3. Arthur Young, *Travels during the Years 1787, 1788 and 1789, Undertaken More Particularly with a View of Ascertaining the Cultivation, Wealth, Resources, and National Prosperity of the Kingdom of France* (London, 1794), vol. 1, p. 147.

4. *Ibid.*, pp. 554, 558. Young took the figures for cloth manufacturing from a report by the inspector of manufactures for Champagne for the year 1782.

5. According to the Troyes census of 1774 there were 322 ecclesiastical personnel (secular clergy, monks, and nuns) and 135 nobles, excluding those under seven years old, residing in the town. Babeau, *Population de Troyes*, p. 11. The Reims census of 1765, which like the Troyes census of 1774 is the latest one available preceding the Revolution, noted 869 secular and regular clergy and 728 "privileged" over the age of eight years old. Henri Jadart, *Chronique rémoise de la fin du XVIIIe siècle* (Reims, 1895), p. 161. The privileged orders of Troyes thus constituted 2 percent of that town's total population in 1774, whereas the privileged orders constituted 8 percent of the Reims population in 1765. Even though the Reims "privilégiés" probably included some nonnobles who enjoyed special exemptions and

privileges, the number of clergymen and nobles in Reims was certainly much higher than in Troyes. In 1789, Reims had 50 resident noblemen and 20 noblewomen who were required to pay the *capitation*; Troyes had 32 resident noblemen and 14 noblewomen who were taxed. The nobles of Reims were assessed a median capitation of 21 livres (in a range from less than 1 to 154 livres), whereas the nobles of Troyes paid a median capitation of 15 livres (in a range from 4 to 81 livres). A.D. Marne, C 2727, "Capitation des privilégiés, 1787–89."

6. In 1789 the bishop of Troyes had a yearly income of 14,000 livres; the archbishop of Reims had an income of 50,000 livres. *Almanach Royal* (Paris, 1789), pp. 59–60. The annual revenues of the Reims religious communities were estimated to range from only 216 livres for the Capucins to 115,535 livres for the Abbaye de Saint Remi. Jadart, *Chronique rémoise*, pp. 165–66.

7. A.D. Marne, C 2506 (1743–63); C 2507 (1763–80); and C 2508 (1780–90).

8. The production of textiles in Troyes was described in a "Mémoire sur les différentes fabriques de la ville de Troyes" (1784), A. N., F¹² 555, written for the Inspector-General of Manufactures. See also Paul Dupieux, *L'Industrie textile en Champagne troyenne de 1784 à 1789* (Châlons-sur-Marne, 1935); and Julien Ricommard, *La Bonneterie à Troyes et dans le département de l'Aube. Origines, évolution, caractères actuels* (Troyes, 1934).

9. Several different kinds of cotton cloths (and even some woolens) were manufactured in Troyes. The most important areas of manufacture were those of cotton calicoes (*toiles de coton*), employing 12,000 workers; draperies, employing 6,000 workers; and *bonneterie* (the weaving of stockings and hats). Each sector had its own peculiar characteristics: the production of draperies, for example, was much more concentrated than the production of cotton calicoes because each loom required two weavers and twelve to fifteen other workers. Merchant drapers owned as many as 60 looms and employed as many as 1,500 workers, and they consequently resembled the clothiers in Reims, whose position is discussed below. See A. N., F¹² 1411 B (this information comes from a letter written by the intendant of Champagne, Rouillé d'Orfeuil, to the inspector-general of manufactures on January 20, 1788).

10. *Ibid.* D'Orfeuil described the Troyes clothiers in his letter as follows: "They are for the most part simple weavers who live from day to day on the fruits of their labor. They have no financial interest beyond the manufacture of one piece of cloth; they sell it immediately and right away begin another on their looms because the smallest interruption in their work would reduce them to extreme poverty. In this state they can expect no help from the merchant, whose own interest is always paramount." (All translations mine unless otherwise noted.)

11. The subdelegate of Reims, Polonceau, reported in June 1788 that Ponce Jean Nicolas Ponsardin, the most important clothier in Reims and a member of the town council, had 100 looms and 1,000 workers. The second most important clothier was Jean Baptiste Sirot, who had 60 looms and 600 workers in his employ. A.D. Marne, C 472, "Etat des fabricants qui sont les plus distingués en Champagne" (report by Polonceau to the intendant). The woolen industry in Reims is described by Gustave Laurent, *Reims et la région rémoise à la veille de la Révolution*, vol. 5 of *Cahiers de doléances pour les Etats Généraux de 1789. Département de la Marne* (Reims, 1930). According to Laurent, 30,000 workers were employed in manufacturing textiles in Reims and its surrounding area. There were 3,120 handlooms in the town and 955 handlooms in the countryside nearby. He bases these figures on a report to the inspector-general of manufactures in 1790 (p. xxxv).

12. Officials, in their reports, repeatedly emphasized the nefarious effects of the expansion of textile production. Many feared that it kept peasants from their agricultural labors. See, for example, the report by inspector Bruyard in 1784, "Mémoires sur les fabriques de la Champagne et de la Picardie," A. N., F 12 650. The destruction of guild discipline is forcefully described by André Colomès, *Les Ouvriers du textile dans la Champagne troyenne, 1730–1832* (Paris, 1943).

13. The most mechanized branch of the textile industry in Troyes was *bonneterie*, which utilized the spinning jenny (*mécanique à filer*). In 1746, stocking looms were set up at the Hôtel de la Trinité, where orphans worked up to ten hours a day producing cotton, woolen, and silk stockings. After this date stocking-making began to expand rapidly. See Ricommard, *La Bonneterie*; see also Emile Chaudron, *L'Assistance publique à Troyes à la fin de l'Ancien Régime et pendant la Révolution, 1770–1800* (Paris, 1923).

14. The argument here is a specific instance of the general argument made by Colin Lucas: "The primary articulation in Ancien Régime society was not the distinction between the privileged and the Third Estate; rather, it was between those for whom manual labour provided their livelihood and those for whom it did not. . . . There was, then, an important and real sense in which all levels of the bourgeoisie and nobility attained in very general terms a community of interest in face of the vulgar mechanic classes and of the vile and abject poor." "Nobles, Bourgeois and the Origins of the French Revolution," *Past and Present*, 60 (1973), pp. 87–88.

15. Picard, "Topographie médicale de Troyes en 1786," *Mém. de l'Aube*, 10 (1873), pp. 192, 200, and 201.

16. For a suggestive, general analysis of the difference between the realm of freedom (politics) and the realm of necessity, see Hannah Arendt, *The Human Condition* (Chicago, 1958).

17. The number of male taxpayers in Reims in 1792 was 2,058 (for the register of the *contribution foncière* see A.C. Reims, registre 194, fonds

moderns). My calculation of the percentage of adult male *rémois* that this represents is based on population figures for 1793 (A.C. Reims, carton 866, fonds moderns, "Etat de la population, 9 octobre 1793"), which show 6,288 men between the ages of 25 and 60 in the town, with an additional 1,283 men in the army. Discounting men in the army entirely, 32.7 percent of the adult males in Reims were assessed for the *contribution foncière*; if we include half of the soldiers as falling into the 25–60 age group (since most soldiers were young, no more than half should be included), then the proportion assessed drops to 29.7 percent. The record of tax roles is spotty at best: I could not locate the rolls for the *contribution mobilière* of the early years of the Revolution in either Reims or Troyes, and the only tax roll I found for Troyes was the register of the "*deux vingtièmes*."

18. See, for example, Jean-Pierre Bardet et al., *Maisons rurales et urbaines dans la France traditionelle*, vol. 1 of *Le Bâtiment, enquête d'histoire économique, XIVᵉ–XIXᵉ siècles* (Paris, 1971) and especially the section by Jean-Pierre Bardet, "La Maison rouennaise aux XVIIᵉ et XVIIIᵉ siècles: économie et comportements." Bardet distinguishes between a "centre coûteux" and the "périphérie moins chère" (p. 334).

19. There is no capitation roll for Troyes in the local archives. At best, the capitation is a crude measure because each occupational group paid a certain predetermined range of taxes. Each member of the occupational group was assessed individually, but the basis for assessment varied from town to town and from group to group. See Marcel Marion, *Dictionnaire des institutions de la France aux XVIIᵉ et XVIIIᵉ siècles* (Paris, 1923), pp. 69–71. Nobles and royal officials were listed in the *capitation des privilégiés* (A.D. Marne, C 2727). The tax for royal officials was based on the rank of the office rather than the income of the officeholder, and consequently it offers little useful information.

20. In 1750 districts 2–5 paid 44.3 percent of the town's capitation bill; in 1760, 43.8 percent; in 1770, 59.4 percent; and in 1780, 57.1 percent (A.C. Reims, registre 640 [1750], 650 [1760], 660 [1770], and 670 [1780], fonds anciens). Apparently, the key decade of change was the 1760's.

21. A.C. Reims, registre 679, fonds anciens, "Capitation de 1789."

22. The highest numbers of women per 100 taxpayers occurred in one of the wealthiest and one of the poorest districts (district 2, with 16.5 women taxpayers per 100, and district 9, with 17.8 women taxpayers per 100). The figures for the other districts are as follows: district 1, 8.1; district 3, 8.7; district 4, 16.4; district 5, 16.4; district 6, 11.4; district 7, 16.5; district 8, 9.1; and district 10, 15.1. Domestic help is not included among taxpayers.

23. If we include those textile workers who were taxed, then 59 percent of the male taxpayers on the roll of the *contribution foncière* were artisans or shopkeepers. See Table 1.

24. I used a sample of the capitation roll—the first section or *connétablie*

of each district, or about one-fourth of the roll—to determine residential distribution of socioprofessional groups. The highest concentration of liberal professions was in district 4 (38 percent); most of the merchants lived in districts 3 (35 percent) or 5 (48 percent); most of the clothiers lived in districts 5 (39 percent) or 7 (39 percent). The poorer clothiers lived in district 7; they paid a median capitation of 7 livres, 4 sous as compared to the median tax of 11 livres, 12 sous paid by clothiers in district 5. It must be remembered that nobles and royal officials were not included in the ordinary capitation roll but were listed instead in the *capitation des privilégiés*; most of them lived in districts 2, 4, 5, and 6. Most textile workers lived in districts 1 (25 percent), 7 (16 percent), 8 (26 percent) or 9 (15 percent). By contrast, no district housed more than 20 percent of the town's artisans and shopkeepers, and only two districts (8 and 9) housed fewer than 5 percent of them. A.C. Reims, registre 679.

25. For the purpose of comparison, I used a similar sample—i.e., the first section in each district—from the *vingtième* roll in Troyes. The vast majority of members of the liberal professions lived in district 1 (78 percent), which included the parish of Sainte Madeleine, the home of most of the town's magistrates. Almost half of the merchants (48 percent) lived in district 2, which included the parish of Saint Jean, the home of the town's ruling merchant families. Over half of the textile workers lived in district 4, the southeast quarter of town. As in Reims, shopkeepers and artisans were relatively evenly distributed: the fewest (14 percent) lived in district 1; the largest number lived in district 3 (39 percent). A.C. Troyes, registre F 346, "Les deux vingtièmes, 1789."

26. The results of the questionnaire have been published in Jadart, *Chronique rémoise*, "Statistique des quatorze paroisses de Reims en 1774," pp. 158–60. A similar picture of Reims emerges from the figures on poor relief gathered in 1791. Over 9,500 people (29.2 percent of the population) were considered needy. Between 38 and 44 percent of the parishioners were indigent in the parishes of Saint Jacques and Sainte Madeleine (district 1), Saint Timothée (district 7), and Saint Julien and Saint Maurice (district 8). Less than a fifth of the population needed assistance in the parishes of Saint Pierre (district 2), Saint Hilaire (districts 3 and 4), Saint Etienne (district 5), Saint Denis (district 9), and Saint André (district 10). Only 8 percent and 6 percent needed help in the parishes of Saint Michel and Saint Symphorien, respectively (both district 5). See Jadart, *Chronique rémoise*, "Population de Reims par paroisses au 10 janvier 1791," p. 163.

27. Much of what follows in this chapter was first printed as "Local Elites at the End of the Old Regime: Troyes and Reims, 1750–1789," *French Historical Studies*, 9 (1976), pp. 379–99.

28. For an excellent description of the development of the office of subdel-

egate, see Julien Ricommard, "Les Subdélégués des intendants aux XVIIe et XVIIIe siècles," *Information historique* (1962), pp. 139–48, 190–95; (1963), pp. 1–7.

29. On the town councils, see Jacques Paton, *Le Corps de ville de Troyes, 1470–1790* (Troyes, 1939); and Gaston Humbert, *Institutions municipales et administratives de la ville de Reims sous l'Ancien Régime* (Paris, 1910).

30. On the chief police magistrate, see Julien Ricommard, *La Lieutenance générale de police à Troyes au XVIIIe siècle, 1700–1790* (Troyes, 1934).

31. The most notable attempts at reform were the so-called Laverdy reforms of 1764–65. For an account of the effort and its results, see Maurice Bordes, *La Réforme municipale du Contrôleur Général Laverdy et son application: 1764–1771* (Toulouse, 1967).

32. The Paillot family held the office of subdelegate in Troyes throughout the entire eighteenth century. There was more turnover in Reims, but the candidates were always prestigious royal officials. See Ricommard, "Les Subdélégués" (1963), pp. 1–7.

33. Most artisanal corporations chose two delegates each, but higher-ranking socioprofessional groups—e.g., the "bourgeois living nobly," the cloth merchants, the clothiers, and the dyers—might have the right to choose as many as six each. The complete breakdown of corporations and their delegates is given in "Corporations de la ville de Troyes qui concouraient par des députés à l'élection des anciens maires et échevins, avant 1789," *Annuaire de l'Aube*, 20 (1846), pp. 112–14.

34. The "Règlement pour l'administration municipale de la ville de Troyes" of December 18, 1773, prescribed the quota for the sixteen town "notables" as follows: one clergyman; two nobles or military officers; one bailliage official; one member of another jurisdiction; one bourgeois living nobly; two advocates or doctors; four merchants; one officer from the militia; one notary or proctor; one barber-surgeon, printer, or other member of the *arts libéraux*; and one clothier or artisan. Paton, *Le Corps de ville*, pp. 165–71.

35. Laurent, *Reims et la région rémoise*, pp. xxii–xxvi.

36. In 1789, the Troyes council included one goldsmith as the representative of artisanal groups. The two delegates chosen from the guilds in Reims held office for only four years—as compared to the regular nine-year terms of the other elected deputies. The occupations of the Reims electors in 1789 show how limited participation in town elections was at the end of the Old Regime. The 90 electors comprised twelve advocates or royal officials, ten notaries, seven proctors, one army officer, ten militia officers, thirteen wholesale merchants, nine small merchants, fourteen artisans, and fourteen without listed occupations. (A.C. Reims, registre 116, fonds anciens, "Conclusions du conseil de ville, 1787–90," *procès-verbal* of March 8, 1789).

37. Ricommard describes in great detail the effects of the introduction of the office of the chief police magistrate in Troyes in *La Lieutenance générale de police*. The office was first established in Paris in 1667 and then extended to all major towns in 1699.

38. Since 1522 the archbishop of Reims had exercised the right to tax all grain sold in the Reims market; in 1727 this was extended to all grain sold within four *lieues* of Reims (B.M. Reims, CR I MM, "Mémoire à consulter et consultation pour les lieutenant, gens du conseil, et échevins de la ville de Reims" [attributed to Blavier]). The tax was equal to about 1/28th of the grain's value, and it was protested by everyone, including the subdelegate. See, for example, A.D. Marne, C 410, letters of the subdelegate (1774–77) describing the advantages of suppressing the *droit de stellage*. The archbishop's singularly powerful position also provoked factional conflict within the Reims council. In 1760, for example, the merchants of Reims successfully protested against the election of one of the archbishop's partisans as *procureur-syndic*. When the merchants' candidate, Cliquot-Blervache, won the office in a new election, the merchants organized a *charivari* directed against several officials linked to the archbishop (A.D. Marne, C 322).

39. Alphonse Roserot, *Dictionnaire historique de la Champagne méridionale (Aube) des origines à 1790* (Troyes, 1942), vol. 4, p. 1522.

40. *Armorial général ou registres de la noblesse de France* (1868–1908; reprint edition, Paris, 1970), vol. 1, p. 429.

41. A.D. Marne, C 2978.

42. Bonaventure Nicolas Sourdat was the *lieutenant-criminel* from 1751 until 1763. Roserot, *Dictionnaire historique*, vol. 4, p. 1530.

43. A.D. Marne, C 2507, folio 259, "Lettres de noblesse à Gérard Jacob, prévôt de l'échevinage de Reims (mars 1776)." In 1756 Jacob had purchased the office of president of the *traites foraines* in Reims (A. D. Marne, C 2523, folio 49).

44. François-Joseph Souyn was 69 in 1789. He married into the Lépagnol family, another prominent noble family in the Reims region. See Pol Gosset, "L'Emigré rémois Souyn à Quiberon," extract from *Courrier de la Champagne* (Feb. 13, 1900), B.M. Reims, CR V 1707 *bis*. Basic information on all town councillors can be found in the local almanacs: *Almanach historique de la ville et du diocèse de Reims*, 1789, and *Almanach de la ville et du diocèse de Troyes*, 1789.

45. On Dessain de Chevrières, see A.D. Marne, C 2225, folio 146 (1773), and A. N. V¹ 519 (1785). On the clergymen councillors, see Emile Bouchez, *Le Clergé du pays rémois pendant la Révolution et la suppression de l'archevêché de Reims* (Reims, 1913). Ponce Jean Nicolas Ponsardin inherited his father's business, which was founded in 1730 (see n. 11 above). Claude Ruinart de Brimont bought the office of *secrétaire du roi* in 1777. He was 58

in 1789. According to his dossier (A. N. V² 45), he had married into the Tronsson family of wealthy wholesale merchants. One of them, Etienne Tronsson-Tronsson, also sat on the town council in 1789. The Reims council also included three members of the liberal professions and two other royal officials in addition to Dessain de Chevrières.

46. Huez's uncle and cousin had also been members of the Troyes court. In 1789 Huez was 65. See A. N. V¹ 335, letter of provision of office, 1743.

47. Henri de la Perrière, "Notes sur l'époque révolutionnaire tirées de la correspondance commerciale de la Maison Fromageot, Berthelin et Fromageot de Troyes," *Mém. de l'Aube*, 94 (1931), pp. 97–145. The Troyes council also included one doctor, one lawyer (*avocat*), one parish priest, one goldsmith, two nobles, and one tax official.

48. I have found tax records for nineteen of the 26 Reims town council-lors. They paid an average *contribution foncière* of 894 livres (median of 600) as compared to an average for all taxpayers of 285. The nobles paid an average tax of 1,940 livres. The next wealthiest group, the merchants, paid an average of 527 livres. If anything, this comparison underestimates the wealth of the prerevolutionary rulers since many of them suffered econom-ically during the Revolution. See Table 1 above.

49. I found marriage contracts for eight of the 23 Troyes councillors. They averaged 84,230 livres (median of 39,000), whereas the average for the en-tire population making marriage contracts was 8,884 livres for the period 1770–89.

50. Of the five Troyes councillors who were not listed among the town's 340 highest taxpayers, at least one had died by 1791 (A.C. Troyes, G* 1).

51. On this point, compare the findings in André-Jean Tudesq, *Les Grands Notables en France (1840–1849): Etude historique d'une psy-chologie sociale*, 2 vols. (Paris, 1964).

52. A wide-ranging treatment of the bailliage courts can be found in Philip Dawson, *Provincial Magistrates and Revolutionary Politics in France, 1789–1795* (Cambridge, Mass., 1972).

53. The Reims *Almanach* of 1789 lists one president, one honorary president, three lieutenants, three councillors, and one king's proctor. The Troyes *Almanach* of 1789 lists two lieutenants, eleven councillors, one king's proctor, and two king's advocates. To determine noble status I used the lists provided by Louis de la Roque and Edouard de Barthélemy in *Catalogue des gentilshommes de Champagne qui ont pris part ou envoyé leur procuration aux assemblées de la noblesse pour l'élection des députés aux Etats Généraux de 1789* (Paris, 1863).

54. Gustave Laurent, "La Faculté de droit de Reims et les hommes de la Révolution," *A.H.R.F.*, 6 (1929), pp. 329–58.

55. My information on the buying of offices is based on the letters of

provision of office issued between 1750 and 1789. These can be found in A. N., série V¹, and most of them are duplicated in A.D. Marne, série C (*bureau des finances*), and A.D. Aube, série 1B, "Mandements du roi." The listings in the Archives Nationales are the most complete.

56. The Troyes councillors paid a median finance charge of 600 livres as opposed to a median of 486 livres for the Reims councillors. The finance charge, which was listed in the letter of provision of office, represented a fixed proportion of the value of the office.

57. In 1758 the subdelegate Sutaine-Maillefer attributed the problems of the Reims bailliage court to its relatively small jurisdiction. Since the ducal bailliage, the archbishop's court, was much more powerful, the subdelegate had difficulty finding prospective magistrates: "For more than fifteen years the discredit of the offices has made it difficult to sell them; and most of those that have been filled are held by councillors who have gone to live in other towns or who have taken other employment" (A.D. Marne, C 321 [1758]). The president of the Reims court in 1789 was Antoine-Raoul Sutaine-Duvivier, the son of the former subdelegate Sutaine-Maillefer. The Sutaines were a large noble family with several branches in the Reims region (B.M. Reims, CR V 1709, "Notice biographique sur M. Sutaine-Duvivier," 1855). Jean-Simon Lévesque de Pouilly, Sutaine-Duvivier's predecessor, came from a Reims family that had been noble since 1698. See Henri Jadart, "Jean-Simon Lévesque de Pouilly," *T.A.N. Reims*, 131 (1912–13), pp. 349–77.

58. Camusat-Descarrets of the Troyes court was the son of a merchant. He married the daughter of a local noble in 1777 (A.D. Aube, 2E 6/136). It is possible that one or two other magistrates had merchant fathers, since I do not know the social origins of all of them. Merchant families formed dynasties paralleling those of the magistrates. Some members became noble, but the merchants did not retire from business as soon as they had enough capital to invest in land. The Berthelins of Troyes, for example, had been important in the region since the sixteenth century. Once ennobled, some members of the family retired to country estates, but the eldest son continued the textile business. Although one Berthelin had bought an office in the bailliage court, this did not inaugurate a family tradition. Edme Berthelin, the brother of the former mayor, bought the office of *secrétaire du roi* in Lyon. Jean-Edme Berthelin, the former mayor, bought the office of *trésorier* in the Parlement of Pau. See n. 47 above.

59. N.-F. Dereins was ennobled in 1775 for his service as *lieutenant-criminel* of the bailliage court and as mayor of Troyes (A.D. Marne, C 2507, folio 221).

60. I compiled information on offices purchased in Montpellier from A. N. V¹ and checked the names against those in Pierre Vialles, *Etudes historiques sur la Cour des comptes, aides et finances de Montpellier* (Montpellier,

1921), and in Louis de la Roque and Edouard de Barthélemy, *Catalogue des gentilshommes en 1789 et des familles anoblies ou titrées depuis le premier Empire jusqu'à nos jours, 1806–1866, publié d'après les procès-verbaux officiels* (Paris, 1866), vol. 1, pp. 15–23. At least three were nobles.

61. In Troyes, councillors held office a median of 21 years; in Reims, twelve years; and in Montpellier, fourteen years.

62. The addresses come from the almanacs and various tax rolls.

63. Etienne Georges, "Les Soirées de la rue du Bourg-Neuf (1787–1788) chez le Conseiller J.-B. Comparot de Longsols," *Annuaire de l'Aube*, 62 (1888), pp. 17–37.

64. See A.D. Aube, 2E/291, August 6, 1775, marriage contract of Louis-Nicolas Paillot.

65. The Troyes rulers are defined below. Unfortunately, I do not have data comparable to that in this paragraph for Reims. The information on the merchant councillors is based on witness lists given in the marriage contracts in A.D. Aube, série 2E. From the same source I have information on the fathers of nine bailliage magistrates; seven of them were the sons of royal officials, one was the son of a merchant, and one the son of a village notary.

66. The average *contribution foncière* paid by 32 of the 46 Reims "rulers" (as defined earlier) was 765 livres (A.C. Reims, "Contribution foncière, 1792"). I located the marriage contracts for 35 percent (18 of 52) of the Troyes rulers, and they averaged 85,282 livres (A.D. Aube, 11C Supplément 36, "Table alphabétique"). Compare n.49. Inventories of property-holdings for nine Troyes rulers are filed in A.D. Aube, série 40, "Dossiers des émigrés."

67. For French Masonry in general, see Alain Le Bihan, *Loges et chapitres de la Grande Loge et du Grand Orient de France (2e moitié du XVIIIe siècle)*, Commission d'histoire économique et sociale de la Révolution française, Mémoires et Documents, 20 (Paris, 1967). Emile Socard describes the activities of two lodges in Troyes in "La Franc-Maçonnerie à Troyes," *Mém. de l'Aube*, 14 (1877), pp. 119–48. One of these was an organization of military officers that never requested affiliation with the Grand Orient. Consequently, it has been excluded from consideration here. The Reims lodges are described by Gustave Laurent, *Aperçus sur l'histoire des loges maçonniques à Reims du XVIIIe au XXe siècle* (Reims, 1937). This typed manuscript can be consulted in B. M. Reims, RBM 567. Information on lodge membership comes from the Fonds Maçonniques of the Bibliothèque Nationale in Paris: FM² 491, Troyes, Union de la Sincérité, roll for 1787; FM² 362, Reims, Parfaite Amitié, lists for 1786 and 1789; FM² 365, Reims, Triple Union, roll for 1787–88. The one lodge in Troyes, Union de la Sincérité, had 32 members in 1787. Nine were merchants, and ten were either advocates, notaries, or proctors. The lodge also included an assortment of

shopkeepers, professors, and low-ranking professionals such as barber-surgeons. Two merchants and a professor of design became members of the revolutionary committee of 1789; the professor and one of his colleagues took office in the 1790 municipality; and a notary was elected to district office in 1790. Only two of the lodge members had ever held office under the Old Regime: one sat on the town council in the late 1770's (the same successful professor of design), and one was a salt-tax official.

68. A.D. Aube, série 4Q.

69. François Furet, "La 'Librairie' du royaume de France au 18ᵉ siècle," in François Furet et al., *Livre et société dans la France du XVIIIᵉ siècle* (Paris, 1965), vol. 1, pp. 3–33.

70. Most of the town houses listed in the dossiers in A.D. Aube, série 4Q, were estimated to be worth between 5,000 and 10,000 livres. Truelle de Chambouzon's town house was evaluated at 16,000 livres (4Q/79). All these figures are for the year II, and consequently must be assumed to be underestimations since by then most former rulers had retired with the bulk of their possessions to the countryside.

71. The estimate of daily wages for textile workers (1786 rates) comes from a report written by a departmental official in 1790 cited by Emile Chaudron, *L'Assistance publique à Troyes à la fin de l'Ancien Régime et pendant la Révolution, 1770–1800* (Paris, 1923), p. 11. Glaziers earned 18 livres a month in addition to their board; tanners earned 1 livre, 16 sous a day; coopers earned 1 livre, 10 sous a day; and roofers earned 2 livres, 2 sous a day. Some highly skilled artisans, such as printers, might earn as much as 3 livres a day. On incomes of artisans, see Laurent, *Reims et la région rémoise*, pp. lxiv, lxv. The figure for Huez comes from A.D. Aube, 2J 244; that for Berthelin, for the years just prior to the Revolution, comes from A.D. Aube, 4Q/4.

72. The economic difference can be seen in the marriage contracts. I have found the contracts for four of the eight merchants sitting on the Troyes town council in 1789. Upon marriage, 85 percent of the wealth of these four was listed as *mobiliers*: profits of trade, inventories, commercial paper, and investments in manufacturing and commerce. In contrast, only 35 percent of the wealth of the royal officials at marriage was in *mobiliers*. The royal officials invested primarily in *immobiliers*, or immovable wealth: land, houses, and *rentes*. All the marriage contracts were in A.D. Aube, série 2E. The four merchants were Bourotte (7/300), Fromageot (10/1126), Jeanson-Bajot (10/1151), and Lemuet (9/138). The royal officials were Cadot (9/102), Camusat-Descarrets (6/136), Comparot de Longsols (10/1153), Coquart (10/1127), Dereins (10/1186), Gauthier (10/1196), Gentil (9/127), Huproye (9/110), and Massey (11/156).

73. The chief police magistrate collaborated with officials from the various

royal jurisdictions and the town councillors whenever high prices threatened to provoke riots. Ad hoc committees were formed in Troyes, for instance, during the shortage of 1782–83. This practice was revived by the rulers in 1789. See Ricommard, *La Lieutenance générale de police*, chap. 6. Thus although the crown may have financially controlled and exploited the towns, local rulers were still expected to provide energetic leadership in times of crisis. For an emphasis on government "tutelage," see Nora Temple, "The Control and Exploitation of French Towns during the Ancien Régime," *History*, 51 (1966), pp. 16–34.

74. This may be taken as the political concomitant of the economic community of interest uniting bourgeois and noble described by George V. Taylor in "Noncapitalist Wealth and the French Revolution," *American Historical Review*, 72 (1967), pp. 469–96.

Chapter 3

1. The textile crisis varied regionally. The decline in cotton and wool production began earlier than the slump in silk production, which meant that the northern half of France suffered first. Moreover, there was less unemployment in the silk industry than in either cotton or wool. Charles Schmidt, "La Crise industrielle de 1788 en France," *Revue historique*, 97 (1908), pp. 78–94.

2. One measure of the textile crisis is provided by the records of the *droits de marque des étoffes*, a tax levied on each piece of cloth produced (A.D. Marne, C 477). Fluctuations in the amount of tax collected reflect fluctuations in production. Using 1783 as the base, the index of taxes collected (and hence of production of cloth) was as follows:

Year	Troyes	Reims
1783	100	100
1784	121	99
1785	120	108
1786	132	152
1787	177	177
1788	121	161

If records were available for 1789 and 1790, they would most likely show a continuing decline.

3. André Colomès, *Les Ouvriers du textile dans la Champagne troyenne, 1730–1832* (Paris, 1943), p. 32; A. N. F[12] 678, letter to Bruyard from Inspector Taillardat de Sainte-Gemme, Oct. 9, 1788.

4. A.D. Aube, C 1926, letter to Lambert, Contrôleur-Général des Finances, Aug. 17, 1788. My translation.

5. Taillardat de Sainte-Gemme, Oct. 9, 1788, A.N. F[12] 678.

6. According to C.E. Labrousse, the grain price rise in the late 1780's was greatest for Champagne (rising from an index of 100 in 1786 to 226 in 1789). In the central and east-central provinces, prices rose about 75 percent; in the west-central and southwestern ones, about 60 percent; in the western and northwestern ones, about 50 percent; and in the southern and southeastern ones, only about 25 to 35 percent. Labrousse compared the minimum annual average price of the cycle (1784, 1785, 1786, or 1787, depending on the region) with the annual average price in 1789. Nationally, grain prices rose about 50 percent over their 1786 level. However, the difference between the seasonal low price of 1788 and the high price of 1789 was much greater: wheat (*blé*) prices rose by two-thirds, and rye (*seigle*), rose by three-fourths. *La Crise de l'économie française à la fin de l'Ancien Régime et au début de la Révolution* (Paris, 1944), especially pp. 155–58. See also *Esquisse du mouvement des prix et des revenus en France au XVIIIe siècle* (Paris, 1933).

Comparison of price rises from town to town and from month to month confirms the pattern of regional variation. Between January and July, 1789, the price of wheat (*blé*) dropped 3 percent in Toulouse and 15 percent in Montpellier. At the same time, the price of *froment* rose 41 percent in Reims and *blé* rose 60 percent in Troyes. The price of rye followed the same trend: it dropped 11 percent in Toulouse and 25 percent in Montpellier between January and July, 1789, while it rose 37 percent in Reims. For comparison I have used the average monthly prices. For Toulouse, see Georges and Geneviève Frêche, *Les Prix des grains, des vins et des légumes à Toulouse (1486–1868)* (Travaux et recherches de la Faculté de Droit et des sciences économiques de Paris, no. 10; Paris, 1967), p. 74. For Montpellier: A.D. Hérault, C 5942, "Etats du prix des grains et autres denrées donné par les marchands de Montpellier, 1789." For Reims: A.C. Reims, registre 689, fonds anciens, "Vicomté: Mercuriale des grains, 1759–89." For Troyes, see Figure 3.

On the question of the national market, see the argument by Louise Tilly based on prices in Paris, Beauvais, and Toulouse in "The Food Riot as a Form of Political Conflict in France," *The Journal of Interdisciplinary History*, 2 (1971), pp. 23–57. Regional variations in prices often were much more significant in the short run of crisis situations than in the long run.

7. A massive, computerized study of demography in Reims is being prepared by Antoinette Chamoux using the parish registers. For a description of the project, see "Reims au XVIIIe siècle: une population urbaine," in *La Ville au XVIIIe siècle: Colloque d'Aix-en-Provence* (Aix-en-Provence, 1975), pp. 153–60.

8. Marcel Marion, *Dictionnaire des institutions de la France aux XVIIe et XVIIIe siècles* (Paris, 1923), pp. 27–28.

9. Pierre Renouvin, *Les Assemblées provinciales de 1787* (Paris, 1921).

10. The list of deputies is given in the *Almanach . . . de Troyes* for 1789.

11. *Ibid.* Seven deputies for the Third Estate in the élection of Troyes had occupations listed: they were Huez, the mayor; Jaillant-Deschainets, king's proctor in the bailliage court; Noché, councillor in both the bailliage and élection courts; Guérard, president of the élection court; Lerouge-Daudier, honorary councillor in the élection court; Martin, officer of the maréchaussée; and Berthelin de Rosières, nobleman and brother of the former mayor. The remaining five—Lafferty, Rapault, Guérapain, Duclozet, and Auger— had no occupations listed and gave residences outside Troyes (Berthelin de Rosières also listed his residence as outside Troyes).

12. The assembly in Reims was called the *assemblée du département* according to the *Almanach de Reims* for 1789. The almanach listed only eleven of the twelve Third Estate deputies. The Reims residents were Jacob, chief police magistrate; Savoye, merchant and former town council member; and Mopinot, merchant and former town council member. The other eight listed were Pinon, Mitoux, Jobart, De Flegland, Pierret, Marguet, Roucy, and Daudigny.

13. A clear example of conservatism was provided by the assembly of Troyes. When a deputy to a parish assembly died, it decided not to call the required elections to replace him, reasoning that "since the electoral meetings of the municipalities were necessarily numerous and composed of rural people, simple farmers, it is to be feared that their choice will be determined by cabal, especially for the members of the Third." Quoted by Albert Babeau, *Histoire de Troyes pendant la Révolution* (Paris, 1873–74), vol. 1, p. 78 (my translation).

14. For a detailed discussion of this period, see Jean Egret, *La Pré-Révolution française, 1787–1788* (Paris, 1962). See also Etienne Georges, "Résistance du bailliage de Troyes aux réformes judiciaires en 1788," *Annuaire de l'Aube*, 64 (1890), pp. 3–25.

15. Jules Michelet, *Histoire de la Révolution française* (2d ed.; Paris, 1868), vol. 1, p. 89.

16. "Règlement arrêté par le Roi pour les Etats-généraux à Versailles" (January 24, 1789), *Recueil de documents relatifs à la convocation des Etats Généraux de 1789*, ed. Armand Brette (Paris, 1894–1915), vol. 1, pp. 64–87.

17. The authors of most of the corporate grievance lists are unknown. Usually, each group chose one or two men to write the grievance list, which was then reviewed and revised by the assembled corporation. The lists thus expressed articulate opinion rather than the average awareness of the political situation. Several historians and sociologists have used quantitative methods in comparing the *cahiers de doléances*, and some have used sophis-

ticated methods of computer analysis. See, for example, the essay by Gilbert Shapiro and Philip Dawson, "Social Mobility and Political Radicalism: The Case of the French Revolution of 1789," in William O. Aydelotte, Allan G. Bogue, and Robert William Fogel, eds., *The Dimensions of Quantitative Research in History* (Princeton, N.J., 1972), pp. 159–91. A recent progress report on an ambitious study of the cahiers is Gilbert Shapiro, John Markoff, and Sasha R. Weitman, "Quantitative Studies of the French Revolution," *History and Theory*, 12 (1973), pp. 163–91. See also George V. Taylor, "Revolutionary and Nonrevolutionary Content in the *Cahiers* of 1789: An Interim Report," *French Historical Studies*, 7 (1972), pp. 479–502. Taylor emphasizes political consciousness and its relationship to urbanization.

18. French historians have recently shown much interest in linguistic or semiotic analysis of the cahiers. See for example Régine Robin, *La Société française en 1789: Semur-en-Auxois* (Paris, 1970). The use of Enlightenment rhetoric in the corporate grievance lists of Reims was analyzed by André Burguière, "Société et culture à Reims à la fin du XVIIIe siècle: la diffusion des 'Lumières' analysée à travers les cahiers de doléances," *Annales: E. S. C.*, 22 (1967), pp. 303–39.

19. The textile workers who invaded the meeting were listed most frequently on the *procès-verbal* as "workers," weavers, carders, combers, shearers, finishers, and day-laborers (*journaliers*). *Cahiers de doléances . . . Département de la Marne*, vol. 4, p. 189. On Hédoin de Pons Ludon, see Victor Diancourt, "Deux originaux rémois: les Hédoin de Pons-Ludon, 1739–1866," *T. A. N. Reims*, 75 (1833–84), pp. 335–95.

20. After this brief appearance in the political arena, Hédoin withdrew into relative obscurity, modestly observing and recording the events of the Revolution in his journal. *Journal de Pons Ludon, rémois (la Révolution, 1789–1795)*, published from the manuscript in the Bibliothèque de Reims by Pol Gosset, *T. A. N. Reims*, 152 (1939–41), pp. 1–124.

21. The grievance list for the town of Reims can be found in *Cahiers de doléances . . . Département de la Marne*, vol. 4, pp. 204–25; that for the town of Troyes can be found in *Cahiers de doléances du bailliage de Troyes . . .*, vol. 1, pp. 210–88.

22. This is a comparison of the sections entitled "Administration de la Justice" in the Troyes list and "Legislation civile et criminelle" in the Reims list. Any such comparison is difficult because the Troyes list often included many demands in each article. Here I have simply compared the number of articles rather than the number of demands.

23. *Cahiers de doléances . . . Département de la Marne*, vol. 4, p. 225.

24. This can be inferred from pamphlets written in later months. One of the apologies written for the Troyes committee specifically cited the conduct of the town council during the March meetings as one of the chief causes of

the revolution in Troyes. See *Réplique au mémoire des sieurs Parent et Gillet* (Troyes, 1789), signed by Truelle de Chambouzon (president of the August committee), Perrin, Noël, and Dorgemont (especially pp. 5 and 6).

25. *Cahiers de doléances du bailliage de Troyes*..., vol. 1, pp. xiii–xiv. The "Règlement par le Roi, pour fixer le nombre des députés que les bailliages de Laon, Reims, Troyes et Vitry doivent envoyer aux prochains Etats-Généraux, du 2 mars 1789" was published in the *Journal de Troyes et de la Champagne méridionale* in its issue of March 18, 1789.

26. For the *procès-verbal* and the grievance list of the clergy of the bailliage of Troyes, see *Cahiers de doléances du bailliage de Troyes*..., vol. 3, pp. 87–139. An account of the meetings of the clergy of the bailliage of Reims is given in Gustave Laurent, *Reims et la région rémoise à la veille de la Révolution*, vol. 5 of *Cahiers de doléances... Département de la Marne* (Reims, 1930), pp. 326–39. The general grievance lists for the bailliage of Reims were published in *Archives Parlementaires... 1ère série*, vol. 5, pp. 520–37. Minor corrections of the text are given by Beatrice Fry Hyslop, *A Guide to the General Cahiers of 1789* (New York, 1936), p. 196.

27. The canons and regular clergy of the Troyes region protested against many of the articles in the grievance list in their "Réclamations et protestations des chapitres, communautés regulières des deux sexes, commendataires et bénéficiers simples du bailliage de Troyes," *Cahiers de doléances du bailliage de Troyes*..., vol. 3, pp. 124–39. They wanted greater representation in future meetings, and they especially opposed article 60, which demanded freedom to assemble for parish priests: "les curés ont prouvé à l'assemblée des trois Ordres du bailliage de Troyes, et de presque tous les bailliages, combien il serait dangereux de leur accorder leur demande" (p. 135).

28. For a description of the incident, see Georges Boussinesq and Gustave Laurent, *Histoire de Reims depuis les origines jusqu'à nos jours*, vol. 2, *Reims moderne de 1610 à 1914* (Reims, 1933), chap. 10.

29. For grievance lists of the nobility for Troyes, see *Cahiers de doléances du bailliage de Troyes*..., vol. 3, pp. 161–74; for Reims, see note 26 above.

30. The meetings of the Third Estate of the bailliage of Reims are described in Laurent, *Reims et la région rémoise*. Those of Troyes are described by Babeau in his *Histoire de Troyes*, vol. 1, chap. 7.

31. Laurent noted that two articles were crossed out of the original version of the town grievance list. These two articles were not included in the bailliage list. *Cahiers de doléances... Département de la Marne*, vol. 4, p. 217, n. 3.

32. *Cahiers de doléances du bailliage de Troyes*..., vol. 3, pp. 184–211.

33. Colin Lucas, "Nobles, Bourgeois and the Origins of the French Revolution," *Past and Present*, no. 60 (1973), pp. 84–126, quote on p. 121.

Chapter 4

1. This anecdote was told by Adrien Duquesnoy, a deputy for the Third Estate from Bar-le-Duc. Robert de Crèvecoeur, ed., *Journal d'Adrien Duquesnoy* (Paris, 1894), vol. 1, p. 4.

2. See the description of the May 4 ceremony in Jules Michelet, *History of the French Revolution*, trans. Charles Cocks (Chicago, 1967), pp. 95–99. The quote cited is from p. 98.

3. For Troyes, see the *Journal de Troyes et de la Champagne méridionale*. For Reims, see the *Affiches, Annonces, et Avis Diverses de Reims* (Bibliothèque Municipale de Reims). Henri Jadart describes the *Affiches* in his *Chronique rémoise de la fin du XVIIIe siècle. Récits et documents originaux* (Reims, 1895). An analysis of the political content in the *Affiches* on the eve of the Revolution can be found in André Burguière, "Société et culture à Reims à la fin du XVIIIe siècle: la diffusion des 'Lumières' analysée à travers les cahiers de doléances," *Annales: E.S.C.*, 22 (1967), pp. 303–39.

4. These letters are described by H. Diné, "Le Journal des Etats Généraux de Camusat de Belombre, député du Tiers Etat de la ville de Troyes (6 mai–8 août 1789)," *A.H.R.F.*, 37 (1965), pp. 257–69. The letters themselves can be found in "Dossier de l'abbé de Champagne," *A.N.*, W 306 (89 pp.). See also the letters by the marquis de Sillery, deputy from the nobility of the bailliage of Reims: *A.N.*, KK 641, "Journal des Etats Généraux du marquis de Sillery, 1789"; and KK 647, "Correspondance générale de Monsieur le marquis de Sillery pendant la tenue des Etats Généraux en 1789." Sillery's letters were not nearly as informative as those of Camusat de Belombre.

5. *A.N.*, W 306, letter of June 7, 1789 (p. 27).

6. *Ibid.*, letter of June 18, 1789 (p. 37).

7. *Ibid.*, letter of June 20, 1789 (p. 39). I have modernized the spelling.

8. *Ibid.*, letter of June 24, 1789 (pp. 44–45).

9. *Ibid.*, letter of July 9, 1789 (p. 61).

10. *Ibid.*, letter of July 10, 1789 (p. 62).

11. Price rises have been calculated using the price in the first week of March as the base: the percent rise equals the price in the first week of July minus the price in the first week of March divided by the base price. Prices are taken from Julien Ricommard, *La Lieutenance générale de police à Troyes au XVIIIe siècle* (Troyes, 1934), appendix; and A.C. Reims, registre 689, fonds anciens, "Vicomté: Mercuriale des grains, 1759–89."

12. My translation of a quote in Etienne Georges, *La Révolution de 1789 à Troyes: Notice anecdotique d'après des autographs inédits* (Troyes, 1895), p. 8.

13. *A.N.*, W 306, letter of July 12, 1789 (p. 63).

14. *Ibid.*, letter of July 13, 1789 (pp. 64–65).

15. *Ibid.*, letters of July 14 ("Les nouvelles qui arrivent ici de Paris à tous les instants annoncent que la tranquillité commence à se retablir. . . .") and of July 15, 1789 (pp. 67–70). In the latter, Camusat refers to "l'exécrable horreur d'une guerre civile."

16. The "electors" were the men chosen to represent the city of Paris in the elections for the Estates General. For the history of Paris during this period, see two articles by Henry E. Bourne, "Improvising a Government in Paris in July, 1789," *American Historical Review*, 10 (1904–5), pp. 280–308, and "Municipal Politics in Paris in 1789," *American Historical Review*, 11 (1905–6), pp. 263–86.

17. According to Daniel Ligou, Rouen's municipal revolution began before news arrived of the dismissal of Necker. Rouen was not simply following the lead of Paris. "A propos de la révolution municipale," *Revue d'histoire économique et sociale*, 38 (1960), pp. 146–77, 154.

18. For a general discussion of the urban revolution of 1789, see Lynn A. Hunt, "Committees and Communes: Local Politics and National Revolution in 1789," *Comparative Studies in Society and History*, 18 (July 1976), pp. 321–46.

19. A.C. Troyes, AA carton 55, "Correspondance, 1789," letter of July 20, 1789. On July 21, Camusat de Belombre wrote to Troyes saying that he had heard about "le commencement d'une fermentation dans Troyes . . . ." (Army commander Saint-Georges had written to the noble deputies from the bailliage.) Camusat hoped to calm the agitated spirits in Troyes by conveying the news that Paris had quieted down. A.N., W 306, letter of July 21, 1789 (p. 77).

20. As might be expected, the trouble in Reims was attributed to "gens sans aveu," who were exciting the people to revolt. A.C. Reims, registre 116, fonds anciens, "Conclusions du Conseil de Ville," July 20, 1789.

21. A.C. Reims, registre 226, fonds moderns, "Délibérations du Comité permanent, 20 juillet 1789–29 décembre 1789," July 22, 1789.

22. The participation of these four men in the events of July and August is described in detail in A.D. Aube, Nouvelles Acquisitions 6199–6201, Maréchaussée: "Procès des assassins de Claude Huez." See also Alexis Gillet and Nicolas Parent, *A Nosseigneurs de l'Assemblée Nationale* (Troyes, 1789), and the replies to them in Truelle de Chambouzon et al., *Réplique au mémoire des sieurs Parent et Gillet, soi-disants Députés de la ville de Troyes par les Députés du Comité général et provisoire de la même Ville* (Paris, 1789).

23. Emile Chaudron, *La Grande Peur en Champagne méridionale* (Paris, 1923).

24. A.C. Reims, registre 254, fonds moderns, "Correspondance, 1789," letter of August 12, 1789.

25. A.C. Reims, registre 116, fonds anciens, "Conclusions du Conseil de Ville," August 17, 1789.

26. Taxes for 34 (69 percent) of the 49 elected deputies were located. Taxes for 32 (67 percent) of the 1788–89 rulers were located. A.C. Reims, registre 194, fonds moderns, "Contribution fonçière, 1792." This comparison is not altogether reliable and may underestimate the wealth of the former rulers (some of whom emigrated early). The same is true of the *contribution patriotique*, which moreover was not rigorously or uniformly assessed. The elected deputies paid an average patriotic contribution of 2,164 livres (23 have been located in the lists) as compared to an average of 1,318 livres for the Old Regime rulers (23 of them have been located in the lists). A.C. Reims, registre 251, fonds moderns, "Contribution patriotique." The list of contributions made prior to February 1790 was used.

27. A.C. Reims, registre 116, fonds anciens, "Conclusions du Conseil de Ville, 1789–1790," August 28, 1789.

28. A.C. Reims, registres 226 and 227, fonds moderns, "Délibérations du Comité permanent."

29. On grain prices, see A.C. Reims, registre 689, fonds anciens, "Vicomté: Mercurial des grains." The average number of arrests per week declined steadily from 5.3 in September to 3.8 in January.

30. A.C. Reims, registre 226, August 28, 1789.

31. This estimation is based on a sample of the first *connétable* of each of the nine militia companies. A.C. Reims, registre 679, fonds anciens, "Capitation, 1789." In the poorest districts (1, 8, and 9) only 10 to 20 percent of the adult males were eligible, but in the town's center (district 3, in particular) as many as 90 percent of the male taxpayers were eligible for guard service. Since the capitation roll did not include all the adult males in Reims, considerably less than 40 percent of the resident males qualified for militia service. The regulation for the Guard aptly described it as "bourgeois sous les armes." Article 20 of the regulation for the Garde Nationale Rémoise, A.C. Reims, registre 226, August 28, 1789.

32. Town councillors had better attendance records than the elected deputies in four of the seven bureaus. I used the signatures at the end of the *procès-verbaux* of the bureaus to establish attendance averages. Each bureau contained nine to eleven members: three or four from the town council, and six or seven elected deputies. A.C. Reims, registres 226 and 227.

33. The narrative of events in Troyes has been reconstructed from a comparison of conflicting reports. On the one side were the official apologists of the counterrevolution, Gillet and Parent (see n. 22). On the other side were the spokesmen for the committee eventually elected on August 28. The Committee of Reports of the National Assembly received letters from both sides (A.N., D XXIX 80, "Troyes"). The court records for the case of Huez's

murder contain lengthy statements by witnesses (A.D. Aube, Nouvelles Acquisitions 6199–6201). In addition to all these, there is a journal for the period: Abbé Trémet, "Notes historiques de ce qui s'est passé à Troyes, 1770–90," (B.M. Troyes, MS 2322). See also the detailed though biased account given by Albert Babeau in vol. 1 of his *Histoire de Troyes pendant la Révolution* (2 vols.; Paris, 1873–74).

34. Saint-Georges had married into one of the town's leading families. One of his wife's sisters married a noble town councillor, and another married the subdelegate's son. A.D. Aube, 4Q/36, "Fadate de Saint-Georges, émigré."

35. "Extrait de la délibération des officiers nommés pour la Milice citoyenne et provisoire de la ville de Troyes, du 25 août 1789," *Journal de Troyes et de la Champagne méridionale*, vol. 8, issue of September 2, 1789.

36. Most of the pamphlets written in favor of the committee elected on August 28 claim that Saint-Georges and Huez gave the order to fire. More details are given in a letter signed "De zèles compatriotes," in A.N., D XXIX 80, January 1, 1790. This version is denied by Gillet and Parent, *A Nosseigneurs*, p. 11.

37. Gillet and Parent, *A Nosseigneurs*, p. 11.

38. Abbé Trémet, "Notes historiques."

39. There was some controversy over who participated in the committee elections. According to the committee's detractors, Gillet and Parent, three-quarters of the town's citizens were excluded from the elections: "La nomination des Commissaires ne fut donc point l'ouvrage de la Commune ... elle fut seulement le voeu de quelques particuliers, spécialement des Maîtres des Jurandes, Corps et Corporations" (*A Nosseigneurs*, p. 13). The committee's spokesmen maintained that all the inhabitants were included: "les journaliers établis, les femmes veuves, les filles tenant ménage, enfin tous les habitants *privilégiés* et *non privilégiés*, les Officiers Municipaux et M. Parent lui-même, y ont contribués" (*Réplique au mémoire des sieurs Parent et Gillet*, p. 1).

40. A.C. Troyes, A registre 54, "Assemblées des conseillers notables, 1786–90," August 29, 1789.

41. The eight bureaus were "Police and Market Supply," "Town Security and the National Guard of Troyes," "Revenues and Expenses," "Charity Workshops and Poor Relief," "Works and Repairs Financed by the Town," "Road and Bridge Maintenance, Fire Control, and Town Lighting," "Water Supply," and "Troop Lodging." A.C. Troyes, Anciens Cartons Locaux, No. 605, "Distribution des bureaux du Comité Général et Provisoire de la Ville de Troyes."

42. Attendance was recorded for eight of the thirteen committee meetings from August 29 to September 15 (the signatures on the *procès-verbal* have

been used as attendance records). Eight men attended six or seven meetings: Collet (medical doctor); Dusaussay-Rabiat (merchant); Bouquet (proctor); Bourgeois-Rollin (merchant, the only one of the eight who had sat on the town council [his term had ended in April]); B̄. Chaperon (bailiff); Jobert (bourgeois); Laurans-Chatel (merchant); and Truelle de Chambouzon (bailliage magistrate). A.C. Troyes, D* 33, "Registre des procès-verbaux du Comité Général et Permanent (4 septembre–5 octobre 1789)," and A registre 54, August 29–September 29, 1789.

43. "Qu'à considérer plusieurs des membres qui le composent, et leur profonde ignorance dans tous les genres d'administration, on ne sait si l'on doit être plus étonné de l'audacieuse présomption d'autres, qui après avoir échoué dans leurs affaires, ne peuvent apporter dans les affaires publiques que le même désordre qui fait gémir leurs créanciers, ou de ceux qui n'ayant ni existence civile, ni domicile, ni droit de cité, n'ont pu acquérir le droit d'administrer ceux dont ils ne sont pas mêmes les concitoyens. Ce sont cependant ces individus qui ont osé renverser de leurs sièges les Magistrats légitimes. . . . L'esprit de cabale a pu seul diriger une telle novation. . . . Que par une incohérence indéfinissable, et qui ne sera pas crue de la génération à venir, des individus sans qualité, sans titre ni mission, se sont érigés en tribunal, ont forgé des loix, les ont dicté, et ont fait porter au-dehors comme au-dedans de la ville des ordres appuyés de menaces et de projets de violence." This passage is from Parent's report to the bailliage court on September 29, A.C. Troyes, AA carton 55, "Correspondance, 1789" (Extrait des minutes du greffe du bailliage).

44. "Après différentes tentatives la Commune parvint enfin à former le 29 août dernier, un Comité Civil et Militaire, mais les Officiers Municipaux et ceux du Bailliage, leurs coopérateurs habitués à commander en Despotes, ne purent lui pardonner cette entreprise hardie." Truelle de Chambouzon et al., *Précis pour le Comité Général et provisoire de la ville de Troyes* (Troyes, 1789), p. 2.

45. Information on Truelle de Chambouzon was put together from a variety of sources. His letters of provision of office can be found in A.N. V¹ 387, 1756 (*conseiller en l'élection*) and V¹ 430, 1766 (*conseiller au Bailliage civil*). For his role during the Maupeou reforms, see Théophile Boutiot, *Histoire de la ville de Troyes et de la Champagne méridionale* (Troyes, 1870–80), vol. 4, p. 615. For information on his family, see A.D. Aube, 4Q/79.

46. The role of the Chaperon brothers is detailed in the sources described in n. 33. Jean-François's marriage contract was located in A.D. Aube, 2E 6/151.

47. Marriage contracts were located for nine town councillors as of April 1789 (39 percent); they made marriage contracts averaging 67,171 livres (30,000 livres median). Contracts were located for sixteen elected deputies

(25 percent); their contracts averaged 18,223 livres (7,700 livres median). A.D. Aube, série 2E. This pattern is confirmed by the list of citizens paying 50 livres tax or more in 1791 (about 340 taxpayers). Two-thirds of the 1789 town council were found on this list, as opposed to only 41 percent of the elected committee members. A.C. Troyes, G* 1, "Etat des citoyens de la ville de Troyes payant 50 l. impositions et au-dessus."

48. Three committee members had their marriage contracts witnessed by members of the 1788–89 ruling group: Milony, an architect; Matagrin, a merchant; and Lalobe, also a merchant. These three were among the wealthiest committee members; their contracts were evaluated at an average of 30,213 livres. Most of the rulers witnessing their contracts were also merchants; only one was a royal official.

Chapter 5

1. A.C. Troyes, D* 33, "Registre des procès-verbaux du Comité Général et Permanent," September 5, 1789.

2. *Ibid.*

3. The meeting of the guild masters was described by Gillet and Parent, *A Nosseigneurs de l'Assemblée Nationale* (Troyes, 1789), pp. 20, 21.

4. *Ibid.*, p. 21.

5. *Ibid.*, pp. 21, 22.

6. This was the position taken by a group of anonymous citizens in a letter written to the National Assembly on January 1, 1790: "Si on s'assure, que le commandant et les officieurs municipaux, étaient associés avec des négociants et les plus riches artisans, pour le commerce des grains; qu'ils ont par ce moyen mis la famine dans la ville; on verra facilement, que leur conduite a forcé à la vengeance et que la mort du maire, et les désastres qui l'ont suivi, sont l'effet de leur odieuse administration, de leur vil commerce et de leur injustice." A.N., D XXIX 80 (Troyes), letter signed "de zèles compatriotes."

7. A.C. Troyes, D* 33, September 9, 1789.

8. Gillet and Parent, *A Nosseigneurs*, pp. 22, 23.

9. A.C. Troyes, D* 23, "Registre de Correspondance de la Municipalité entre 1766 et 1792," letter to Interior Minister Saint-Priest from Truelle de Chambouzon, president of the committee, September 10, 1789.

10. The narrative of events on September 9 has been reconstructed from pamphlets, court records, and various secondary materials. See especially Albert Babeau, *Histoire de Troyes pendant la Révolution* (Paris, 1873), vol. 1, chap. 12.

11. A.C. Troyes, D* 23, letter of September 13, 1789.

12. A.D. Aube, Nouvelles Acquisitions 6200, "Procès des assassins de Claude Huez." Many suspects were detained only briefly; hence there were

some fragmentary lists. The most informative list contains the names of those interrogated by the court.

13. A.C. Troyes, A registre 54, September 11, 1789.

14. A.N., D XXIX 80 (Troyes), no. 5064.

15. *Ibid.*

16. A.C. Troyes, D* 23, September 13, 1789, letter from Truelle de Chambouzon to Saint-Priest.

17. A.C. Troyes, A registre 54, September 15, 1789. The minutes of the committee report only that the vote was not unanimous.

18. A.C. Troyes, AA carton 55, "Correspondance, 1789," September 13, 1789.

19. *Ibid.*, August 31, 1789.

20. Etienne Georges, *La Révolution de 1789 à Troyes. Notice anecdotique d'après des autographs inédits* (Troyes, 1895), p. 15.

21. A.N., D XXIX 80 (Troyes), January 17, 1790. The letter was signed by Paillot, Comparot de Longsols, Babeau, Sourdat, Coquart, Jaillant-Deschainets, Corrard de Bréban, Héroult de la Clôture, and Gauthier. With the exception of Sourdat, all were bailliage magistrates.

22. A.C. Troyes, AA carton 55, "Correspondance, 1789," extract from the minutes of the bailliage court, September 29, 1789.

23. *Ibid.*

24. Georges, *La Révolution*, p. 19.

25. A.C. Troyes, A registre 54, October 6, 1789.

26. B.M. Troyes, MS 2322, Abbé Trémet, "Notes historiques de ce qui s'est passé à Troyes, 1770–90."

27. Gillet and Parent, *Observations* (Paris, 1789), p. 3.

28. A.C. Troyes, Fonds François Carteron, vol. 25, "Règlement pour la formation d'une Garde Nationale Volontaire."

29. A.C. Troyes, AA carton 55, "Correspondance, 1789."

30. *Ibid.*

31. Georges, *La Révolution*, pp. 33–34. The letter went on to ask what the new volunteer militia companies would do in the event the committee was reestablished.

32. René Demogue, "La Criminalité et la répression en Champagne au XVIIIᵉ siècle, 1715–1789," *T.A.N. Reims*, 125 (1909), pp. 103–93. The Troyes prison consisted of a room called "the calamity," where those arrested for criminal offenses, deserters, and beggars were mixed together; a room for noncriminal offenders; an infirmary; and a room for women. After an epidemic in 1783 three other rooms were added: a military room, an interrogation room, and a meeting room.

33. A.D. Aube, 1B, registre 1325, "Registre du lieutenant criminel au bailliage: Prisons, mai 1789–nivôse an X." Between June 1 and December 31, 1789, entries were recorded for 239 people. The conditions in the prison of

Troyes concerned the National Assembly. On October 24, 1789, the president of the Assembly asked the *comité des recherches* to investigate the "malheureuse affaire de Troyes": "Il y a plus de quatre-vingt accusés, les prisons en sont remplies, il y en a jusqu'à vingt dans un cachot: les prisonniers sont à chaque moment exposés à perdre la vie." *Archives Parlementaires*, vol. 9, p. 517.

34. A.N., D XXIX 80 (Troyes), letters received on October 3 and October 8, 1789.

35. A.D. Aube, 2J 549, "Jugement prévôtal et en dernier ressort," November 27, 1789.

36. The 52-year-old self-styled "bourgeois" was banished from the province for nine years. Only six of the fourteen could sign their names; only one of the five sentenced to die could sign his name. A.D. Aube, Nouvelles Acquisitions 6200.

37. Demogue, "La Criminalité en Champagne."

38. The Cour Souveraine was established in 1740 for special cases: smuggling, illegal assemblies, employee thefts, and perjury. It continued to operate until 1789. *Ibid.*

39. A.D. Aube, 2J 549, "Rapport du procès instruit et jugé au siège de la maréchaussée à Troyes, contre les auteurs du massacre de M. Huez, Maire, et de pillage et devastation de maisons" (February 9, 1790), pp. 2, 4, 5.

40. *Archives Parlementaires*, vol. 10, p. 498.

41. Babeau, *Histoire de Troyes*, vol. 1, chap. 13.

42. Trémet, "Notes historiques," p. 56 (entry for November 1789).

43. A.C. Reims, registre 254, fonds moderns, "Copies de lettres," August 18, 1789.

44. A.C. Reims, registre 116, fonds anciens, "Conclusions du Conseil de Ville," September 1, 1789.

45. A.C. Reims, registre 226, fonds moderns, "Délibérations du Comité permanent," September 27, 1789.

46. *Ibid.*, October 23, 1789.

47. A.N., D XXIX 67 (Reims).

48. A.C. Reims, registre 116, November 2, 1789. The procureur-syndic reported the rumors to the town council meeting.

49. A.C. Reims, registre 254, "Copies de lettres," January 15, 1790.

50. Letters on this issue can be found in the files of the Committee on Reports of the National Assembly. A.N., D XXIX 67 (Reims) and 80 (Troyes).

Chapter 6

1. Mirabeau advocated local autonomy on the model of the United States of America. Mounier considered local autonomy dangerous. This debate

began in reference to Paris. *Moniteur (Réimpression de l'Ancien Moniteur)*, vol. 1, pp. 191, 197.

2. Jacques Godechot, *Les Institutions de la France sous la Révolution et l'Empire* (2d ed.; Paris, 1968), part 2, chap. 3.

3. Bankrupts and men under arrest were also excluded from the franchise. *Archives Parlementaires*, vol. 10, p. 567.

4. R. R. Palmer, *The Age of the Democratic Revolution* (Princeton, N.J., 1959), vol. 1, p. 523. See also Jean-René Suratteau, "Heurs et malheurs de la 'sociologie électorale' pour l'époque de la Révolution française," *Annales: E. S. C.*, 23 (1968), pp. 556–80.

5. Godechot maintains that the large towns generally had a greater proportion of "passive" (nonvoting) citizens than the small towns. *Les Institutions de la France*, p. 76.

6. Reims reported 5,539 active citizens to the department in the spring of 1790 (A.C. Reims, carton 843, fonds moderns, liasse 211). In estimating what percentage of all adult males that figure represented I used population figures for 1793, as described in Chapter 2, note 17. In 1793 Reims had 6,288 men aged 25 to 60, 1,283 men in the army, and 2,977 people of both sexes over 60. Taking half of the people over 60 and half of the men in the army, we get an upper limit of 8,417 adult *rémois*. The figure of 5,539 represents about two-thirds of that (66 percent). Troyes reported 2,760 voters to the department in May 1790 (A.D. Aube, Lm 2a 188). If we take even a rough estimate that one-fourth of the total population consisted of adult men (as in Reims), then Troyes in 1790 must have had 6,000–7,000 adult men (one-fourth of 25,000–28,000). Hence 2,760 voters were less than 50 percent of the adult men. Troyes and Reims had slightly different criteria for enfranchisement: a day's wage was set at 19 sous in Reims, and at 20 sous in Troyes. This difference was too minor, however, to account for the substantial difference in numbers of voters.

7. This is my calculation based on the nominative lists given in A.C. Reims, carton 843. "Service workers" includes gardeners as well as unskilled laborers. The figures for social groups of the "upper classes" were royal officials, 2 percent; liberal professions, 4 percent; bourgeois, 2 percent; clergy, 3 percent; merchants, 2 percent; clothiers, 4 percent; farmers, 2 percent. Six percent did not list occupations. Noble titles were not indicated.

8. "Liste des citoyens éligible pour la formation de la municipalité, 1790," B.M. Reims, CR I 1050.

9. A.C. Reims, registre 116, fonds anciens, "Conclusions du Conseil de Ville," February 1, 1790.

10. A.C. Troyes, A registre 54, "Assemblées des conseillers notables," January 18–20, 1790.

11. *Ibid.*, January 23 and 30, February 3 and 5, 1790.

12. A.C. Reims, carton 816, fonds moderns, February 7 and 22, 1790.

13. In his letters, Camusat consistently opposed local violence, but he understood very well the need to placate an angry populace. ". . . Je connais tous les droits et toute la force actuelle du peuple: j'en ai été ici le témoin dans diverses circonstances." A.C. Troyes, AA carton 55, "Correspondance," letter from Camusat de Belombre to the town council, August 31, 1789.

14. A.C. Troyes, A registre 54, lists given by the town council on January 30 and February 3, 1790. Albert Babeau gives a slightly different list of newly elected municipal officers because he includes only those who accepted election. Milony, the architect, refused election, and Truelle de Chambouzon eventually resigned in order to take a post with the district council. Truelle was replaced by Sissous, one of the most active pamphleteers in defense of the Chaperon brothers and the committee. For an account of the election, see Albert Babeau, *Histoire de Troyes pendant la Révolution* (Paris, 1873), vol. 1, chap. 13. Babeau's judgments, though based on extensive research, must be taken with a grain of salt.

15. A.C. Troyes, A registre 54, list given by the town council on February 9, 1790.

16. A.C. Reims, carton 826, list of new municipal officers, February 20, 1790.

17. *Ibid.*, February 22, 1790.

18. Godechot, *Les Institutions de la France*, p. 111.

19. Abbé Trémet, "Notes historiques de ce qui s'est passé à Troyes, 1770–90," B.M. Troyes, MS 2322, p. 58. The former rulers felt the same way about the department elections. "Nous n'avons recueilli, des débris de l'ancienne administration, que M. Fromageot . . . et le vicaire général Clergier," wrote Abraham de Lafferty, a member of the élection assembly, to Comparot de Longsols in a letter dated July 13, 1790, and quoted by Etienne Georges in "Progrès de la Révolution à Troyes de 1790 à 1792," *Annuaire de l'Aube*, 50 (1896), p. 10.

20. "Journal anonyme du XVIIIᵉ siècle," *T.A.N. Reims*, 110 (1900–1901), p. 300.

21. The names and professions of the Troyes electors are given in A.D. Aube, Lm 2a 188. The Reims electors are listed in A.C. Reims, carton 843, liasse 211. Very little detailed information on the district and department elections remains.

22. The list of the Aube electors can be found in A. N., F¹ᶜ III Aube 4. I did not find a comparable list for the Marne department.

23. Raymond Nicolas, *L'Esprit public et les élections dans le département de la Marne de 1790 à l'An VIII* (Châlons-sur-Marne, 1909), list of names and professions in appendix III. The Troyes *Almanach* did not list the professions of those on the Aube department council.

24. Pierre Bréon's marriage contract was located in A.D. Aube 2E 9/88 (1758).

25. Edme Herluison-Cornet's contract was found in A.D. Aube 2E 6/133 (1774).

26. Marriage contracts were located for 33 percent of the new rulers in A. D. Aube, IIC Supplément 36, "Table alphabétique des contrats de mariage," and série 2E.

27. For the 340 highest taxpayers in 1791, see A.C. Troyes, G* 1, "Etat des citoyens de la ville de Troyes payant 50 l. impositions et au-dessus."

28. Too many addresses for artisans and shopkeepers are missing to justify a more exact statement. Seven new rulers listed addresses in the Beffroy quarter, and twelve gave addresses in the Croncels quarter. Addresses are in the *Almanach de la ville et du diocèse de Troyes* (Troyes, 1791).

29. The marriage contract of Truelle-Sourdat is in A. D. Aube, 2E 7/309 (1781). It was evaluated at 60,000 livres.

30. Jouvant's career can be traced through several sources: his letter of provision of office as king's advocate in the bailliage court of Reims is in A.N., V¹ 404 (1760); his letter of provision of office as *lieutenant particulier* is in A.D. Marne, C 2524 (1768); and his name is inscribed in the Triple Union membership roll of 1778 (B.N., FM² 365, Reims).

31. Guittard's capitation tax is listed in A.C. Reims, registre 679. He was listed on the 1778 membership roll of the Triple Union lodge (B.N., FM² 365). The property taxes of 74 percent of the new rulers were found in A.C. Reims, registre 194, fonds moderns, "Contribution fonçiere, 1792." Addresses of the new rulers come from the *Almanach de la ville et du diocèse de Reims* (Reims, 1791) and from the property tax roll just cited.

32. Cobban's claim that "in the main the administrative personnel of the *ancien régime* was taken over with little change by the Revolution" is correct, if at all, only in reference to the departments. Even the department councils, however, had many new men. The municipal governments were dominated by men who had not held office in the Old Regime. Alfred Cobban, "Local Government during the Revolution," *English Historical Review*, 58 (1943), pp. 13–31, quote on p. 18.

33. Rabaud de Saint-Etienne explained the meaning of the new administrative division in his "Nouvelles réflexions sur la nouvelle division du royaume": "ces décrets régénérateurs qui substituent l'égalité politique de toutes les villes et de toutes les portions du royaume au monstrueux et contradictoire amas d'inégalités, dont le temps, le hasard, les abus, les privilèges, la faveur ou le despotisme, avaient composé la chaos" (*Archives Parlementaires*, vol. 10, p. 37). This is the kind of rationalizing impulse that Edward Whiting Fox analyzes in *History in Geographic Perspective: The Other France* (New York, 1971).

34. See the discussion about the new administrative structures on November 3, 1789, and especially the comments of Thouret, the spokesman for the Committee on the Constitution: "Toutes les provinces sont mainten-

ant réunies en droits et en intentions; elles avaient du se créer des corps assez puissant pour résister à l'oppression ministérielle; mais à présent, ne rendons pas ces corps aussi forts. Elus par le peuple, leurs membres acquérront une trop grande prépondérance" (*Moniteur* [*Réimpression de l'Ancien Moniteur*], vol. 2, p. 126). The decree of December 14, 1789, clearly subordinated the municipalities to the departments and the districts (see Articles 50 and 51). *Archives Parlementaires*, vol. 10, p. 566.

35. The names of the new judicial officeholders can be found in the 1791 volumes of the *Almanach de Reims* and the *Almanach de Troyes*.

36. Alexis de Tocqueville, *L'Ancien Régime et la Révolution*, ed. J. P. Mayer (Paris, 1952).

37. Some of the limitations placed on public gatherings were opposed in the National Assembly as contrary to the liberty of the citizens. On December 1, 1789, when this point was debated, Defermon, Rewbell, Mirabeau, and Duport opposed the limits on the rights to assemble and to denounce municipal governments. *Archives Parlementaires*, vol. 10, pp. 344–45. The Committee on the Constitution successfully defended its articles on the grounds that local governments should not be encumbered by easily lodged complaints.

Chapter 7

1. For a more detailed discussion, see Lynn A. Hunt, "Committees and Communes: Local Politics and National Revolution in 1789," *Comparative Studies in Society and History*, 18 (July 1976), pp. 321–46.

2. In Montpellier, for example, the committee elected on August 28 included 21 merchants, twenty members of the liberal professions, fourteen officials of the Cour des Aides, and six officials in the various royal jurisdictions among its 99 members. J. Duval-Jouve, *Montpellier pendant la Révolution* (Montpellier, 1879), vol. 1, pp. 64–65.

3. A.C. Orléans, AA (Suppl.) 13, July 19, 1789. (The inventory lists the names and occupations of the deputies.)

4. My figures for Paris are based on the lists of names given by Paul Robiquet in *Le Personnel municipal de Paris pendant la Révolution: période constitutionnelle* (Paris, 1890), pp. 205–11, 213–29.

5. The royal officials (19 percent) and the artisans and shopkeepers (22 percent) did particularly well in the 1790 municipal elections in Dijon. Henri Millot, *Le Comité permanent de Dijon* (Enquêtes sur la Révolution en Côte-d'Or, n.s., fasc. 1, Dijon, 1925).

6. Zoltan-Etienne Harsany, "Metz pendant la Révolution: la chute de l'Ancien Régime (1789)," *Mémoires de l'Académie Nationale de Metz*, 142, 5e sér., 6 (1959–61), pp. 4–45; my calculations based on list of names given on p. 26.

7. Hannah Arendt, *The Human Condition* (Chicago, 1958).

A Note on Sources

THE LITERATURE ON the French Revolution in general, and on the provincial towns in particular, is so enormous that I have chosen not to list secondary sources here. In the absence of such a list, a word is in order on the nature of the secondary materials available for research on Troyes and Reims. Many local historians in the late nineteenth and early twentieth centuries contributed valuable information about various aspects of life in their communities in the eighteenth century. They wrote primarily for their friends and neighbors in local scholarly societies, and they often published extracts from original documents in their journals. Many of the sources they used are now lost. Without the painstaking labors of these devotees of local history my work would have been extremely difficult, if not impossible. In Reims most publications appeared in the *Travaux de l'Académie nationale de Reims*. In Troyes there were three useful serials: the *Annuaire de l'Aube*; the *Révolution dans l'Aube*; and the *Mémoires de la Société académique d'agriculture, des sciences, arts et belles-lettres du département de l'Aube*.

Two reference works are essential for anyone discussing this period: Gérard Walter, *Répertoire de l'histoire de la Révolution française: travaux publiés de 1800 à 1940. Lieux* (Paris, 1951); and Philippe Dollinger et al., *Bibliographie d'histoire des villes de France* (Paris, 1967).

Unpublished Sources

The materials listed in this section—a wide assortment of tax records, marriage contracts, letters of provision of office, and various other political and legal documents—formed the foundation of the collective profiles of the various ruling elites on which I have based most of my conclusions. Only general designations of sources are given below; full citations will be found in the Notes.

ARCHIVES NATIONALES

BB^{30} 87. "Emeutes, 1789."

D IVbis 47. "Population des villes suivant les états envoyés par MM les intendants des provinces, années 1787 à 1789."

D XXIX. Comité des rapports. Letters to the National Assembly from Troyes and Reims.

F¹ᶜ III. Aube. Elections for the department, 1790.

F¹². Statistique: Reports on textile manufacturing.

F²⁰. Results of the census of 1793–94.

H. Reports by the intendants on local disturbances.

KK 641. "Journal des Etats Généraux du marquis de Sillery, 1789."

KK 647. "Correspondance générale de Monsieur le marquis de Sillery pendant la tenue des Etats Généraux en 1789."

V¹. Letters of provision of office, 1750–90.

W 306. "Dossier de l'abbé de Champagne." Letters of Camusat de Belombre, deputy from the Third Estate of the bailliage of Troyes (89 pp.).

ARCHIVES DÉPARTEMENTALES, AUBE

Série 1B. Prison and court records.

Série C. Records of the intendant.

Série IIC, Supplément 36. "Table alphabétique des contrats de mariage, 1754–an VI," bureau de Troyes (provisional classification).

Série 2E. Notarial records of marriage contracts.

Série 2J 549. Printed documents from the trial of the suspects in the killing of Mayor Huez.

Série L. Departmental records.

Série 4Q. "Dossiers des Emigrés."

Nouvelles Acquisitions 6199–6201. Maréchaussée: "Procès des assassins de Claude Huez."

ARCHIVES DÉPARTEMENTALES, MARNE

Série C. Records of the intendant.

ARCHIVES DÉPARTEMENTALES, HÉRAULT

C 5942. "Etats du prix des grains et autres denrées donné par les marchands de Montpellier, 1789."

ARCHIVES COMMUNALES DE REIMS

Registre 116, fonds anciens. "Conclusions du Conseil de Ville."

Registre 233, fonds anciens. "Déclaration des biens et revenus du chapitre et de l'église de Reims, 25 février, 1790."

Registre 679, fonds anciens. "Capitation, 1789."

Registre 689, fonds anciens. "Vicomté: Mercuriale des grains, 1759–89."

Carton 673, fonds anciens. "Dénombrement de la ville, 1777."

Registre 194, fonds modernes. "Contribution foncière, 1792."

Registre 226, 227, fonds modernes. "Délibérations du Comité permanent."

Registre 251, fonds modernes. "Contribution patriotique."

Registre 254, fonds moderns. "Correspondance, 1789."
Carton 826, fonds moderns. "Elections, 1790."
Carton 843. fonds moderns. "Electeurs, mai 1790."
Carton 846, fonds moderns. "Garde Nationale."
Carton 866, fonds moderns. "Etat de la population, 9 octobre, 1793."

ARCHIVES COMMUNALES DE TROYES

A registre 54. "Assemblées des conseillers notables, 1786–90."
AA Carton 55. "Correspondance, 1789."
D* 23. "Registre de Correspondance de la municipalité entre 1766 et 1792."
D* 33. "Registre des procès-verbaux du Comité Général et Permanent."
G* 1. "Etat des citoyens de la ville de Troyes payant 50 l. [livres] impositions et au-dessus."
Registre F 346. "Les deux vingtièmes, 1789."
Anciens Cartons Locaux. No. 605. "Comité Général et provisoire."
Fonds François Carteron. Vol. 36, pièce 3. "Etat des citoyens actifs et éligibles" (undated).
———. Vol. 25. "Règlement pour la formation d'une Garde Nationale Volontaire."
———. Vol. 26. "Tableau des contributions patriotiques."
———. Vol. 38. "Observations sur le tarif et la boulangerie de Troyes, 1786," and "Suite des observations sur le tarif et la boulangerie de Troyes, 1787" (Truelle de Chambouzon).

BIBLIOTHÈQUE NATIONALE

Fonds Maçonniques FM² 362, 365. Reims.
———. FM² 491. Troyes.

BIBLIOTHÈQUE MUNICIPALE DE REIMS

CR I 1050. "Liste des citoyens éligible pour la formation de la municipalité, 1790."
CR V 1189. *Affiches, Annonces et Avis Diverses de Reims et de la Généralité de Champagne*, chez M. Havé.
CR V 1666 M. Genet, J.V., "Une famille rémoise au XVIIIᵉ siècle" (Reims, 1881).
CR V 1709. "Notice biographique sur Sutaine-Duvivier" (Paris, 1855).
RBM 567. Laurent, Gustave, "Aperçus sur l'histoire de loges maçonniques à Reims."

BIBLIOTHÈQUE MUNICIPALE DE TROYES

Manuscrit 2322. Abbé Trémet, "Notes historiques de ce qui s'est passé à Troyes, 1770–90."

Published Primary Sources

ALMANACS

The almanacs of Troyes and Reims provided vital information on office-holding. For few towns in France are collections are complete as for Troyes and Reims before 1789. For Troyes I used the *Almanach de la ville et du diocèse de Troyes* (Troyes, 1776–an IX [1801]); for Reims, the *Almanach historique de la ville et diocèse de Reims*, also entitled *Almanach historique, civil, ecclésiastique et topographique de la ville et diocèse de Reims* (Reims, 1752–94).

SOURCES FOR THE ELECTIONS OF 1789

Cahiers de doléances du bailliage de Troyes (principal et secondaires) et du bailliage de Bar-sur-Seine pour les Etats Généraux de 1789. Edited by Jules-Joseph Vernier. 3 vols. Troyes, 1909–11.

Cahiers de doléances pour les Etats Généraux de 1789, Département de la Marne. Edited by Gustave Laurent. 5 vols. Epernay, 1906–11; Reims, 1930.

Recueil de documents relatifs à la convocation des Etats Généraux de 1789. Edited by Armand Brette. 4 vols. Paris, 1894–1915.

MUNICIPAL RECORDS

Actes de la Commune de Paris pendant la Révolution. Edited by Sigismond Lacroix. 15 vols. Paris, 1894–1942.

Archives législatives de la ville de Reims. Edited by Pierre Varin. 4 vols. Paris, 1840–52.

Procès-verbal des séances et délibérations de l'assemblée générale des électeurs de Paris, réunis à l'hôtel de ville le 14 juillet 1789. 3 vols. Paris, 1790.

LEGISLATIVE RECORDS

Archives Parlementaires de 1787 à 1860, recueil complet des débats législatifs et politiques des Chambres françaises, 1ᵉ série (1787 à 1799). Edited by Jérôme Mavidal, Emile Laurent, et al. 82 vols. Paris, 1867–1913. Volumes 8–32 cover the years 1789–91.

NEWSPAPERS

Journal de Troyes et de la Champagne méridionale (Troyes: veuve Gobelet, 1783–89). Weekly.

Gazette nationale, ou le Moniteur universel (Réimpression de l'Ancien Moniteur, Paris, 1847).

PAMPHLETS

Gillet, Alexis, and Nicolas Parent. *A Nosseigneurs de l'Assemblée Nationale.* Troyes, 1789.

————. *Réflexions ultérieures.* Troyes, 1789.

Truelle de Chambouzon, Jacques, et al. *Précis pour le Comité Général et provisoire de la ville de Troyes.* Troyes, 1789.

————. *Réplique au mémoire des sieurs Parent et Gillet soi-disants Députés de la ville de Troyes par les Députés du Comité général et provisoire de la même Ville.* Troyes, 1789.

————. *Résumé pour le Comité Général et provisoire de la ville de Troyes.* Troyes, 1789.

Index